# *Fire For Effect!*

## Artillery Forward Observers in Korea

by

Anthony J. Sobieski

authorHOUSE™
*1663 Liberty Drive, Suite 200*
*Bloomington, Indiana 47403*
*(800) 839-8640*
*www.AuthorHouse.com*

*First published by AuthorHouse 04/26/05*

*ISBN: 1-4208-3836-9 (sc)*

*Printed in the United States of America*
*Bloomington, Indiana*

*This book is printed on acid-free paper.*

**Fire For Effect –**

1. **Fire which is delivered after the mean point of impact or burst is within the desired distance of the target or adjusting/ranging point.**
2. **Term in a call for fire to indicate the adjustment/ ranging is satisfactory and fire for effect is desired. (Army)**
3. **That volume of fires delivered on a target to achieve the desired effect. Also called FFE.**
4. **See also final protective fire; fire mission; neutralize; suppression.**

# Dedication

***For My Hero, My Dad***

***And***

***For all Forward Observers of all wars***

# Foreword

**By Major General Robert H. Scales, Jr.**

First some truth in advertising: I'm an artilleryman with over 34 years of service. My father, also a professional soldier, spent over two years in Korea fighting with the Second Infantry Division. Finally, I've been assigned to Korea three times and during the four years I spent there I served as an artilleryman, first as an artillery staff officer in the seventies, then as a battalion commander of the 17th Field Artillery, the "Guns of the DMZ" in the eighties and finally as the assistant division commander of the Second Division in the nineties. So there's a great deal of personal emotion and professional baggage for me in this piece. As is usually my habit I intended to scan this book, pick out a few meaningful quotes and provide a few worthy comments. Instead, I was transfixed. I read it twice over a period of two weeks. In a sense the words transported me back to a war that most of the world has forgotten to a function in war that many have marginalized in this era of smart bombs and cruise missiles that kill the enemy surgically and from great distances.

What makes Tony's book so compelling are the personal stories of the gunner Forward Observers most of which are told to a public audience for the first time in almost half a century. In their voices you can sense the relief and gratitude that someone at last has taken the time to hear their stories. Like most veterans they remember the small things: bad food, the chilling cold, sleepless nights, humping SCR artillery radio sets and the tedious boredom that seems to characterize most wars. They also speak about the fear of experiencing the enemy for the first time. But they also recall the power of their arm: without personal hubris they recount what it's like to call in hundreds of rounds of steel and explosive in the midst of a charging enemy... and the impersonal feeling of watching enemy soldiers die horribly in large numbers in front of them.

Also important to me was the inevitable comparisons that veterans will make about the firepower systems in Korea, Vietnam and the Gulf War. The first impression I had was the change that this war made in the minds of maneuver commanders as they learned (often painfully) that limited wars demanded a limited expenditure in human lives. Firepower from ships, aircraft and artillery of every caliber would replace manpower as the principle means of achieving effect on the battlefield. And the orchestration of that symphony of firepower would be placed in the hands of junior sergeants and lieutenants. Forward Observers shared the dangers of their supported infantry units and from their accounts you can trace the difference between their relatively limited engagement in the early years to their overwhelming importance later in the war when infantry units would call on them and their supporting batteries to deliver hundreds of thousands of rounds to support even the most modest attacks.

Several of these FOs speak about their independence and authority. Where else can a young man of twenty hold the lives of hundreds of men in his hands and command the expenditures of killing power that might cost the entire budget of a small city during a final protective fire or a Time on Target? In the end this work shows the incredible uniqueness of the American artilleryman. He knows that in the close infantry fight he is responsible for not only killing the enemy but for keeping alive those infantrymen who depend on his skill and bravery to be the eyes and brain of guns located thousands of yards to the rear. Now at last Tony Sobieski has frozen in amber a moment in history long forgotten. Generations of gunners will look to this work to understand their pedigree. And I will refer to it time and again as I try to relive my own time as a member of that exclusive club of Forward Observers in combat.

Major General Robert H. Scales, Jr. U.S.A. (Ret)

# Introduction

In the year 2000, after the publication of my first book, *FIRE MISSION!* About the 213th Field Artillery Battalion, my Dad's unit in Korea, in which I included a chapter on Forward Observers, I realized that there was a great untouched wealth of information that had never been completely told about the Korean War. In listening to my Dad recollect his FO experiences, along with other 213th FO's, was when I decided to do a historical project on Forward Observers in Korea. The vivid mental images that were explained to me, sometimes in detail, made me intrigued by the whole FO story. What was it like to actually see a human wave of men and to then systematically destroy it? To actually see artillery rounds hit their target? To live as an infantryman, but not be considered one? Surely, of all the duty positions to serve in Korea, the Artillery Forward Observer was at the top of the list when it came to respect. I have had numerous infantry officers and men recount to me that the FO and his team were treated like kings (maybe this is why the artillery is referred to as the 'King of Battle!), because it was known that at any given time this man with his EE8 field phone or radio could save yours and your men's lives.

After I decided to do this project, I started to collect information in the summer of 2000. By the time 2001 had come, I was knee deep in information. Letters, e-mails, phone calls, I was inundated by the shear volume of responses I had gotten from requests put in the American Legion, VFW, and Korean War Veterans respective magazines. I knew I had made a good choice in my subject topic! There were many men, whom, now in their later years, that were willing to shed some light on their battlefield experiences, most for the first time to anyone, not even their families. However, all that changed in September 2001. I am in the military, and when the attacks happened on the WTC and Pentagon, everything that I had been working on was put immediately on hold. This 'hold' lasted almost 2 years, and it was only until May 2003 that I was able to even pick up a letter from a former FO and read it, or respond back to an old e-mail, or phone call. How many of those that had contacted me previously had by now passed away? I will never know, but it is in theirs and all Korean War FO's memories that I present this work.

These interviews are nothing more than the words of the men themselves. I have not embellished these accounts, these recollections, these life-changing events. When starting this project, I developed a questionnaire that was designed to elicit a certain type of response from a Forward Observer. The type of response I was looking for was the 'matter of fact' style of recounting one's experiences from 50 years ago. These men are not fresh from the battlefield; they have been tempered by 50 additional years of living. For those of us who are veterans of current conflicts, how will we reflect on our experiences 50 years from now? These FO's and the vast majority of Korean War veterans are not telling their story for bragging rights, "I fought on Porkchop" or "I was at the Frozen Chosin", rather these men wear their experiences as a quiet badge of honor, knowing that they did what their country asked them to do, and they did it better than anyone could have expected. One of the questions that I asked on the questionnaire is if the FO's family was aware of their military service and record. A surprising number answered, no, not fully. Some wrote comments such as "My family didn't seem to make a big deal of it, so I didn't." How many of these families did not realize that they were living and sharing their lives in the company of heroes?

***The Author***

# Table of Contents

# Chapter One

## *Artillery, The King of Battle*

*Korea will forever be known as The Artillery War.* At one time or another, over sixty different United States artillery battalions served on the Korean Peninsula. Regular Army, Marine Corps, Reserve, and National Guard battalions all played a part and served with distinction. Additionally, U.S. Navy ships from destroyers to battleships added their heavy 'punch' to the mix of available firepower at the hands of the Forward Observer. The original and final intent of 8th Army was to eventually have a breakdown of units divided evenly between the three Corps, I, IX, and X. Infantry divisions all were assigned four artillery battalions each, usually consisting of three 105mm units for direct support, and a 155mm unit for heavier general support, although the 2nd, 3rd, 24th, and 25th Infantry Divisions all had one additional 155mm artillery battalion attached to their chain of command. There were three field artillery observation battalions, the 1st, 187th, and 235th. These units did not have any artillery pieces assigned to them. Rather, they were units that specialized in locating enemy guns through various means, including radar and 'flash and sound' observation posts, and then would proceed to call for fire on them. The plan called for one of these 'special' observation battalions cover each corps sector, although in the beginning the 1st FOAB covered the entire front. As with the field artillery observation battalions, there were three 8-inch howitzer units that served in Korea, the 17th, 424th, and 780th. Again, the idea was to have one 8-inch howitzer battalion in each sector. The three observation battalions and three 8-inch battalions were not assigned to any one division, but rather were Corps units. In April 1953 two battalions, the 213th and the 159th, were converted in place to the 240mm howitzer, the largest artillery piece used in the war. These units also were Corps battalions, with the 213th covering IX Corps and detached a battery to support the X Corps sector, while the 159th supported combat actions in the I Corps area.

When starting this research, the goal was to interview at least one FO from each of the 60+ US Army artillery battalions to serve in Korea. Shortly after advertising my request for information, I became overwhelmed by the responses I received, not only from the Army, but Marines also. It was evident of the need for the services of someone who knew and understood the use of and employment of artillery in a strategic situation. This stemmed down from 8th Army, to the three US Corps and three ROK Corps, to the divisions, regiments, battalions, companies, and individual leaders of patrols and small units throughout the front lines of Korea. The Korean War had both the outright brutality of fighting that WWII had in the Pacific, while drawling from the battlefields of Europe in it's etiquette on fighting. The brutality of the Pacific war, short battles of pure intensity, there was no falling back and regrouping, thousands of men, trained to slaughter their enemy, collocated on a small area of land. And then the war in Europe, with its huge armies thrusting and counter thrusting, moving over large areas of land, sometimes encompassing an entire country in a particular battle. In the beginning stages of the war from 1950 to 1951, movement of artillery in Korea was very similar to that of WWII, firing and movement, firing and movement. The mobility of artillery units was invaluable to the successes of the infantry and movements of the UN forces in general. By the beginning of 1952, when the war entered what is generally considered the 'stalemate' phase (although there are plenty of combat veterans from that time that would strongly disagree with that statement) and on into 1953, the Korean front began to resemble the trench warfare of WWI, with shells raining down on both sides of the front lines (hence the term that WWI veterans had 'shell-shock'). Through all of this, all artillery units used some form of artillery spotters, or Forward Observers. These ranged from FO's that served with the infantry units directly, sometimes never even knowing or seeing anyone in their firing unit for months, to FO's who were positioned in bunkers (either on or in front of the MLR) to aerial observers flying in an un-armed, un-protected scout plane. Also, many an infantrymen doubled as FO's in their duties when artillery battalion FO's were wounded or not available.

For the men assigned to Forward Observer duty, this meant being literally on the front lines, close enough to see and observe enemy actions, for the purpose of giving fire support when ever and where ever needed. These men regularly became the focus of unwanted attention by the enemy, sometimes even being caught right in the middle of a raging firefight. Artillery battalion Observation Posts (OP's) were almost daily shelled by enemy artillery and mortar fire, and at times took small arms fire. Sometimes a simple entry in a unit's daily morning reports, such as a statement like 'OP #2 received rounds' was a very polite way of saying that that position was being targeted and fired on. The communists realized that knocking out these OP's meant eliminating some of the allies' ability to fire at them. Divisional OP's tended to be located and numbered across the front from one to whatever number of OP's were required by Divisional Artillery (DIVARTY) or by the battalions or tactical situation. These OP's were for the heavier divisional artillery units in general support. For direct support artillery units, established OP's were not generally used, the FO parties serving directly with the assigned infantry unit they were supporting. These OP's were fluid according to the tactical situation. Corps artillery units used their own OP's which they established in their support roles of divisional artillery. These OP's were not numbered with the divisional artillery OP's and, depending on what units they were supporting, they were frequently located with UN or ROK forces. These OP's also sometimes overlapped divisional artillery OPs in their respective Corps area.

The Korean War, and artillery, was before the time of computers and satellites and high speed electronics. Today, the US military is researching mobile artillery mechanisms that can plan, calculate, load, and fire ten rounds of 155mm ammunition in less than one minute, at a target ten miles away, with deadly accuracy, all with a crew of two, simply by pushing a few buttons. During the Korean War, all of this was done by the human brain and physical strength. The Fire Direction Center (FDC) worked directly with the Observation Posts, and was the brains behind the brawn. Each Battery had a FDC, and they were all linked into the Battalion FDC, who had overall control of the combat situation, and directed the battalion where it was needed the most. The Battalion Commander ran his unit through the FDC, and the Air Observers and the FO teams worked with both the Battery and the Battalion FDC's. Each FDC was manned by approximately eight men and two or three officers. Tracking the tactical situation was the life blood of the artillery battalion, and the effectiveness of the Forward Observers was directly related to the ability of the FDC to do its job well. Connecting the FDC to the OP's and the batteries were the wire section crews, using thousands of yards of phone lines to get the job done. This meant being fired at on more than one occasion, and each wire section man has his own personal 'close call' story. Sometimes these wire crews found themselves even navigating enemy held ground to do their jobs. Lastly, there is a long history of pilots and ground troops or artillery working together to suppress the enemy, going back to World War I. In Korea, artillery units used 'spotters', Air Observers who were flown over the battlefield by brave pilots usually in a small single engine airplane called an L-19. They were no more than flying targets, and had provided little protection and had no armament, except flares they would sometimes use to mark targets. These crewmen were U.S. Army personnel attached to the artillery units. These men sometimes rarely even knew the men of the firing batteries, flying out of airstrips miles from their units.

The fact that so many FOs have called fire onto their own positions brings to light a startling realization of what Winston Churchill said 'Uncommon valor was a common virtue'. These men KNEW what they were doing. They had a choice: be killed or captured, or fight it out and possibly lose their life and the lives of their FO team also. This was not a decision made lightly. I have come across quite a number of FO stories where the FO called artillery fire onto his own position because they were being overrun. What FO does not readily know or understand what they are asking their firing battery to do? And at the same time, what FDC and firing battery does not understand what they are hearing on the radio or field phone? A man that they more than likely knew, yelling to them to shoot high explosives at them, knowing that this might be the last time their voice is ever heard on this earth? That the 'cause and effect' rule is in full swing, fire a 37 or 100 pound shell filled with high explosive at a specific coordinate and destroy (kill) whatever is at that coordinate.

In the beginning, the Korean War was fought with antiquated equipment, mostly 'leftover' items from WWII. Not many improvements were added to the US Army from 1945 to 1950. The attention was on demobilization, return to civilian life, down sizing, crating up, and putting away in storage the items of war. The US participation in WWII, the last 'good war' left a distinctive taste in the mouths of those who fought it and suffered from it. No one wanted that kind sacrifice, but it was done, hence the term 'The Greatest Generation'. When the fighting in Korea splashed across the headlines of American newspapers, most said 'Where?' The fact that our forces were going into combat again caught some by surprise, but the thought process was that we had the best army in the world and that we would take care of business. The US military became woefully depleted by 1950, not just with men, but with supplies and equipment. The service members who were on duty, and those that were called up reservists, certainly were the best. But times had started to change, and their equipment wasn't ready for it. Not until later in the war did our fighting men see improvements, such as 'Mickey Mouse' boots, Flak vests, and bazookas that could knock out a tank. These new assets did not make the fighting any easier on our troops, but it gave them the advantage of preparedness. US artillery was no different. Loading, aiming, and firing artillery had not changed much, and the weapons not at all, since WWII. Most if not all artillery shells were of WWII vintage as well. Korea was a very different type of war indeed. By 1953, trench warfare reminiscent of WWI was the standard, but the use of more accurate artillery, with better knowledge in fire direction planning, shell trajectories, types of shells, and overall destructive power were incredible. Not before or since Korea can it be said that artillery ruled the battlefield. It truly was 'The Artillery War', and one of the major factors in making all of this possible was the men and teams who performed Forward Observer duties.

The men who fought in Korea were a mix of men that could be broken down into very specific groups. First, there were the WWII veterans, these were the men that fought the majority of the early battles in Korea, some who survived the hedgerows of France and Germany, or who had fought island by island across the Pacific. These were the 'old breed' who knew battle, and many who came through WWII would end up losing their lives in the coldness of Korea. The next identifiable group was the younger brothers, sons, and nephews of those who fought in the 'Big One'. These were the men who were maybe 15 or 16 during WWII, who followed the war in the newspapers and on the radio, or were told stories by their older brother or even father who came home from 'the front'. Some saw and heard what war was like and had no illusions about it, while others had what some WWI veterans had before they went over to France, a chivalric view of service in the military and to fight in a war. The next group was the draftees. Remember, this was at a time in our country's history when something like a draft was not considered a bad thing, or 'infringing' on someone's rights. These draftees realized that they were being called on by their country to perform honorable military duty for a just cause, and they did just that. The Korean War was also the first major US conflict after the decision to de-segregate the military. Black men were now allowed to serve with, and over, white men in the armed forces. Support units such as the artillery battalions were some of the first units that became de-segregated, and it became common place by 1953 for men of both colors to serve side by side with honor and respect for each other.

To help understand the role of artillery and specifically of the Forward Observer in Korea, the need for a general understanding of the knowledge required by the Artillery Forward Observer is given below. The following information was compiled with the grateful assistance of 1st Lt Joseph Reynolds (936th Field Artillery Battalion), who served in Korea in 1952. The Army prescribed a set method of making fire request information to the Fire Direction Center in order to minimize confusion and to facilitate rapid fire as much as possible. These commands are designed to be logical and in an easily used manner. Fire requests must contain certain information to enable the Fire Direction Center to compute the firing data. In divisional artillery battalions, each firing battery usually used the standard method of having two Forward Observers and crew on the MLR. The use of two Observation Posts usually covered the complete arch of trajectory of the firing battery. In Corps support units, any number of OP's was used to support the tactical situation, sometimes one, sometimes three OP's per battalion. The 'tools of the trade', the binoculars and BC scopes, included a graduated reticule that enabled the Observer to measure lateral distances with some degree of accuracy. The value of the 'mill method' of measuring angles was effective in that with the mill method, there was an arc of 1 unit in 1,000. When an Observer, with the use of the reticule, measures a lateral distance of 20 mills and the estimated range to the target is 3,000 yards, then the lateral adjustment would be 60 yards. Vertical graduations are 5 mills each, and vertical scale would be used for such positions as machine gun emplacements. Horizontal graduations are 10 mills each. Military maps, when available, show contour lines that enable the Observer to better identify the target location coordinates. In layman's terms, the BC scope was to a Forward Observer as was an M-1 rifle to an infantryman.

Some Fire Request types are as follows:

- *Identification of the Observer.* The fire direction must know who is requesting fire. This can be a code name or any other method acceptable to the commander.
- *Azimuth.* Direction which the observer is looking at the target. This is very important especially if the observer is at an angle to the direction of fire from the guns.
- *Target location.* This location can be in many different forms. It can be identified as coordinates, range and azimuth from a known location, and range and direction from the observer to the target, or shift from a previously fired upon target and others. Circumstances determine what method the observer will use in identifying the location of the target.
- *Substance of the target.* The fire request should identify the type of target for the fire direction to order the proper shell and fuse type.

These are examples of fire requests made by Forward Observers. They will vary in content but notice that they generally follow a set procedure in transmission. Not all fire missions were done in this format, taking into account the expediency of the mission being called. If a position or OP were about to be overrun, or were already overrun, as was the case numerous times in Korea when faced with the Chinese 'human wave' attack style, some missions tended to be called in somewhat 'colorful' ways. As 1st Lt Joe Adams (213th Field Artillery Battalion) recollected when talking about the Battle of White Horse Mountain, Hill 395, in October 1952, he remembers when the Chinese stormed over his OP and surrounding positions, his call to the FDC went something like "*The Chinese are all over the fucking place start shooting at my bunker!*". Sometimes units set up a 'Final Protective Line' where pre-registered final protective fire coordinates would be given so as to, again, deal with an assaulting force that was about to overrun a position. These were at times referred to as 'Flash Fires' such as were used during the defense of Pork Chop Hill in 1953, when the order was given by 2nd Lt Richard Jaffe (57th Field Artillery Battalion) "*Give me Flash Pork Chop!*", which in essence meant for all available artillery to fire directly onto the hill.

**FIRE MISSION #1.**

Observer is from Able Battery, and is their second observer. Target is small group of enemy setting up a mortar. The target is in an area easily identified on a map and the coordinates of the target can be determined with some degree of accuracy but adjustment will be necessary.

Request #1: "*Fox Oboe Able No. 2, Fire Mission! Azimuth 2300, coordinates 236-421, enemy mortar digging in. Will adjust!*" The Fire Direction Center transmits confirmation to the firing battery and will repeat the information, adding such information as "*Battery one round in effect*". This means the eventual fire for effect will be six rounds, one round per tube.

The initial fire would be two rounds fired simultaneously which the observer would adjust from the center of the burst of the two rounds. The classic adjustment would be a left or right adjustment to get the rounds on line with his line of sight and the target. From there he would give add or drop with the first adjustment of 400 yards; then 200 yards followed by 100 yards and then an add or drop of 50 yards, then the command "*Fire for effect*" is given. This method was generally used but after becoming familiar with the target area a Forward Observer would quite often make adjustments for line of sight along with the initial add or drop and many times the initial rounds would be within 100 to 200 yards of the target.

**FIRE MISSION #2.**

Observer is from Baker Battery and is the Observer number 1. Target is near Check Point 210. The target is enemy squad in open.

Request #2: "*Fox Oboe Baker No. 1, Fire Mission! Azimuth 3200, from Check Point #210, right 300 add 500, Enemy squad in open, will adjust!*" The Fire Direction Center transmits confirmation adding such information as "*Battery one round fuse VT in effect*".

**FIRE MISSION #3.**

Observer is from Charlie Battery and is the Observer number 1. Target is 1000 yards from the observer. The target is an enemy bunker.

Request #3: "*Fox Oboe Charley No. 1 Fire Mission! Azimuth 0400, Coordinates 234-146, Range 1500, enemy bunker, request precision fire, will adjust!*" Fire direction transmits confirmation and adds such information as "*Precision fire, fuse delay in effect*".

The battery will fire one round on adjustment and then when fire for effect is called for, the guns will fire fuse delay and a succession of rounds will be fired with the observer reporting the landing point of each round in regards to the target. Fire direction will average 'overs', 'shorts', 'lefts', and 'rights' to make corrections until the target is destroyed.

**FIRE MISSION #4.**

Observer is from Charlie Battery and is the Observer number 2. Enemy is in attack on a front of some 500 yards. The Observer sends estimated target center and calls for additional fire.

Request #4: "*Fox Oboe Charley No. 2, Azimuth 2800, coordinates 354,456. Spread sheaf 500 yards, enemy infantry in attack. Request all available fire!*"

Fire direction responds by repeating the request to the Observer and adds: "*One battalion in initial fire, requesting support from Corps. Report observation!*"

The list below is of U.S. artillery battalions and associated units that served in the Korean War, most of which are covered by at least one interview in the following chapters.

**1ST Cavalry Division -** 1st Cavalry Div Art HQ
61st FAB – 105mm    77th FAB – 105mm    82nd FAB – 155mm    99th FAB – 105mm

**2nd Infantry Division -** 2nd Div Artillery HQ
12th FAB – 155mm    15th FAB – 105mm    37th FAB – 105mm    38th FAB – 105mm
503rd FAB – 155mm

**3rd Infantry Division -** 3rd Div Artillery HQ
9th FAB – 155mm    10th FAB – 105mm    39th FAB – 105mm    58th FAB – 105mm

**7th Infantry Division -** 7th Div Artillery HQ
31st FAB – 155mm    48th FAB – 105mm    49th FAB – 105mm    57th FAB – 105mm

**24th Infantry Division -** 24th Div Artillery HQ
11th FAB – 155mm    13th FAB – 105mm    52nd FAB – 105mm    63rd FAB – 105mm

**25th Infantry Division -** 25th Div Artillery HQ
8th FAB – 105mm    64th FAB – 105mm    69th FAB – 105mm    90th FAB – 155mm
159th FAB – 155, 240mm

**40th Infantry Division -** 40th Div Artillery HQ
143rd FAB – 105mm    625th FAB – 105mm    980th FAB – 105mm    981st FAB – 155mm

**45th Infantry Division -** 45th Div Artillery HQ
158th FAB – 105mm    160th FAB – 105mm    171st FAB – 105mm    189th FAB – 155mm

**5th Regimental Combat Team**
555th AFAB – 105mm SP

**187th Regimental Combat Team**
674th FAB – 105mm Tow

**Field Artillery Observation Battalions**
1st FA Ob Bn (no guns)    187th FA Ob Bn (no guns)    235th FA Ob Bn (no guns)

| **I Corps** | **IX Corps** | **X Corps** |
|---|---|---|
| I Corps Artillery HQ | IX Corps Artillery HQ | X Corps Artillery HQ |
| 176th AFAB – 105mm SP | 75th FAB – 155mm SP | 92nd FAB – 155mm SP |
| 204th FAB – 155mm Long Tom | 145th FAB – 155mm Long Tom | 96th FAB – 155mm SP |
| 623rd FAB – 155mm Tow | 213th FAB – 105 SP, 155 Tow, 240mm | 196th FAB – 155 Tow |
| 936th FAB – 155mm Tow | 937th FAB – 155mm Long Tom | 999th FAB – 155mm SP |
| 955th FAB–155mm Tow | 987th AFAB – 105mm SP, 155 SP | 300th AFAB – 105 SP |
| 780th FAB - 8 inch | 2nd Rocket FA Battery – 105mm | 17th FAB- 8 inch |
| | 424th FAB – 8 inch | |

**11th Marine Field Artillery Regiment**

| | | | |
|---|---|---|---|
| 1st Btln – 105mm | 2nd Btln – 105mm | 3rd Btln – 105mm | 4th Btln – 155mm |
| Anti-tank Company | Comm Platoon | Headquarters Battery | Service Battery |
| 1st 4.5 Rocket Btln | 1st ANGLICO Det | 1st 90mm Gun Btln | |

# Chapter Two

## *1950 – The Business of War*

Scarcely five full years had passed since the end of WWII, the greatest military operation ever known to man. WWII covered four major continents, and almost every country in the world to some extent. By 1950, the world had changed, some for the better, some for the worse. On June 25th, 1950, on a little known peninsula bordered by China in the north, war broke out yet again in the Pacific/Asia region. The vast majority of US forces had left Korea only a short time before in 1949, part of the post WWII contingent that was left in Korea after the surrender of Japan. The only American forces were the KMAG, or Korean Military Advisory Group. That was soon to change drastically. The United Nations was about to cut their teeth on international affairs, and by overwhelming vote, decided to defend South Korea from the attackers, who had a communist plan and agenda for all of Korea when they were done. The 24th Infantry Division, on occupation duty in Japan, were alerted and told to prepare a defensive 'stopping force' to be sent to Korea until further US and UN forces could be deployed. Lt Col Brad Smith was assigned the task of leading 'Task Force SMITH', comprised of the 21st Infantry Regiment and 'A' Battery of the 52nd Field Artillery Battalion. Task Force SMITH and the 52nd Field Artillery were the inauspicious entry of US artillery into the battlefield to be known as KOREA...

**1st Lt Donald J. Miller**
**159th Field Artillery Battalion 1950-51**

"I was a Forward Observer with 'B' and 'C' Batteries 159th Field Artillery Battalion. The 159th was a 155mm unit, and we were part of the 25th Infantry Division. At about 15 July 1950 upon arriving in Korea, I was with 'C' Battery, and we were sent to the east coast supporting the 23rd Infantry Regiment. After a couple of weeks we pulled back, eventually to the Pusan Perimeter. During this period I was a Liaison Officer and Forward Observer with 2nd and 3rd Battalions of the 24th Infantry Regiment. I was an FO during the breakout and movement into North Korea, and during this time I was awarded the Bronze Star for action on 29 August 1950. I was relieved as FO in December of 1950 for assignment to Service Battery, but by January 1951 I was recalled to 'B' Battery as an FO prior to crossing the Han River, and was assigned to a tank company for recon and targets of opportunity. I participated in the Han River crossing on March 7th, 1951 and was wounded on March 8th. They evacuated me to the 279th General Hospital in Osaka Japan. That for all purposes was the end of combat for me. I did return to Korea after eleven weeks but was assigned administrative duties until august 19th, 1951, when I returned to duty in the US. I have six campaign stars with the 159th while in Korea."

**Sergeant Carl Stepp**
**11th, 52nd, & 99th Field Artillery Battalions 1950-51**

"I was a Radio Telephone Operator for a Forward Observer team with the 11th Field Artillery Battalion in 1950 in Korea. I also was an FO for 'B' Battery, 52nd Field Artillery and later in January of 1951 for the 99th Field Artillery of the 1st Cavalry Division as the 24th Infantry Division was reorganizing. I was transferred at my request to join the push to the Yalu River, and I was part of the first FO team to re-enter Taejon and secure the air strip with flat trajectory fire. I was under the command of Captain Henry P. Carrington, a very brave officer who later was KIA. We had to know a lot about artillery support for the infantry and engineers. A lot was involved in knowing when to lift fire for the infantry and air attacks. Short rounds were a constant worry due to interference of sound waves from F-86's and F-80's. Air Observers was the choice way to direct fire, and the Air Force Observers were very important also. The L-17 and L-19 were great little planes for this because they were ideal to slow to about 80 knots, they were very light and landed on any short runway dirt or any other surface. As the old saying goes it was a good way to see the whites of their eyes while flying by the seat of your pants! I participated in the crossing of the Han River in July 1950. My OP was overrun but I destroyed my radio and I escaped back to my battery. We knocked out six T-34's and stopped an infantry attack on a forward aid station. I passed 25 feet from a T-34 in the river bed and had I had a weapon I would have tried to get him as enemy infantry were riding on top but I had to hide and wait my day. I was awarded the Bronze Star on 24 April 1951."

**Sergeant Edward Damaso**
**10th Field Artillery Battalion 1950-51**

"I joined the RI National Guard in 1947 at age 14 with an altered birth certificate. From a broken family, I was a ward of the State. The system was a little loose in the control area and I wasn't really watched very closely. I joined the 103rd Field Artillery Battalion, 43rd Infantry Division. A year or so later, I used the same dubious documentation and established no enlistment to enter the regular army. I was assigned to the 10th Field Artillery, a part of the 7th Infantry Regimental Combat Team, 7/RCT, 3rd Infantry Division, then stationed at Fort Devens, MA. We were on TDY from Devens to West Point to provide training troops for cadet summer training when the Korean War broke out. We were returned to Devens and began the long deployment to Korea. Prior to the outbreak of the war, the 7/RCT was a near full strength unit. We were extremely well trained and, for the times, combat ready. We had trained for and participated in Operation PORTEX, a practice amphibious landing on Vieques Island near Puerto Rico. I was assigned as a radio operator on an FO team for the operation. At the outbreak of the war our well trained units were decimated by individual MOS levies and the loss of the 3rd Battalion of the 7/RCT and 'C' Battery of the 10th, these units were immediately deployed to Korea and integrated into the 1st Cavalry Division then in Korea. They became Charlie Battery of the 99th Field Artillery, and the 3/8th Infantry Regiment respectively. As a part of the reorganization of battalion resources, I was reassigned from 'A' to the new 'C' Battery, 10th Field Artillery Battalion, 7th Regimental Combat Team, 3rd Infantry Division. The remainder of the division, the 15th and 30th RCT's were at Fort Benning, GA. After the earlier departure of the full strength battery. We were left with about twenty-five men per battery and only six howitzers in the battalion, two per firing battery. The 10th was a 105mm towed howitzer battalion, and the normal compliment should have been eighteen howitzers! After our arrival in Japan in early September, we began receiving some individual reservist replacements, but not nearly enough to bring the unit to any semblance of sufficient strength. This was remedied by a large infusion of ROK personnel and after a very short period of training in Japan, we deployed to Korea, landing at Wonson sometime in November, 1950. We were shortly thereafter assigned to the X Corps. We received so many dragooned ROK replacements that the story went around that when our CC Major General 'Stumpy' Soule reported to General McArthur, he was asked 'Who sent you, the communists?'

I served with the 10th Field Artillery from November 1950 to November, 1951. I became an FO by way of volunteering. I was originally assigned to the communications wire section. There were insufficient personnel and little time to formally train FO team sergeants before the need for them suddenly arrived. The wire section was a convenient place to get and quickly train people without curtailing the efficiency of the firing battery. My realistic FO training on operation PORTEX helped in my selection. I should add here that in the 10th, all FO's per se, were commissioned officers. A FO team usually consisted of a lieutenant FO, a team sergeant and a radio telephone operator/driver. As the war progressed an extra man was added in the form of a starving South Korean civilian who would be unofficially assigned the duties of 'radio facilitator' but was in actuality a 'humper'. This was not the case in all teams, but it was so in mine. Also, not all FO's allowed their team sergeants to handle fire missions on their own. Although I had several different lieutenants over the year, all but one allowed me to handle missions. In the era of WWII and the Korea War, there usually were three RCT's per division, three battalions per RCT, three rifle companies per battalion, etc. The artillery was organized into three six-gun firing batteries per battalion. Each firing battery had three FO teams, with additional teams for relief purposes. When a 105mm artillery battalion was tasked into direst support of a RCT, one battery was tasked to each infantry battalion and one FO team to each rifle company to provide observed, directed artillery support. When the 10th Field initially entered the fight, we moved north in the attack on the remnants of the North Korean Army. When the Chicom's entered the war and the 1st Marine Division forward positions at the Chosin Reservoir became threatened, the 3rd Infantry Division reverted to an effort to extract trapped troops to the north. The 7th RCT was assigned to Task Force DOG, and the force was sent forward to hold open the Marine retreat route through the Funchilin Pass to the south. In this capacity we served in a major part of the battle at the Chosin Reservoir. At some point the 10th was relieved from the task force and replaced by the 92nd Armored Field Artillery Battalion, 155mm self-propelled, I assume because of their better mobility in the restricted, mountainous terrain of the area and their longer reach. As the embattled Army and Marine troops at the Chosin began their withdrawal, we were reassigned to direct support of the 65th Infantry Regiment from Puerto Rico, which was newly joined to the division to replace the 30th Infantry which had remained at Fort Benning. We took part in the rear guard action to cover the evacuation of the retreating Army and Marine forces from the Chosin Reservoir area and the evacuation of the city of Hamhung and then the evacuation of all friendly forces through the Port of Hungnam. We were a part of the last defensive perimeter around the evacuation harbor. As the perimeter shrunk and our guns were outloaded we reverted to adjusting naval gunfire in support of the defense. I heard the overhead passing of 16-inch shells from battleship USS Missouri that was an indescribably awesome experience. Sergeant Bob West, who was an FO team sergeant with another company of the 65th, and I departed on one of the last two LST's to leave the harbor. It was Christmas Eve afternoon, 1950. As we left, we watched another awesome sight, the demolition of all harbor facilities in one gigantic explosion.

Upon arrival in the south we went into positions on pre-prepared defensive positions. A short time later we began the new push to drive the Chinese back north. I can remember being in an OP on the south side of the Han River, a short distance to the right of the main railway bridge into Seoul, which was blown of course. We were in what had been a dentist's office. We had a clear view of the river and the sand flats leading up to the first buildings on the far bank. From this position we brought much thunder from above on the enemy on the other side. It was while in these positions that a member of our team and an old friend from the Devens days, George Brattain, was seriously wounded and evacuated to later return to duty. After Seoul was retaken we moved into the attack in Operation KILLER, and our main mission I believe was to relentlessly pound the retreating Chinese and NK forces causing as many casualties as possible. There were some bitter, fast moving battles during the next few weeks. My memory blurs and it is difficult to pick out any certain one action. After one of these forward movements I remember walking through a hurriedly abandoned Chinese casualty treating point and the hideous sight of large numbers of amputated limbs and bloody bandages. When the reality hit that most of the horror was inflicted by our supporting fires, it was a sobering sight not to be forgotten, ever. On 16 May, 1951, the Chinese hit us hard on the east central front. The ROKs were routed, and we as part of the 3rd Division, who was then in reserve on the western front, was tasked with making a seventy mile lateral movement to plug the gap. This move was done in record time and the gap was plugged and the entire enemy drive was stopped cold. We called it the 'End Run' or the 'Flying Tackle' as it was called by the NY Times in a later article. We were again in direct support of line units and I participated in several company and platoon sized patrols aggressively patrolling in a fluid 'movement to contact' the retreating enemy forces. One of these night patrols stands out vividly in my memory. At about 0200 we waded a fast moving river, the Imjin, I think, and when that icy cold water reached the level of certain hanging body parts there was a chorus of subdued moans and deep intakes of breath, however, discipline and stealth were maintained regardless of discomfort and the patrol was a success.

As an FO, I always felt a little independent. We were a small, close knit unit, usually three or four men, mostly operating apart from our parent unit and its disciplines. While deployed we lived and acted as any other infantry soldier. At the very beginning, I shed my M2 carbine as an ineffectual weapon outside the battery. I acquired a Garand MI rifle and a Colt 1911 .45 caliber pistol. I carried these throughout my time in Korea until I finished my tour. I gave these unauthorized weapons to my replacement when I returned to the battery and my M2 carbine. My thoughts were to get the job done and to stay alive. We were always welcome in any infantry unit we joined because they all knew that we packed a pretty big punch and could make the difference in a tight situation. Although we directed the fire of only one 105mm battalion with eighteen howitzers, we could, when justified, call upon the fires of the entire division artillery and beyond. I remember one Corps ToT where the massed fire of all available Corps artillery units was massed on one target. The result was awesome, we were being heavily attacked and in danger of being overrun at the time. My thoughts were simply, 'Wow, did we really do all that?' We supported all the infantry units in the 3rd Division at one time or another, the 7th, 15th, and 65th Regimental Combat Teams. And in one case, we supported the Turkish Brigade. I don't believe we ever supported the ROKs directly. We were always welcome in the infantry units due to our ability to bring massive fires in support of operations. I'd like to point out that on many occasions the FO team spent more time on patrolling activities than the average infantry soldier. Patrols were always rotated among the infantry squads and platoons. There was only one FO team to draw on for patrols, and we were it. If an FO was required for a patrol we went on it, regardless of frequency. We also had the heaviest radio equipment to carry, the SCR 610 or 619 radios, as opposed to the comparatively much lighter SCR 300 or 536 'walky-talky' radios of the infantry. We did not use trenches but whenever in a defensive posture always dug individual fighting holes as required. All of my experiences, except for the brief time in the pre-prepared defensive line, were, for the most part, in fluid forward moving operations. We almost exclusively fought the Chinese. By the time we arrived in-country, the North Koreans were pretty battered and although they reorganized later, they were never again as potent a force as they were in the early days of the war. We may have gone against them, I just don't remember. Back then they were just 'Gooks'. In hindsight, they were damn tough and aggressive enemies.

I do not recall any specifically named OP's during my time there. As I said, we were mostly involved in typical, fluid infantry combat operations. These were mostly attack and defense and, in the case of the Chosin Reservoir in the north, retreat. We normally operated OP's in the forward areas of an infantry company operating areas so as to provide prompt, accurate observed fire adjustment onto enemy targets. When in any temporary static defense position., we operated from the Outpost Line of Resistance, which was forward of the Main Line of Resistance and that was way out there! The naming of these positions started after we entered into fairly static positions and I was long gone as an artilleryman. If our battalion was tasked with direct support of an infantry regiment that was totally committed there could be as many as nine FO's in the field in support of infantry units, based on one FO to each deployed infantry company. We were always located in forward positions where the best observation points allowed clear vision of the target area. I can only remember one numbered hill, Hill 337, just to the north of Uijongbu, overlooking a highway that later became the Main Supply Route, as we pushed further north. We had successfully attacked the hill in the early morning and as we topped the crest of the hill, the call came for the FO to come forward. We went forward of the crest to a heavy machine gun position, a water cooled .30, which was busy firing at Chinese soldiers frantically trying to beat feet to their rear. A large group had taken refuge in a defilade position where the machine gun could not range. We called in salvoes with Variable Time fuses which created deadly air-bursts. The carnage was complete in a short time and we busied ourselves calling in adjusted defensive fire concentrations, while the infantry consolidated the position and prepared for a counterattack.

The counterattack did not materialize in strength and we settled in for the night, as this was our final objective for the day. During the night our positions were aggressively probed by enemy patrols and we were busy calling fire missions which we adjusted from the already registered concentrations, or check points. Life and work as an FO was pretty close to and sometimes more harrowing than the life of a typical infantry grunt. I think all FO's were a little cocky and self assured because of their fairly nomadic and very often dangerous life style. I know that I sometimes felt a little like a swashbuckler. We were pretty much on our own when not in direct support actions. We had easy access to vehicle transportation as each team was equipped with a 1/4 ton truck or jeep, and trailer. When not directly on duty, we sometimes ranged far and wide and were known for our re-supply capabilities, or in layman's terms, scrounging. When we worked, we worked, but when we didn't work, well, we just didn't! I remember one time Sgt Bob West and I were traveling back to the battery area when we came upon a roadside shower point. We were both filthy as we had just come off the line. As we approached the entrance we noticed that there were two lines, one for officers and the other for us enlisted men. Our line was very long and there were only two or three in the officer's line. Since we were just off the line and we wore no rank insignia and we both wore sidearms, we agreed that what the hell could they do to us, send us to the front? I loudly said to Bob 'Well Lieutenant West, this shower sure will feel good'. He replied 'Yes Captain Damaso, I'm really looking forward to it' or words to that effect. We kept up the banter until we had successfully completed our showers and were leaving, with huge superior grins.

Although there were many fire missions called during the evacuation in the north, only the adjustment of naval gunfire at the evacuation of Hungnam stand out in my memory. Some of these and some of the later missions were under heavy enemy pressure and very harrowing in nature, but they do not specifically stand out in my memory. During the drive back to the north, again there were many, but only the OP on the Han River, Hill 337 and the 'end run' stand out in my memory. That is not to say that some others were not much more significant and or more dangerous, though. I remember one of the calls signs that we used, 'Whitehorse'. 'Whitehorse' was the call sign for our Fire Direction Center, 'Whitehorse Charlie 3' indicated that we were in support of the 3rd battalion of whatever RCT we were supporting at the time. A typical fire mission might be as follows, 'Whitehorse,

Whitehorse this is Whitehorse Charlie 3', 'Whitehorse Charlie 3, this is Whitehorse, over!' 'This is Whitehorse Charlie 3, Fire Mission, over!' 'Whitehorse Charlie, send your mission, over! 'This is Whitehorse Charlie 3, from concentration Able Nan 360, left 250 add 250, enemy infantry in the open, request one round Willy Peter, will adjust, over!' Here FDC would repeat the fire mission data and state 'Roger Wait!' FDC would then compute the firing data and relay the fire commands to the guns. When fired, FDC would respond with 'Whitehorse Charlie 3, this is Whitehorse, one round WP on the way, over!' 'On the way, Roger wait!' When the ranging round was observed the FO would make an adjustment to bring the round onto the target, for the sake of brevity, we will assume that this FO is really good and his initial data was close, but no prize yet. 'Whitehorse, this is Whitehorse Charlie 3, left 50, drop 50, Fire for Effect. Request fuse VT, request battery three rounds, over!' FDC repeats and says 'Roger Wait! Whitehorse Charlie 3, battery three rounds, fuse Variable Time, on the way, over!' Then after the target is hit, 'Roger, Wait. Whitehorse, this is Whitehorse Charlie 3, cease fire, end of mission. Enemy infantry dispersed with heavy casualties. Over!' 'This is Whitehorse, cease fire, end of mission, Roger, out!' Bringing a ranging round onto a target in three rounds was considered a brass ring. This guy was really good!

When we returned to the west central front we continued the relentless attack to the north which, for me ended up at the 'Iron Triangle', Pyongyang, Kumhwa, and Chorwon. Somewhere in there I was hospitalized for a period with bronchial pneumonia and returned to the battery on light duty. This effectively ended my FO days and I was assigned other duties in the battery until my rotation home a short time later. I did return for a second partial tour during that later static period, but I returned reincarnated as an infantry soldier. My FO experience stood me in good stead as I initially led a weapons company 60mm mortar squad and later became the weapons platoon sergeant on my second tour."

**2nd Lt Milton Grismore**
**15th Field Artillery Battalion 1950-51**

"At age 15 I joined the Army National Guard in Denver, Colorado. I was a troublesome boy and in and out of trouble so to get away from the bad family situation I transferred into the Regular Army in October 1947. My first overseas assignment was to the 6th Infantry Division in Korea, 1948. I transferred to Japan with the division in December '48 and was assigned to the 24th Infantry Division, 52nd Field Artillery Battalion. I rotated home in March 1950 and into the 2nd Division, 15th Field Artillery Battalion. And many others were extended for the Truman year and I went back to Korea, arriving 31 July 1950 at Pusan. I was in Korea from July 1950 to 16 July 1951. I was assigned to a recon' party because of my own words. I happened to mention when assigned to the 15th that in my previous time in Korea I had in the Infantry and was assigned to pull maneuvers in the same area outside of Taegu. I spent thirteen months on line with in artillery reconnaissance, part of Headquarters Battery and Forward Observation parties. The Forward Observer artillery party was infantry without the infantry MOS. We laid landlines, and maintained AM or FM radio communications with divisional rear, either battalion or regiment. Our life was that of the frontline infantryman, hot and cold, dirty, hungry, tired, bored and unhappy, except when they rested we had to stay alert. Our basic load was often much more than the infantry. Our own field gear, radio, wire, phone, weapons and ammo. We were in those days the elite, better trained, the gung-ho individualistic soldier who could and would do the type of combat sorties today rendered by Rangers, Scouts, and Special Forces types. I fought along the Naktong River line at the Pusan perimeter, where we used a lot of interdiction fire and counter battery fire as we drove north in September1950. I was the driver RTO at the time. From there,

Anthony J. Sobieski

I fought at Kunu-ri, the River and the 'gauntlet'. I was temporarily assigned to a firing battery of the 503rd Field Artillery Battalion, they fired 155mm's, to work fire control in FDC. They had had many killed or captured. Then In December 1950 I was transferred into 'C' Battery, 15th Field Artillery, and patrolled Wonju Pass during January 1951. In February 1951 we moved into Hoengsong to support the 38th Infantry Regiment who in turn supported a ROK Division.

During August 1950 artillery fire was restricted to six rounds per gun per day, or 36 rounds per battery, 108 rounds per battalion, or 424 rounds per Div/Arty. It normally took three ranging rounds to register a base point, hence accuracy was demanded. On the Naktong River line, near the Pusan Perimeter, this restriction curtailed many targets of opportunity, counter-battery fire was a key need. September saw an increase of ammunition supply and fire missions became more able to cover the infantry and take targets of opportunity. After crossing the Naktong River, at our first action we were beset by North Korean artillery and two enlisted parties of two enlisted each were dispatched to climb nearby peaks, using BC scopes, and during the night took azimuth of the distant flashes of enemy artillery, battalion fire control triangulated and a fire mission destroyed the enemy pieces. In Kunu-ri our action against the attacking Chinese was defensive firing and in many cases hand to hand fighting with the enemy who had infiltrated our positions. The 15th Field Artillery, as part of the divisional rearguard, set up in a circular position, and many truckloads of ammo was fired into surrounding enemy infantry. Then we spiked the guns, removing firing pins to disallow enemy use, we were in convoy with the 23rd Infantry Regiment, where some armor and engineers made a route march out of the containment back towards P'yong-yang. Going through a refit somewhere south of Seoul I was transferred into a firing battery, and an FO section. North of Wonju we participated in long range patrols into and through Wonju pass, it was cold and no one wanted to fight.

An artillery Forward Observer was anyone in an FO party, be he commissioned, the reconnaissance sergeant, radio operator or driver. It was common practice in our unit for each member to be able to direct fire. I began as the RTO and learned the trade from there. An FO was an infantryman with artillery MOS. He had to maneuver and walk with his Infantry Company. We spent months on line and seeing our Battery on infrequent rest periods. My thoughts? Am I going to be able to come out of this, did I nail 'em all, the wire has to fixed, I stink. Then at last no thoughts other than laying a good base point registration to provide both defensive and offensive fire. An artillery recon party spent a lot of time doing ground surveys, patrols, relaying fire commands and running wire. As your experience and knowledge increased more responsibility became yours. We provided fire support for the 9th RCT, 23rd RCT, 38th RCT and many South Korean Units, and we were involved with both North Korean and Chinese communist forces. During my time in Korea trench warfare had not been introduced yet, and for FO duties we used the foxhole and reinforced bunkers. We did not designate the OP's by name or number except for the hill number. To my knowledge each Battery manned three OP's, one FO team per line company of infantry. Our life was busy, climbing slopes, adjusting fire, fighting as infantry, doing forward recon's, being cold and hot, wet or sizzling, hungry and tired, dirty and smelly. Calling a fire mission followed a set protocol. Laying a registration well was crucial so adjustments could be made by eyeball and finger. Firing into an enemy concentration became a dangerous chore for you and to stay down so small arms fire didn't hit you. With incoming, you hoped your hole was deep enough to cover you. In short it was exhilarating to be so effective.

There were many actions that I and the 15th fought in, some large some small. One particular fire mission I remember I called that stopped an enemy advance of at least regimental to divisional strength, having started with battery and finishing with everything up to and including the 8-inch howitzer. In August of 1951 somewhere in the Taebuk Mountains north of the 38th parallel a quite night was interrupted by the sound of movement in front of our position. There were two of us sergeants together this night so we called for an illuminating round. There were Chinese troops climbing up our forward slope. I called the 60mm mortar Observer over to do a fire mission, this was his first night on line, and, yep, he forgot what to do. I started the forward slope fire mission for him then called in my fire mission. The illumination round exposed the enclosed valley below to be full of enemy troops. I asked for 'Battalion, ten rounds, mixed ammunition HE, then WP, then Time fuse'. By the time morning arrived we had fired everything including the 8-inch howitzers. The infantry unit was ordered off of the hill following that incident. The smell was terrible, and it was estimated that we had decimated at least a regiment size unit. With ammo to burn we could have a grand shoot!

On the night of 12th of February the ROKs were hit by the Chinese and dispersed through us. The Chinese overran our position and we fought as infantry. They infiltrated our battery position causing great death and damage. We fought as we could, sniping and engaging in frontal situations. The afternoon of the same day after coming through a, for the lack of a better term, a gauntlet and coming to three pieces of our battery, with prime movers and ammo sitting there, I with another FO member bore sighted the weapons, and with mixed ammo fired 'fuse quick' we fired into the enemy hordes until dark. Most all of the FO sections were decimated, as were the firing battery and motor pool personnel. I was told to go for help and under extreme incoming of small arms and mortar fire I was wounded, and evac'ed to Japan. After a six-week hiatus in the hospital and return to my battery I saw mostly all new faces as I rejoined the infantry on company and battalion size patrols and actions in the Kumhwa valley. I became recon' sergeant and seconded my FO officer. The commissioned attrition was terrible at the time, and I began to lead my own FO party in May of '51. Involvement on the mountainous battles saw our FO parties firing heavy concentrations of directed fire in support of the infantry mission. Because of a shortage of qualified artillery officers as FO's, NCOs were used in that capacity. There were three such in my battery and all were as effective as any would require, we fired on 'Heartbreak', 'Bloody Ridge', and into and through the 'Iron Triangle'. I participated on the Chorwon valley campaign and 'Porkchop' too, some before they had names.

On the Naktong River I and my recon' officer spent several hours on a small hill overlooking the valley as North Korean Infantry and Armor advanced towards us. The Division was in CSMO and we were their eyes. We evacuated our position and returned to the main lines and took stragglers with us. While doing this, a T-34 tank came up behind of us and chased us south, but we were moving too fast and erratically for the tank to shoot at us. Coming upon tail end of our friendly column there were some of our vehicles and we alerted them, I we passed a 155mm section we yelled 'T-34!'. The section chief got his crew together, tied a rope on the lanyard, loaded the piece and aimed line of sight, knocking the tank out. At Kunu-ri, in North Korea, about fifteen air miles from the Yalu River for me are a wipe out. I remember the first and last days of the fight. The other five are missing. I started out in the FDC of a 503rd Field Artillery 155mm Battery. My next remembrance is at the crossroads where our battalion and the 23rd Infantry RCT were 8th Army rear guard. We fired all ammo, destroyed the breech blocks and everything we could not take out and rather than going through the gauntlet went out along the South China Sea where when we stopped we were bombed by a Chinese reconnaissance plane, with hand grenades. Hoengsong was more an infantry action with each man acting for himself or with small groups against the Chinese infiltrators. Sometimes for me, my memory is not easily accessed, but sometimes a sound, smell, or color will bring me back to Korea and my time there."

**Sergeant Harold Huston**
**90th Field Artillery Battalion 1950-51**

"It was in the fall of 1948 that three of my buddies and I from Rushville, Illinois decided to hitch hike to Quincy, which was about 60 miles west, to join the Navy but only two of our group passed the physical. The following day the remaining buddy and I hitch hiked to Springfield, another 60 miles east, to try our luck there to join the Navy where he passed but I did not. So on the following day, I hitch hiked to Chicago, 320 miles north, to try to join the Navy but again, I did not pass my physical. Where upon, when I arrived back in Rushville, I went to the pool hall and told the Army recruiter that I wanted to join the Army. We got into his car and went to Quincy where I was taken in without a physical being given! Yes, I did not receive a physical so, finally I made it into the military where I took my basic training at Camp Breckinridge, Kentucky. From there, I was sent to Fort Worden, Washington. It was in early July of 1950, while based at Fort Worden that I and another fellow from another company were called into my orderly room and were informed that a person with our M.0.S. was needed immediately in Korea. Since the other fellow was married, I agreed to go. Even though I was flown over immediately, that position had been filled from an outfit in Japan, by the time I arrived, so I was sent to HQ Battery, 90th Field Artillery Battalion, where I was informed that a jeep driver on one of the FO crews had been killed, so I inherited that position. The 90th was a 155mm gun Battalion, and while I was with the 90th there were several unusual events that happened. One time they called back the FO crew while 'B' Battery was told to go to the front lines to fire point blank at enemy positions in order to rescue an infantry company. In another extraordinary circumstance, 'A' Battery was called upon to help the infantry clear out a village that had enemy soldiers in it. My most excruciating experience during my months in Korea, which was from July 1950 to November 1951, was the night that our FO crew was spotted and we had to hurriedly gather our equipment together and move out. In doing so, I stumbled while carrying my radio, tent roll and rifle and rolled down the mountainside. As a result of my blunder, our FO crew was separated and we were listed as Missing In Action. This prompted my mother to try to get me back home as she felt she could not deal with any more trauma. Needless to say, her efforts were in vain. One time when our outfit was overrun, the only vehicles that were saved from HQ Battery was the HQ truck, maintenance, mess vehicles and my jeep. Later, when the area was retaken, we were able to take pictures of the equipment that was destroyed by the enemy or ourselves. During my tour of duty while fighting against both the North Koreans and Chinese, this was the only time that we lost any equipment. During one of the encounters with the Chinese, while supporting the Turkish Army, it was a thrill to see the Turks to fix their bayonets and charge the Chinese with great success. Like all of the U.N. units in Korea between July 1950 and the later part of 1951, our battalion covered almost all of Korea from North to South in several 'strategic withdrawals'. It was after one of those that I was able to get a much-needed break on R & R to Japan. During my tour in Korea I earned the Korean Service Medal, Purple Heart and five bronze stars. It was while being transported in a basket hanging below a helicopter after being hit, that I fully understood the meaning of the phrase, 'Frozen Chosin'. Shortly before my being rotated from the Frozen Chosin, I received a letter stating that I had been involuntarily had my three year enlistment extended for another year. I was rotated home in time for Christmas 1951 and after a 30-day leave I was sent to Camp Polk, LA. from where I was discharged."

**1st Lt Francis Kennedy**
**10th Field Artillery Battalion 1950-52**

"I was with the 10th Field Artillery Battalion, 3rd Infantry Division. We fired everything from 105mm to 16-inch Navy guns. I joined the military in the Second World War. I volunteered to be drafted in place of a friend of mine, because he was awaiting an appointment to the Merchant Marine Academy. That was March 3, 1943. I was assigned to the Army and joined the 359th AAA. I later applied and was accepted to the Air Corps for pilot training, but my class, 44K 'Air Cadets' was overloaded with pilots as was the U.S. Air Corps, so many of us became Aerial Engineers. I was in the training command in B-17's, when the atom bomb was dropped, and shortly afterwards in 1946, I was discharged from the United States Air Corps. I went to St. Bonaventure College, joining the ROTC, and was commissioned 2nd Lt., Artillery. After graduation I was assigned to the 10th Field Artillery Battalion of the 3rd Infantry Division at Fort Devon, Mass. I went to Fort Sill, Oklahoma, and had excellent training for FO work, and generalized training as an artillery officer. I was a member of the 10th Field Artillery with 'B' Battery. We were school troops at the U.S. Military Academy at West Point, when our division was directed to go to Korea. By the time we embarked for the Far East most of our units in the 3rd Division were at fifteen to twenty percent manned. We went to Kyushu Island in Japan and our vacancies were filled with Korean Civilian Replacements. Raw recruits who didn't speak English, and we GI's who couldn't speak Korean, what a fun time that was. We trained the ROK'S as best we were able and on October 20-25, we were landed in Wonson, North Korea. As an Air Observer and Forward Observer I participated in and was awarded Five Battle Stars, the CCF Intervention, CCF Spring Offensive, 2nd Korean Winter, 3rd Korean Winter, and the 1st U.N. Counter Offensive.

Because I was a flyboy in WWII, and a trained FO in the ensuing years I was ordered to the 10th Field Artillery Air section as an Air Observer. I flew fifty-six combat missions as an Air Observer with a real great pilot named Lt. Don Platt. We were north of the Chosin Reservoir at least twice a day directing artillery, support aircraft, and Navy gun fire on targets of opportunity. On December 22nd about fifty miles from the Hungnam Beach something happened to our L-19 aircraft. It started to shake violently after a round of some sort went off nearby. I mentioned that Platt was a great pilot. We started loosing altitude as we headed toward the evacuation at Hungnam, but Don Platt nursed that baby back to the beach where we landed in one piece. After inspecting the plane for quite a while we discovered that the plexi-glass panel above the cockpit had popped out causing the air stream over the center part of the wing to oscillate and cause the plane to vibrate. We had to destroy that great little plane, and felt bad about that. I was now an Air Observer without an airplane, but headquarters soon took care of that. I was now an FO on the beach and was directing fire of the ships that were there to support the evacuation. I called fire missions in as usual to the 10th Field fire direction center, and word came back, 'You are now firing the BIG MO.' What a thrill that was for me, but a bigger thrill was looking up and watching my 16-inch rounds flying over. I watched the Marines come back from the Chosin Reservoir, Hagaru, Koto-ri, Hamhung and they were physically beat, but in no way defeated. They had their dead with them, they are a very proud outfit and well they should be. On December 24th, 1950, I was ordered off the Hungnam Beach. I was very glad because I was assigned to depart on the last LST at the dock. Rumor had it that the engineers would be blowing the dock within the hour. We had quite a hard time pulling away from the dock because we were overloaded. As we were 500 to 600 yards away from the dock, on our way to our assigned ship, the dock exploded into a spectacular display. Thirty years later I was visiting my cousin and her husband Bob Trapp at Cape Cod, and he had mentioned that he heard that I was in the Korean War. He said he had also served in Korea, in the Navy. I told him that I loved the Navy, because they got us off Hungnam Beach, and sure annihilation. He then said that he had command of an LST. I then told him I was the last LST to leave the dock on December 24th. He just shook his head and said 'Frank, that was my boat, I was your skipper'. It sure is a small world.

At first the 10th was assigned to X Corps under General Almond. When we were evacuated from Hungnam, we were redeployed to Pusan, and our division was assigned to 8th Army support. When we landed in Pusan, on December 28th, 1950, division headquarters gave me orders to report to the 5th Air Force unit known as the 'Mosquitoes'. This was the 6147th Tactical Control Group. I was given a jeep and a driver, and then headed for Seoul, Korea. I was told that the Mosquito unit was located at K-2 Airfield in Seoul. When we got to the airfield, I went to flight operations and everyone was scrambling to get out. I asked about 'Mosquitoes' and a master sergeant pointed to a C-47 and said, 'That's the last plane out of here, you better haul your asses over there, to get out of here'. I told my driver to get back to Division Headquarters ASAP and got in the C-47. As we took off the end of the runway was lined with Chinese Soldiers firing at us. We got out with a few bullet holes and flew to our new field in Taejon, about eighty miles south of Seoul. We had unarmed AT-6's in the Mosquitoes. Our mission was to fly support for our infantry, and most of the time we were no higher than five hundred feet. We picked up targets of opportunity and would call in to the Air Force, Navy, or Marines for fighters to give the infantry support. In January, February, and March 1951, I flew one hundred combat missions with the Mosquitoes. Our missions were four hours, twice a day most of the time. I was very fortunate to have a great pilot, Captain Bill Dodson who was one of the best in the business. Of all the missions I flew with Mosquitoes, I was in only one plane that was lost, flying my 63rd mission with a high school friend from Sayre, Pennsylvania, Captain Jim Hoag. As we took off about 600-800 feet, our airplane engine caught fire, and Jim immediately did a 190 and landed on the same strip that we just took off from. It was an unbelievable maneuver, but he saved us. I'll never forget his great ability and quick thinking. In the Air Force after 100 missions the pilots were rotated out of Korea. We TDY Army Observers were rotated back to our units, and that's when I started my years as an FO Now the toughest part of the Korean War had started for me.

From March until December 1951, I served as an artillery Forward Observer with the infantry. We supported Companies 'L', 'I', and 'E' of the 7th Infantry Regiment, 3rd Infantry Division, Company 'K' of the 65th Infantry Regiment, 3rd Division, and the 28th and 29th Regiments of the 9th ROK Division. I considered myself an infantry man, more than an artillery man in those months. When you serve that long with these men you become one of them. I'll always have the highest regard for the infantry. No one asks you about your job or your branch of service. As you get to know each other they begin to realize that you can give them great support when it's needed. We artillerymen always got kidding about short rounds, and once in awhile that happens. You can fire 20,000 rounds at the enemy, but have one short round land in your company area and your name becomes 'Lt. Short Round'. One thing I know, there is no such thing as 'Friendly Fire'. I don't care where it came from, it isn't 'friendly'. Being with the infantry companies was pretty much the same. We were cold, hot, wet, dry, sleepless most of the time at night and bored as hell in the day. My thoughts were all about getting home to my wife and three boys. My first replacement was Lt. Stokes, he was with me only two days and was killed. My recon sergeant Dennis Sugrue, was killed on June 3rd 1951. In that same action my radio operator lost his leg. My second replacement was with me for seven days, was MIA and later listed as a POW. My thoughts began to wonder if I'd ever get out of Korea alive. My third replacement, Lt. Tillotson, was a great young officer who later returned to the States. Now that I look back, I begin to realize how poorly at the time we were trained to work with the infantry. I was a member of the 10th Field Artillery since 1948 and never once did we train in conjunction with the infantry assimilated situation. This flaw in my training nearly got me and my crew killed. I was told to go with 'L' Company, 7th Infantry Regiment. I arrived, met the company commander and was told that we were to attack a small well fortified hill next morning. That next morning, at 5am we left the staging area and started to attack. I was with my crew about half way up the hill of the objective, when I realized that the infantry had broken off advancing without our knowledge. We were left high and dry and when the enemy counter attacked we were alone. We kept firing as we fell back, but it was too close for comfort. I never found out why we were not notified of the infantry's withdrawal, but it taught me a great lesson, to stay in close contact with the company commander at all times. After this incident, when I was assigned to an infantry company, I made sure I met with, and got to know the company commander and his intentions on everything.

In July 1951 we assaulted Hill 355, later known as, 'Pork Chop'. Most of our OP's were hill elevation numbers, like Hill 596, called 'Little Gibraltar'. We usually manned twelve OP's for divisional support, but while I was there, seems we were all over Korea. The 3rd Division was very mobile, as were all units who served in Korea. Little Gibraltar, Uijongbu, Pork Chop, at the time we didn't name our outposts or hills when we were there. Other units named some of these hills, and locations such as the Punch Bowl, Heartbreak Ridge, and so on, but the 3rd Division was too busy fighting a war to take time to name hills. But, there were moments of hilarity even then. On hill 355, a funny thing happened on a middle of a July day. We had little or nothing to do, and a fellow 10th Field Artillery Forward Observer and I were looking over the same target area. His name was Ira Goen, one of the most humorous, nicest officers I have ever known. Ira was from Louisiana and a real Southern gentleman. He and his crew from 'F' Company next to us came to visit us in our boredom. We jointly decided that the crews at our batteries needed some exercise, so we determined that the wooded area in front showed signs of enemy activity. I told Ira that, 'I thought I saw a truck moving in the area.' He said, 'That's strange, because I thought I saw a tank in that same wooded area.' Keep in mind Ira and his crew from 'C' Battery and me and my crew from 'B' Battery were suppose to be about a mile from each other and normally we were. I told Ira I would call a fire mission and as soon as I got FDC's attention he was to call in a mission on the same area. I called my fire mission in and started to adjust with Ira standing next to me, although he was suppose to be a mile away, started to call his mission in. Both batteries started firing at the wooded target area for about twenty minutes, pounding the area with at least sixty rounds of 105mm shells. I gave a cease fire and damage report. Ira gave his report and both crews had a good laugh at the whole thing. In about fifteen minutes after our cease fire we saw secondary explosions, heavy oil and fuel explosions and fires. Soon the whole damn woods were burning and exploding. We all looked at each other and couldn't believe what we were seeing. Later reports indicated that, we great FO's and our crews that didn't have any idea of what we were doing, set off a secret enemy supply dump that was to be used as a planned offensive in the next few days, and that offensive did not materialize. Generally, life was, 'a day at a time'. After adjusting your defensive fire for the attack you expected that night you had time to clean up and at times boredom was your companion. This was a time you enjoyed your men's company and a time to write home. I had great crews, we all knew and respected each other and unfortunately we were close and when my recon sergeant Dennis Sugrue was killed and Jim Scully was badly wounded and evacuated, I never got too close with anyone again. I'm ashamed to say for the rest of my time on the OP I never got close to any of my crew. I respected them, but kept my distance. I never remembered anyone who I served with on the OP after Sugrue was killed. I truly loved him and Scully, like younger brothers, their loss was too much for me. Life in the trenches for the FO was the same as life in the trenches for the infantryman. It was cold, wet, hot, dry, hungry, sleepless, dirty, terrifying, and you thanked the Good Lord for the morning that you never thought you'd see. The infantryman in any army has it the toughest, I thought, period.

Two fire missions that I called stand out above all the rest. The first, I was told that Division Artillery was to fire a 'Time on Target' mission for General MacArthur on Hill 538, north of Seoul. I was very surprised when an entourage of brass arrived and MacArthur got out of a jeep. He was directed to me by one of his aides. I saluted and explained the mission. I called Fire Direction Center of the 3rd DIVARTY and told them that we were ready for the ToT on Hill 538. In a very short time I could hear the 8-inchers, the 155mm, and the 105mm, go off at their respective times and standing next to, but a little behind the General watching his expression when the whole top of Hill 538 exploded simultaneously. I have never seen a ToT any better at the Artillery School in Fort Sill, Oklahoma. I thought the corn cob pipe would fall out of the General's mouth, when the top of the Hill 538 erupted all the same time. He turned to me and said, 'Lt. what outfit did you say this was?' And I proudly said, 'The Third Division Artillery Sir.' He said, 'Yea, that was great.' I agreed that they were excellent. The 3rd DIVARTY really dished it out. The other significant mission that comes to mind was at Uijongbu, in April 1951. We were supporting the 65th Infantry Regiment 3rd Division. We were in the midst of the Ridgeway 'Meat grinder.' It was decided that the OP north of Uijongbu was where we would make our stand. I had seen massive attacks of Chinese against the Marines at Chosin, but this was different, because that was infantry against infantry. This was absolute madness. In broad daylight, about a quarter mile away the Chinese by the thousands just kept coming, and I just kept firing with massive artillery. I told Sugrue and Scully that this was just a slaughter, it made no sense. This went on and on and finally FDC told me that I had all division artillery at my command. For well over four hours that afternoon we killed over twelve thousand Chinese. I never understood why they sacrificed as many of their troops as they did. Forty-five years later, I read, 'Enter the Dragon,' by Russell Spurn. In the Epilogue of that book, I quote, "The former Nationalist Corps, the 50th Field Army, was virtually wiped out in the final battle for Seoul. Taiwan propagandists claimed the turncoat troops were deliberately scarified. This was untrue. The 50th stood and fought and fought well, as Sergeant General Wantu had promised, he was one of the few survivors. One-eyed Colonel Pang died leading a mass charge at Uijongbu.' It is clear to me now that, the 3rd DIVARTY had become the executioners of the Chinese 50th Field Army for the Chinese Communists.

When the infantry company commander decided to dig in at a position, I first look over the immediate target area. Identifying land marks such as cross roads, hills, bridges, and I would locate these on my maps of the area. I would determine the coordinates of the land mark and start my defensive fire plan from these coordinates. It went something like this. The Battalion's call sign was 'Pointer'. I would call the fire direction center, 'Pointer, this is Pointer Baker over'. They would respond with 'Pointer Baker this is Pointer, over!' And then I'd call a fire mission, 'This is Pointer Baker, fire mission, over'. 'Pointer Baker send your mission over', 'This is Pointer Baker, coordinates 25001250 request two rounds H.E. will adjust over'. The FDC will then repeat your fire mission and give you a, 'Roger, wait'. The FDC then computes the data and sends it to the firing battery. The FDC then comes back on with 'Pointer Baker this is Pointer, two rounds H.E, on the way, over'. You respond, 'On the way, Roger, wait'. When these rounds are observed in the general target area, the FO then adjusts the ranging rounds to the target. I found that the first rounds were mostly long so I might say, 'Right 100, drop 400, over'. FDC repeats this command and gives you an 'on the way'. Once you've adjusted in on the target you request a, 'fire for effect' to the FDC At this time you specify the type of rounds, usually H.E. High Explosive, Fuse, variable time fuses, or VT, and number of rounds requested, such as 'battery four rounds, over.' The FDC repeats your command and gives you a 'Roger wait.' The FDC then sends 'on the way, over.' You respond Roger, 'on the way.' After you determine that this is your desired target you and the FDC give it a concentration number. You can then call the FDC at any time and designate concentration number '268, fire for effect.' It saves many minutes and many lives of your fellow soldiers, when you are under attack. I found that determining good defensive fire in the daytime paid off at night when you were normally under attack. It worked for me.

On Thanksgiving Day 1951 Easy Company of the 7th Regiment was to replace the British forces on 'Little Gibraltar'. I and my crew were very fortunate to find an old bunker at the very top of the western most hill. I was surprised to see that the British didn't dig any holes and quite frankly, was very critical of them until I saw some of the GI's of 'E' Company doing their best to dig in. As it turns out the whole top of the mountain was nothing but slate. Who ever dug the OP Bunker we were in must have been an engineer with a lot of help, because it was an excellent Sheltered OP This was November 25th, 1951. I remembered on Thanksgiving the previous year, 1950, they hit us with all they had in the Chosin Reservoir area. It was the big push to annihilate the U.S. X Corps and the U.S. Marines. Fortunately, the Navy saved our bacon and the Hungnam evacuation took place. My Battery Commander Captain Donald McConnell called me on the land line to wish me and my crew a Happy Thanksgiving, and told me that the battery would be sending up a crew with our Thanksgiving dinner, turkey, potatoes, and all the trimmings. Soon after this call I was looking over the valley north of us and the whole front came alive with massive fire. I grabbed my phone to call in a fire mission for counter battery fire and we were hit with every kind of artillery, rockets, and mortar fire. I looked out again and everywhere I looked I saw flashes from all kinds of field pieces. It was continuous steady fire and our area was being hit with the bulk of this onslaught. I was then aware that my phone lines were out, so immediately grabbed my radio. I called to the FDC and could not receive or send to them. My radio was also out of order. Now here I was a Forward Observer without any communications with the largest target I've ever had to fire on, and no communications. I counted at least one hundred field pieces firing at us. This was a new Chinese tactic and it was very effective. I looked out of our bunker and saw only dead soldiers. They were not only dead, but most of what I saw was blown apart. They had no fox holes to get into and they were vulnerable. At least seven infantry GI's joined me and my crew in the bunker, they were the only live infantry men I saw that day. Our Bunker was hit at least fifteen times with heavy rounds and it looked like it would collapse at anytime. The infantry platoon leader that was able to make it to the bunker was badly wounded in the head and face. I told one of the men with him to get him back to an aid station. They left and I was sure that he was so badly wounded that he would never make it. The barrage went on and on. I would guess for at least a couple of hours or so, but time goes very slow when you are under that kind of incessant concentrated artillery, so I really had no idea of how long. It seemed like a life time.

A big round hit our bunker and I felt the left side of my face burn and my hearing was affected. I felt my face, it was bloody and it stung. I was surprised, because I didn't expect that to happen. The reason for my disappointment was that I, in April, was given a novena to the Blessed Virgin Mary, by my Recon Sergeant Sugrue. Dennis' sister was a nun and had sent him this novena. He passed it along to me. After reading the promise of the novena I was determined to complete it. For nine days I diligently said the novena with the promise that on completion that no violent end would come to my life. Further, I would not be burned and no metal would pierce my skin. As a soldier in close combat this was something I couldn't resist believing in. I was comfortably safe in my own mind. Now, as I looked out of the bunker, artillery hitting everywhere around us like machine gun fire, I found myself saying, 'Oh God, please let me get home to see Patrick, my new son that I had not yet seen, and I will never ask another thing from you.' All of a sudden a complete calm came over me. I turned to the men in the bunker as said, in a calm voice, 'We will leave this bunker and get back out of range of this devastating fire'. And with that, we left the bunker. I again cannot gauge the time, but it was long enough that our artillery started to come in on our position, and our planes started to strike the area. To say the least it was a tough trip back to headquarters. I ended up in battalion HQ where my old friend, Captain Kanamuitau Ito gave me a bottle of V.O. The next thing I knew I was at the aid tent being attended to. I guess I was given a sedative but just before I fell asleep I heard the Doctor say, 'Your face is a mess, it's got wood splinters, mud, and rock embedded in it, but I can't find any shrapnel or metal at all.' For the next ten to fifteen years when I would shave, I would find wood pieces in my face. Guess what, I never found metal either. I really never knew about events that occurred at the aid tent after Little Gibraltar. It was fifty years later that I was with my Battery Commander, Donald McConnell at a 10th Field Artillery Battalion reunion at Fort Sill, Oklahoma. He and I went for a ride together and gave us a time to talk. He told me that I was delirious after being wounded, and that I punched the doctor, the chaplain, and my Battalion Commander Colonel Smith. All of them were trying to help me, but I was angry that my radio and telephone communications had gone out and was unable to return counter Battery Fire to all the field pieces that were firing at us."

**Sergeant Joseph Lennox**
**10th Field Artillery Battalion 1950-51**

"I enlisted in September 1948 in the Regular Army for two years. I was stationed at West Point as cadre training cadets. My enlistment was up on Sept 28th, 1950, but President Truman extended all military personnel for a period of one year. On the 28th I was in the middle of the Pacific Ocean on my way to Japan. From when I enlisted, I spent all three years with 'A' Battery, 10th Field Artillery Battalion, 3rd Infantry Division. We were a 105mm battalion, I believe we were initially under the X Corps, but after being evacuated from Hungnam in December 1950 we became part of I Corps. When we landed at Wonson and moved up to the west bank of the Chosin to Sachang-Ni, and that was when we were hit by the CCF which began the long retreat to the port of Hungnam. Ninety-five percent of the time I was assigned to 'B' Company of the 7th Infantry Regiment, and additionally I spent anywhere from three to five days on and off with 'B' Company of the 65th Infantry Regiment and the Belgian Brigade. When we landed in Wonson in November of 1950 the North Koreans had been decimated and we did mostly mop up operations on our way north. The Marines and the 7th Division were moving towards the Yalu River past the Chosin Reservoir, so all of our major contact was with the CCF. The Chinese were good soldiers and I held them in great respect. I did not have any animosity towards them. They were GIs just like us. I served in Korea with the 10th from November 1950 to august 1951. In July of 1950 'C' Battery along with a battalion of the 7th Infantry Regiment was deployed in their entirety to fill up the 1st Cavalry Division, and this left us woefully under strength and the CO asked for people who were good with a map and compass. I was, so I volunteered.

I vividly remember the night battle at Sachang-Ni in November of 1950. The CCF overran 'A' and 'C' Companies and got into the infantry battalion headquarters and burned it to the ground. By dawn we had air cover and the CCF pulled back. We got hit the next night but held the ground. That was when we learned that the CCF had crossed the Yalu River and entered the war. By afternoon we were ordered to burn what we could not carry and that we were flanked on both sides and even they had gotten behind us. The retreat was a constant fire fight but our air support was greatly responsible for our success. The CCF had no planes except for a few Russian MIGs that ventured over us once in a while, but mostly stayed hidden during the day. Each night was a bitch because that's when the CCF operated. I cannot recall the names of the places but during our retreat to the Port of Hungnam in mid December 1950, I was attached as an FO with 'B' Company 1st Battalion 7th Infantry Regiment when a platoon that was left to cover our movement to the rear was cut off. The CO of 'B' Company, Capt John Powers, who was one of the bravest men I ever served with, asked me to put fire on both sides of the valley. My Battery 'A' must have fired at least 100 rounds of ammunition and I raked both sides. He then took me, three tanks, and a platoon of riflemen and we went out and beat off the enemy but had many casualties. After Hungnam we went to Pusan and then North to Osan-ni. My memory is vague but we pushed north and set up an OP on the south bank of the Han River. It was a solid bunker and we used a B.C. scope for most of the month of March. We crossed the Han and pushed north of Uijongbu. 22 March of 1951 stands out clear. The spring offensive by the CCF was fierce. Their objective was to capture the capital city of South Korea to celebrate May 1st, the communist holiday of May Day. We pulled back to what I recall was the 'golden line'. General Ridgeway told us we will stop them here or die. We fought the CCF for about five days both day and night and we held the line. They suffered massive casualties both dead and wounded and that operation was the last big battle of the war for me. Shortly after that, talks began at Panmunjon to negotiate a cease fire, and we moved to an area called the 'Iron Triangle', where it was mostly patrol action and smaller operations.

What was it like being an FO? I liked it. We were very important to the infantry. They relied on us for heavy support and treated us kind of special. When we secured a hill, the CO of the infantry company would lay out his defensive plan for us and always asked where we thought our OP would be best to support his defense. He also would assign a rifle squad around our OP to make sure we had ample fire power. I carried a .45 pistol and carbine as did my radio operator. I guess the best way to express it is that we were treated with great respect. I felt good to have GIs thank us when we called in fire on the enemy and kept them from making a success out of their attack. Normally, artillery batteries have three FO teams. I was a member of FO team #2 therefore I was assigned to 'B' Company, FO #1, 'A' Company, and FO #3, to 'C' Company. So we always had three FO teams in the field as OP's. Our OP's were always with an infantry company. The only hill I can remember is Hill 155 near Singone-ni. We generally fired support both offensively and defensively but during an attack if the CCF made in-roads into our position they were too close to chance artillery fire so we would then revert to riflemen. In addition to our .45 caliber pistols we carried M1 carbines and basically used ourselves and infantry riflemen. We always dug a fox hole and one of us would be awake all the time. If we expected an attack then sleep did not come easy. At night you never got out of your hole. The nights were scary. A funny thing is that during a battle I was never really scared but afterwards I would have a dreaded fear of the next fight. When it rained we got soaked and conditions were bad. We were dirty, tired, and homesick.

One time, I spotted three CCF artillery guns firing on our position. I called in the fire mission and my azimuth and coordinates were so exact that the first round fired, which was the adjustment round, hit right smack on target and I then ordered each gun to fire three rounds, for a total of eighteen rounds. We knocked out all three guns and a patrol went out and found all three guns destroyed and ten enemy KIA's. Using a compass you shoot an imaginary line from your position to the target. This is called an azimuth. Then locate the target on the map. These are the coordinates, and this is plotted using the map that is coded on the left side and top of the map. I remember the call sign of the Fire Direction Center for the 10th Field was 'Pointer Dog'. My call sign was 'Magazine Queen'. After determining the azimuth and coordinates this is the sequence using the radio 'Pointer Dog this is Magazine Queen, fire mission over. Magazine Queen this is Pointer Dog send your mission. Pointer this is Queen, azimuth 3510, coordinates Charlie 6.50 three artillery pieces dug in, fire one round to mark target over. Queen this is Pointer azimuth 3510, coordinates Charlie 6.50 is that correct over? Pointer this is Queen. Roger. Fire when ready'. The target is then plotted by the Fire Direction Center. 'Queen this is Pointer. Rounds on the way. Pointer this is Queen. Roger wait'. When the round hits, depending on relation to the target you adjust it either left, right, up or down. Binoculars are graduated in a scale, as you look through them you see millimeters. The formula is that one mil is 1,000 yards which equals 1 yard. If you say you are 1,000 yards from the target and the round hits 100 yards to the left and 50 yards below you count off using the binocular scale and make the adjustment. In this case you would, being so close to the target, then call the FDC using the call signs I have mentioned 'Right 100. Add 50 and fire for effect' I can request any number rounds including air bursts and white phosphorus, but, it was not always that easy. Sometimes the first requested round would hit behind the target. You could hear it hit but could not see it, which would then cause me to request a smoke round for a visual.

The winter of 1950 was unbearable. I have never been so cold in my life. Temperatures dipped to 20 and 30 degrees below zero and from November of 1950 until I was evacuated at Hungnam on Dec 24th I never had a roof over my head and the only article of clothing I ever took off was my helmet and gloves. The ordeal of our retreat to Hungnam still haunts me. I do not in God's name know how we made it. We fought almost every day. A hot meal was a rarity. We were also short of winter gear because General McArthur said we would be home by Christmas after we defeated the North Koreans, but I guess he had not counted on Chinese intervention. My feet are still cold."

**Sergeant A.P. Robert Mixon**
**2nd Battalion, 7th Marine Regiment, 1st Marine Division 1950-51**

"I had joined the Marines at 16, my high school graduation day. WWII was winding up and though I saw no combat, I did learn that I did not want to be infantry. When things broke in Korea, I thought it was the beginning of WWIII. At that time, the Marines would let you pick your area or MOS field if you signed up for four years. So for the second time in my young life, I volunteered. I was sent to Camp Pendleton and got there about 10a.m. and by 2a.m. I was loaded aboard the USS Bayfield with a rifle in my hand and was assigned to the 81mm Mortar Platoon, Weapons Company, 2nd Battalion, 7th Marine Regiment, 1st Marine Division. From the time I hit Pendleton, I was yelling that I was supposed to be 'Aviation Duty Only', but no one listened. Once again, I was a grunt! I went in to Korea at Inchon and stayed until 9 May 1951. I had gotten into some trouble with a squad leader and he was putting some heavy duty on me, every water and ration detail had my name on it. In the Seoul operation, we lost some FO people and the call was out for volunteers and I took it on in order to get away from this vindictive sergeant. My first battle was the Inchon landing and Seoul. I was an ammo bearer until Seoul where I went into radio/FO training. Second campaign was the Chosin campaign. I went in at Wonson and was attached to Fox Company and remained with Fox Company until they were detached and then was put on OP duty at TokTong Pass. At that time, I came back to the Mortar Platoon for some 'rest'. I went with the platoon to the Reservoir and on the 28th when our other two companies, Dog and Easy, were slaughtered, I was still in the valley with the guns. On the 30th when they tried to form a new battalion out of the remnants and various others such as drivers, cooks, band people etc, I was re-assigned with the new Dog Company 2/7, now called the Damnation Battalion. I stayed with this unit until we boarded ships at Hungnam. My third campaign was what we called the 'Pohang Guerrilla Hunt' but if my memory serves me they called it Operation Thunderbolt. It was not impressive, in order to attack the small bands of guerrillas, they spit us up into small units. We did a lot of walking but little fighting, only one firefight in a month. The fourth campaign I was in was about mid February and called Operation Killer. We jumped off in central Korea in a town called Chungju. My fifth and final campaign was the CCF Spring Offensive that started sometime in early April of '51 and we were in the Hwachon area.

Being an FO was a heavy responsibility. In the Marine Corps, a company commander is a very powerful man. He has at his disposal, 24-hours a day, 250 highly trained assault troops that are very esprit de corps and motivated. But in addition to this, he has at his command 81mm Mortars, 105mm and 155mm artillery, air assault and naval gunfire and each of these specialties are represented by Forward Observers. In addition, if conditions require, he may also have such strengths as tanks, heavy machine guns, 4.2 mortars, anti-tank weapons, etc. In other words, this captain has a full arsenal at his instant disposal. He doesn't have to clear with battalion or regiment or division, if he needs it, he so orders. As a result of these groupings, most of us FO's were near by the Company CP and the captain although some of us such as heavy machine guns and the 81mm mortars, the lighter weapons, may be attached to the point platoon. I found this to be the case most of the time. Life of an FO was pretty much like the life of a grunt. The exception being that every two or three weeks we were rotated and got to go back to the gun emplacements where we could sleep better, eat better, and live better although we were the second line of defense. Nothing is like being on the front lines. There is a love, a trust, a comradeship that does not exist anywhere else like it does between ground troops, and though they occasionally let us slip into their fraternity, we are still only half breeds. My thoughts then and now are uttermost respect for anyone who was infantry. You ask what it was like being an FO and for me it was constant fear. Fear of pain, fear of death, and fear of failure. I did everything I could to see that I was ready when called upon, scared to death, but ready. At the end of each day, unless in a stationary position, I would zero my guns in on the most likely attack routes. If an attack came, and I could identify the route, I would have one or more guns already on target with the remaining guns able to convert to the attack target. We were welcomed and the grunts were thankful for us. That is especially true of the Air FO, this cat could lay down some serious hurt on the enemy and the grunts knew it and respected it. They also had a reverence for the Navy Corpsman and were extremely protective of him.

I was on a lot of OP's but I can't recall their names. I got my second wound while on an OP in late April, but I don't remember the name, if I ever knew it. Most firefights required me to merely call in my mortar fire. On occasion, things became more serious and I was required to enter the firefight as well as call in fire missions. I was a young man from rural South Carolina, accustomed to the outdoor life with lots of hunting and fishing, but, I don't recall a single day in Korea where I thought to myself 'what a beautiful day!' It seemed every day had something seriously wrong, too hot, too cold, too dry, too wet, too muddy, and too sandy. Nothing was right and I dreamed and prayed for the day I'd get out of there. My most vivid memories of combat in Korea most often do not involve fire missions. I do recall one that I called in at the Reservoir in which I caught a detail of Chinese crossing a body of water which of course was frozen solid. They were hoping to join others in an encircling movement and I happened to spot them and brought in big time fire on them and if the metal didn't get them the ice did. I would evaluate the target, infantry, tank etc. and the terrain and determine which form of ammo I felt would be most effective, whether it be HE, WP or whatever to fire for effect or search and traverse. I relayed these choices to the gun crew and waited for the first round to hit to see if corrections were in order, unless doing a search/traverse mission. I recall many actions in which I was involved, I probably called in a hundred or more missions and each was specific just some stand out more than others. I think the most exciting events I had was when we were under mortar or artillery attack and I knew that there was an FO out there with his glasses on us, just as I had mine on them. I would try to locate the area I felt the FO might be located and on a few occasions, I think I got to him. At least on a couple occasions, the firing would cease and I could imagine that I got the FO location."

**2nd Lt Robert Teitelbaum**
**15th Field Artillery Battalion 1950-51**

"I originally enlisted on August 22nd, 1940 in the Army Signal Corps. When Korea came along, I went from Ft. Lewis, Washington to Pusan, Korea in June 1950. I was assigned to the 2nd Infantry Division, 15th Field Artillery Battalion, 'C' Battery. The 15th was a 105mm unit. I served in Korea from the beginning in July of 1950 through September of 1951. I first was a Liaison Officer for an Infantry Battalion Combat Team, then as a Liaison pilot starting around Aug 11th 1950. The first five battles I was in were as an Army aviator and Air Observer. I found that most of it was just do what was necessary and expedient. We worked with the 37th Infantry Battalion of the 2nd Infantry Division, I also was used to instruct other FO's how to adjust artillery fire. I was also assigned to KMAG about the beginning of 1951. My whole time there we fought both the Chinese and the North Koreans. There were just too many fire missions to mention. Things that stick out in my mind were being behind the 105's that were drawing enemy fire, night attacks by enemy tanks, knocked down aiming stakes, which made the job difficult."

**Sergeant Nathaniel Nicholson**
**159th Field Artillery Battalion 1950-51**

"I volunteered for the Army. My mother was a religious person and I didn't want to continue going to church so I joined the Army. I was stationed in Nara Japan in 1948 and sent to Korea on July 12th, 1950. I was a radio operator assigned to the 159th Field Artillery Battalion, we fired 105mm howitzers and were part of I Corps around Yong Dok. I served from July 12th, 1950 to April 15th, 1951, My original M.O.S. was as a medical technician, but they converted it to Forward Observer. We fought every day, and everyday was another hill. The summertime was hot, flies, mosquitoes, no nets, cold, wet, ice, snow, sometimes no food. The 159th supported 24th Infantry Regiment, they were glad to have us. We were called the automatic artillery. We also supported some ROK units, but I'm not sure which ones. At that time in the war, the very beginning, we fought against the North Koreans. My assignment was with 'C' Company 1st Battalion, 24th Infantry Regiment. We had four FO teams, three working and one in relief. We had OP's located on Bowling Alley, Baldy Mountain, Pork Chop Hill, the River Bed, Horse Shoe Road and Engineer Road. I remember at Masan, the Riverbed on September 1st, 1950, the enemy attacked and we had to defend ourselves. I was wounded and saved the last 105mm, I received a Purple Heart and a Silver Star for that action. I always knew where the enemy was at all times. We moved so often, there was no time to dig trenches because when we got on the OP we had to set up the guns, but many times the infantry would dig a trench. There was so many fire missions I don't remember, but there was one at Yechon where we had 150 enemy killed, that was in July 1950.

In July 1950, shortly after arriving in Korea, the Marines encountered combat. The Army's Triple Nickel, the 555th Infantry Regiment supported them and we set up our guns to support them both with artillery. The North Koreans were on the hills on both sides and the Marines and the Triple Nickel went down the middle between the enemy. The Marines went first and the enemy spread out and 'opened the door' as it is called and let them go through. Then all of a sudden, the enemy broke loose and closed ranks behind them and the Marines saw that there were more enemy combatants than they had planned on. They tried to fight their way out but the enemy annihilated them. A group of Marines and members of the 555th was captured and killed. Their bodies were hidden in a schoolhouse. Meanwhile, our 90th Field Artillery Battalion was also attacked. They had to abandon their guns, block the tubes, and explode them so that the enemy couldn't use them. My friend, James Burnett, was on the radio, talking to the airplanes that were supporting the Marines that were trying to get out of there. We had a .50-caliber machine gun mounted on the roof of the cab of an ammo truck. I manned that truck and began shooting to try and keep the enemy off of our men. My gun jammed while I was shooting it and a soldier named Francis Mackey un-jammed it and started shooting until the enemy killed him. That could have been me instead of Francis. God spared my life. On July 17, 1950, I was called upon a mountain to observe the enemy. An American tank was stranded and we were trying to free it. As well, the infantry needed some artillery. I was the jeep driver for the Forward Observer, and my jeep needed oil for the transmission. As a driver for the FO, I was on the front line of battle. I was up on that hill for two days waiting for oil but no one would bring it to me or send a replacement jeep. Heavy fighting incurred and we had to get out of there quickly. I had no choice but to try to drive the jeep. It was my sole means of escape. Although I didn't expect it to operate, it did. It was stuck in second gear but miraculously brought me to safety. Later when the mechanics inspected the jeep, they saw nothing but steel in there. The gears had been grinded down to nothing. They couldn't believe that I drove the jeep but I did. I was reprimanded for doing that, and was admonished never to drive a jeep again and ordered to serve in the mess tent. However, when more men were needed to go to the front line, guess who was ordered to go? Me. I would be on the front line throughout my duration of the Korean War.

August 24, 1950, marked a bit of a turning point in my life. We were in a riverbed like a stalemate, not able to really progress because of the enemy. We were headed to Inchon, but would not arrive until after September 15th, the day the United States launched a surprise attack against the North Korean Army. I was up on Battle Mountain. It was a steep climb to our position. After we took the hill, the enemy counterattacked us and we were forced to retreat down the hill. As I was running, I heard a moan. It was the moan of a wounded soldier. So much was happening around me. The Reds were moving in on us real fast. UN soldiers were trying to get down the hill. In spite of all that was happening, I couldn't bear the thought of leaving this wounded soldier behind for the enemy to just ransack. Clutching him, I tried to drag him down the hill. It was difficult but I managed to move him a considerable distance. Finally, I came to a clump of bushes. He said, 'Leave me here and go. Someone will find me.' I tried to secure assistance for him but with chaos all around me, I couldn't do it. The enemy was fast approaching. He kept reiterating, 'Go. I am too heavy for you.' It was hard to do but I had to go for two reasons, one, if I had any hope of escaping at all and two, if I had any hope of securing help for him. I got to the bottom of the hill in tears crying for this soldier when the commanding officer of 'C' Company said, 'Let's go up on the hill again.' I was relieved in the sense that the soldier would have a chance of being rescued, but I was feeling ill and could not endure the trip uphill again. I shouted for a medic and was taken to the aid unit. I had a fever of 103 degrees and had to stay put. Meanwhile, the solder was rescued but died en route to the aid unit. Nonetheless, he did not die at the hands of the enemy. It wasn't until 40 years after the war that I received news of him and even until this day, I do not know his name.

On September 1, 1950, at approximately four o'clock in the morning, a missile hit a tank in front of our position in a riverbed in the city of Masan. The 2nd Battalion collapsed. On the other side of the riverbed was a road and behind the road, a mountain. We had our attention toward the low hills but the enemy attacked from the mountain area. Some of the South Korean troops that manned the front line were unreliable in standing their ground and as well, we had a weak regiment. A considerable amount of stragglers left their positions without leave. Earlier that day, the pay truck had been there to pay the men their wages. Everyone felt better after receiving their pay. We were listening to music when mortar shells started coming in, more than 50 or 60. The Reds blew the pay truck to pieces. Everybody scrambled into a hole. The first machine gunfire came from our outpost. That signified that they were coming in a great force. The regiment was on the line in front of us and the enemy had broken through. One company from the reserve was sent up to try to close the back line but it was in vain. The enemy had succeeding in breaking through. We had no infantry watching over us. Earlier on, they had been relieved and had gone back about five miles. A soldier named Willie Boone was on the outpost where the road went into a little farmhouse, or barn, approximately 300 yards away. Boone was holding the enemy off with a .50-caliber machine gun. About two o'clock in the morning, he needed some ammunition and I grabbed two cans and ran 200-300 yards through the riverbed, down the road, and yet down another road to where he was. Then I ran all the way back. Bu the next day Boone disappeared. We never knew what happened to him. His body was never recovered. Some questioned whether he was actually there, but I took Boone his ammo so I know for a fact that he did not run away. Eventually, he was listed as MIA. I have seen the casualty reports showing his name twice on the list, once on August 31, 1950 and again on September 1, 1950. I really don't know what happened to Boone. It's a mystery. The report stated that he went down shooting but his body was never recovered, neither did he receive an award for bravery.

As day was breaking, we started shooting rounds point-blank. We depressed the muzzles and sighted through the tube. There was a gully on the other side of the road and as the Red raised their heads to come over, we'd shoot at them. They were forced to find some way around us. They couldn't come straight at us from the front. It would be an understatement to say that we shot everything we had at them. We even fired smoke shells. They weren't doing any damage, but at least the enemy was kept back. We just wanted to make a boom some sort of way. They had no idea what to expect. We shot everything else we had and was finally down to our last high explosive shells, WWII stuff. There's a timer on the head of the shell and if it's set to explode just before hitting the ground, more casualties are incurred. That was our 'smart bomb' in those days. Actually, it is dangerous to fire high explosive rounds with the tube close to the ground because the round is timed. The timers are preset and could engage at any time. But, that was all that we had left to fight with. We were reduced to one type of shell. We had to take our chances. Finally, after much intense fighting, we were down to nothing. Our CO, Captain Franke, said, 'Close stations, march order. We can withdraw.' Four men, including myself and one B.A.R., were able to hold the enemy off until our troops safely withdrew. Before I know what happened, the B.A.R. was shot out of my hands. It was about 8:00 a.m. and it appeared that everyone left except me. 'What did I get myself into' I thought. Then, I saw a truck. Lieutenant Kenneth Ingraham, my Forward Observer suddenly appeared, and I wasn't alone after all! He said 'Wait! We have to get the last gun!' Two other men and the lieutenant hooked it up to the truck and Lieutenant Ingraham said, 'Let's get out of here!' As I positioned myself to drive, they jumped on the shields of the gun which one could stand on. An enemy mortar round was lodged in the radiator but the truck started when I turned the key. It didn't have any water in it and it ran hot but it ran! Someone was calling, 'Come on out this way!' It was Captain Franke, he was in Burnett's weapon carrier leading the way out. Suddenly, a bullet came through the windshield past my chest and went through the big muscle of my left arm. However, I could still drive with one arm. I said to myself, 'Nick, get out of here quick!' I continued to drive, following behind Captain Franke when the truck started steaming. It was overheating and I couldn't continue to drive it anymore. The captain noticed our plight and pulled over so we could switch the gun to the weapons carrier and pull it, and us, to safety. I am proud to have been part of the 'C' Battery. It was the only battery in our battalion that never lost a gun. The entire division lost guns, but we never lost a single one.

Captain Franke took us to 'Engineer Road'. The 77th Engineers had built a road, I didn't even know that it was there. In a report by the division artillery, they said they saw no reason to build a road just for one battery. However, if they hadn't built it, we would have been trapped. That day, I, a black soldier of the 159th Field Artillery Battalion, received recognition and honor. For my act of bravery in combat, I was awarded the Purple Heart and the Silver Star. Finally, we stopped at a place called Horseshoe Road. Our plans were to move there if we had to, we had ammunition that was stockpiled there. We set the guns up again and shot everything we had from high explosives to smoke just to keep the enemy away and to regroup. This allowed us to test all of our equipment also. It was obvious that my wound needed medical attention and I was taken to the hospital. After being there for two days, it was surmised that I had a flesh wound. My arm was put in a sling and I was sent right back to Horseshoe Road. Thirty soldiers, including myself, had been admitted to the hospital from that fight and twenty-nine had been granted R&R in Japan. As for me, I was sent where I always was since setting foot on Korean soil, the front line! It appears as though nothing could prohibit me from having to serve on the front line. Whether due to my skill and expertise, or simply because that's where I had always been, I seemed doomed to the front line. I thought for sure that I would be granted R&R right along with everyone else and God knows that I needed it. That same night that I was discharged from the hospital and rejoined my outfit, I went to sleep alongside the recovered gun that we transported back to Horseshoe Road from our last battle. I was sleeping deeply seeing as I had not slept for an entire day and had engaged in fierce combat coupled with the fact that I hadn't had a regular sleep pattern in weeks. While sleeping, I dreamt I heard my mother call my name, and I woke up and just at that time, heard the enemy coming through again. We had hung out some brass shells in front of our position and I could hear the 'ping, ping, ping' of the shells clicking together. I woke everyone up and crawled over to Captain Franke. 'Someone is coming up the hill on gun four' I told him. Instantly, there was gunfire, the enemy was trying to destroy the area. I approached but couldn't see anything. I told the captain to give me some hand grenades. I threw them down the hill and the enemy finally left, causing no harm. I went back to the radio jeep where Burnett was and stayed with him that night. We found out the next day that one enemy soldier had been killed.

I remained in combat right up until the time that I was sent home. On Easter morning, 1951, I was on the front line and a Chaplain Deveaux went from foxhole to foxhole praying for each soldier. I thought to myself, 'He must certainly be a man of God.' God was definitely with him because the enemy could have picked him off any time as he walked in the open. He prayed for each of us. I prayed that I would be able to go home and within two weeks, I was on my way home. I had been in combat for ten months and finally, I was on top of the list to go. Throughout my duration in the war, I could not go on R&R because I was on the front line and never got to rest. That's the reason I slept often in my jeep or slept hard. I had to steal sleep whenever I could because sometimes days would elapse before I got a solid 6 hours sleep and oftentimes, I survived on only 2-4 hours of sleep. When I was summoned to come off the battlefield, a jeep was appointed to take me back to my CP Just as I was about to get on the jeep, a report came in that a jeep had just blown up because the road was mined. I refused a jeep ride and instead, ran the five miles back to my outfit on foot. Obviously, I somehow avoided the mines as well as the enemy. Upon arrival back to my outfit, I acquired a temperature of 106 degrees. I had malaria, and I feared I would not be able to go home. Through the grace of God, however, the medic, Captain Booker, put cold water on me to break the fever to send me home. When my temperature reached 98 degrees, he signed the papers for me to go home. If he had not broken my fever, I would not have been released to go home. Thus, I received a final triple blessing, prayers answered, mines avoided, and fever broken! Hallelujah! I was going home!"

**Sergeant James Daly**
**10th Field Artillery Battalion 1950-51**

"I enlisted in September 1948. A few of us had about twenty days left on our two year enlistments, and while on a three day pass in Highland NJ, one of my sisters called and told me I had a telegram to report back to Fort Devens immediately. We who were waiting for our enlistments to be up now had an additional one year to serve. I was with the 10th Field Artillery Battalion, 3rd Infantry Division, 'C' Battery, and served in Korea with the 10th Field from November 1950 to September 1951. We had 105mm towed howitzers, and from what I remember we supported the 65th Infantry Regiment most of the time. I originally became the CO's driver, from what I heard it was my attire, I was just learning to drive, but my pants and shirts were always creased, I had them sewed that way! I volunteered to be on a Forward Observer team because as I believed we were paid a little more for every day of combat. If one team came down from the hills usually another would take their place, but mostly I was on a team with the same 2nd Lt, Lt Sawyer, who was from my area of the Bronx, NY. Being a Forward Observer, it was lonely, wet, but most of all I remember the cold. A lot of us were Gung Ho or John Wayne types, Ed Damaso, Jack Lennox, a few others, all great guys who I remain close friends with today 50+ years later. Going to Korea was a number of steps of reality that kind of hit us along the way. Hearing that Tom Reed from Battery 'A', who had deployed earlier, had been seriously wounded. We also began to hear rumors that our old Battery 'C' which had deployed earlier as part of a Battalion Combat Team that had been badly mauled. It was at this point that some of the excitement began to wear off and little reality began to sink in. When we got to Japan, we were billeted at Camp Chicamauga, which the 19th Infantry Regiment, 24th Infantry Division had just left for Korea. Some of their equipment was still in the barracks. This didn't last long. After a few days we were moved to a desolate training area at Camp Jumonji for intense training. At Jumonji we received our first replacements, ROK's. Now the fun began as we trudged up and down every hill in Southern Japan. I remember the admonition 'lock your knees' as we trudged up these seemingly vertical mountains looking for a 'top' that I don't remember ever reaching. It was for the good, the hills in Japan were only molehills compared to Korea. The highpoint of our arrival at Wonson, Korea was having vertical bars welded to the front bumpers of our vehicles to snag wires stretched across roads to decapitate careless young studs. Reality was really setting in."

**Corporal Robert Gutting**
**2nd Battalion, 11th Marines 1950-51**

"I was raised in Chicago, Illinois and in 1944 when I was 15 I ran away from home, lied about my age and got papers to sail in the Merchant Marine, the only service I could get into. I sailed for four years, mostly Liberty ships and oil tankers, and in August 1948 I returned from a seven month trip on a tanker to the Persian Gulf and back to Germany several times. While in the Gulf I suffered from heat stroke and felt the sea had lost its charm. At about that time the US started the draft again, and I decided to join the Navy. A friend of mine, who had been in the Marine Corps at the end of WIT, talked me into joining the Marines. He said he was going to reenlist, and we could probably serve together. I signed up and left on a Friday for Boot Camp and he was supposed to be sworn in the following Monday, but he changed his mind and so I was in the Marine Corps. After boot camp in Platoon 222 at Parris Island, SC, they put a group of us in the back of a 6x6 truck and drove us to

Camp Lejuene, NC. They pulled up in front of some barracks and told us to get out. We were now in the 10th Marines, a 105 Howitzer outfit. The battery had been almost stripped of manpower due to the expiration of enlistment of many two and three year men who had signed up in 1946 and 1946, so they were glad to see us. I was placed in Baker Battery under Captain Cable, who later was severely wounded on the outskirts of Seoul, Korea in Sept. of 1950 when he drove to the front to visit our FO team. His driver was killed and the chaplain riding with his also severely wounded when their Jeep hit a landmine.

At that time, the Marine Corps was down to roughly 60,000 men in two divisions and guard, ship and consulate duties around the globe. The battery was short wiremen, so I was told that was what I would be. They never sent me to school, just taught me in the field. Subsequently the Corps disbanded anti aircraft batteries and sane artillery batteries and condensed us into two 4- gun batteries with a skeleton compliment. As I remember it, we only had one sergeant, two corporals and one gunny sergeant in the battery. Gun Crew Chiefs were all acting corporals. At that time 'B' Battery was disbanded and the remnants went to Charlie Battery 10th Marines. In May of 1950 I was promoted to corporal after only 20 months in the Corps and felt I had arrived! We then drove up to Camp Geiger, Virginia for our annual firing exercise in June, 1950. The evening of June 25th while we were all sitting on the ground at an outdoor movie screen waiting for the film to start it was announced over the PA system that the North Koreans had invaded South Korea. There was a lot of cheering from the Marines who were undoubtedly bored with peacetime duty. We then packed up and drove back to Camp Lejuene, were told to send our footlockers and other personal effects home and got ready to board a train for California. Morale was high as the troops did not expect it to be much of a deployment. We arrived in California after six days on the train and prepared to go overseas. I was placed in Fox Battery, 11th Marines. We also picked up a bunch of reservists from Los Angeles, California including quite a few Hispanics who wore very likeable kids. At that time I discovered that the reserves were more like a social club, they met once a week for drill and then at the end of the month when they got their paycheck they chipped in for a keg of beer and had a party. Training was, to say the least, lacking. I remember one young Hispanic from the reserves that did not know how to load his weapon or field strip it. I had to show him how. He also had never been to boot camp or fired his weapon. This caused the Marines to set up a boot camp in South Korea after the Chosin Campaign to teach these now combat veterans how to march and salute. However, the older NCOs and officers were almost all WWII veterans and fought in such places as Iwo Jima and Okinawa, so there was plenty of experience.

My officially assigned unit title was Fox Battery, 2nd Battalion, 11th Marines, 1st Marine Division, Fleet Marine Force. We were assigned to the X Corps, and I was attached to Charlie Company, 1st Battalion, first manned under the leadership of legendary Col. 'Chesty' Puller. I was in Korea from the landing at Inchon on Sept. 15th, 1950 until August of 1951. My battery had two Forward Observer teams, FO1 and FO2. I was on FO2. I landed at Inchon with Charlie Company and climbed the seawall at Blue Beach, south of the town. Approaching the wall in our Higgins boat most of the Marines were stretching their necks trying to see what was going on as all of the Navy ships were laying down a heavy barrage. Then a few rounds of ammunition came whistling over the top of the boat and everyone instantly became a combat veteran and instinctively ducked down as much as they could in the crowded craft. At the time I climbed the wall I was carrying the top and bottom parts of my field pack, shelter half and blanket rolled up, carbine and plenty of ammo, a roll of telephone wire, one EE8 telephone, wireman's tool, bayonet, two canteens of water, first aid pack, three days rations, etc. When we got ashore we were told to put our packs in a pile, the bottom half containing extra pair of shoes, dungarees, socks and underwear, and we would retrieve them later. I never saw that pack again!

The first night at Inchon we moved as far as we could before it became dark then dug into a cabbage patch. Next morning we secured Inchon and made our way toward Seoul. Near Seoul is an industrial town called Yong-dung-po, and there were two hills, 80 and 85, overlooking the roadway and a branch of the Han River behind Hill 85 with a burned out bridge crossing it. The North Koreans wore dug in on these hills and Charlie Company attacked. The FO team I was on was behind the assault force and in front of the reserves of Charlie Company. Lt. John Guild and his runner crested the top of Hill 85 and were cut down by machine gun fire. Lt. Commiskey had given his carbine to a BAR man whose weapon had jammed, and assaulted the machine gun nest with a .45 calibre pistol, killing the two crewmen and then killing two more Koreans who were shooting at him with burp guns. His pistol was then empty and he jumped on the remaining Korean who had a burp gun. Lt. Commiskey was straddling this man, who was trying desperately to free up his burp gun so he could fire, when Commiskey's runner came up and handed him a carbine, with which he shot the Korean in the head. Commiskey later was the first Marine awarded the Medal of Honor in the Korean War. Lt. Guild was awarded the Navy Cross posthumously. He and his runner were dragged to the foot of Hill 85 and covered with blankets, including mine, but both died during the night. We were not yet in a position to establish lines of communication with the rear and when we dug in it was in a 360 degree front.

We then pushed on to the Han River and crossed in DUKWs and advanced down the road to the suburbs of Seoul. We set up our position for the night overlooking Seoul. There was a Christian church on the hill that had been desecrated by the North Koreans, and Maggie Higgins visited the site that evening and was escorted around the area by two of the Charlie Company sergeants. The most impressive sight that night was the swooshing of shells overhead hitting the city below. It was all lit up like the 4th of July. They said the battleship Missouri was pumping shells into the city from over 20 miles away in the harbor at Inchon, and when these huge shells hit it wiped out an entire block. The rumor was that these 16 inch shells cost five thousand dollars, at that time the price of a new Cadillac, and every time one of these huge shells swooshed over, someone would comment 'there goes another new Cadillac'. The next morning we moved out into the city of Seoul. We advanced down the main street, ending up at the main train station. About 100 yards down the street from the station the NKPA erected a barricade of rice sacks and fortified it with machine guns and two old bolt action anti-tank guns they were shooting toward the train station with. We later captured one of these guns and it had something like a 6-foot barrel on it. One of the Marines fired a round thru it and almost broke his shoulder from the recoil, so we abandoned the weapon. When we entered the main doors of the train station, at a dead run due to the fire coming our way, we found the bodies of a young man and woman along with two small children that had been killed by the NK. I remember the babies looked like rag dolls lying in the rubble next to their parents. After we drove the NK out of Seoul into the surrounding hills we were relieved by Army units and dug in as reserves for about a week. At that time I once again suffered from heat stroke and just lay in my foxhole for three days until I felt better. If we would have had to move out I could not have made it. One of the things I remember about this period of time is the terrible stench in the area. There was a dead North Korean soldier somewhere and it took several days of searching before they found him in a camouflaged hole and buried him.

We then returned to Inchon and boarded ship for a landing in North Korea. We landed at Wonju and took trucks south to Koto-ri, a small village, as a blocking force for any remnants of the NK Army trying to escape north. At Koto-ri our guns dug in along the shore with a railroad embankment to our front. I was temporarily back with the battery for a rest, but we weren't there long. The NK survivors staged a night attack on our positions in the hills overlooking the bay. They overran one position, bayoneting Marines in their sleeping bags. I helped load several of the bodies on a 6x6 truck the next day. The best I can remember, there were about 75 dead and numerous wounded. We dug in that night expecting the worst. I had a machine gun nest with three other artillerymen dug in to the right and slightly in front of the battery. We were told if the infantry was overrun, they would come across the railroad embankment on the run yelling 'I'm a Rebel bastard' and we were to hold fire. That night the mortar section tried to fire illuminating flares left over from WWII and they fired several boxes and none of them worked. Fortunately, the dinks had continued on northward. One unfortunate incident that occurred that evening was when Republic of Korea Marines attempted to reinforce us from the sea in barges. It was reported that the barges were filled with the enemy, and we turned one of our guns seaward and opened fire, sinking them. Don't know how many friendlies were killed by 'friendly fire', it was the fog of war. After our stay at Koto-ri we moved north to the base of the mountains to a town called Ehittung-ni. We were still in reserve there, and I again had a machine gun outpost set up about 100 yards from the battery. We all thought the war was over, and rumors were that we would all be home for Christmas and would be guests of the Rose Bowl New Year's day. So much for rumors!

When the Chinese entered the war, I was again placed on the FO team and joined Charlie Company. We moved up to the base of the mountains and set up in squad tents for about a week. During that time, the British commando's stopped by and warmed themselves up in our tents for a while. We did not know they wore part of a relief force that was going to the aid of the Marines in the mountains. They all wore red berets with airborne badges on them, and we tried to barter for them to no avail, they just would not part with their red berets. Later we learned many of them were killed or wounded in an ambush. At that time, Charlie Company was given the job of opening the road from Chinhung-ni to Koto-ri, which was blockaded by the Chinese. The lieutenant and corporal we had from Inchon to Seoul were reservists from Los Angeles and they left the battery and I never saw them again. I was then made the Wire Team Chief for FO2. Our officer was Lt. Doezsma, who was wounded in the Seoul campaign and had trouble carrying his pack due to a shoulder wound. But he managed to survive and later retired as a Lt Col. Charlie Company jumped off in a snowstorm and assaulted Hill 1085, the most prominent peak above Koto-ri. They only lost six men killed and a handful wounded due to the snowstorm. It was such a formidable peak it would have been costly to assault it in clear weather. My job at this point was to get a telephone line from the infantry to a radio jeep usually at the bottom of the hill, in this case the base of the mountain. I also had to keep it in working order. This was not always an easy job with people tramping around and tanks and trucks moving along the road, which was not much more than a goat trail that had to be constantly widened by the engineers or we would not have been able to move much equipment along it. Charlie Company subsequently held the high ground and kept the road open and the division withdrew, followed by our unit. The one thing that I remember most about this campaign was the intense cold. We probably had more casualties due to cold weather than we did to the Chinese gunfire. After the Chosin battle I participated in 'The Great Guerilla Hunt'. We were so badly depleted at the reservoir that after we got to Masan and Pusan we had to rebuild the 1st Marine Division with fresh replacements. Some units had a lot more replacements than they did original members. After we rested and came up to full strength we were deployed to root out remnants of North Korean units that had been bypassed and had taken to the hills to continue fighting as guerillas. Although they were called guerillas, I believe some of the outfits we attacked were simply bandits, because the local natives told us they had been operating in the area for five years, since WWII ended in 1945. In fact, they were using Japanese equipment and on one occasion I liberated a Japanese bayonet. From September to November, 1950, we faced North Koreans and pretty much annihilated them. By the time we got in North Korea, they were almost finished as a fighting force. After November 1950, I remember almost entirely fighting Chinese. The NK were better equipped and better led than the Chinese but they were a lot more savage than the Chinese in my opinion. They executed a lot of American and allied POWs, especially after we landed at Inchon and got them on the run. We recovered many bodies of soldiers with their hands tied behind their backs with communication wire and shot.

My initial thoughts upon landing at Inchon were I could not believe we were actually going to be allowed to go ashore and kill people. It seemed somewhat insane, but I also remember being very scared most of the time. At the Chosin Reservoir operation the one thing I remember the best is how cold it was. They said it was 30 below zero but with wind chill it could have been 40 below. A lot of the Marines were from the South and California, and many of them had never seen snow. Three of my close buddies were from Jacksonville, Florida. All three were wounded and suffered frostbite, but managed to get out of the reservoir. After the months went by it got to be like a bad dream. You saddle up, advance, climb a hill, come down and then climb another hill with all the shooting and explosions going on around you. During action once we were set up and calling in artillery support, the main the Forward Observer. On several occasions Infantry, due to the Marine Corps concept of every Marine a rifleman. We were constantly on the move in the attack or withdrawal around this time, and did not have any permanent OP's. Whatever the elevation of the hill we were on became our OP, such as Hill 80, 85 or 1081.

In the Marine Corps the FO units always supported the same infantry company so I was exclusively with Charlie Company except for one interesting two-week period when my FO team supported a Republic of Korea Marine unit. They did not have FO teams, so when Charlie Company was placed in reserve, we were sent to provide artillery support for the Korean Marines. It was a real experience. They actually carried a .50 calibre machine gun as a company weapon. It was also at this time that the Chinese launched a spring offensive and hit the Korean Marines at night. That was probably as scared as I had been. I wasn't feeling too bad until our Lt. called us together and gave us a pep talk about 'It's not when you die, its how you die'. I felt pretty good up until that time. The Chinese launched a probing attack against the Korean defensive positions, and the Koreans opened up with the .50 calibre machine guns. Every time the .50s opened up it lit up the whole area. I thought that would get us all killed, but the Koreans killed ten Chinese armed with Thompson machine guns. The Koreans put them in a pile and I thought I would get one for my personal weapon. I picked one up and it felt like it weighed a ton. I promptly put it back down. We gave the weapons to a Jeep driver. At 5:00pm the day after the Chinese attack we were told to pack up and out. The Chinese had broken thru the center of the line and we were sitting out front like a bulge. We marched for twenty miles at the double until we came to a river about midnight and then crossed in DUKWs or 'Alligators'. We were then at the Reservoir, and went into reserve again. While we were with Koreans, Charlie Company was put into the line and suffered extreme casualties at Horseshoe Ridge, and the FO team that took our place had two men killed.

Being on an FO team in the Marines was about as close to being an infantryman without having the infantry MOS. We ate, slept, hiked and fought with the infantry. One thing about the Marines, every Marine is trained as a rifleman first and then whatever specialty 2$^{nd}$, such as cook, truck driver, quartermaster, etc. And in many cases all of these people were put on the line to act as infantry, particularly at the Chosin Reservoir. Three of my close friends in the artillery were wounded while fighting as infantry at the reservoir. One died soon after the war from head injuries and another is in a wheelchair due to his Korean wounds. With the infantry, we stayed in the lines until relieved and seldom had a chance to clean up until after we went into reserve. One time I remember in July 1951, we pulled back in reserve temporarily after having been on the lines for over thirty days. The lieutenant asked me if I wanted to go to the rear and pick up the mail. Any chance to get off the hill was appreciated, and I went off the hill and 'borrowed' a Jeep and drove to the rear. I happened to pass a portable shower unit that had been set up and stopped to clean up. After I took a shower, they took my old utilities and underwear and gave me a clean set. After I got the mail and returned to the hill occupied by Charlie Company I could not believe the stench. As long as I smelled as bad as everyone else, I did not notice how bad everyone smelled, but after cleaning up, the smell was overpowering. Since I served with the infantry when they were on the line and returned to the battery when the company went in reserve, I experienced both 'lifestyles'. One thing about the Marine infantry is that they were 'gravel crunchers' all the way. I do not remember ever riding in a vehicle while with the infantry. Even when they formed up to go into the attack, they marched sometimes several miles before reaching the jump-off line. On the other hand, the artillery always had to move by truck, and when set up in a semi-permanent position, always had hot chow. Each battery had their own cooks with them and the first thing they would do when possible is set up a mess tent and cook hot meals. Also the Marine infantry seldom advanced on roads. We were always 'running the ridges' from one point to another. Also the Marine infantry had few vehicles, the only one I remember is a Jeep for the company commander who seldom used it. Another fact of life is that casualties were of course much higher in the infantry. All of our dead and wounded artillerymen occurred when they were with the infantry. The only other battery casualties occurred in accidents, especially when our prime movers went over the steep embankments on the Korean roads, or when they hit a landmine. The only other casualty I recall was due to one of the gunners setting a trip flare around the battery perimeter and making the mistake of having his head over the tube when he removed the safety pin. The flare went off, hitting him in the face and killing him instantly.

The first fire mission I remember was called when we were on the Hill 85 at Yong-dung-po. Two T-34 Russian made tanks were on a road across the river from the hill we had just taken from the North Koreans, and they were firing at us. Their guns had a flat trajectory so as long as we stayed on the reverse side of the hill we were relatively safe, but the explosions were unsettling to say the least. Our FO officer called in a mission and the sounds of the shells whizzing overhead was a welcome noise, and both tanks were disabled. However, later on the outskirts of Seoul we were by the bank of a dry river, possible a tributary of the Han River. An island sat in the middle of the dry river bed and the company commander, Captain Wray, wanted to lay an artillery barrage on the island before we advanced and would all be out in the open. He felt the artillery could disperse any possible enemy troops. The FO officer called for a round to be fired several times, but we all strained but could not see where the shell hit. He than called for a round of smoke in order to orient himself. One of the Marines thought he saw it hit on the far side of the island so the lieutenant called in an adjustment and called for the battery to fire all six guns. They did, and as we all stood there looking intently at the intended target, there was the swoosh of incoming fire, and all six rounds landed about a half a block behind us. We obviously gave the wrong coordinates to the guns. Capt. Wray was reluctant to use the guns for a while after that! At about the same time a low flying B-26 was staffing the city when a shell from another battery hit its left wing, knocking if off. The plane nosed into the ground with its entire crew. Later when we occupied the train station in Seoul, the North Koreans had a barricade blocking our advance. Tanks were not able to knock it out, so our FO officer called a fire mission and walked the artillery right up the street and onto the barricade. This really impressed the troops. On another occasion we were preparing a fire mission for the company commander. Since he wanted the shells to fall close to our position, the captain ordered some of the Marines dug in on the forward positions to leave the foxholes and come back further to the rear. As two of the Marines complied and were getting out of their fox holes, one of the six 105's fired a short round that landed between them and killed them instantly. A check of the guns back at the battery showed that the Gun Crew Chief had misunderstood the command of the Fire Direction Officer and had put the wrong elevation on the gun causing the short round. The Crew Chief was relieved of his position, but the damage had been done. It's hard to place blame on these occasions. Of course, this often caused hard feelings between the infantrymen and the artillerymen on the FO team.

Another time in the late spring we were on a low ridge overlooking a village with a long hill on the other side of it. By this time I was serving under my third FO officer, Lt. Peabody, who also retired as a colonel. The North Koreans were dropping mortar rounds on us and we could see movement on the hill on the other side of the village. Lt. Peabody called for marker rounds, but after several were fired we could not tell where they hit. Lt. Peabody adjusted the range downward and asked for another round to be fired. We heard this one whistle over our heads and hit a house on the far end of the village near the enemy occupied hill. We could see smoke rising and people yelling and saw some villagers running around in a panic. At that time we stopped firing as the North Koreans had also ceased dropping mortars on us and apparently had left the hill. A short time later a Korean man came into our lines with his brother, who had been hit by our shrapnel. Both were dressed all in white as was the custom at that time, and one man was covered in blood. They told our interpreter, a ROK officer, that the man and his family had just sat down to eat a meal when the shell hit his house and killed his wife and children and seriously wounded him. The ROK officer told the man it was the North Koreans who had shelled the village. Our corpsman treated the man and sent him to the rear for medical attention, but I do not know if he survived. It was always interesting to me that when the Korean civilians needed help they always cane into our lines instead of the North Korean lines, even though they were kinsmen. Talk about a bad day, we really felt bad and it was one of those things that made the infantry look at us with less than admiration in their eyes. Of course during the eleven months I was in Korea we fired literally several hundred missions destroying tanks, troops and supplies and helping to soften up the defenses on numerous hills before being assaulted by the infantry, but the disasters stand out. Another quaint aspect of the Korean culture is that they were curious. We could always tell in the early stages of the campaign when we were about to approach an enemy position. The hills around would be full of standing and sitting Koreans waiting for the show to begin."

**1st Lt Leo Johnson**
**99th Field Artillery Battalion 1950-51**

"I entered active military service on 29 October 1940, at Fort Sill, Oklahoma, and completed basic training in six weeks and was assigned to Battery 'C' 77th Field Artillery Battalion as battery clerk. By 1945, I was the 1st Sergeant of the battery, and had fought in North Africa, Sicily, the Anzio Beachhead, Southern France, and on into Austria. After WWII, I re-enlisted in March 1946 in the Grade of Master Sergeant, and attended the Ft. Sill NCO Course #2. Upon completion I was reassigned to ROTC duty at Virginia Tech University in Blacksburg, VA. I was the administrative NCO and Instructor for the artillery unit there. In May 1950 I was transferred to FECOM, and then in July I received a direct reserve commission as a 2nd Lieutenant. In Teague, Korea, I was assigned to the 99th Field Artillery Battalion, 'A' Battery, and further was assigned as a Forward Observer to a company of infantry, a duty I performed until I was wounded in July 1951. The 99th was a 105mm direct support artillery battalion to the 1st Cavalry Division. During my assignments in Korea, I was awarded six battle stars, participating in such battles as Yong Dong and the Teague perimeter. I was serving with the 5th Battalion of the Thailand Army, part of the UN contingent, when wounded. They awarded me the Noble Order of the Crown of Thailand medal for my service with them. When I was assigned as a Forward Observer, I never realized how much hell the infantry actually went through until I went up as a FO the first time. We normally supported the 1st Battalion, 8th Cavalry, and the Thailand Battalion, 1st ROK Division. We were always treated 1st class by the infantry folks. The battery had a couple of observation posts, some with names like 'Rampart 27' and 'Clawhammer 27' but we normally manned one per battery. As for significant things that I remember, on November 3rd 1950, the Chinese over-ran our position, that was a tense time. The most significant fire mission I recall was one fired on 'Liberty Bridge' in April 1951 in support of the ROKs. Calling a fire mission, after six battles in WWII as Chief of Firing Battery, it came natural to me. I was wounded in July, and by August '51, I was evacuated from Tripler General Hospital in Hawaii to Ft Hood, Texas, and assigned to the 1st Armored Division."

### Sergeant Kenneth Collins
### 10th Field Artillery Battalion 1950

"In June 1948 the draft was re-instituted because of the Russians closing off Berlin. I was going to be drafted or I could join for two years without any reserve time, so I joined on July 30, 1948. In June 1950, the North Koreans attacked. Our outfit, the 10th Field Artillery Battalion, was at West Point training the cadets. I was due to get out on July 29th and was sent back to Ft. Devens, MA to be discharged. President Truman froze all discharges on July 28th. Needless to say I wasn't thrilled to have another year tacked on. Then in August the 3rd Infantry Division was ordered to Korea. I spent my entire time, well almost, three years in the 10th Field Artillery of the 3rd Division, including infantry basic training, and we fired the 105mm howitzer. We were assigned to two different corps, but most of the time to X Corps I believe. We left Ft. Devens on August 25, 1950 and left San Francisco September 1st, arriving in I-Ionsue, Japan on the 16th for training and working ROK troops into our depleted outfits. We arrived at Wonson in North Korea just after Bob Hope's troupe. We went north to the Chosen Reservoir and came back and tried to go West through the mountains to hook up with I Corps when the Chinese hit. Then back to Hungnam where we were the last field artillery unit off the beach, Our FO's adjusted fire on the Chinese from the USS Missouri. Back down to Pusan then back up the peninsula across the 38th parallel for the May Day attack by the Chinese in 1951.

I was in the Fire Direction Center in the early months in Korea, and they did not have any lieutenants for the Air Observers so I was asked to do this as a Corporal. This was fine with me since I got to sleep on a cot in a tent and it was bitter cold that winter. The first big battle was the Chinese attack in December 1950 in the North. This was our baptism of fire and the 10th did well. The next battle was in January in the North under Ridgeway in 1951. We chased the Chinese back across the 38th recapturing Seoul. The third was the May Day attack by the Chinese that pushed us back to Seoul but we held. In the first battle I was in the fire direction center. In the latter two I was an Air Observer. I was covering the advance by various outfits including the Turks and the French in addition to our own 3rd Infantry Division regiments. Being an Air Observer was much different than an FO because we were 10, 15, and even 20 miles sometimes ahead of our lines looking for the Chinese. Sometimes we covered advancing troops, spotting the enemy. I then drew a crude map and dropped it to the lead scouts. Adjusting fire from the air turned out to be rather easy. I could normally be on target in three rounds before we fired for effect. Once in Seoul we came under anti-aircraft fire. We were in L-19's, a Stinson single engine two-seater or a Piper Cub which was canvas covered. This was rather frightening, sometimes we came under fire from dug in troops who lay on their backs and just aimed their burp guns at us, we were hit several times but not in any place that did harm.

Air Observers were kind of different, we lived at the air strips not at our units so our contact was by radio. We supported the 7th, 65th, and 15th Infantry Regiments, the three regiments assigned to the 3rd Division, plus the ones I mentioned earlier, and the British Highlanders. In the spring May Day attack in April and May '51 we were under intense pressure so much so I didn't sleep for 36 hours. This was true for most of the other FO's and FDC personnel too. I remember a specific mission when McArthur came to the front in April '51, we were south of the Han River ready to assault Seoul. For his visit they wanted a division artillery barrage on Seoul and I was assigned to make the initial adjustment and ask for a 'converged sheaf' or for all guns to aim at my target. It was a tremendous 'shot' but of course the Chinese had left but 'ol' Mac' thought it was great! I was, as far as I know, the first to try to adjust artillery fire at night from the air. This was on Seoul also and it wasn't very effective and we did forget one thing, our landing field didn't have lights! So they burned some 55 gallon drums of gasoline to light the grassy field. We also marked the targets for carrier based aircraft. I'd fly low, twenty to thirty feet, open the door and drop smoke grenades to mark the targets. This is when they would lay on their backs and shoot. Unfortunately, I also observed disasters, in January 1950 the Air Force caught a large contingent of Chinese troops south of Seoul and Suwan on a cold, snowy night. We were sent up to fly over and give a report. There were hundreds, if not thousands, of casualties along a twenty mile strip of road, all civilians! A sad sight but the Air Force could not tell they were civilians I'm certain. During the evacuation of Hungnan we were on an LST in the harbor when the docks were blown up. I've seen this in newsreels many times, it rocked our LST and I spent Christmas Eve in my sleeping bag in a 20mm gun turret and was happy to do so! As a FDC staffer, sometimes I was listening to the FO call in their mission and it was like listening to a full scale attack, sometimes heart wrenching to hear them call for fire on their own location. I was sent back home on May 14th, 1951. We left Inchon that date to Sasebo, Japan then Camp Drake near Tokyo, then we left Yokohama on May 30th for Ft. Lewis. We arrived on June 9th and I was discharged on July 28th at Ft Knox, KY."

### 1st Lt Abraham Epstein
### 64th Field Artillery Battalion 1950
### (A letter written by General Sidney Berry, USA retired)

"As Able Company's commanding officer, 'Able Six', I must have been a cross to bear to the commander of 'A' Battery, 64th Field Artillery, who provided artillery Forward Observers to Able Company. I was demanding and hard to please and sent several FO's back to their home battery and demanded competent replacements. The source of conflict was my high regard for artillery's effectiveness in putting my infantrymen on the objective with minimum loss of life and limb and my expectation that artillery lieutenants would be as physically fit, alert, determined, reliable, and effective as infantry lieutenants. I expected artillery FO's to be an integral part of Able Company in every way, professionally and personally, and I knew that Able Company depended upon effective artillery fire to hold defensive positions and seize objectives with minimum human loss. Perhaps I expected too much of the artillery FO's, most of whom were junior lieutenants with relatively little artillery experience.

Then, in November 1950, 1st Lt Abraham Epstein joined Able Company as our artillery FO. His appearance was unimpressive. Epstein was short, balding, gentle, soft-spoken. He wore thick-lensed eyeglasses and sported a little Hitler-like mustache underneath a large nose. Our new FO looked more like a meek high school teacher than a stalwart soldier. Thankfully, I was unaware that Epstein was an experienced anti-aircraft artilleryman who had never directed artillery fire in direct support of infantrymen. In fact, Abe Epstein proved to be a superb artillery Forward Observer who became a close friend and a valuable source of canned Mexican food that his wife, Wilma, mailed from their home in El Paso, Texas. We soon accepted Lieutenant Epstein as an integral part of Able Company, called him 'Ep' and referred to him as 'Able Seven' an honor we granted to no one else. To his battery commander's consternation, only Ep fully satisfied me as Able Company's artillery Forward Observer.

What made Abe Epstein such an effective artillery Forward Observer? First, he was a friendly, intelligent, poised human being who respected others, had high personal and professional standards, and was willing to work hard at accomplishing common tasks. Second, he was an effective field artillery Forward Observer who understood artillery's role in supporting the infantry, worked hard at learning how he could better supped the infantry, advanced his ideas to improve our combat effectiveness, was tireless in seeking more and better artillery support for Able Company, and respected and coordinated the role of all weapons available to us. Third, he pitched into help the company effort in every way possible and never complained that 'this is not an artillery FO's job'. Finally, Lieutenant Abraham Epstein felt at home in Able Company, and as time passed and platoon leaders were evacuated as casualties, he became one of the company's trusted 'old-timers'.

When Able Company defended, Ep had a central role in coordinating mortar and artillery defensive fires. He placed his radio jeep where best he could direct supporting fires when needed, and stayed in close contact with me. I always knew where Ep was located. When Able Company attacked, I usually followed the lead rifle platoon to sense how the battle was going and to determine when and where to commit other rifle platoons. Ep, the mortar FO's. and the company executive officer normally coordinated supporting fires from a nearby observation point. But when appropriate, Ep and radio would accompany me. For example, about 0100 hours, 28 November 1950, when a close-in Chinese attack panicked one of our rifle platoons, Ep joined the company executive officer, first sergeant, and me in turning soldiers around to retake their position, which they did. Ep later humorously wondered aloud if leading a counterattack was included in his contract as field artillery FO.

I was aware that I complicated life of the commander of Able Battery by sending FO's back as 'unsuitable to Able Company's needs' and requesting Epstein's assignment as our regular FO. I understood the battery commander's desire to rotate FO's among rifle companies, but I was selfish in wanting the best for Able Company. Convinced that effective artillery support was essential to Able Company and its soldiers, I demanded the best available artillery FO, and Lieutenant Abe Epstein had proved best for Able Company. In December 1950 when Able Company manned the regimental combat outpost line along the south shore of the Imjin River, one battery commander spent several days on FO duty with us to determine just what I expected of an artillery FO. When he returned to his battery, he reassigned Ep as Able Company's artillery FO and did so routinely for the remainder of his battery command. My Korean War combat experience as a rifle company commander who enjoyed superb artillery support directed by an outstanding artillery Forward Observer shaped my professional attitude for the remainder of my active military service. I had learned that effective supporting fire permits maneuver units to accomplish their mission with minimum casualties and was convinced that in fighting ground warfare, American military professionals should spend ammunition as if we were millionaires and soldiers' lives as if we were paupers and that field artillery was the Infantryman's best friend on the battlefield."

**1st Lt Richard Kirk**
**58th Armored Field Artillery Battalion 1950-51**

"Like everyone else in my age group I received a draft notice in December 1942, and entered service on 1 Jan '43 and entered a totally different life style for a college student with his own bathroom. After some initial moves, I studied Japanese for two long years, was commissioned and sent to Japan as part of the Allied Translator and Interrogation Section. I went from there to Korea in October '45, commanding a translator team where, with exceptional skill, I manage to screw up enough newspaper translations to put us on the edge of a renewal of hostilities on a couple of occasions! By 1948 I was a civilian again, but figured the Army was the best life I had led up to that time, so I applied for competitive tour, returned to service in August '49 and went to Fort Sill for the Basic course. I decided on artillery as a career because I didn't want to walk everywhere in the infantry and I didn't want to get locked into a tank if the hatch was stuck. I was assigned to an all black armored artillery battalion in Fort Hood, this was before integration, and was doing nicely with all the crappy jobs they would give a second lieutenant on competitive tour for Regular Army when Bingo! Guess what? Just as I discovered the riding stables and the golf course at Fort Hood the North Korean's invaded South Korea and we were put on alert. Our battalion designation was changed to the 58th Armored Field Artillery Battalion and we were hustled off to Korea as early fill out for the 3rd Infantry Division, which had lost one of its artillery battalions in downsizing. We were alerted in August and shipped out September '50 with a short stop in Japan and a quick trip to Pusan in late September or early October, can't remember which but in time to join the break out and the push north to Seoul, passing through Taejon and so on. Always in support of the 65th Infantry Regiment from Puerto Rico because we were a Regimental Combat Team which had arrived in Korea in advance of the 3rd Division which was still in the States. That put us often in support of elements of the 24th and 25th Divisions. So there we were, a black artillery battalion in direct support for a Puerto Rican regiment filled out with Koreans. Interesting.

When the 3rd Division arrived we held on to our basic 65th support role, but we were often in direct support for the 7th and the 15th Infantry Regiments and, later on, the 64th Heavy Tank Battalion where, as an FO, I got to ride in my very own tank on a couple of hairy occasions, and never had a stuck hatch! The 58th fired an armored M7 vehicle mounting a 105mm howitzer, which had a .50 cal machine gun and a basic load of shells. The interesting thing about our armored artillery pieces was that they were all labeled 'Combat Unserviceable' when they left Fort Hood on railway flat cars. I saw them go by with a very sinking feeling and sure enough, they collapsed piece by piece over the year that I was with them in Korea. Sprocket wheels fractured, engines burned out. They were all WWII veterans and we were victims of military downsizing that caught us completely unawares when Korea erupted. We were assigned to X Corps, but determining our location is not so easy. Korea was a yo-yo war, up and down the peninsula. We took Seoul about tour times it seems from what I recall. Name a location and we were probably there! Because I was on competitive tour for Regular Army I got my full share and more of FO'ing. Actually, I preferred it to battery duty. The battery was more or less routine most of the time and the infantry company offered me a chance to be more fully integrated into the scene. Sounds ridiculous now, but it was pretty neat then.

I was in Korea for four major campaigns. The UN offensive, the CCF intervention, the First UN Counter-Offensive and the CCF spring Offensive. During those times there were various Task Forces that we were assigned to as a support unit. For instance, in Task Force 'Dog' we supported the Wolfhounds, the 27th Infantry Regiment, in retaking Kimpo Peninsula. It was kind of a kick. Very little opposition but interesting when one Korean approached the column when it had halted and asked for help for his boss from the old days before the war. They sent him to me because I spoke Japanese. When I told him to bring the wounded man to me it turned out to be old Mr. Han who had managed the Banto Hotel when I lived there in 1945 and'46. He had been wounded by shell fragments and was ripped across the abdomen. I sent him back to battalion aid, they bandaged him up and sent him on his way. I never saw him again. In another instance I was with another unit as an FO when I ended up on the south bank of the Han River, just below Seoul, overlooking a little riverside village on the north bank. It was a place where I had been ice skating just before I left Korea in March 48. There were two couples of us and we both had dogs. The other couple's dog bit a young girl and the villagers demanded compensation from me. I told them it was not my dog, but they didn't believe me. They stole my dog about a week before I left Korea, killed him, ate him, I guess, and nailed the hide to the gate at my house. That didn't make me look upon their village with much sympathy when I was picking targets for defensive fires and points of assembly and attack. When I was with a company for an extensive period of time I occupied myself with teaching the NCOs how to adjust fire and so on. Often, if the casualties had hit the command element I would serve as a platoon leader and take out patrols. I know that is not what the artillery tells you to do when you are at Fort Sill, but in real-time, that is what happens. You do what the situation calls for. It was more interesting because no could talk to the ROK troops except me and none of the Puerto Rican troops could master anything in Korean. One time I had to brief a whole group of Koreans who were entering the US services as ROK replacements. I had them all going in Japanese about fighting for Korean Independence together with us, their duties and how we were all together in this war and how we would live together and fight together and perhaps die together. They had all been applauding and shouting 'Mansei' which corresponds to Banzai and means Ten Thousand Years and so on, but when I got to the dying part there was a noticeable lack of enthusiasm and a sort of shuffling around. Their reaction was totally normal, I suppose. I asked them if they wanted to join the artillery, the infantry or the engineers. I was OK with the infantry and the artillery, but the word for engineer is 'kihei' and the word for cavalry is 'kiiihei', which has a longer sound. I did it wrong and most of them volunteered accidentally for the engineers. I saw a bunch of them a couple of weeks later, up to their earlobes in mud and dirt, carrying logs for a washboard road and they wanted to know where the horses were. I left the area as rapidly as possible.

Since I was with the infantry for long periods it was a feeling of being accepted and integrated and of key assistance in tight moments. You were asked to bring the fire in as close as possible and you did. You were supposed to be able to ring your positions with defensive fire and you tried, praying that FDC knew what the hell they were doing. They did not on one tragic occasion and, while I was on R&R in Japan in Feb '51, my replacement did that, making a horrible mistake with terrible results. I still cannot bring myself to think about it. I went back to that same company later and no one would talk to me. It took time and firefights to be accepted again and still it was never complete. The company I spent most of my time with totally accepted me. When I would join with them it was like coming home again. I had a regular duty station with them and they took care of me. It was a two-way situation. I rode with the tanks on a couple of occasions just before I left Korea in May/June 1951. Once it was pretty tight, beyond the range of the guns who had to displace forward to cover us. Up through a tiny pass where the tanks were actually belly exposed for a moment and into the face of a buffalo gun across the valley. Lots of fire and two tanks blown up. I had to lift my fires for a moment while P-B6s strafed until they ran out of fuel. The tanks called for my fire and I responded as best I could. The day I left I was standing by the road, waiting for a truck to haul me out and the tanks had been up the road on a mission. The commander knew I was waiting for a lift so they took time to put up their flags, open the hatches, stand in their tanks and give me a 'Present Arms' as they passed me. I cried like a baby and I still do when I think about it. Matter of fact I am crying as I write this guess I am just getting old.

My battalion supported the 3rd Infantry Division, specifically the 65th, the 7th and the 15th Infantry Regiments with our primary duties supporting the 65th. As to how they reacted to an artilleryman in the trenches, it was just like any other situation, whether peacetime or war, civilian or military it depended on how you behaved. Some FO's hated the job and might purposely misdirect their fire so that they never hit the target. I had one that did that. He would talk a great game, but when it came time to take over and you had to be with him when he set up his defensive fires it was so bad that you had to believe he was semi-blind or just really wanted to return to the battery which was way the hell and back behind the lines. You just couldn't leave someone like that with the company you knew so well, so you ended up sticking with the infantry. It was not a bad job, you had your own jeep, and your own crew and you lived pretty well. I know it sounds Totally unreal when you think about who will ever read this, but my ROKs took care of me every day, setting up my bunk, getting my clothes washed by the mama sans, cleaning the jeep and my gear, making sure I had plenty to eat, hot water for shaving and washing, a good life. But I took care of them, too. Not only could we have long conversations about America and our society, but I could help them and other ROKs when they had problems, because my linguistic ability enabled me to speak with them, probably better than I spoke with the Puerto Ricans because, at that time, my Spanish was pretty limited. I don't recall supporting any ROK units. As for foreign troops, we supported the 5th Regiment from the Philippines and the Turks on a couple of occasions and also the Brits and the Greeks once or twice. At first, of course, we fought against the North Koreans. In the early phase around Pusan I got the word that a Fort Sill buddy of mine, Hank Farinholt, had been captured for a brief period of time and, during that brief period, the NKs had eviscerated and emasculated him after cutting off his fingers and toes and blinding him. After that, I did not have very good thoughts about the North Koreans. I knew that the 3rd Imperial Marine Division in the Japanese military during WWII had been responsible for a number of war crimes violations with prisoners and captured personnel and, further that this division had been comprised of Korean personnel. The conclusions that I drew from this knowledge and what I personally observed in Korea was not conducive to gentle treatment of the North Koreans. The Chinese, on the other hand, may not have been a hell of a lot better, but the stories I heard were that they were better than the North Koreans about prisoner treatment. In combat I tended to regard both entities the same, our enemies and the reason I was in Korea as a soldier.

We moved so much and so frequently during my time in Korea that we seldom hung around an OP long enough to look fondly upon it and give it a name. My OP's were sets of coordinates for me or 'that hill just west of the OP' or whatever, not names. My firing battery, 'C' Battery 58th Armored Field Artillery, supported the 3rd Battalion, 85th RCT. There were three line companies and one heavy weapons company. That meant that each firing battery had three FO's. My battery supported I, J, K Companies. I spent my time with 'I' Company and I had one OP, making it three OP's that my battery supported. We had three FO's, each FO had one OP to the best of my knowledge. The OP's were all over the place. When you moved on an almost daily basis you picked your OP as the best observation place available and then you fired in your defensive fires, aimed at routes of approach to your position and whatever Harassing and Interdicting you were told to fire or knew about. If you were attacked it was your job to get to the OP, where you should have been anyway, and call in your fires by their concentration number. If you came under attack while moving it was your job to get yourself into a position where you were immediately available to the company commander and follow his requests for fire. It was just that simple and, of course, if it was a planned attack your job usually was to concentrate on targets of opportunity to support the attack. That meant again that you had to have your communications in order and ready to go and you had to be clued in to what was going to happen. We had the mission of each as Move, Shoot and Communicate. Life as an FO was really pretty good. I was pretty much my own boss, unless the officer casualty rate had been high and then I usually had a platoon to worry about. I know, artillery officers are not supposed to be infantry officers also, but you do what you have to do and yes, I took out patrols and all that while FO'ing. But, with few exceptions, you were appreciated and taken care of as a valuable asset to the company. We never stopped long enough, during my tour, to get into the trench system regularly. Being with the infantry was pretty good, I had my own jeep, a recon crew comprised of a recon sergeant and a driver and also had two ROK soldiers. That was my little empire. It was especially good because, as I said before, I was relatively fluent in Japanese, which all the ROKs spoke because Japanese had been their official language for the previous forty-five years, so I had a handle on a lot of conveniences that the language ability afforded me. Actually, I heard later that DIVARTY wanted me at the rear area where they could use my language, but I was on competitive tour and the powers that be wanted me at the front.

Every fire mission was significant and the multiple ones especially so because I lived through them, but I recall a couple that had some different turns. On one occasion, during the attack to the rear from the Chosin Reservoir, I was in the CP late one night, trying to heat up a cup of chocolate when I heard a mortar round just short of our position, in between us and the company to our front. Right after that I heard one behind us, and that caused me to say 'uh-oh'. I was in the company CP and I should have been in my OP. Nothing for it but to tell my recon sergeant to get on phone to the FDC and relay my fire missions while I took my Korean ROKs with me to the OP which was on the high ground to our right flank, which was a good position but a long way off. I had fired in my defensive fires and that meant that I could call in flares, which I did before I left the CP. So here I was, with two ROKs speaking only Japanese and moving through two platoons of Spanish speaking Puerto Ricans to get to my OP. I heard the flares pop and that gave me five seconds to tell my ROKs to freeze, speaking in Japanese, when it occurred to me that the PR troops are going to hear my Japanese and think I am a Chinese or NK infiltrator and my fanny is in deep doo-doo. So, while I am speaking Japanese to my ROKs I am also speaking Spanish to the PR's. My Spanish, at that time, consisted of 'Dos Oervesos, por favor' and 'Deme Ia cuenta' and that was it so here I go, telling my ROKs to freeze when I hear the pop of the flare and ordering two beers and the bill in Spanish. I was tight all over and vastly relieved to get the OP and do something I knew something about, fire my missions. The firefight lasted all night and we were still taking rounds when the mess truck drove up from battalion, taking a round through the windshield. There were other times like when Joe Klezka, another FO, wanted to pull back and kept telling FDC the Chinese were coming on, etc, and finally got the O.K. to pull back. About a minute later I heard Joe calling for the medics, saying his legs had been shot out from under him, and then there was a delay and I heard him cancel the request for medics. I found out the next day that he had accidentally laced his phone wire into his shoe pacs and hotel alpha'd out in a run, only to be caught up short and knocked totally down when he ran to the end of the tied down phone wire, I loved it. There were other times, but it takes too long to spell them out. I remember talking to a captured Chinese sergeant who was leading an infiltration down the road.

They liked to get in between two units and fire into both and then withdraw, leaving the units to fire at each other, thinking they were under attack. Clever. Anyway, these infiltrators had been stopped by a PR patrol, speaking in Spanish. The Chinese sergeant thought it was another Chinese dialect and got friendly, only to have the PR's recover first. 38 NK and Chinese infiltrators, plus an orange painted, bicycle mounted machinegun from WWII, were captured. I loved that, too. We would call a mission by contacting the FDC and announcing 'Fire Mission', then FDC responds by saying 'Send your mission'. You answer with the coordinates, the shell requested, the nature of the target and FDC responds with 'Wait'. Finally, you hear 'On the way'. You respond with 'Roger, wait'. Then you respond with the corrections, so much right or left or add or drop. Finally you split your bracket, when you have it, and call 'Target' if you have hit it and then for 'Fire for Effect'. When you are new to FO'ing you use your binoculars with their mil ratio scale to measure the distance, but when you have been firing daily for some time you usually dispense with the binocs and call your corrections from a scale on the ground, which you recognize from your experience. At least, that is what I did.

Some things that happen in war really affect a person. I think there was a couple of things for me that stand out. One, being told of my Fort Sill friends' horrible death. You are ready for combat deaths, but you are not ready for mutilation and torture. That flavored the war for me for some time. At a later date a Korean man, I can't remember the town he came from, came to me and asked for help for a schoolteacher. I went to the residence and the teacher asked me to assist him in digging up his schoolbooks so he could start teaching again. I got my ROKs and some shovels and we dug for a couple of hours and recovered the books and the papers he needed. He fed us dinner that night and thanked us. We moved on to another position, but before we did we left rations and paint and soon for the rebuilding of his school. So, not everyone was dedicated to torture and mutilation. At that point I think I understood that there was hope for Korea and for our war."

**Sergeant Robert West**
**10th Field Artillery Battalion 1950-51**

"I snuck in the Navy when I was 16 years old in 1944. I went to boot camp at Farragutt Idaho. After boot we were sent for Sea Bee training, but there was a mix-up and we ended up receiving Marine boot training! After WWII I wanted to see Europe, and the Army said they would give me a boat coxswains MOS on the Rhine River, so I joined the Army. When I got to New Jersey to embark for Germany, Ft. Dix was going through some sort of cadre scandal, so I ended up as a D.I. at Ft. Dix! Instead of having German beer and girls, I had to get up at 0400 to wake up the little boys. The Army decided to activate the 3rd Infantry Division and it was made a priority. Half of the 3rd was to be at Ft. Devans MA, and half at Ft. Benning. I was sent to the 10th Field Artillery Battalion, a 105mm Howitzer unit at Devans and eventually became a wireman in the commo section. This was 1948. By 1950, my buddy Edward Damaso and I were on TDY at West Point and it was great duty. Then those stupid North Koreans attacked South Korea and our fun time was over. We were sent back to Ft. Devans and the 10th Field Artillery along with the rest of the 3rd Infantry were shipped out to California to an awaiting Navy ship. The 3rd had 3 Regimental Combat Teams, the 7th, 15th, and the 65th from Puerto Rico. We arrived in Wonson on November 7th 1950. The Chinese entered into the war and all hell hit the roof. The 7th Infantry and the 'C' Battery FO's were sent up to help the Marines out of the Chosin Reservoir, we were called 'Task Force Dog'. The Marines left on December 14th, and we left on Christmas Eve. The Navy gave us maps that had hundreds of squares with numbers. We would call in the numbers and there was this battleship off-shore that would fire. Their shells going over head sounded like box cars on a train. When they hit, all you could say was 'wow'.

Our FO teams were normally two men. There was an FO officer and an recon Sergeant. The sergeant carried a very heavy radio due to wet cell batteries. The division always had one RCT in the rear for a break and to guard divisional headquarters. The RCT's rotated about every 3 to 4 weeks. When back at division rear, the RCT was given a beer ration! The only time the FO's were given a rest is when some guys volunteered to take our place for a few days. There was a PFC Chamber and a Corporal Sugrue who took Sgt Jackson's and my place for three days and they were killed. They were in the FDC section. Needless to say, not too many wanted to volunteer. FO recon sergeants were at the line company's request to accommodate them on patrol. The infantry company has four platoons. Each night or day a different platoon chooses a different squad. Now you can see how much time on patrol a recon sergeant has and how much time an infantry man has on patrol. By rotating the RCT's you can see how much time an FO officer has on the line compared to an infantry officer. Near the end of 1951, the army decided to issue a combat badge for FO's. The guys in congress raised hell and that idea was turned down. We had more time on the lines, fought more battles then the infantry men, but could not wear a combat badge. Because they had no air power, the Chinks liked to attack around 2 a.m. If you had 300 guys on the hill, they would send 1800 since man power was not a problem. They would lay down a heavy barrage of artillery, mortars, and a heavy smoke screen. This made it hard to see any distance even with flares. We used HE, VT, and WP. The Chinks did not like the WP and would run. One time when we were overlooking Seoul, my FO officer, Lt. Donald Langren would shoot fire missions at day and I would shoot them at night with a B.C. scope. We were 'Night Red Charlie' on the radio. Our shells would cause fires in the city and the Reds thought it would be smart to put their tanks behind the fires and shoot at us. I got some of them and after two nights they dropped that idea. In North Korea I froze my hands until I had no feeling at all in them. SFC Vance McBee poured gasoline on the ground and lit it. He made me put my hands close to the fire and it was painful as all hell but I got my feeling back. Later in South Korea I got a small piece of flak in my left hand. I pulled it out and forgot about it. Soon it got infected and I had a red line up my arm. The medic said I had blood poison and gave me some penicillin shots every two hours. Next day the line faded away! When the 10th Field Artillery has a reunion, the FO's all sit together because we are an elite group. There used to be a saying 'put a gold star in the window mother, because your son is an FO"

### Sergeant Lenny Wilde
### 64th Field Artillery Battalion 1950-51

"At the age of 16 years I quit school and went to sea, inland waters of the Great Lakes, hauling from Duluth to other ports of the Great Lakes. I enjoyed sailing, and sailed from 1942-1949. I wanted very much to join the Navy like my father before me and his brother Bob. They served on the U.S.S. Arizona from 1921-1926. I took the test and passed for the Navy. But of course! I wanted to serve aboard a submarine, but I had bad veins in my left leg, which disqualified me for the submarine service. So I left the Navy Department and went on down the hall into the Army Department. Three days later I was on my way to basic training at Fort Riley, Kansas. Finished basic, and then was sent to Camp Carson, Colorado for field artillery training, then on to Camp McCoy, Wisconsin for more artillery training, but before our four months was completed orders came through to return to Camp Carson, Colorado. The troops were unloaded, the trucks and artillery guns and duffle bags were left on the flat cars of the train and sent onward to Oakland, California. We then boarded another train, and we were on our way to Camp Stoneman, California. Stayed there about three or four days, and then went to pier 91 to board a troop ship bound for overseas. We left stateside as the 'C' Battery 537th Field Artillery Battalion. We arrived at the port of Yokohama Japan, just long enough to join forces with the 25th Division while in port aboard the ships which have stayed all night until the next day.

We removed our shoulder patches which were 5th Army then and we had to put on our new patches 'Tropical Lighting' 25th Infantry Division. We were now Charlie Battery 64th Field Artillery Battalion. Our next stop, Port of Pusan, Korea, where we had to fight our way ashore. We fought our way north at the time, I was assigned to the wire section as a linesman and jeep driver. As we fought our way north fighting the North Koreans from Pusan, Taegu, Osan, Suwon, right into Seoul. We pushed the North Koreans above the 38th Parallel and fought them all the way to Sunchon and Hamhung. All the way to and through the 'Frozen Chosen' like being up in Alaska!

The 64th fired a 105mm howitzer. We've got six battle stars for the time I was there. I was in Korea from August 1950 till September 8th 1951, the day I was wounded on Hills 682 and 717. They said we'd be home by Christmas. Sure! What year? After Christmas the war was supposed to have been over. We started on our way south, everyone was happy and excited. We were going home! While me, the sarge, and 1st Lt. was in the jeep heading south we heard noises and flashes way behind us. The convoy stopped, everyone started looking in the direction of the smoke and fire. The CO said, 'Oh, that's only some of our guys blowing up some of the ammo they can't haul anyway.' Then over the radio in the back of my jeep came the yelling 'Bug-out fast! The Chinese are coming by the thousands!' And the convoy stated moving again. We retreated one hundred fifty miles south on the first day, blowing bridges behind us. I was assigned as an FO on day while I was laying wire one afternoon and when I came back into the area, I parked the jeep next to the mess tent and went in and got a cup of tea and smoked a cigar. I sat there with Jacob Whitney, our switchboard operator. He also just got relieved. While we were talking some guy came in the mess tent and yelled 'Yo! The CO wants you on the double.' I got to the CP tent. I knocked on the wooden sign 'CP' At least it made some noise. 'Enter!' a voice yelled. The clerk said 'Wilde's here sir.' He told me, 'You know we pick men from the wire section for our FO parties, don't you?' I replied, 'Yes sir.' 'Well you know your buddy Eddie Wilczkilwicz? Well Eddie got shot in the shoulder while with the FO party on the hill they were on. And he's on his way to a mash unit, probably already there. So that means you're next in line. So go get your jeep and join the sergeant and lieutenant. Harth is getting their gear together so go take the A-frame and wire equipment out of the jeep and get the FO stuff in it.' Two large radios had to be put in the rear of the jeep along with our rifles and ammo, canteens and our personnel stuff. And that's how I and my jeep became FO party pals.

After the Chinese came across the lines from China by the thousand, blowing whistles, bugles, running, riding horses, everyone wanted artillery support I suppose. We fought against the North Koreans from the time we arrived in August 1950 till the after I left, and the damn Chinese entered the war and screwed up everything. I fought against the Chinese till September 8th, 1951. Life was hell. I took infantry basic, ended up in the artillery, joined an FO party, and still ended up almost an infantry rifleman. That's hell! Life in the trenches was hell too! It was scary. I saw guys killed, blown up, blown apart. I was glad to get out of there, and lucky to have gotten wounded. I remember one special mission we called in. A lot of people, old, young, children, and among them were Chinese, they would get in among them to get through check points. And once the Chinese passed, that night they would be behind our lines, where at night they would attack and kill our troops. We could see their guns and ammo, and they wore gym shoes and packs under their long white robes like old papa sans wore. The lieutenant said he had to call it in to stop the attacks at night. The rounds killed a lot of people.

There were only three of us on an FO party. The lieutenant, a sergeant, and corporal as a jeep driver, me. I drove the Lt. and the sarge. I and the sarge played with the radios in the jeep or on a hill.

We had walkie talkies. The Lt. would call back to the jeep and we would call for artillery fire. Or if we planned on staying on the hill for a couple of days, we had the radios carried up the hill to the highest point, inside a bunker. We supported the 35th Infantry Regiment Companies, Love, Mike, Item, King, Dog, Fox, and Easy, and many other units. I can't remember them all. We had OP's with all of them at one point or another, and these OP's were on hills 682, 717, 586, 588, and a bunch of other places all over North and South Korea. Hills 682, and 717 were the worst. While on Hill 717, we were with 'Item' and 'Love' Companies, 35th Infantry Regiment, 25th Infantry Division. Hill 717 was near the village of Yangwon, North Korea. When darkness came the Chinese began shelling Hill 717. They poured artillery and mortar shells on close positions, and the men hovered low in their holes to escape burns and falling debris. We, the Observers, calculated over 1,000 rounds fell on them in thirty-five minutes. The Chinese threw two battalions against us on 717, and the fight went on for six hours. Ammunition was running low, and the GI's were breaking up belted machine-gun ammo to use in their M-1s. Attempts to reach the battery in the rear area were out of the question. The radios broke down. I was in a bunker, but rounds kept coming through the opening. One radio had three bullet holes in it. We called for a supply drop earlier that morning, but a plane came over us between both Hills 682 and 717, like a valley between us. As they attempted to make the air drop, a strong breeze carried three bundles down the one side of the hill, right into the enemy hands.

I got wounded on Hill 717. Right hip, right foot, and also left leg. All I remember, everyone started running off the hill after the Chinese overran us. Out of five of us FO men just me and Hal got off the hill alive. He went to one mash unit and I went to the 8063 MASH unit. They kept sending me south. I lost a lot of blood and passed out. When I finally came to my senses I was in an Air Force hospital in Magoya, Japan, and I stayed there for about a month. Good thing I got wounded or I'd probably still been in Korea! They told us when we got to Korea 'When you guys get yourselves thirty-six points, you rotate home.' HA! Thirty-six hell! When I got wounded I had fifty-six points! Yes I had some good times in the Army and some not so good especially on hills 682 and 717. We got up there on the 6th and things were quiet for a while. I was in the bunker writing a letter home to my girl and listening to a small radio some guys let me use. The infantry guys were all dug in, talking about home, laughing and having a quiet afternoon when about an hour later all hell broke loose. We fought and they drove back and left. We were five miles south of the closest friendly contact and northeast is the Korean City of Pyongyang. Then when they really attacked, we fought all afternoon into the late hour of morning. We ran out of everything, mortar rounds, grenades, .30 cal rounds, .50 cal rounds. Those infantry guys used everything at the gooks. I had a carbine with three 30 round clips taped together that ran out of ammo and I had a sub machine gun I picked up off a dead Turk soldier about a month back. We were close to a hill, near some Turks. They were the next hill from us, and boy, they're blood thirsty bastards sure glad they were on our side. Those Turk soldiers are rough. Well as we cleared out the next morning I came upon a dead Turk, and his sub machine gun and four clips. So on hill 717 I used all my ammo from the carbine and had only the four clips left from tommy gun. It carried .45 shells so I fired all but one clip. I returned to the bunker, used half of those on the two walkie-talkies and the one good radio. The CO yelled and said every man for himself as we started to leave I got hit in the right side, just a flesh wound the medic said, and my friend Walt pulled me inside another bunker, I'm pretty sure it was Walt, his brother told me. I was on one hill, Walt came over from another hill and I was from 'C' Battery and he was from another Battery. He put a first aid patch on my right side, and then off he ran and I also never saw him again. But his brother said before he died in '95 he talked a lot about me.

After being wounded, I got out of the hospital in Japan, and they sent me home. I lived in Detroit, and when I got to the closest camp to my house, which was Fort Custer, Michigan, I got a thirty day leave. I reported back to Ft. Custer, Michigan on my 29th day, told the CO I wanted to go back overseas, and I was sent to Seattle, Washington. I stayed at Ft. Lawton about one week, and then was sent to Camp Drake in Tokyo, Japan, where I was assigned to the 1st Cavalry Division and stayed at Camp Drake two weeks. They sent me to Camp Chitose #1, on an island of Hakkado, Japan, where I was with HQ and HQ Company, 5th Cavalry Regiment. Ten months later I went home for discharge, and then in April 1953 went back to shipping on the Great Lakes as a merchant seaman again."

## Lt (jg) Neal Hammon
## USS Helena (CA75) 1950-51

*Author's note: Even though this is a book about Artillery Forward Observers, I would be remiss in not mentioning the roll of the US Navy and its Fire Control Officers. These Naval officers worked in close coordination with infantry units and artillery battalions along both coastlines of Korea, providing valuable naval gunfire support throughout the whole war. Here is but one sample of their involvement.*

"I enlisted in the Navy at age of seventeen in Springfield, Illinois. I was a reserve officer and attended the USNR at Louisville, Kentucky. I was assigned to the heavy cruiser, USS Helena CA 75 when the Korean War broke out. The USS Helena was known as 'The Hell Ship' and yes they really did call it the Hell Ship! I was well aware that the Helena was a heavy cruiser of the Baltimore class, since I had previously served on a light cruiser of the Cleveland class, and at a glance the two ships looked pretty much the same, except for the main battery. The light cruisers had four 6-inch turrets, two forward and two aft, whereas the heavy cruisers had three 8-inch turrets, two forward and one aft. The super-structure looked the same. I served aboard the USS Helena from about Sept 1950 through the summer of 1951. We did a lot of shore bombardment of the east coast, and there were one or two US officers attached to the ROK division as Forward Observers. Whenever we were available, we would use our 5 or 8-inch guns on targets of their choosing. I also remember that our helicopter would pick up these army officers and bring them aboard our ship, where they would usually take a shower, then sit around the ward room eating ice cream and stuff they didn't get over in the hillside bunkers. People examining the Helena notice the guns first. 'Gosh, you gottalotta guns', people would say. A cruiser was designed as a movable gun platform. There were the triple 8-inch guns sticking out of three large turrets, two forward and one aft. Between these turrets were six 'mounts' each containing two 5-inch guns. In addition the Helena carried a number of twin and quad 40-mm guns in open mounts, and some 20-mm machine guns operated by a single Marine. Normally, after firing one of the 8-inch guns, people on deck can not hear the sound of the projectile when it is in flight. But there are exceptions, sometimes one of the bourrelet bands comes loose as the shell is leaving the barrel. This causes some very weird sounds as the projectile proceeds to the target, sounds like, 'wap,wap,wap'.

In the middle of the ship was the Fire Direction Center installation capable of controlling the guns and searchlights. On our watches, in the director, we usually had four men, the pointer, the trainer, the range-finder operator, and the control officer. The pointer elevated and lowered the sight, the trainer moved the sight right or left, and the control officer could slew the director in any directions when in automatic operation. The idea was for the control officer to get the sights more or less on a target, and let the other three men do the rest. As the men moved the sights to keep on the target, this information was sent down to the plotting room, where it was 'rate-controlled' by the computer, then sent back up to the guns. On my second night aboard ship I had the mid-watch in CIC.

The Helena was cruising along the east coast between Pohang and Yongdok, but nothing was going on. The following evening we moved closer to the battle, and I spent some time on deck watching the tracers go back and forth between the ROK and NKPA forces. Afterwards I went to CIC to stand my watch, and Commander O.S. Dwire came up and assigned us some targets for night interdiction fire. He marked six or eight places on the chart, such as villages, road crossing, or suspected troop concentrations, where we were to fire a certain number of rounds each hour 'But never fire at these targets with any regularity', he ordered. I asked how that was done, and was told by a fellow officer on duty 'Well, what we do is to play gin-rummy, and assign certain cards to certain targets. For example, the jack of spade will be the road crossing. When the card comes up, we shoot at that target.' When it came time to shoot at a target, we would take the range and bearing and send it down to the plotting room, where all the fire-control equipment was located. The guns were set to point to the target automatically. And so it was when we were on interdiction bombardment duty, the ship would fire from 2000 hrs until breakfast the next morning. The following night I again went on watch in CIC, and it started out the same way, with the commander coming in after the dog watch, at 2000 hrs, to assign some targets. He then left us junior officers to do the firing. I thought this war-time duty was all pretty dull until we got a call from the bridge. 'Hey, come out and look. See the fireworks. We've hit an ammo dump'. Sure enough, we had. I went out to look and there was stuff flying around like the 4th of July. We had indeed hit a North Korean ammo dump. I rushed back into CIC to determine which target it had been, and when we looked back at our notes we realized that our super good shot had not been at any of the targets. We had made a mistake. We had accidentally called in bearing 315 degrees, when we had intended to shoot at a target with a bearing of 291. As we expected, the gunnery officer, the commander, and Captain Lawson soon paid us a visit. 'Which target was that?' the captain asked excitedly. 'None of them!' admitted Digger O'Dell, the senior junior officer present. We were pardoned for our mistake without a court martial, but we didn't get any medals either. Afterwards, we paid a little more attention to the range and bearings and less to the card game.

On 14 September, I had the early morning watch, beginning at 0400, which lasted until breakfast. Things in CIC were normal, and we were engaged in interdiction fire as usual. About daylight Ensign Kalin in the director called down, and asks me to come out on the deck and take a look at a possible new target. I obliged and took a pair of binoculars, and scanned the shoreline. It was very foggy morning, but I could see a company of soldiers marching up the road, which was flat and near the beach. I raced back to CIC and grabbed the phone. 'How about firing a round or two at them', asked Ensign Kalin. 'Why not?' I replied. 'Well, this is not one of our designated targets' he answered. So it was all arranged. He called down the range and bearing, and we fired a single round from one of the 5-inch mounts. The range was too great and it exploded several hundred yards beyond the marching men, but Kalin corrected this mistake and quickly fired two more rounds which were right on target. Our little secret was well kept, and only a few junior officers and enlisted men were aware of the incident. I felt like Daniel Boone when he said, 'I believe I have killed enemy on other occasions, but I am only positive of having killed these.' When that was over, we headed south again, and while underway, received a message that we were needed at Changsa-dong, about forty miles north of Yongdok. We were informed that LST 667 was aground, and that a commando force of South Koreans was being vigorously attacked by NKPA soldiers, who had them penned in along the beach. We were pretty close to the area, and arrived soon after to discover the worse scenario. The LST was not only beached, but the waves had pushed it sideways into the sand, and there was a large hole in it's' bottom. That's what we sailors call a bad situation. It was our task to keep the North Korean troops back with gunfire, but we could only do so much. Destroyers Brush and Thomas, and the DMS Doyle, ships that could assist and take up some of the slack, accompanied us. The same afternoon we were informed that there was a landing near Inchon. The marines had landed and taken an island and pushed on toward Seoul. Everything on that front was going good, but there were no signs of the southern front cracking. It was also suggested that our bombardment at Samchock and the landing by the breached LST was part of a planned diversion to the main invasion at Inchon. To keep back the North Koreans, we fired 5-inch VT shells at them. I had never seen VT's used against troops, but they appeared to be very effective. From the ship we would first see a flash, then a black puff of smoke, and then the shrapnel would hit a large area under the puff. The ground would be dug up and trees would loose their foliage. Anybody exposed in the area would most certainly be stuck by the shrapnel and injured. It was a mean shell when used against ground troops. If the first round found the range, we often fired a broadside, consisting of eight 5-inch VT shells at a time.

On 20 September we went back to the end of the firing line, where we could be of real service. We furnished harassing fire to the ROKs during their drive on Pohang. By morning our ROK troops had moved past Pohang, and the Air Force began using the airfield again. We went to general quarters right after breakfast, at 0740, which convinced us that the captain had our best interests at heart. Standing GQ on the dawn patrol is tough on our stomach. We fired with the 8-inch turrets at reported massing North Korean troops. This was the first time I had seen the 8-inch turrets fire at night, which was certainly a show."

# Chapter Three

## *1951 – Infantry Support*

The Korean War was only six months old by the beginning of 1951, and already many large-scale battles and small engagements had taken place. The Pusan Perimeter defense, Inchon landings, and the drive to the Yalu River had all happened. There was the heroic stand at the Chosin Reservoir by the Marines and U.S. Army, and the hurried and panicked pull back down the peninsula after the Chinese entered the fray. There seemed to be an almost set pattern to the constant movement up and down North and South Korea as the United Nations troops battled Communist forces. This continued on into the beginning of 1951, when the build up of American units began to arrive and take their place 'on the line'. At this point in the war was when additional artillery units in particular began to arrive in strength, adding more punch to the U.S. Divisions' already each assigned four artillery battalions. These additional Corps units, many of them National Guard units, bringing with them 105mm, 155mm, and 8-inch howitzers, bolstered the U.N. lines...

**Sergeant Wendell Murphy**
**143rd Field Artillery Battalion 1950-52**

"I went into the service on April the 16th, 1950. I was in the National Guard and they converted some of those positions to the regular United States Army, and I became assigned to the143rd Field Artillery Battalion, a I Corps 105mm unit on the western side of Korea. Even though we were 105mm howitzers, depending on the target we had at our disposal other weapons too, like the 155mm howitzer. I got to Korea in December of 1950, and left in October of 1952. I was wounded on September 24th of 1951 and I went into the hospital for about three months in rehabilitation then came back to Korea. That came about with me stepping on a mine. A lot of people got killed, and I prayed to the good Lord every night. The artillery Observer was the main man for the infantry. You have a radio operator and you have a lieutenant. I had a lieutenant when I first when in but he was killed and there wasn't another lieutenant to take over so I had to replace him. We fought both the Chinese and the North Koreans, and I usually was with one of two infantry companies, Easy Company and Fox Company, where I manned either OP #1 or OP #3 while with them. We supported the ROKs, and I was scared to death. I had one sergeant who could speak broken English, and I told him at night time when he came into my OP that he'd better holler 'sergeant' so that I knew it was him. The 143rd usually would have three OP's that they controlled at any given time, depending on what was going on. I shot missions on Pork Chop Hill, Heartbreak Ridge, and Old Baldy. When I came back from the hospital they sent me back to the 40th Infantry Division again, but I wasn't with them. They sent me back to serve with the 3rd ROK Division, so I served with them twice. While on the outposts, we had two OP's. We had what was called the 'forward' OP to sit out in front of the infantry then we'd come back at night time with the infantry and sit on the line with the infantry. My OP's were usually built with nothing but a trench with some logs over top of it with some sandbags. And I had my binoculars, stand up binoculars, and I could see out anywhere for 45,000 yards. You felt a little bit safer being in the trenches but when you got ready to take another hill out in front of you, something in the air tells you to make the OP over again.

I called hundreds of fire missions. The biggest fire mission I actually had was in '52 and I called it in as a regiment or a division on the Chinese or North Koreans. I called for air strike but couldn't get it, and the Battleship Missouri came in and they shot the mission with sixteen rounds of shells that weighed about a ton a piece. It was tough communicating with the U.S. Navy because they do everything 'port' and starboard' right, and left, or maybe that was reversed, and the Army didn't. It was the first time that I was ever involved with the Navy and I was only about forty days from coming home. I'm glad I wasn't them! That's all I can tell you. It is one heck of an explosion. Most of the time you're sitting on an OP you're on and you look out, maybe a mortar round comes in, your out looking for the flash of a mortar. You call your fire mission on that mortar to knock that mortar out. Any man that's looking, they clean the ditches up and then throw a mission on top of them. Any vehicles you can see in the distance where you can hit you shoot. The BC scope lens is good for having the guns in the caves. They'd lower the gun down and then have to lower it back in. And all you can do was bust artillery and hope you caught them. My last fire mission before coming home I remember it real well. A mortar team was setting up and I watched them come in and set up and I had watched them and said 'They belong to me'. And I had my map made up with coordinates, and we fired the first round and made that the concentration. Then you could look off the concentration off the center of your map. Anywhere you wanted to go, all you had to do when you called your fire mission was say 'Concentration 222 left 1,000 drop 500. Fire for effect'. And I had my map all planned that way. The whole front of my OP was like that. And that was my last day on the hill. I said I'd never get wet or cold again and I don't think I have since then."

**1st Lt LaNard Johnson**
**213th Armored Field Artillery Battalion 1951**

"We used to fly two to four hours a day, trying to make a flight to represent our battalion. I flew for the 213th Armored Field Artillery Battalion, but if it got a little too heavy for us, we were made up of a group of pilots within the area covered by IX Corps, and at that time we could cover several firing units with one observer. We had about ninety percent control on the firing line at that time during daytime hours, and possibly even more than that, to the point of using us completely. We used to fly out beyond the enemy lines and get back in there, maybe ten miles back from the line, you know, and observe from there. We didn't just fly in for our battalion, though. We'd fly out into enemy territory and watch our backs because it was just too massive a firing for us to go through. We used to fly 2-3000 feet off the ground, we wouldn't get too high, and in some cases we picked up anti-aircraft fire or small arms fire. We worked seven days a week, sometimes two flights a day, and if it was a bad situation they might call us out for a third flight, with usually two hours on each situation. And sometimes it was just registering a battery over a ridge or something like that, to prepare them for a night barrage.

I recall one time we were flying, and we observed an awful lot of troops, on a hillside on the roadways. So I dropped down and the troops were waving at us, and we called in the information to FDC. And they asked if we could direct fire on them, and we called back and said 'No, they're friendly troops, they were waving at us, there's no problem' and they said 'Negative, we would like for you to direct fire on these troops'. They were that well trained that they wouldn't fire on us, and we would drop down to 2-300 feet sometimes. These enemy troops would just wave, and they had our panels showing that they was friendly troops. This was the night of a big breakout by the Chinese, and they were so well trained that if they had given themselves away they're surprise wouldn't have been as effective. They come through in the night and moved in on us and most of the U.N. positions in our area. We did alert them a little bit because our intelligence discovered that they weren't friendly troops, and we directed fire on them, and we got some altitude too! We got out of there in a hurry! We flew from fields, roads, and just about anywhere you could kick out a 3-400 foot runway. Sometimes on sandy edges of rivers, we would just put a flag in and that's where we tried to land. When we flew we sat in tandem, the pilot sat in the front and the observer sat in the rear. If there was a location that the observer couldn't see we would discuss it back and forth on the intercom. We were totally unarmed, and thinking back about it, it was pretty hairy sometimes, because we always would have to fly out through our own rounds being fired. We would ask for one round from a battery, and we didn't particularly know where this battery was. And we would give them an 'add 1000' or 'back 1000' or whatever it would be to get it on target and immediately we could get the location of the firing battery. We got a lot of Air Medals, we got so darn many of them that we couldn't pack them on our chest, because every day we were over enemy territory under harassing enemy fire."

**1st Lt Royal James Painter**
**987th Armored Field Artillery Battalion 1951**

"I remember my time in Korea, it was not fifty years ago, it was yesterday. More memories I would like to forget than remember. I was activated on September 5th, 1950, with the Pennsylvania National Guard, 28th Infantry Division. I was sent to Camp Carson, Colorado where I was assigned to 987th Armored Field Artillery Battalion, 105 SP's, self propelled howitzers. We left for Korea in January 1951 and we were assigned to IX Corps. I was in Korea from February 1951 until November 1951. We were involved in the First UN Counter Offensive, the CCF Spring Offensive, and the UN Summer-Fall Offensive while I was there. We supported the 25th and 7th Infantry Divisions and the 1st Marine Division, where we were attached to the 11th Artillery Regiment. After we were over-ran on April 22nd and lost nine of our guns, we stayed with the Marines until we got back to Chinchon. From there we were then attached to the 25th Division for most of the rest of the time. We supported the 2nd ROK Division too, they were okay. We supported the 6th ROK Division also, but on April 22nd they ran out before the battle began and left us. They were no damn good! The OP's did not have any names because we moved so often. We usually had two OP's for the battalion, and our guns moved every day and sometimes twice a day and we were always ahead of the guns laying out the gun positions. We went up as an FO one week at a time, I was up there in September. It was cold and it rained every day that week. There was no shelter. I watched four P-51's making a napalm run in the valley below us. One was hit by ground fire and went in between two mountains. About a month later we were on a task force that left at daybreak and pulled out about two in the afternoon, while going up the valley I saw the P-51 and it had not burned, and there was no sign of the pilot."

**Sergeant Danny O'Keefe**
**57th Field Artillery Battalion 1951**

"I re-enlisted into the Army in January of 1951 and was sent to Korea in the late winter of 1950-51, where I was assigned to the 57th Field Artillery Battalion of the 7th Infantry Division. It was being refilled after a near wipe out at the Chosin Reservoir a month and a half before. The 57th was a 105mm towed howitzer unit that was a direct support unit of the 7th Division in the X Corps area, except for a very short period in 1951 when we were assigned to IX Corps. I was in Korea from early March 1951 and was sent home in January of 1952. I was never assigned as a Forward Observer but spent time as a wireman with the infantry laying wire between artillery and infantry positions. Occasionally I would run an ANGR-9 radio for the FO. I was then assigned to the Fire Direction Center as a computer of data for the field pieces. In September of 1951 the XO asked if I would like to volunteer to fly as an aerial observer. After a tour of the air section, I agreed. So, I served as the very first enlisted aerial observer for the 7th Division Artillery in the fall of 1951. We participated in aerial flight each day looking for enemy troop movements and directing artillery fire from all X corps and 8th Army artillery units located in our battle zone. We called the L-19 a 'tooth paste tube' that we flew in. We flew along the lines and when an 8-inch howitzer fire mission 'on the way' was received we could turn and watch the 8-inch shells coming at us like little Volkswagens. As a result of this action I developed the strongest anal muscles in the United States Army.

I was so far down the chain of command that I never knew or was aware that battles had names. Later I found out by reading books that I was involved in the first Chinese offensive in April and the second Chinese offensive I think in May. Later, when flying, I was involved in what is now called Bloody Ridge and Heartbreak Ridge, the Punchbowl and the Mundung-ni Valley. I even witnessed a tank attack, while in the air, by our forces and watched as they got the hell blown out of them. The Infantry troops always, at least to our faces, treated us with utmost respect, even awe on certain occasions. They were always lost it seems and they always asked us where in hell they were. We always told them and they respected us for that and our guns of course. They loved and respected those guns of ours. As an artilleryman I was always treated with kid gloves by the infantry. As a flyer whenever we encountered an infantry soldier they were in awe of us. They wondered how anyone could be dumb enough to fly that low and under those conditions. Our primary support was rendered to the 31st Infantry Regiment of the 7th Infantry Division. When they were in reserve status, we remained on the line supporting either the 17th Regiment or the 32nd Regiment. Several times we were attached to units and formed a Regimental Combat Team. We supported elements of the Turkish Brigade, the Ethiopians and some of the Korean Capitol Division as well as one or two other Korean Army units whose numeric I don't remember. We fought both North Koreans and Chinese soldiers, primarily though we fought the Chinese most of the time. The North Koreans were meaner than hell, much more so than the Chinese.

We pulled many an infantry unit out of trouble with our support fire. The beauty of flying is that you could watch both sides in the actions. At the time the 2nd Division was trying to take Hill 931 or Heartbreak Ridge in September of 1951, my pilot and I were flying in the Mundung-ni Valley, which was to the west of the Punchbowl and to the East of the Hwachon Reservoir. I spotted the movement of two Chinese soldiers making their way up an east-west ridgeline. I watched through my 7x50 binoculars as they slowly made their way up to the main north-south ridgeline leading south toward what was later called Heartbreak Ridge and the Punchbowl. Once on top they stopped and hunkered down. Guessing that they were scouts and that they would be making their way south toward the Punchbowl and our front lines, I called into DIVARTY, radio call, 'Manslaughter Niner, fire mission'. As I looked through my glasses I noticed at least two companies of approximately two hundred Chinese squatting in a draw several hundred yards east of the two scouts atop the ridge. Manslaughter Niner advised me, 'Send your mission'. I advised I had two companies of Chinese in the draw. I furnished the map coordinates and was advised to contact 'Blaster-Niner' for my mission. 'Blaster' was the 31st Field Artillery Battalion of the 7th Infantry Division, a towed 155mm howitzer unit. It had snowed the previous night and the ground was white. The sun was out brightly and it made very difficult to look at the ground. I called in the following, 'Blaster-Niner, fire mission, coordinates such and such, two enemy companies in the open, request William Peter, will adjust, over'. Shortly after I had an, 'On the way' then a 'Splash'. I spotted the first round and dropped the next sensing round along the gun target line, south fifty meters and left one hundred meters. The second round impacted along the ridgeline just where I wanted it. After adjusting on the ridge, I told Blaster-

Niner to hold fire, and gave the battery a fire mission of three rounds HE at my command, and we waited. It had snowed the night before and the adjusting rounds had blackened the ridge line where the fire had been adjusting. We circled south and away from the area while watching the Chinese all the while. The impacted rounds had made big black blast marks in the snow. After an interlude the two Chinese scouts, who had watched the shelling, waved their comrades up onto the north-south ridgeline. Once on top they headed south as we had guessed. They approached the black shell marks and double timed to the south side of them, then they took a breather on their haunches. I contacted Blaster and said the following, 'Blaster-Niner, Brute 88 here, fire... Over'. Then they responded with 'Brute 88, Blaster Niner, on the way, over' and shortly after that 'Brute 88, Blaster Niner, Splash'. At the splash the rounds began to strike and explode right into the middle of the Chinese formation. It was like throwing a perfect strike in a bowling game. Through the glasses you could see the enemy bodies blown into the air and down the sides of the ridgeline. It was magnificent, it was terrible. I felt good, I felt sick. After that mission, I could only think of going home. There was very little movement below. We had nailed a company of replacements for the Chinese front lines. Our boys would not have to worry about these guys."

**Sergeant Dennis Jones**
**99th Field Artillery Battalion 1951**

"I was a Sergeant E5, served from 7 September 1950 to 7 September 1951. I arrived in Korea on about 1 April 1951, joined 'B' Battery 99th Field Artillery Battalion, 1st Cavalry Division. I had my training at Ft. Riley, Kansas and then on to Ft. Sill. I was not nineteen years old when I completed my artillery training so for some reason I stayed at Ft. Sill until March. Our battery was part of a battalion combat team and went to Kaesong, when the first peace talks started. While at Kaesong, I did the things they tell you never to do. I asked out of the guns. They made me a recon sergeant, gave me the title, but not the rank, I was still a PFC! As an FO, I remember one day they told us to pack up. We were going back to the battalion, the fall offense had begun. I was assigned to Lt. Lee, lucky for me, he had been in Korea from the beginning. We were attached to King Company 8th Cavalry Regiment and went into attack on Hill 272. We laid everything we had for a day and a half, a lot of attempts by infantry to get into the trenches. There was a lot of dead and a whole ton of wounded. Our company was down to less than one platoon, and then another company relieved us and took on the attack. We went back down into the valley, rearmed, got food and water and went back up. We got to the top of the hill with the other company, there were a lot of dead and wounded. When I went up there, there were dead all over the hill, our dead. You do not know how I thank God for my Lt. Lee who taught me how to stay alive and do my job. I wanted to do more than I did but I don't know what else I could have done, there were so many dead. We stayed with King Company until the fall offense was about over. Lt. Lee was rotated home after fifteen months in Korea, I was sad to see him go. I had other lieutenants, but not like him.

Later on, I was attached to 'E' Company of the 8th Cavalry for a while. We were at Hill 334 for several months. One night we got hit with a lot of artillery fire. The Thailanders on our right got hit with infantry. The next morning I was asked by the infantry battalion CO what he could do for me. I told him all that I wanted was a Combat Infantry Badge. I told him he might not be able to do it because I was in the artillery. He said that he would look into it. Well, right after that, the first landline call was for my lieutenant. All of the lines had previously been out, and our jeep driver came up and told me what he had heard on the line. He said that the artillery battalion liaison officer told my lieutenant that he was going to court-martial me for insubordination. I called them a few names to get the 'fire' I wanted. I asked our jeep driver what our lieutenant said. He said that that would be hard to court-martial me because the infantry battalion CO was putting me in for the Bronze Star for Valor. That is the last I ever heard about it until I got back in the states and looked at my 201. There it was, the decoration all drawn up but a note saying 'not brave enough but should stay in 201 file'. We were relieved by the 40th Infantry Division and left Japan around the tenth of Dec 1951, and I was rotated home in April 1952."

**2nd Lt Alan Hartshorne**
**31st Field Artillery Battalion 1951-52**

"I was assigned to the 31st Field Artillery Battalion of the 7th Infantry Division. We were a 155mm Howitzer unit. I served in Korea from the spring of 1951 to the spring of 1952, and got my training and baptism of fire under the watchful eye of an old WWII veteran Forward Observer on 'Heartbreak Ridge' during the summer of 1951. I believe he was a reserve officer who was called back to service for Korea. I took over as the chief of all FOs for 31st Field Artillery in the summer of 1951 during the campaign north of the Hwachon Reservation in North Korea. I became Staff Sergeant at this time too, and I remember we had some support from a Colombian patrol, and hit an enemy headquarters 1.5 miles behind their lines and I was the FO for the action. I spent my 23rd birthday on Heartbreak Ridge. We took back the ridge in December of 51 after the 2nd Division was pushed off. The temperature was down to -30 at that time. In early 1952 we participated in Operation 'Clam-up' campaign, while the Chinese made a build up it seems. We had no fire missions and were told not to be active, just observe. When the enemy hit us we had a surprise for them. Searchlights in the rear lit up battlefield like daylight. All areas of the battlefield were covered with fire from all units at our disposal, and they were repelled.

During the early spring of 1952 the 7th Infantry Division pulled back into reserve but our guns and I stayed on line to support the ROK 5th Division on the Chorwon Reservation in central North Korea. During my stay on this hill we made use of 8-inch 'Long Toms' from a unit that had just moved into our west. We used them to hit approximately 300 to 400 enemy on 'Old Baldy' straight north of my position but out of range of my unit's 155mm guns. At other times I fired missions to knock off 200 to 300 enemy troops at the base east of 'Pork Chop' and 'T-Bone' Hills. I remember being visited by a Corps general and his staff. Using my BC Scope, the general spotted a great target and pointed it out to me. I took three rounds to bracket and one volley of three guns 'fire for effect' to knock it out. It turned out to be 76mm gun emplacement and ammo supply, and the fire mission blew out the whole ridge! Within a week, the general offered me a commission to fly Air Observer for Corps Artillery, but I was due to rotate home within two weeks and declined. I broke in two ninety-day wonders, replacements, before leaving Korea in late spring of 1952, and that was it for me."

**1st Lt. Ray Duerkson**
**213th Field Artillery Battalion 1951**

"I was a pilot, having been a flight instructor in World War II, but officially I wasn't a pilot as far as the 213th Armored Field Artillery was concerned, I was a Forward Observer. Unofficially, I did a lot of flying over there anyway. We flew missions not just for the 213th, but whoever was nearest to the area, that's who they would call to go up. We fired all the battalions. The only thing was, the 213th, we had a terrific Fire Direction Center, and if they could the infantry would always call for the 213th to fire on these targets of opportunity. We flew for all of them, and it would be coordinated through the liaison. There were times when some of the fire direction, and some of the batteries that were firing, didn't seem like they got the right coordinates. Sometimes, we took our .45s out and fired them out the side of the airplane as we were flying over the targets, as sort of a joke! There were so many direct hits that the destruction was horrific. We could see the fire come in, and you could see sometimes a lot of those Chinese men, those rounds would come in and heck, those guys would fly around in the air like cork wood. Those morning flights, were the one's that were really pretty, all those tracer bullets, you know, it was all lit up just like fireworks, rounds flying from the machine guns of people firing at each other. We would call in air strikes, that's when the Air Corps P-51s would come in and drop napalm. It was quite a sight. The Air Force planes a lot of times would be able to get things that the firing batteries couldn't get to. Flying as an Aerial Observer, since I was one of the newest officers with the 213th, I was one of the last to rotate home. By that time the Chinese started to get some Russian weapons in with them to fire at us. And they started to have capability to where the rounds that would start to come in would start to knock some of us down, and I remember that one of the guys that came after me was shot down and they never did find him."

**Sergeant Elmer Hasenmiller**
**1st Field Artillery Observation Battalion 1951-52**

"I was drafted on September 15th, 1950, and was assigned to a Heavy Mortar Company at Fort Carson Colorado. I was a Forward Observer for the 4.2-inch mortars, and since there weren't any 4.2-inch mortars around, they put me in the artillery. When I got to Korea, I was assigned to the 1st Field Artillery Observation Battalion, which further assigned 'B' Battery to X Corps. We fired all different types of artillery from 105mm, 155mm, 155mm Long Toms, 8-inch self-propelled, and also fired a few times the Battleship U.S.S. Iowa. It was seven miles out at sea, and we were seven miles inland. 'B' Battery, while with X Corps during the time I was there, was north of Yanggu, Korean Satari Valley. I was in Korea approximately from June 15th of 1951 to May 1st of 1952, I had 42 points to rotate home. During the battles of Heart Break Ridge and Bloody Ridge, we fired at targets of opportunity as support to the infantry. We normally supported the 24th Infantry, but at any given time we would be supporting the Turks, French, English, Ethiopian, and Korea Marines. I remember supporting the ROKs on two occasions, too. At this stage in the war we fought mostly the North Koreans. I served on OP's on Hill 821, and others on Bloody Ridge and Heartbreak Ridge, which was in the eastern sector seven miles from the coast. The battery normally manned four to five OP's all together. We had men on the scopes 24 hours a day. There were four American GIs, and two Korean carriers in the back-up crew. We were not in the trenches most of the time, but rather usually on the highest point behind infantry, where we established we established bunkers. The fire missions I remember most were firing the Battleship Iowa on targets that we couldn't select for regular artillery. Their 16-inch guns sure make one big hole. Most of our targets were targets of opportunity, mostly on troops or motor units and supply people. On several occasions North Korean Infiltrators got through the lines and among us. The OP to my right had several wounded one time because of that. Another time our own F-84 jets strafed us. One of my crew got shrapnel in his back, and one of the infantrymen had his hand shot off."

**Sergeant James Luger**
**3rd Battalion, 11th Marine Regiment 1951-52**

"I was an FO for the 11th Marine Regiment, 1st Marine Division. One of the members on my team was Sergeant Carl Chester Perryman a very colorful black Marine from Alabama, I remember he had received the Silver Star, Bronze Star, Navy Medal and Purple Heart while performing FO duties. Our team was on the line with all infantry regiments, the 1st, 5th and 7th Marines. I was a volunteer.

I was reassigned from the Naval Reserve to the Marine Reserve and requested active duty, and then shipped out from San Diego on the USS Weigand in May l951. I was assigned to George Battery, 11th Regiment, 1st Marine Division. George Battery was a 105mm battery, and we were assigned to the east central sector from June 1951 through May 1952, above Yangu. Working as an FO on the front lines, I thought it especially nice to be alive, considering. Our FO team was pretty relaxed. I remember a new addition to the team was a 1st lieutenant, and when he joined us he asked what he could do to be of help. Well, we suggested every day he could go to the rear to fill canteens, which he did. He was a reservist, a school teacher from Wisconsin. We stayed on the line as the infantry regiments, the 1st, 5th and 7th Marines, rotated up and to the rear. The 'gravel crunchers' respected us due to our volunteer status. I remember a Korean Marine Corps unit was tied into one of our flanks a lot, and we fought mostly the Chinese it seems. George Battery controlled three OP's, all of which were south of Hill 1052 which the Chinese controlled. These OP's usually were on the ridge lines only. Duty and living as an FO, we were dirty, unshaven for months on end. It was dangerous work, and some things you never forget, like the c-rations, lice, mortars, and anti-tank flat trajectory weapons you always had to contend with. I remember we used white phosphorous to start a fire followed up with H.E. that was set for about twelve feet off the ground. There were many casualties inflicted with this format. It was an exhilarating experience when called in with the right coordinates. Other things stick in your mind, like I remember one time being shot out of a tree while laying wire, and another when a stupid colonel set up in a valley for a hot Thanksgiving dinner. Chinese mortars wiped out about twenty men."

**Sergeant Daniel Mecca**
**13th Field Artillery Battalion 1951-52**

"I was drafted in September of 1950, and did basic at Fort Bragg, then was sent to Fort Lewis as a cadre in March of '51. I shipped out to Yokohama in June of '51, and was sent to Inchon with the 24th Infantry Division in July. There I was assigned to 13th Field Artillery Battalion, 'B' Battery. The 13th was a 105mm unit that was assigned to the X Corps and was located in central Korea, and I served with the 13th in Korea from July of '51 to January of '52. I was not assigned as a Forward Observer, I volunteered. I was part of a three man team which I was one of the radio men and then we had a lieutenant.

Being an FO was a gung ho experience. After being in the rear, I finally got involved more closely in combat. It was exhilarating, and gave me a feeling of importance as if I was truly in the heart of this war. The FO was held in high esteem by all, and it made me proud to be an FO, and I earned the respect of all those around me. As an FO I was normally assigned to 'George' Company, 19th Infantry Regiment of the 24th Division. They depended on us and held us in high esteem. We were the equivalent to an air strike on the ground. Life as an FO was interesting. I had a ring side seat after being back with the 105's. At times we ran out of water to drink, and October was unseasonably hot. As an FO, I was always dirty, dusty, and thirsty. After a while of performing this duty I was getting burnt out, and I didn't want to be there anymore. They couldn't find anyone to come up and take my place, so I had to stay longer than what was anticipated. The longer I was up on the hill, the worse it got. We did not support any ROK's, but we did have two ROK divisions on either side of us to protect our flanks. We fought against the Chinese while I was there. The Chinese set up a defense line, and we were there to demonstrate that we still had fighting potential. It was a continual offensive struggle with little chance of setting up any outposts. There was no break to do so. At one point in November of '51 we set up an outpost overlooking the Kumsong Valley and north of Kumhwa. At that time I think we were the farthest northern unit in Korea. There were no names for the hills that

I was on. We went from one hill to another in rapid order. We were moving so rapidly from one hill to another day and night, that supplies could not keep up with us. Calling a Fire Mission was fairly simple, you would radio back your location and targets and coordinates. If we were calling a mission 'Peanut one to Peanut two', which was the Fire Direction Center, and the procedure was to call for one round WP, then you would adjust your fire according to the WP and target, then say ,maybe, 'left 500 or right 500', and when they hit the target, you would say 'Fire for Effect, three rounds of HE.' Then you would say 'End of Mission'.

One of the largest battles I fought in was 'Operation NOMAD' which began on 13 October. The division jumped off into a strongly fortified main line of resistance. The battle was a continual offensive operation. My first day on the hill, the antenna on the radio was hit by shrapnel, and we had no communication with the 105 battery, but we didn't need them anyway, because there were no targets to fire on at that time, the enemy was in full retreat. The antennas were always the favorite targets for the enemy because it would give them our locations where we were. That first day, I looked across the ridge and saw yellow blotches. I commandeered a light 30, and directed fire from the light 30 to the blotches. All I could do is assume the outcome of that action because it was remote from the direction we were going. Right after that, as we were moving, mortar shells started coming in. The lieutenant and I jumped in a hole, and that was when the shrapnel got my antenna. Throughout this operation we were bombarded with mortar and straight trajectory fire. Prior to the jump off, the FO team had a liaison with the column moving to the jump off area a little before dawn. As we were moving up, they called for a cigarette break. The other radio man and I leaned up against the hill with the rifle company. As we were smoking, a half track came by, detonated a mine right in front of us. I called the medic, because our team member's eyes were bleeding from the explosion. I was ok except for gun powder in the lungs. Now he was sent back to the rear before we jumped off, so I had to carry his radio as well as my own, which added to 72lbs plus my other equipment. Our Lt. was at the head of the column, unaware of what just transpired. I was in a rage with the situation. I was running to the front of the column with all this equipment on my back mad as hell, maybe even a few tears in there, trying to get to the Lt. We finally got to the jump-off area, and what a show there was. Heavy bombardment, half-tracks, anti-aircraft guns, quad-50's, everything going on at once. We finally jumped off. At this point, the Lt. relieved me of the other half of the radio. Now it was he and I against the world, watching each other's backs for snipers. When we got to the top of the hill, there were enemy bodies lying all around. The bunkers they had were heavily fortified. This might have been Hill 585, I'm not quite sure. Then we set up a CP with all the brass. We were watching a platoon attacking a hill. I happen to turn around, and there was a water cooled .30 set up, and I looked at it and strolling a little away from the CP and saw a Chinese starting to come out hesitantly out of a hole. When he saw me, he raised his hands in fear. Behind him were more of them. They were all terrified and injured. As soon as I spotted them, I yelled for help 'Somebody come over and throw a frisk on these guys, and watch that heavy thirty'. I didn't know anybody's name up there. The only GI I even talked to for any length of time was sitting next to me on a reverse slope to get away from the harassing fire from a pack howitzer. We thought we were safe from it on a reverse slope, but a shell hit a stump on the ridge and it hit him in the back of the head and he went down the hill. I ran after him and called for medic, but it was too late. Then we moved on to another ridge.

There was another action and firefight, after that, it finally hit me I was in a war when I saw all the guys laid out dead. In the process of taking another ridge, I was on another reverse slope, and a Lt. came over and asked me if I can get the infantry on the radio, but I told him no, because of the antenna. He went back over the ridge and I heard automatic fire, and he was gone. We were getting a lot of fire. We had to go to the next ridge through Chinese dug trenches that were lined with bodies with gaping holes in them. That was truly an experience I will never forget. About this time a 'choogie' party came up with some supplies and two letters from my mother. I opened the letters and couldn't read them. I waited till I was able to get to the rear. So I must say, being up on the hill, I experienced all kinds of emotions, some that never go away."

**1st Lt John Kneuer**
**189th Field Artillery Battalion 1951-52**

"I was assigned to the 189th Field Artillery Battalion, a direct support 155mm towed howitzer battalion with the 45th Infantry Division, and I believe the 45th was in I Corps. I served with the 189th in Korea from 1951 to 1952. As a Forward Observer, I had mixed feelings, because it was something between ecstatic with what I wanted to do which was get out and work, and also I had thoughts of not being home for quite a while and that was sure enough. I fired primarily for the 45th Division, the 160th, 170th, and the 180th Infantry Regiments. However we would fire to the left of us into, I think it was the 3rd Infantry Division area on occasion, and on the right I cannot remember exactly, but it could have been the 40th Infantry Division which was the National Guard division out of California. We mostly supported the FO's from the 105s to give them a little heavier support and also give us some recon essence if we had to move forward. We always looked forward to moving forward and to check out new positions. Walking out there is the best way to find out sometimes because aerial photographs didn't help tell us everything in those days what was out there. It also gave us what our field of view was, especially what kind of ridge or mountain might be in front of us for our asking range. We had fixed Observation Posts, however we would go out every now and then on a special mission. The only thing I can remember about the OP's in the Chorwon section where I was first assigned was, well, one was called Hill 300, about 300 meters total, and that overlooked Old Mount Baldy. The second one I was on was Hill 400 which was about 480 meters which looked directly up the Chorwon Valley, directly up through what we called T-Bone. It had ridges, very high ridges that looked just like a T-Bone. I was up there for six days at a time about every third week, and there were a total of three in my crew, myself, a sergeant, and a commo sergeant. I had a good feeling believe it or not about being a Forward Observer. I had a good feeling about it and I knew I was helping the infantry, because I was helping them in quite a few missions. And most of us did not have time to be scared because we were always working, no matter at night or during the day time. And most of our work was at night time however, so we slept during the day and during the evening we took turns observing and seeing what we could do. And when we did get something to fire on, all three of us would be up in the OP helping each other because many things were going on. One time the Chinese started going after me and you could hear the shells creeping up the mountain side. I got a call from a friend of mine from the 1st Field Artillery Observation Battalion, and they said they had their radar clicking on the shells that were coming in. They said 'Don't fear, we're going to knock that piece out in about a couple of minutes'. And they did. So the nearest a shell go to me was about probably 500 yards, so I was perfectly safe. That did get my adrenaline running, though, you could see the shells creeping up the side of the hill!

There were so many unnamed skirmishes and battles, but I remember specifically one time that I did fire on our own outpost at the very south end of the T-Bone ridge, and the Chinese had overrun us in the early evening and I got through to the infantry officer with us there and I asked him, 'Do you need cover fire?' and he says 'Hell yes! Get it to me!' So I got permission back from DIVARTY. The Chinese were really overwhelming our infantry and I brought in the overhead fire and then I got permission to roll the fire right up that ridge almost to the main intersection with another mountain range that was perpendicular to us. And we kept that going until 4 in the morning. And because there was what we call the communication line for them, the trenches, they'd run up and down these trenches, they gave me permission to use not only the 155s but I had the 8-inchers firing for me that night too. I told the infantry lieutenant what I was going to do, and I fired for a long while, overhead fire with proximity fumes, and they were just coming over us, Hill 400. I'll tell you, I buried myself way under, but we didn't get anything going off over above us. This was early in January of 1952. We had just been deployed there a month and a half before. That was my first real baptism of really catching it! Well I did not have any rounds fired at me that night. The Chinese did not go after my OP, and my fear was really my own rounds coming over the very top of it, hoping they'd stay up at least 60 yards so that the proximity fuses would not go off. That one I fired at the end of T-Bone Ridge stuck out really in my mind because I had to fire on the infantry, but they were dug in and buried. Something like you saw in the Pork Chop Hill movie.

Another time I had to fire continuously from about 9 o'clock at night to four in the morning to support the infantry. During one of those times we were supposed to be in a quiet time but all of a sudden all hell broke loose and the Air Force couldn't get in with their flares so I fired continuous flares and what they called Willy Peter, white phosphorus, and I bounced white phosphorus off a rock. And I wish I had some pictures of that for you! That was something at night time to see those things first hit the rock and then skid upwards and explode! It gave the infantry time enough to see things because we did not have enough flares. The Chinese were all over in front of us. The infantry held them back, thank goodness. I gave them covering fire which hopefully helped. We had one tank out in the front that was disabled and the engineers had filled it with napalm and they set that off, and we could see the men. And later on in history, like a month later, the Chinese set up a 120mm mortar inside that tank and fired at us. That's when we knew we had to get the tank recovery team in there and get that tank out of there! The Chinese would come to us in waves that evening and the first wave was usually drunk and they had two grenades, and they'd throw the grenades at our line and they'd fall on the barbed wire. And then there would be a second wave of men and they would actually walk over their fellow countrymen and throw their grenades and that's how they got over the barbed wire usually. By the time the third wave had finished up, the regulars would come in and try to cross over, you know, walking over the bodies of their own countrymen. And that was something to stop. We had quad 50's up there, which were supposed to be triple A at that time but we used them for ground support direct fire. So consequently, Baldy out in front of me had dozens of dead Chinese on it and luckily it was winter time because the smell would have been terrible and we finally took that hill in early spring and we moved all of the bodies. I was not in that team thank goodness.

They kept the trucks rolling all night just for me carrying in white phosphorus to the battalion that was behind me and the Chinese never did get up in my OP That was when I was on the OP opposite of Old Baldy, it was 300 meters high, maybe 320. Another time, which was a little more self satisfying, General Muldrow, who was the division artillery general, he had gotten the word that I had hit some mountains and got good secondaries. I mean the whole side of the hill would blow up, and it was something he didn't believe right away so he came up to my OP And I got to know the general very well. And he says 'give me a good fire mission and see what I can do'. So I gave him a couple of hillsides and he says 'well, I'll take this one'. And he went into fire for effect within about four rounds and he was getting big secondaries. He said 'How'd you get to all the good targets? Can I stay up here a little longer?' And I said 'General, you'd better head back because they may be after us here in a little while'. He'd come up every now and then and ask for a good target to shoot at. He was the general from the 45th Infantry DIVARTY, he'd been with the 45th Division for years. In fact, he was over in Italy during WWII as the commander of the 189th. The general visited to me quite often. When I say quite often I mean maybe once every other time when I was up on the hill, because he knew that I had usually spotted some good targets and he'd like to shoot at them. He got what he wanted.

In the summertime we had moved from the Chorwon area to the central area and then to the Punch Bowl. In the Punch Bowl area, which is near the east coast, the Chinese looked down upon us and we were under smoke continuously. At that time I was not doing much FO'ing. However I was helping train a battalion on line of ROKs and it was the 195th ROK Field Artillery Battalion of 155s. But I did get some FO'ing in every now and then I'd take some of the Koreans out and show them what to do. Then I'd leave them and come back. So my stays were only something like less than twelve hours up on the hill with them because I was needed back in the battery area as well as in Fire Direction Center. We trained that battalion essentially on line from central Korea all the way over to the Punch Bowl."

**2nd Lt. Phil E. Squire**
**213th Armored Field Artillery Battalion 1951**

"I was assigned to the 213th with the Utah National Guard. We were getting more equipment and training when I received orders to go to Artillery Basic Officer's Course at Fort Sill, Oklahoma. The course started early December, and we were called back to the unit in early January to head for Korea. The 213th landed in Korea at Pusan in mid February 1951 and we played war games till we were tested 'battle ready'. My assignment was Reconnaissance and Survey Officer in the battery. As most of the moves were handled on a battalion basis, I spent my time as a Forward Observer assigned to different units we were supporting. This was one way to say how I was on the OP so much, but there was another reason worthy of note. I was at battery headquarters one day when the call came in to see which kind of whiskey I wanted. I said, 'None.' They let me know I had been getting one every time. I said, 'Nope, I don't want any.' It turned out that my captain had been ordering one for me so he could have double ration. The next day I was on the OP! I had a few interesting experiences I had on the OP's that were memorable. I was assigned to a ROK infantry unit, it seemed I was never sure when they were going to 'fall back'. When my interpreter was with me, he was always upwind so I could get the full benefit of his garlic when he belched. It was good manners to belch after enjoying a good meal. I was also assigned to the Queen's Own Scottish Borderers, commanded by a tall lanky colonel. He was like a goat when he would get his walking stick and start up a mountain. He would out-climb many of his younger officers. On top of one of the mountains he pointed out a range of mountains and said, 'This is our line, gentlemen. We will move only one way, forward. No retreat'.

Another time with a Columbian unit, my interpreter showed me my bunker just before dark and left me saying, 'Stay here, I'll be back'. There were three hills lined here and a company on each with the one I was with in the middle. Shortly after he left, a skirmish started. The North Koreans attacked and kicked the companies off each side of us. I sat there listening to the dogfight, but I didn't dare go out without my interpreter till daylight came. Then I got in some good fire missions as the friendlies recaptured the hills. Another memory was from the top of one of these hills. I could walk around in the daylight all I wanted, but pick up a pack or a box and walk toward the front of the hill and it would bring in mortar rounds. It was so cold, we kept the spotting scope in its box, and I guess they knew that. So I had to set it up before daylight or not use it. After light, I could saunter over to it and watch. One of the last times I was relieved from an OP to go back for a bath and to wash my clothes, as I started down the back side of the hill, mortar rounds started coming in, and I could see what looked like a foxhole just ahead, so I made a dash for it. As I left the ground to jump into it, I could see it was a slit trench quite full. I grabbed my seat and carried myself to the other side of the dirt mound, rolled down the hill a ways, but did not come up smelling like a rose!"

**Sergeant First Class Fred E. (Gene) Proft**
**1st Field Artillery Observation Battalion 1951-52**

"I just missed the draft for WWII, but was in the first one for the Korean conflict. November 30th 1950, I was inducted into the Army and assigned to the 653rd Field Artillery Observation Battalion In Fort Sill, Okalahoma. On July 3,1951 I landed in Pusan, Korea, and boarded a small gauge train for Paejon. On July 6, 1951, in the early morning hours, I arrived at Battery 'B' of the 1st Field Artillery Observation Battalion located in the X Corps Sector on the East Central front. A sergeant met me and asked 'Are you Proft?' I said 'yes' he then said I was his replacement and ticket home. He showed me where to sleep and met me for breakfast. After showing me around, he informed me I was not to leave the area without his presence, as he didn't want anything happening to me before he started for home. Later I was told he had been called up from a Utah National Guard outfit and had a large family waiting for him stateside.

My first week with the battalion was spent in orientation of the battle line, our battalion's job, and what each soldier was to do. I was assigned to the Flash Platoon. In essence, the Flash Platoon's function was to be the eyes of the Field Artillery, setting up observation posts on the front lines with the infantry. We would seek out enemy troop movements and targets and call in for fire missions on them. We also gathered such intelligence information that might be valuable to X Corps. One day when the sergeant went to check on OP #1, I asked to go along just to get some idea of what it was like to be on the front line. That trip was a disappointment for me both physically and mentally. First, having been raised at sea level all my life, I almost gave out trying to climb that mountain. Second, when we got to the top of the hill I didn't see one enemy soldier, and not even one enemy shell landed anywhere near our position. To keep from exposing ourselves to the enemy, we walked on the reverse side of the ridgeline, watching our footing on the narrow trail. I was able to get some idea of what it was like on an OP and, after about an hour, we headed back down the trail to the battery area. Believe me, I slept like a bear that night.

I will never forget the first OP to which I was assigned. They told me it was on a hill. Where I came from, they called them mountains. One often wonders what its like or how they are going to feel going into combat for the first time. I'll never forget my reaction, for it's one of those things a fellow thinks about for a long time before it happens. I didn't worry too much about it when I was in basic training or when I got my shipping orders, although, I knew that someday I would probably have to take the life or lives of the enemy while lighting. On the troop ship going overseas, however, I did a lot of thinking along those lines. Around mid July, 1951 our lieutenant called me aside one night and told me that we were to establish an OP on grid coordinates 11111715, in the Marine Division's sector. The Marines already had an OP up there and we were supposed to occupy it when they were pulled into reserves. After getting the layout and instructions from the lieutenant, I got my gear together, informed the fellows going with me to do the same, and set out bright and early the next morning climbing mountains again. Loaded down with everything I felt was needed, I didn't think I would make it to the top. My leg muscles and knees were killing me. The veterans and Korean cho-gee boys would slow down every so often to let me catch up. After a month of climbing those hills, I could keep up with the best of them. We arrived at the position where we were supposed to set up our OP. and it was a big disappointment. The OP was just a foxhole in the ground, and the lieutenant wanted one so a person could stand up in it. We started digging in rock and sun baked clay. I put a couple of guys digging in the instrument bunker where we'd put our spotting scope and put the others digging in some sleeping bunkers in which to sack out. On Hill 715 the main line of resistance was running roughly east and west. At our hill, however, the line dropped south for a couple thousand yards, so that Hill 715 was really a 'corner' or 'point' in the main line. From our position, we could look to the southwest and see Hwachon Reservoir where the Marines really had a fight.

We had a water-cooled thirty-caliber to our front, an air-cooled thirty-caliber to our right, a BAR team that set up position on the west slope of the hill at night, a thirty-caliber light machine gun to our right rear, and riflemen scattered around the hill. We had plenty of firepower, but we were in an exposed position. We chose our sleeping bunker, another corporal and I, down on the west slope a few feet, making it necessary to climb up to our instrument bunker from our sleeping bunker. Later on this proved to be a big disadvantage because we had to move around at night when we changed watches, and that always made everyone on the hill jittery. I was pretty tired when night finally overtook us. After assigning the men their watches and checking my carbine and ammo, I retired to my bunker. I was asleep as soon as I hit the sack. I awoke with a start, someone was shaking me and whispering, 'Get up corporal, a gook patrol is out front'. The first thing my waking ears heard was the staccato of two 30-caliber machine guns, interspersed with short bursts from carbines, crack of M-l's and the exploding whomp of grenades going off in front of the hill. I grabbed my carbine and web belt and started to survey the situation. Strangely, and much to my relief, I wasn't scared. I was amazingly calm. I asked 'Pineapple', a name we had given a Hawaiian in our outfit, what the situation was, and he was ready to give me advice. He knew I was fresh from the States and was determined to take care of me. He told me my best bet was to stay in the opening of the bunker and help guard the west slope of the hill. But, after a short time in the bunker, I wanted to get out and see what the hell they were all shooting at, I crawled out of the bunker and took up a position behind a stout tree trunk, which was a foolish think to do, I was covered from the front but exposed to the left and rear. We were getting some return fire from down the hill, and I could hear fragments of grenades and bullets clipping the leaves in the trees on the bill. I didn't see a damn thing to shoot at, but I felt like I had to shoot something. So I cut loose with a burst from my carbine down the forward slope of the hill. I believe that's all the rest were doing, just shooting in the general direction of the enemy. After a while, things quieted down again and I checked with my crew once more before going back to sleep.

To get the best unrestricted view of enemy territory, our OP's and especially the instrument bunker were most always established on the highest point of a ridgeline. One night a strong and frigid north wind was sweeping the ridges and valleys. I was on watch in our instrument bunker, my sleeping bag wrapped around my shivering body, so I started a small fire to help keep warm. My companion told me I was crazy as the gooks would see the light from the fire and come to investigate. I then told him if those nuts were going to climb a frozen mountain in this ungodly weather, in their tennis shoes, that's what most of them wore, and meager jackets, then they could have me. But I sure the hell wasn't going to freeze to death. No one, I mean no one, friend or foe, bothered us that night. I can feel the cold just thinking about that night! One night, while crawling from one bunker to another to stand my watch, I found myself looking into the muzzle of a .45 held by a sergeant who forthwith advised me that 'the next time you crawl around at night you'd better be whistling Dixie'. To this day I swear that the barrel of that .45 looked as big as a 105 howitzer's. That incident added ten years to my life and made me a much wiser soldier.

One day we had a particularly successful fire mission on some enemy troops detected moving through a valley. We surprised them with a battery of Fire for Effect on a concentration we had previously established. I requested 'Victor Tare' shells, which exploded in the air and blew shrapnel in all directions. The results were effective and awesome. I could see the dead and wounded troops in my spotter's scope. I told the gun battery what I had seen, that they were right on target, and thanked them. I always tried to keep the gun batteries appraised of the target and the success of the mission, I felt they needed to know their efforts were appreciated. Anyway, I was feeling pretty good about what we had done and happy about the whole mission. Then, 'Whoa, wait a minute, Gene!' I heard the voice of my conscience. You're patting yourself on the back for killing people. Where's the boy Mom and Dad raised to be kind to people and animals, and the Fifth Commandment that says 'thou shalt not kill'. It's one thing to do your job and do it right but to be proud of taking the lives of others? I thought about this for a long time. I remembered that in the Old Testament of the Bible, God had aided his people in destroying their enemies, sometimes without mercy. Two sayings came to my mind 'War is hell' and 'It's kill or be killed'. Many days I was frustrated because the peace talks were on again, off again, and from the news I got from home, it seemed the papers just carried brief paragraphs about skirmishes on the front. But those actions were taking lives, some very close to me. I feel sure these same types of thoughts entered the minds of many of our soldiers. However, it's something you can't dwell on. You react to your training, and most times that reaction has to be made quickly in order to stay alive. I never had to kill anyone face to face or in hand to hand combat, but I feel I would have reacted to my training and the instinct of self-preservation.

On one of my last OP positions I was standing the night watch when I noticed what appeared to be moving lights a long way off, too long through our spotting scope. I could see what appeared to be vehicle lights going through a pass. I counted over forty of them. Looking at my map, I could see that they would be out of artillery range, but I took azimuth reading to them and left my scope set on where the lights had been seen. When daylight came, I could tell that the lights I had been looking at were indeed a considerable distance from us, almost on the horizon. On our map I drew a line on the azimuth from our OP to where I had seen the lights. Studying the terrain along the line, I picked out two mountain passes where the lights could have been located. I reported what I had seen to battery headquarters as well as a 155mm gun battery with whom I had fired missions. They confirmed it was out of their range but would pass it on to the Air Force. I saw the lights a few times after that, and then I stopped seeing them, I don't know if the Air Force worked those passes and roads over, or the enemy found a new way to bring supplies up.

One of the more humorous highlights of my tour of duty in Korea had to do with searchlights. Now this searchlight deal was something new to me, and I had never heard of it being used in ground warfare before, but it has a good purpose. The night I rolled into the outfit to which I was assigned I saw searchlights being used for the first time to aid the infantrymen in their cause. I peered out of the truck in which I was riding and the land and sky were lit up with artificial moonlight. It gave everything an eerie setting in the cold, misty hours just before dawn. These searchlights were in batteries of about two or three and were situated about five miles behind the lines, depending a lot on the terrain and enemy positions. The lights were really effective on overcast nights, as the beams could be reflected off the underside of a cloud layer and deflected into no man's and this artificial moonlight was really helpful to the men on the line as they could see the area in front much better and deter any surprise attacks. Also, if there was a firefight, a fellow felt better if he could see what was in front of him. An observer stationed on the front line controls the searchlights. This observer may be an FO to the searchlight battery itself, but most of the time someone who had a good knowledge of the terrain and positions of the front line troops directed the light. So it was that that a Lt. Potter, Forward Observer for the 15th Field Artillery battalion got the job. Lt. Potter and his crew really added color to our stay on Hill 715. They holed up in a bunker next to ours, and his crew consisted of a Sgt. Snow and a Korean houseboy that did all the dirty work, like carrying rations up the hill, going for water, etc. Lieutenant Potter was a talker, and the way he talked in itself was humorous. Every night, about an hour after sundown, Lt. Potter would receive a call from the searchlight battery saying they were ready to adjust the searchlights. This was when the fun really began. They would turn on the searchlights, and usually the beams were set too high This was done so that they wouldn't light up our positions on the hills and give our location away. The chinks knew where our line was and had an idea of our defenses, but they didn't know where everything was pinpointed, nor did we want to disclose it. I've never seen a searchlight up close and don't know how to adjust them, but it must be intricate. Taking into consideration the distance they were from the front, just a minor adjustment would make a big difference where we were.

The lieutenant would tell the searchlight battery to lower the beam a specified number of degrees, like three degrees. Well, the next thing you knew our hill was bathed in light so bright you could read the fine print in a contract by it. Lt Potter would wince and then tell the battery to raise two degrees, pronto, because we didn't like being lit up like a Christmas tree. The next thing we knew, we would be receiving the full beam of the searchlight with none going into enemy territory. When this happened, the lieutenant would jump about three feet straight up, grab the phone and yell, 'Up, up, you blankety-blank, lunkheads! I said two degrees up, not down! Now give us about ten degrees up!' Well, the next thing you knew that searchlight would stab the sky like it was looking for enemy planes. The lieutenant would give out a string of cuss words that would put a retired sea captain to shame, throw down the phone, stomp around cussing like a sailor, then try to gain his composure. He'd pick up the phone again and, in a manner of dignity, would say, 'Let's start all over again'. Well, they would start easing the beam of light down again and the next thing we knew it was as bright as day again The lieutenant would throw both hands up in the air, throw the phone to the sergeant, and tell him to adjust the damn thing. The sergeant couldn't make them understand either, so the lieutenant would take over again. And so it went about an hour of this, and the searchlights would finally be pretty well adjusted. The lieutenant and everyone on the hill would settle down to their watches, when something would happen to the searchlights, which threw them out of adjustment All hell would break loose again if the beam fell on us or if it were deflected upward, the lieutenant would usually sigh, turn over, and go to sleep!

I had the unique experience of working with units of the Turks, French, British, and Ethiopians. In talking with these various United Nations forces, I found out they knew more about America than I did about their country. Once, when the French were on the line with us, they sent out a probing patrol to Hill 651. It was just across the Satari Valley from us. They were doing great, they got across the valley undetected and got almost to the top of the hill when all at once they started shouting 'Viva La France' and yelling in French as they scurried up the slope. Needless to say, this woke up the enemy who started rolling grenades down the hill and laying down a curtain of fire causing the French to pull back. I later asked one French soldier why they started yelling when they had the element of surprise in their favor. He replied, 'Oh, Qui, that's the spirit of battle'. I enjoyed being on the line with them, they were very entertaining and interesting. When the Turks were on the line with us, I felt safe and secure. I had heard tales about their tactics and their fierceness in battle. They would set up an ambush on the line by deploying a squad of men in a perimeter around a campfire where one or two men would sit as decoys. When the enemy would come to investigate, they would allow them inside the perimeter then kill them. Eating with two Turk officers one day, I asked them about their country and what they had heard about the United States. They told me that in Turkey, the people thought that everyone from Chicago was a gangster and everyone from Texas was a cowboy. They got this idea from the movies they saw. I remember the time a British gun battery was firing a mission for me on enemy troops I observed in a valley. We were just getting on target when a British officer got on the phone and said they were suspending the mission for 10-I5 minutes. When I asked what the problem was, he said it was teatime. He said they would get back to me after the break. I told him to forget it; the enemy would be long gone by then.

A lot of fire missions were counter-battery or harassing fire. You didn't know if you destroyed what you were firing at, especially at great distances or in wooded areas. On one particular day I happened to be scanning a valley in front of us when I saw these three flashes, heard the booms, and then the explosions of the shells. It looked like the three flashes came from the top of a ridgeline that protruded into the valley. On looking at my map, however, I could see that there was no room for artillery up there. So, They had to be in the valley below the ridge, but, how far? Knowing the elevation of our OP and the elevation of the ridge in front of us, I calculated where the guts might be keeping in mind the terrain and ground features in the area. I gave my coordinates to the gun battery, told them what we were up against and they agreed to work with me. Meanwhile, I had kept the cross hairs of my scope where I had seen the last flashes. When our gun battery put a round right where the flashes had been, I called for Fire For Effect. Several weeks later, after we had secured Heartbreak Ridge our Commo Sgt called to me and said he had been in the valley I had fired into and had seen the enemy guns. All three were damaged beyond repair. Sure makes a guy feel good to know his efforts were not in vain.

One time a Marine spotter from the Battleship Iowa used our OP instrument bunker to fire the ship's 16 inch guns on an enemy position across the valley from us. The enemy had dug Caves into the mountainside. They brought up artillery that they would move out to fire and, then, pull back in. The spotter was good and was on target with the third round. Time in flight of the shells seemed like it took forever, and they came roaring in like a freight train. He worked that fortification over good, but would you believe, about thirty minutes after the shelling stopped, we could see some of the enemy soldiers come out of their caves staggering around like they were drunk! I didn't think anyone could survive that pounding. Another day, I was looking through my scope searching for enemy targets and I started scanning the enemy trenches and bunkers on the ridgeline nearest us. I saw this guy in a brown uniform with red epaulets and a cap with a red band around it. A Russian advisor, I thought! Hot, diggity dog! Because their ridgeline was so close to ours, I thought I'd try my hand at getting him with an M-l rifle. I had one of my OP men looking through the scope telling me where my rounds were hitting and what corrections to make. Well, I never hit him but I got close enough to make him take cover. Next day we all paid for my foolishness. They brought up an anti-tank gun up and proceeded to work over every bunker on our ridge. They were good, too! When they got to our bunker, the first round was high, the second was below us about ten feet; and moments after we scrambled out of our bunker, the third round went through the observation slit and tore up our maps, phone, instruments, and gear. When it was all over, one of the infantrymen came over and said they didn't want us drawing army more enemy fire on their positions!

There was the time I was sitting at the switchboard in the Flash Platoon OP. The Lieutenant was back at Battery HQ attending a meeting, when this call comes in from some general asking what we were doing to stop the enemy artillery raining down on his men. I told him our OP's were trying to locate the artillery causing all the havoc. He then said with emphasis, 'Trying isn't good enough I want it stopped... Now!'. His language, adjectives, and verbs were pretty explicit. So I turned to Elmer Hasenmiller, with whom I had been talking, told him what the General said, and asked him if he wanted to go with me to make shell crater analyses. You know what that is, when a shell hits the ground and explodes, the dirt is thrown out in a fan shape from the impact point. You ascertain the furthermost edges of the "fan', determine the mid-point between the two edges, and with a compass, take a reading from the deepest point of the shell hole to the 'fan' mid-point. The azimuth in theory should point to the gun. Well, we got a jeep and a volunteer driver to take us to the valley that was receiving the bulk of the enemy shelling. We left the jeep and driver behind a hill, and then Elmer and I waited for an incoming shell to hit. When it did, we ran like hell and dove into the crater. We got an azimuth from that crater, dashed to another new shell hole and took a reading then to another and another. We tried to get readings from shell holes that were spread out so we could get crossing azimuths. We got four or five readings, then high-tailed it back to the jeep. The infantry on the line thought we were crazy. but we didn't think about it then. We got back to the CP and plotted the azimuths on our map and came up with a valley from which the artillery had to be firing. Hasenmiller asked what we were going to do. I told him we were going to fill that valley with so much William Peter that those gooks were either going to gag or lose their sight. And that's what we did. The General had said all his gun batteries would be at our disposal. Well, it must have worked, because the enemy stopped shelling and the General called back to tell us we 'did a damned good job'. Lt. Barnes wasn't too happy when he returned and found out what we had done. He said the General should have gone through him. We could have been killed. I told him we were only doing our job, and when a General says 'jump', I'm going to jump. Just before I was discharged at Fort Sill, a General presented me with the Bronze Star with V device for our action. Sergeant Hasenmiller had been discharged, but they called a National Guard muster in Iowa and presented him with a like medal."

**Sergeant William Gerardino**
**5th Marine Regiment 1951-52**

"I enlisted in the Marine Corps and my MOS was a radio operator. I was ordered to Korea as part of the 12th replacement draft in 1951. When I got there I was assigned to the 5th Marine Regiment, 1st Marine Division. I served as a radio operator for 81mm mortars, part of Weapons Company, with two different FO's. I spent 11 months 'on the hill' as it was described. While I was there I saw action on both coasts on Korea. I participated in three rather large battles, Operation 'Killer', Operation 'Clambake', and another that I can't remember the name of. Our FO team was always alert, we had to be accurate and be quick. We fought against both Chinese and North Koreans, I remember supporting some ROK units, but they were not trained very well. We called our OP 'Baker', and our unit had one per company. I think some of the hill numbers our OP was situated on at one time or another were 881, 1242, and a few others. Being part of an FO team was dangerous, independent duty, and it always seemed to be cold and wet. The fire missions that we called, it required complete concentration and staying calm while watching for enemy fire. All of the missions that were called were deemed significant, no matter what, even dealing with probes and guerilla style tactics."

**1st Lt Howard Maki**
**37th Field Artillery Battalion 1951-52**

I was sent to Korea as a replacement in late summer, 1951, and was assigned to Battery 'A', 37th Field Artillery Battalion, 2nd Infantry Division, as a Forward Observer. Although the three firing batteries 'A', 'B' and 'C' of the 37th Field Artillery's organic weapon was the 105mm howitzer, I had occasion to fire larger artillery weapons, from the 155mm howitzer, 155mm 'Long Tom' to the highly accurate 8-inch howitzer. Which weapon responded to my request depended upon the target and how quickly I needed fire support. The quickest response for fire, the ability to mass fire on multiple targets and volume of fire was always my own battalion of 105mm howitzers. The other artillery weapons provided reinforcement and backup as needed.

I left the casual atmosphere of the Incoming Replacement Section of the Eighth Army and arrived at 2nd Division Headquarters in about one hour. A series of official orders assigned me from Camp Drake to EUSAK to the 2nd Infantry Division. At each level of headquarters I signed in and signed out until I arrived at Battery 'A', 37th Field Artillery Battalion. I thought, 'Well, it's been a long trip from Fort Bliss way back in July.' As always, it felt good to be 'home' and off the transient status even though I didn't know a soul here yet. I already knew a lot about the 2nd Division. And I was here because the NCO at Camp Drake had advised me to stay away from an assignment to the 2nd Division because it was too much in the thick of things. His comment helped me make the decision that what unit I wanted to join was one that was involved in doing something. The requirement for field artillery Forward Observers was higher priority. Many Observers were needed for assignments to infantry rifle companies to provide artillery fire support. The need was critical because of the high turn-over rate of FO's. I wasn't upset or uneasy about my assignment for I could see the logic. Fortunately, I knew how to direct mortar fire and had become familiar with field artillery procedures during OCS training at Fort Riley. This assignment would be different only because of the caliber of the weapons and the language used and accordingly the changes were not difficult. The FO's were assigned to work as closely as possibly with the same infantry unit in order to promote rapport. Battery 'A' FO's were assigned to the rifle companies of the 1st Battalion, 23rd Infantry Regiment, Companies 'A', 'B', and 'C'. Battery 'B' FO's were assigned to companies in the 2nd Battalion, and Battery 'C' FO's to companies of the 3rd Battalion. I received a new identity, actually a code name, when I was sent to work with a rifle company. This eliminated sending the given name of the Forward Observer. In addition, it was easier to give the code name during telephone or radio transmission. Individuals at the FDC knew immediately who and where the caller was. When I was with Company 'A', I was 'Easy 7' with Company 'B', 'Easy 8' and most of the time I rotated between 'A' and 'B' companies. Toward the end of my Korean tour I worked with the French Battalion. With the French, my code name was 'Impede 2' the designated code name of my job as Battalion S-2, Intelligence Officer.

On two occasions I was on line for over three weeks, followed by a three-day rest period. It was so nice to shower, sleep and relax before returning to work with the infantry! I was sent to Heartbreak Ridge to 'learn the ropes' under the tutelage and guidance of an experienced FO It was a very undesirable place to be. The hill was battered, the scene was gray with clouds and drizzle, and it was very noisy. Smoke obscured the landscape out front. All the rocky intermediate ridges, large and small, all the valleys and depressions were known intimately by my guide. My impression was similar to what I remembered about the craggy terrain in northern Italy, bad. War is always hell. I wondered why I had volunteered to be here. After a couple of days my orientation visit was over and I returned to the relatively safe Battery Area. In our sector, two units of the 1st Battalion, 23rd Infantry were in defensive positions on the front lines. A reinforced rifle platoon from 'B' Company was the most forward unit and guarded a major line of approach. Approximately 800 yards southeast of the platoon across a small valley, Company 'A' was situated on another hill. The distance of both units was approximately 2,000 yards in front of the MLR. Chinese outposts were scattered on a series of high ridges and hills directly in front of the platoon, the closest on Hill 400, approximately 400 yards away. In order to provide artillery support, Forward Observers were assigned to each unit on the MLR. During the day each side watched warily for hostile actions by the other. At night, patrols from each side continued to probe and harass the other. Brief fire fights occurred several times as opposing patrols encountered each other in the dark. Because of the isolation of the platoon, our Battery Commander decided each available FO would draw straws to determine who would be with the platoon from Company 'B' at its outpost position. I thought that was not a fair way of selection, and said so. Some of our FO's had just been relieved after several days on line and deserved a rest. Since I had the least amount of work on line, I told the Battery Commander to put away his straws, I would go. My trip to the outpost occurred during daylight. Dangerous, but it would have been even more so at night. Night movement would have had to be without lights, and finding our way along the narrow jeep trail would have been too difficult. Also, the chance of encountering an enemy patrol was highly possible. As we traversed the narrow, winding jeep trail, we knew we were under enemy observation. 'Charlie', as the Chinese had come to be called, had observation posts on all the distance hills. He saw every move we made, on foot and by vehicle. Knowing that we were being closely watched gave us an eerie feeling. Our trip didn't seem too bad at first, as we passed through our own forward positions on the MLR, waving back to the GI's when they waved to us. But upon looking back, we realized the friendly faces had disappeared. Now we were vulnerable, in the open, on our own. One jeep, one driver, my NCO assistant, and I, alone in the wilderness of no-man's land!

I hated that ride for I felt so vulnerable. The jeep engine purred, but it seemed too loud. What if Charlie decided to send a few rounds our way? We wouldn't hear them coming over the noise of the jeep. I watched the side of the road for a likely bail-out spot in case founds did come in, explode on our flanks, in front, or to our rear. The jeep made a lot of noise! We wouldn't hear nay warning sound before an artillery round hit! But nothing unusual happened as we negotiated one small curve after another on the way to the outpost. Two thousand yards is just a little over a mile in a straight line. Not too far, but our route was longer than that. I touched my.45 caliber holster giving me a feeling of security. I know it was ridiculous but nonetheless if I had an M1 rifle, I would have felt more secure. I trusted that weapon! The map coordinates showed Old Baldy to be on the right of my destination. As I stared at Old Baldy, I thought the name was appropriate for the top of the hill and several hundred yards below the crest showed nothing but brown earth. I checked my map again. Company 'A', 23rd Infantry was on an intermediate hill, actually a series of ridges overlooking a river between Old Baldy and the smaller hill occupied by the platoon from Company 'B'. The river, one of the many swift flowing rivers in Korea was narrow, winding and shallow with a rocky bottom. It cut sharply in a northerly direction and disappeared in an area of higher hills occupied by Chinese forces. A long expanse of rice paddies covered most of the valley we traversed. The jeep's windshield was folded forward on the hood and covered with a piece of canvas. This was common in a combat zone. The purpose was to eliminate glare reflected from the sun that could signal enemy observers of a vehicle's presence even when the vehicle was hidden behind obstructing terrain features. I wondered if the Chinese had copied the nasty German trick o stringing piano wire across a road, about throat high of the jeep driver and front-seat passenger.

Arriving at the outpost, the platoon commander, a 1st Lieutenant, said cheerily, 'I heard you were coming, and watched you coming down the road.' 'Yeah,' I said, 'and I wonder how many other eyes over there was us,' and nodded toward the distant hills. 'I'm sure they saw everything you did.' Following a few words of welcome, the platoon leader took me around the position to familiarize me with his defense layout. He pointed out the location of his area of responsibility on the map, and identified the physical features on the ground corresponding to the terrain features depicted on the map. He said he had been at this position for only three days, it'd been quiet except his listening posts had reported movement of Chinese patrols passing by the platoon's position each night. Evidently they had been sent to probe positions along the MLR prior to returning to their own lines before dawn. Occasionally there was a fire fight along the main line located well to the rear. When this occurred, tracer bullets from the rear whined and sparkled overhead, almost like the 4th of July. It was a weird feeling to have fights behind the position where we were, in the middle of no-man's land. At times the Lieutenant's perimeter personnel had brief encounters with the Chinese who upon being discovered withdrew immediately. One Chinese patrol was successful in cutting the telephone line to his company command post. However, telephone communication was re-established before sunrise. When we were in a defensive position, I shared my living quarters with my NCO assistant. This consisted of a bunker with a dirt floor, sand-bagged walls and roof. Every attempt was made to locate the bunker on the reverse side of a hill that faced the enemy. The bunker was equipped with a gasoline lantern, an air mattress for each of us, and a small space heater during cold weather. Warm food was delivered twice each day from kitchens in the rear, and C rations were available but were a supplement to regular rations. On the forward slope of the hill, I had an OP that had a commanding view of the terrain out front. A high-powered spotting scope and a special set of binoculars mounted on a tripod allowed the Observer a 'wiggle proof' sight picture of the target area and ability to send accurate azimuth readings to targets. The OP was dug into the hill and protected to some extent by sandbags. In order for us to see the enemy, it was necessary for the OP to be opened on the side facing the enemy. This meant that at our most forward positions the enemy could easily see our Forward Observer. The FO was subject to be fired upon at any time by sniper and a variety of weapons including machine guns. He was a prime target, to get rid of the Forward Observer and eliminate the eyes of the artillery.

Knowing we were isolated some 2,000 yards in front of the actual front line or MLR was somewhat frightening. Our hill position was higher than the vast rice paddies that surrounded us but lower than most of the other hills within the sector. Had the Chinese wanted to take the hill away from us, a mere platoon, they cold have done so. We knew we could be surrounded like Custer at Little Big Horn and overwhelmed before any assistance could arrive from our friendly lines far behind us. It was somewhat consoling to know Charlie would have to use a much larger force than ours to accomplish this. We were protected by barbed wire, well-dug in bunkers with machine guns strategically placed to provide interlocking fire. Still, we were vulnerable for our ammunition would not last long enough to beat back repeated human wave attacks. Chinese night patrols periodically cut our telephone lines between us and our main forces. Radio backup was available but cutting of the line heightened suspense over what might happen next. Supplies and mail runs occurred only during daylight hours because night traffic was too hazardous. A night ambush could occur almost anywhere along the dirt road leading to our position. At dusk our position was buttoned up until dawn. That tight feeling of closed-in isolation strongly increased when darkness approached. No external lighting was permitted. When there was no moonlight or stars, the black of night squeezed us into our little outpost making it seem even smaller. Just before the light diminished to zero, everyone checked his weapon and unlocked the safety, pulled the bold back just far enough to make sure there was a round in the chamber, released the bolt to lock, and reset the safety to the "ON" position. Preparedness was complete for whatever might come before dawn. I kept busy during the daylight knocking out Chinese bunkers on distant ridges. I often called on the 8-inch howitzers to knock out these bunkers, because the 8-inch howitzer was the only artillery weapon that had the range and pin-point accuracy to do the job. Other artillery weapons such as the 155mm gun affectionately called the 'Long Tom' had the range but its dispersion ratio was too great. 'Close' was not good enough to penetrate and destroy strongly-built bunkers. The round had to actually hit the target. Direct-fire weapons such as tank guns could but were unavailable during this time. The dispersion of several 8-inch howitzer rounds fired by one weapon at the same settings, however, was very small. Once the target was zeroed in with point-detonating rounds, I asked for subsequent rounds to be fired with time-delay fuses. The delay was not long, perhaps 0.5 seconds, but it was enough for the 196 pound projectile, loaded with HE, to penetrate the thickly constructed bunkers and destroy them along with the occupants and their weapons. I continued my bunker-busting mission until most of the bunkers were destroyed, or it became too dark to see. A concentration number was then assigned and the range and azimuth settings were recorded for late use, if required. After arriving at the infantry unit to which I was assigned, I notified the FDC and asked fro a concentration number for my actual location. The purpose was to call for massive artillery fire in case it became apparent we would be unable to fight off a sustained Chinese attack, and our defended sector was about to be overrun. None of the infantry commanders disapproved of this action. Fortunately, I never had to resort to this drastic maneuver to inflict maximum casualties on enemy forces.

The Chinese proved they are good, diligent workers. For example, after 'walking' the heavy howitzers along a distant ridge destroying bunkers one at a time, I would count what remained on the ridge at dusk. The next morning, however, it was evident that many of the bunkers I had destroyed the previous day had been rebuilt during the night! And additional bunkers had been added that had not been there the day before. At first, I suspected the Chinese wanted to show they had the capability to build faster than we could destroy them. I felt a tinge of discouragement, but rationalized the new construction probably were decoys. I renewed calling fir emissions on only those bunkers that had been on the ridge previously, assuming these to be occupied. At the end of each day I had to give an estimate of damage. I lost count of the number of bunkers I destroyed, but over a period of two weeks, it must have been several dozen. Especially rewarding was seeing a large secondary explosion follow immediately after the projectile hit suggesting ammunition or fuel had been stored in the bunker. When these secondary explosions occurred, I always let the gunners know. I thought they should have some reward for their efforts especially since they couldn't see the results and sustaining a rate of fire of one round every three minutes loading and firing their large artillery rounds was heavy work.

During the three weeks I was with 'B' Company's reinforced rifle platoon there was no serious retaliation by the Chinese in our sector. This surprised me because many of their bunkers had been destroyed and they had afforded protection for weapons and personnel. Perhaps they didn't know the location of the individual who was directing the artillery fire on his area. I began to have the feeling he was going to find this 'Easy 8' guy and retaliate. On the morning of the 21st day of my tour on the hill, I was relieved and returned to the relaxed atmosphere of my home, the Forward Observer's tent at Battery 'A'. The hot shower and change of clothing was great! That night I listened to guns firing and thought, 'I wonder how the boys out there are doing'. In a few days it would be February, and I'd be going back up. But at least I wouldn't spend another January day on the hill. It was no surprise when I was told that I was going back after three days of doing nothing but resting and relaxing. I was a little surprised, however, to learn I was going to Company 'A', 23rd Infantry. It was located on the MLR where I had spent the previous three weeks, except it occupied a position several hundred yards behind and to the right of where I had been. After packing my meager gear, I loaded my jeep and left without taking the time to say good-bye to anyone. Just a pack with a few personal things, stationery and shaving stuff, a bedroll, air mattress and a shelter half. In addition, I had a pistol belt with canteen and .45 caliber pistol, a pouch with two clips of ammunition, a trench knife and a first aid pouch. It was too warm for a parka and my Mickey Mouse boots. We found the trail past the main line and headed out across the same valley we had traveled over three weeks ago, and where the trail split we took the path to the right and arrived at Company 'A' without incident. My confidence was higher than it was when I first looked at the wide expanse of rice paddies and clumps of bushes along the trail, I was alert but left my holster cover snapped shut. After the usual informal introductions to the key members of the company, I was taken to my quarters, a bunker located on the reverse slope of the hill. Someone had spent a lot of time and effort digging and reinforcing the place. The narrow door was a double shelter-half held in place at the top with three sandbags. There were no windows, only a six-inch square hole cut through the sandbagged wall. The hole was an escape for stale air and exhaust fumes from a Coleman lantern used for illumination. I hardly noticed the musty smell of unwashed bodies, lantern fumes, and carbon residue. I hadn't expected plush, anyway. I looked around the interior and saw that the bunker was large enough for three people to sleep and permit limited relaxation such as writing letters or reading. Two empty ammunition boxes lying side by side served as a combination desk and nightstand. I tossed my belongings on one of the makeshift bunks, the one with the gray cotton mattress and nearest the makeshift door. I wondered where the mattress had come from, but didn't ask, nor did I think of bugs; it looked inviting! My perusal of the interior of this home away from home for the next few days or weeks took no ore than a few minutes. My guide was waiting for me outside, and I knew he was anxious to continue my familiarization tour of the company's position.

The OP provided a wide, panoramic view. Directly to my front the same Hill 400 still loomed as a major landmark. Because of the different angle and higher elevation, it seemed closer than it had when I was with the 'B' Company rifle platoon. Everything I had been able to see from 'B' Company I could see better now, with greater detail, even the blown up chaplain's jeep in the ditch by the small bridge. To the left and at a greater range, the position occupied by the platoon from Company 'B' looked small and vulnerable. I saw no movement over there, even when using binoculars, the daylight discipline was still high. I tried to locate my old OP but couldn't, only the small knoll where it was located was visible. While I was there, I thought it wasn't well camouflaged, but from this distance and angle of observation it was indeed well hidden. Nonetheless, I felt safer now that I was with Company 'A', secure in knowledge that I was with more troops and on higher ground. The position occupied by Company 'A' was far more extensive than the smaller hill occupied by the platoon from Company 'B'. While the latter position was well-defended, limits existed as to what a platoon could occupy, and greater restrictions on comfort. I hadn't noticed the crudeness of my surroundings while I had been with the Company 'B' platoon, but now, however, it was evident. Company 'A's defensive position was far superior. The bunkers were better built, pathways were mostly dug in trenches, and the OP was built of heavy timbers, thick walls and roof. The only open area of the OP, toward the Chinese lines, afforded a better than 180-degree view of the front. My sense of security was optimistic and hopeful, yet had they wanted, the Chinese could have surrounded and overwhelmed our puny infantry company with their hordes of bodies. A daily ritual helped ease tension during those cold January days on the OP. Everyone looked forward to 1700 hours each day when it was a time to 'exercise' our weapons for fifteen minutes. Every weapon in the company opened up, rifles, machine guns, carbines, and pistols. The noise was great, as was the elation! It was a way to relieve any feeling of tightness, to overcome the tenseness accumulated during the previous 24-hour period. In a word, it was a release. The reason for this daily firing of weapons was twofold, to provide an outlet for emotions and, to prove to everyone that his assigned weapon would fire under adverse conditions of snow and ice. After the 15-minute period, each man had something else to do, namely, clean his weapon!

We had plenty of ammunition. Large stores of ammunition were on hand and replenished daily. After each noisy and flashy episode of smoke and hundreds of tracer bullets firing from our hilltop toward the Chinese positions we wondered what their feelings were! Crazy Americans! All that ammunition! Laughingly, we referred to each day's expenditure as rotating stocks. One day while the exercising fire was going on, one of the infantry platoon leaders and I were walking along a narrow path that meandered along a small ridge. He was carrying a carbine, one capable of firing full or semiautomatic. I was armed with the standard issue Colt .45 Army pistol. Rather than pointing our weapons toward the Chinese lines and firing at an angle of about 45 degrees we looked for a suitable target to fire upon, a stump, a box, anything. We spotted a rusty GI helmet lying downhill, about 25 yards below our path. He said, 'Watch this', and sprayed a quick burst of about a dozen rounds toward the helmet. Snow and mud around the helmet flew into the air but none of the rounds hit the helmet. I said, 'What a lousy shot, you missed', and laughed. 'Now watch this', and I drew my .45-caliber pistol from its holster. I was kidding, bragging for nothing, because I am a very poor shot with the weapon. I fired, and much to my amazement the helmet jumped and began a slow roll down the hill. I fired again. Again the helmet jumped and began rolling faster. Poker faced, I said, 'That's enough', snapped the safety on and holstered the pistol. My companion had a look of disbelief on his face as he asked, 'Jeez, where did you learn to shoot like that? Slowly, word got around about my shooting prowlness!

The first ten days of February were relatively quiet but not without activity. It was never totally quiet and dull at the front. On one occasion, peering into the darkness from the relative safety of my position, I was aware of a sudden eruption of rifle and machine gun fire, verifying patrol activity of some kind. Until our men returned to report what they accomplished, it was not known whether we or they had fired first, and why. Sometimes a single shot in the dark beyond our perimeter brought us to an increased awareness that something was out there. Maybe a rifle was fired by a nervous occupant of a Chinese listening post, or perhaps someone fired unintentionally. Perhaps it was the Chinese version of H&I fire. Whatever the reason, it got our attention. Unless there was moonlight, it was so dark at night one could not see the front sight of his weapon when looking down the barrel. We took little comfort in the fact that there were extensive coils of barbed wire and antipersonnel mines in front of our position; a silent defense for protection and security. What a temptation it was to shine a flashlight toward the direction of the slightest noise. Maybe it was a rat, maybe an enemy recon patrol, or the rattle of something disturbed by the breeze. The first hint of dawn was always welcome, however, the gradual minute by minute sight of familiar objects did not mean we could now relax. The enemy was known to attack suddenly at dawn. A master of stealth and tactical night movement, the Chinese could move thousands of men into position without being seen or heard by our observers. Daytime was the time for the majority of the infantry to relax, sleep, and attend to minor chores. Weapons during anytime were manned, but at night the tense, silent shift work began with two men in a foxhole, two hours on, four hours off. I didn't perform shift work; I stayed in my "quarters" with my Recon Sergeant. A telephone from the Company Command Post was always within easy reach. Each morning, I went to the OP to look for any changes that might have occurred overnight along the Chinese lines. As mentioned earlier, new bunkers had been built along the far ridge lines where our 8-inch howitzers had knocked out over a period of several days. I wondered whether the new bunkers were real. Charlie was a great builder, but I questioned the active construction of so many new bunkers, especially under night conditions. Why would they rebuild along an open ridge line where they had already lost so many? Perhaps they were decoys placed along the ridge line to truck us into wasting ammunition. However, bunker-busting continued through the remainder of the winter. The building activity was reported to higher command headquarters and resulted in a scheme of hitting these locations in darkness after the daylight destruction missions were fired. This action caused heavy losses among enemy work parties.

As mentioned earlier, the OP was on the forward slope of the hill facing the Chinese lines. Access to the OP was provided by a narrow path from our protected area on the reverse slope of hill. The path continued past the OP through a narrow opening in the expanse of barbed wire for about 50 yards, and disappeared behind a series of small knolls and ridges into enemy territory. This was one of the paths our patrols would take at dusk and upon their return in the morning. Each morning, GI's shuffled by on their return from perimeter watches and listening posts, some responding to my greeting of, 'Good morning', others looking in my direction and saying nothing. I could tell their time spent on the hill by looking at their faces and their clothing, and each succeeding day their eyes were more hollow. Shaving was a daily requirement even though we were in a combat environment, and short haircuts were the rule as well. I agreed with these rules of sanitation. Keeping one's self and sleeping area clean was considered food for morale and discipline, even when laundry facilities were unavailable. The simple act of using one's helmet as basin for warm water, a handkerchief for a washcloth, and a bar of soap helped dispel war's distractions. We were in a so-called static or defensive position, so everyone had adequate time to keep reasonably clean. During this period weapons firing along our outpost line was almost totally limited to the daily late afternoon routine of exercising weapons, and H&I firing of artillery, with favorite targets such as known road junctions, likely areas of troop concentration and equipment storage. Occasionally a large secondary explosion and fire would cause us to wonder what we had destroyed. Patrol activity occurred mostly at night. However, daylight patrols were also sent out to determine visually what was on the reverse slope of hills in front of us or search out other areas where the enemy might be located. Sometimes caches of enemy weapons and ammunition were located., and if found they were destroyed. Daylight patrols permitted members to see, but their movement could also be seen by enemy observers. As usual, I was informed of the patrol's planned route to a designated location via a map reconnaissance. From the OP, critical terrain features on the map were identified on ground and numbered. In the event the patrol leader needed my assistance at or near any of these locations, he would call me directly giving me his code location. Within minutes artillery rounds were on the way.

Early one morning while I was in the OP, the patrol leader called to say they had captured a Chinese soldier and were about to return to our lines. He whispered that numerous Chinese patrols were in his vicinity but so far he and his men had avoided detection. Almost in the same breath I saw the arc of tracer bullets split the darkness into my right front. The voice on the radio gasped, 'Charlie's got us pinned down at A-14, get us out of here!'. A-14 was code for a draw about 200 yards to our right front, I know exactly where it was, thanks to our pre-planning. I rang the phone to the FDC and said, 'Impede 3, this is Easy 7, fire mission.' Back came the command, 'Easy 7, send your mission.' I said 'Concentration 15, battery 3 rounds, fire for effect.' That point on the ground had been zeroed in and designated as 'Concentration 15'. The data required to fire on this point was quickly passed to the gunners, and within seconds the first of three rounds from each of the guns in Battery 'A' was on the way. The platoon leader later said he had heard everything I said and decided to stay hidden until he heard the first incoming rounds. When the first rounds landed among the Chinese, he and his men ducked and ran the 200 yard distance to the perimeter of Company 'A'. The entire patrol and the prisoner made it safely. During this time the company commander was present in the OP. He had alerted a rifle platoon to prepare to move out on a rescue mission if necessary to provide cover for the patrol in order for it to get back. This move proved to be unnecessary because the artillery fire had eliminated the threat to the patrol. We were elated! The patrol leader came to the OP, shook my hand and told me, 'You saved our tails out there. Those rounds were right on the button!'.

We are all familiar with the old expression, 'You never hear the one that gets you,' meaning, if you hear the bullet whiz by, it missed you! Immediately after the sound, you feel especially alarmed when you realize you're the target. On two occasions, I was the target. Both times this happened was when I was on the hill. In late January 1952 when I was with Company 'A', 23rd Infantry on an outpost some two thousand yards in front of the MLR. We occupied defensive positions on a high knoll west of Old Baldy and approximately four hundred yards south of Hill 400, a strongpoint occupied by Chicom forces. Early one morning I left the relative safety of my bunker, turned to the right and began walking to the observation post, or OP, some thirty yards distance. It was cold, it had snowed during the night and the path was slippery underfoot. The path was more like a trench, about two-feet deep, narrow and commonly used by men going to or coming from patrols. This morning, the path had only one set of footprints that led in the same direction I was going, these evidently were from my recon sergeant who had left for the OP a few minutes earlier. A few icy spots along the path made me walk slowly and carefully with my head down; there was no hurry to get to the OP. I was about half way there when suddenly, my concentration on moving carefully changed from unhurried to urgent. The next thirty seconds seemed like eternity. Without warning, the sound of a half dozen or so ear-numbing machine-gun bullets ripped through the snow about two feet left of the trench I was walking in, churning the mud under the snow, and scattered it in a dirty trail several feet beyond the point where each round had hit. I didn't duck, I hit the path with my elbows and chest, hard! Looking forward, I saw what had to be smoke from a machine gun on Hill 400 about four hundred yards in front of me. Instinctively, I realized I was in a direct line of fire of the gunner and his weapon so I had to move quickly, to continue lying on the path would only allow the gunner time to adjust his aim carefully, about two clicks left deflection and spray the path I was lying with more bullets.

Fixing my eyes on Hill 400, I rose to a crouch and started sprinting forward toward the OP in the direction of the distant machine gunner. This time I saw the second burst of fire from the weapon, a split second later the rounds tore through the snow and mud, this time on the right side of the path. He had me bracketed! I had to get off that path, now! Running back to the safety of my bunker was one way, but it'd be faster if I ran to the OP, the heavy layers of sandbags there would protect me from the bullets and give me a chance to call a quick fire mission on Charlie's position. I knew what I had to do, but the distance seemed so far! I continued running while in a crouch, slipping and sliding on the ice. It seemed I was barely making headway. The icy condition of the path caused me to slip and fall just as I reached the juncture where I was to turn right and run the remaining ten steps into the safety of the OP. A quick glance revealed the recon sergeant crouched in the open doorway, a look of concern and fear on his face. He yelled something, but I didn't hear. My ears were ringing from the loud staccato sound of the bullets as they whizzed by. It was fortunate that I slipped and fell because at that point another burst of machine-gun fire tore into the snow on each side of the path between me and the door opening. If I hadn't fallen I'm sure I would have been exactly in the line of fire from that last burst! I got up quickly, ran through the doorway and hunkered in the protection of the sandbagged wall. I was safe! The sergeant asked, 'Are you all right, are you okay?' I said, 'I'm fine, hand me the phone.' Knowing Hill 400 was already zeroed in, I called in a fire mission with time-delay fuses. When the Fire Direction Center said rounds were on the way I raised up to peer through the BC scope. The top portion of Hill 400 erupted in smoke and dust. I saw what appeared to be the form of a man, spread eagled as his body twirled through the air. A smaller object, which I believed to be the machine gun, along with pieces of unidentified equipment, flew upward in another direction. Perhaps both objects were figments of my imagination, to satisfy a feeling of revenge for this individual who had chosen me as a target just minutes before. True or not, the intended result was achieved, the fire from Hill 400 was neutralized. I reported the incident to the company commander and told him I was convinced the Chinese had seen me walking on the path to the OP many times over several days. The short distance between Chinese outpost positions and our own could have revealed what I looked like to a person peering through a well-hidden high-powered telescope. I believe they waited for me to appear on the path and decided to get me, 'that troublesome enemy Forward Observer.' They came close. Despite their failure, they tried again, not with a machine gun but with sniper fire. Protection afforded by the OP was excellent except for the narrow side entrance and the opening in front that faced the Chinese lines. This wider opening provided no protection from about chest high up to the reinforced roof, about two feet higher.

A second 'close one' occurred a few days after the Chinese machine-gun incident. I was in the OP with one of the infantry platoon leaders. We were tracing his upcoming patrol route on a map, pointing out and identifying actual terrain features on the ground that would be investigated later that evening. Although crackling gunfire somewhere along the line was a common occurrence, the initial sound would catch our attention briefly, but be disregarded if the sound came from a distance and posed no threat to us. This day, however, our conversation was interrupted by the loud crack of a single rifle bullet that hit very close to the OP. Then another. The second sound was a louder crack that passed over the top of the OP. I glanced at the platoon leader who was with me, then toward Hill 400 to see if I could see where the rounds had come from. Nothing. Another round hit a steel barbed wire support about five feet to the right side of the OP. The platoon leader said, 'Sniper! I think he's trying to zero in on us.' I quickly searched the far hills and ridges with my binoculars for tell-tale smoke. Still nothing. I said, 'He must be using smokeless ammo and I can't see any place close in, maybe it's long-range stuff.' At that instant, a bullet hit a thick horizontal timber between and slightly above us, scattering pieces of wood and dust, struck a second timber, ricocheted and fell to the ground between our feet. The noise of the bullet and violent tearing of the wood within the confined space of the OP was so loud it deafened our ears. It happened too quickly to know immediately how close the bullet hit, but as we both ducked, I saw the bullet on the floor with a wisp of vapor rising above it. It was melting a hole in the snow between our feet! I reached down to grab the round, still hot to the touch. With both ears ringing, my voice sounded tinny when I looked at the platoon leader and said, 'This is my souvenir of Korea!' I still have that bullet in my display case. It's a .30 caliber round, but when it hit it sounded more like a .50 caliber. We rose, cautiously looked out over the wall, but saw nothing.

We never spotted the sniper. We guessed the rounds had come from a long distance because at short range, a good marksman using a telescope sight would not have missed. The first three rounds were zeroing in rounds, the last was meant for one of us although I had the feeling it was more than likely meant for me. The elapsed time for all four rounds was about twenty seconds. Later, when I got thinking about that close call, I came to the conclusion the guy was either a lousy shot or a rookie sniper. A good sniper doesn't zero in on his target with three rounds, a good sniper takes only one shot to accomplish his mission. During the first three weeks of January 1952, I was assigned as a Forward Observer to a reinforced rifle platoon of Company 'B', 23rd Infantry Regiment that was located on an outpost position in the Old Baldy sector approximately two thousand yards in front of the MLR. When I arrived, I asked the infantry platoon leader what was it that made his platoon so 'reinforced.' He said, 'You, you're our reinforcement in case we need supporting artillery fire in a hurry.' All I could think to say at the moment was, 'Oh'. In a way, that felt good even though we all knew that in spite of our carefully laid out minefields, booby traps, barbed wire entanglements and heightened ability to direct artillery fire, our defenses would be by-passed or over-run in the event of a strong Chicom offensive. At best, our mission was to provide advance warning and delay the enemy's effort, at worst we were expendable. A dominant hill mass, numbered on the map as Hill 1200, was located in Chinese forces' territory about one thousand yards northeast of my OP. By using my 20-power spotting telescope I could make out a foot trail leading almost to the top of the hill. Periodically, I would check the hill to see if I could spot enemy activity but most of the time I saw nothing. One day one of our Piper Cub spotter planes approached the hill from the south. As I looked through the scope toward this hill, I saw an enemy soldier and his machine gun come into view and begin firing at the plane. The plane, apparently untouched, turned and flew in a slow arc back toward our main line, made another turn and flew parallel to the front between the main line and the outpost line where I was. Maybe the pilot didn't realize he was being fired upon every time he came within the machine-gunner's range. I continued to watch as the plane made another turn, then another. He was flying in a wide circular pattern.

I began to fear for the plane and the life of the pilot. Nothing happened. The plane made another slow arc, then disappeared in the clouds further east. I called a fire mission to blast the top of the hill with a battery of 105mm shells where the gunner had appeared. It was an impressive sight to see the rounds explode, however, I was convinced the gunner could hear the incoming rounds and retreated to safe cover in well-constructed bunkers dug deep into the hill. Maybe I could time a concentration of artillery fire to arrive at the top of the hill at about the same time as the gunner appeared! But first, I needed a plane and a gutsy pilot to fly over Hill 1200. There were several problems involved with that plan. There was no way to explain the plan to personnel at the Fire-Direction Center over my telephone and timing was critical. The plane had to be close to the hill to draw the gunner out into the open, and simultaneously, some distraction, perhaps the noise of the airplane engine could mask the sound of incoming artillery to the gunner. Otherwise, the machine gunner would have time to disappear into the protection of a bunker dug deep into the top of the hill before the rounds arrived at his position. He and his weapon had to be in the open. The answer was provided by a volunteer, my battalion commander, Lt. Col. Robert Backes. The afternoon of the next day, Lt. Col. Backes paid a routine visit to the OP. I summarized the activities that had taken place since my arrival and mentioned the gunner on Hill 1200 taking shots at spotter planes. When I told him about my plan to eliminate the machine gunner he said, 'Good, let's try it tomorrow at 1400. I'll tell the FDC about the plan and I'll be the guinea pig in the plane. I'll radio 'Easy eight, okay' when I'm in position to fly close to Hill 1200.' 'Easy eight' was my call sign. He finished with 'You call in the fire mission and just before the FDC says the rounds are ready to fire, tell me via radio. I'll fly over the hill when you say, 'Sunday shoot, FIRE', this will be the signal for the guns to fire, the pilot will rev-up the engine, then we'll get out of there fast. See what happens and let me know.' The plan worked out just as planned. The machine gunner came out of his hole to fire at the plane but the combination of the airplane's buzzing noise, plus the chatter of the machine gun, apparently kept him from hearing the incoming sound of four artillery rounds. Almost simultaneously, they exploded on his position while he was still in view of my telescope. When the smoke and dust cleared, the gunner and his weapon were no longer visible. I called in 'Impede three, this is Easy eight, TARGET, cease fire, end of mission.' About fifteen minutes later, Backes called me on the phone to ask how it went. When I told him what I'd seen, he said, 'Great job!' It wasn't I that deserved the accolades, it was the two guys in the airplane. Backes and his pilot had guts! I reported the above story of heroic action by Lt. Col. Backes and his liaison pilot to higher headquarters, however, to my knowledge it was never recognized. Perhaps this was due to my being the only witness."

## Corporal David Fife
## 1st Field Artillery Observation Battalion 1951-52

"My original outfit, the 653rd Field Artillery Observation Battalion, which originated from Ft. Douglas, Salt Lake City, Utah as a National Guard outfit, was called to active duty September 1st, 1950 and sent to Ft. Sill Oklahoma for further training. We were to be the replacements for a unit already in Korea. We had heard they were overrun and lost all equipment and were converted to a 105mm Howitzer firing outfit. I was assigned to Charlie Battery of the 1st Field Artillery Observation Battalion. We were stationed at different points on or above the front line. My crew and I served as Forward Observers for the Corps artillery. We were in the sound ranging part of the 1st Field Artillery, and we saw plenty of action and set up many artillery barrages. My time of service in Korea was from August 11th, 1951 to May 24th, 1952. My crew and myself also called in several air strikes, Marine Corsairs, P-51 Mustangs, and Jets on targets of opportunity. We were on an outpost, which was dugout 3,000 meters in front of the front line. We sure were like sitting ducks. Our outfit arrived for the spring offensive, when we kicked ass until we were above the 38th parallel. My group's last outpost was in front of Hill 1062 elevation, and the nearest town was Kumhwa."

## Sergeant Robert Hollowood
## 2nd Battalion, 11th Marine Regiment 1951-52

"I enlisted in the Marine Corps in January 1951 at Buffalo, NY and went to Boot Camp at Parris Island, SC as one of a platoon recruited from western New York and Pennsylvania. Upon completion of Boot Camp the majority of the platoon received orders for Camp Lejuene, NC. I was assigned to Casual Company at Headquarters, Parris Island awaiting orders. A call went out in late April '51 for volunteers to fill out a draft for Korea. I volunteered, was accepted and was soon on a troop train headed for Camp Pendleton, CA. At Pendleton we were sent to the 2nd Infantry Training Regiment and were given two months of intensive training culminating in the classification of MOS 0311, rifleman. The 11th Replacement Draft was formed and left for Korea in July 1951. I was, for the second time, in a Casual Company awaiting orders and was finally assigned to the 12th Replacement Draft. We boarded the MSTS General Meigs at San Diego and sailed for the Far East, hitting port in Kobe, Japan in Mid-August 1951. We stayed in Kobe for a couple of days loading C rations, Ammo and sundry other items and off loading our seabags. Liberty was allowed and then it was on to Pusan, Korea. After de-barking at Pusan we were trucked to the United Nations Replacement Depot and spent several days there getting our 'land legs' back, conditioning hikes occupying most of our time. I thought it was fairly amusing that we Marines were situated between the Turkish and Greek soldiers. The way their countries got along it could've proved to be the proper introduction to a war zone. We were flown about 200 miles north to the airfield at Chunchon and from there trucked to 1st Marine Division HQ where we were given our unit assignments. I was an 0311 rifleman so I fully expected to go to one of the Infantry Regiments, the 1st, 5th, or 7th Marines. I was completely surprised to be sent to the 11th Marines, the Artillery Regiment instead. I was not aware of the fact that I had been given an 0800, Basic Artilleryman, as a secondary MOS but very aware that I knew nothing at all about artillery. Trucked on up to 11th Marines HQ I was further assigned to Fox Battery, 2nd Battalion located near the 'Punchbowl'. The 1st Sergeant of Fox Battery asked me where I was from, if I had ever hunted the hills or done any outdoor farm work, and then gave me a choice. My options were as a cannoneer or as an FO team communicator. I chose the FO team though I wasn't really sure what FO meant, or which end of it I would be on. It proved to be the right choice for me because even though FO team members were given the option to return to the battery at their request, but stayed with the

Fox Battery FO team for all but the last several days of my tour. I arrived in Korea on 15 August 1951 and was detached for return to the U.S. on 15 August 1952.

The 11th Marines are the artillery regiment of the 1st Marine Division. In Korea the 11th Marines consisted of three battalions, the 1st, 2nd, and 3rd Battalions, that had three batteries of six 105mm howitzers in each, and one 155mm howitzer battalion also having three six-gun batteries. In general each 105mm battery directly supported an infantry battalion with an FO team attached to each of the battalion's companies. For instance if Fox Battery was in support of the 1st Battalion, 1st Marines, 'Fox-1' would be with Able Company, 'Fox-2' with Baker Company, and 'Fox-3' with Charlie Company. The 4th battalion of 155mm was available on call to any team but did not have direct FO teams of its own. When I arrived in Korea the 1st Marine Division was part of X Corps and was located in the far northeastern part of the MLR. The ROK I Corps was on the division's right occupying the part of the MLR that terminated in the coast in the Sea of Japan. In March 1952 as part of Operation Switch, the 1st Marine Division was moved west to a position blocking the historic invasion corridor from the north to Seoul and became a part of I Corps with the 1st ROK, 1st Commonwealth and 45th Infantry Divisions. When I joined Fox-l we were in support of Able Company, 1st Battalion, 1st Marines in Division reserve. I was introduced to my duties as a wire-man by manning an OP in the Punchbowl area with the other team members as we waited to be committed back into action. This was strictly a secondary OP but very useful to me in terms of what was expected of me as a member of the team, from watch standing to manning the commo gear and becoming a member of the team. The team consisted of an FO officer, who was a 1st or 2nd Lt., a scout/observer, usually an NCO, a radio operator and three or four telephone wiremen. As I was to learn, like every other team operation in the Marine Corps, all members of the team were cross trained in the others duties and could operate proficiently outside of their specialties.

There were only two major battles that our unit had part in or were of sufficient magnitude to be considered battles. The 1st took place early in my tour and the 2nd was near the end. In early September 1951 the 1st Marine Division was engaged in operations to secure several dominant terrain features in their sector of the MLR. Hill 749 was one of these objectives and because of fanatical North Korean resistance would be very difficult to take and secure. The 7th Marines started the assault and after sustaining heavy casualties, were relieved by the 2nd Battalion, 1st Marines who continued the attack until they too were badly mauled by minefields and the heavily bunkered defense. We, the 1st Battalion, 1st Marines moved into 2/1's positions under cover of darkness and after sustaining a barrage of mortar and 76mm cannon fire during the night, continued the assault on the following morning. The hill was secured after a hard days fighting and a counter attack that night. The North Koreans continued harassing mortar and cannon fire, and even threw in a few rounds of anti-tank rifle shells. Our scout/observer Archie Estes was wounded in the right arm badly enough to be evacuated. He was the only member of Fox-l to be hit by enemy fire while I was with the team. My activities during the assault besides following behind laying telephone wire were to observe our flanks for any enemy movement. This was my first exposure to an offensive operation and I suppose I was no different than many others before me. It seemed chaotic most of the time with the only clear objective being to move forward and upward until the hill belonged to us. The cost of doing this was evident by the bodies laid out under ponchos after we had pushed the North Koreans off the summit and controlled the terrain. When we had everything sorted out the next morning the FO, Lt. Guynes gave me his field glasses and told me to sweep the valley to our front, reporting anything unusual. I had been using the glasses for quite a while without seeing anything and some of the terrain had started to blur on me. I was just about ready to ask for relief when I saw a NK break cover from a brushy gully and run into the entrance to a canyon that ran roughly parallel to our ridgeline on the other side of the valley about 1000 yards away. He was followed a short time later by several others. Lt. Guynes had no problem locating their hiding place and within minutes had a fire mission on the way. He covered the gully and then used both HE and VT fire on the canyon. This was the first fire mission that I had any part in and was extremely satisfying. The rest of the time that we were in X Corps was a mixture of MLR duty with the patrols and occasional brief firefights or small patrol actions. It wasn't until we moved over to the western sector and joined I Corps that we were once again in a heavy engagement. On 28 May 1952 while Fox-1 was in support of Able Company 1/7, we were part of an assault to take and hold high ground to the front of the MLR, designated the 'Jamestown Line'. Able Company was to seize Hill 104, roughly at the tip of the triangle of objectives. We moved out before dawn and by around 0800 were in control of Hill 104. That was the high spot of that morning. The air cover we were supposed to have to support the attack was grounded by heavy overcast and the enemy reacted to our assault with extremely heavy and accurate mortar and artillery fire. Accounts of the action state that it was the heaviest concentration of enemy fire in the war to date with over 4,000 rounds of incoming counted during the 24 hour period. I don't recall much incoming, if any, prior to our assault on Hill 104, nor a lot of it after we were finally able to break contact and return to the rear, so I believe that those 4,000 rounds were compressed into six or eight hours. It sure seemed like it!

The incoming was being fired from behind high ground to our front and could only be countered by random efforts at likely targets because of our inability to observe beyond the masking hills. Lt. Noakes, our FO officer could do hardly more that make sure that enemy infantry did not mass against us for a counter-attack. I was kept very busy trying to keep telephone contact open back to the MLR and our artillery liaison. Because of heavy casualties the other elements of our assault had been ordered back to the MLR so there we were out on our own with no easy way to break contact and move back or to suppress the incoming we were taking. Late in the morning a flight of four F-80's showed up and even if they were only on station for a very short time we got a respite from the incoming, but as soon as they left though it resumed with the same intensity. Around noon, to the best of my recollection a flight of Skyraiders arrived and we were able to organize a rear guard, get our more seriously wounded and dead aboard tanks and make an orderly return to the rear. We had been mauled badly enough, nine killed and over one hundred wounded, that we went directly to reserve. The 1st Battalion, 5th Marines took over our sector of the Jamestown Line. The Skyraiders were masters of close air support and kept the bad guys totally quiet. If we had them in support earlier as planned it would've made the outcome of our raid much different I'm sure. We rotated in and out of that sector of the line for the rest of my tour, remaining attached to A/1/7 the whole time. I never called a fire mission during an offensive or defensive action we were involved in but I did communicate, both by telephone and radio, the SCR 619, in the missions. I thought and still do, that I was able to handle my duties in a calm and competent mariner. The FO officer or the scout calling the mission could have the best possible information for the mission plotters but if it couldn't be communicated it wasn't any good. It was also important to me that I did not let down any of the Marines I was with, my team or the men of the infantry units we were supporting.

When I got to Korea the 2nd Battalion 11th Marines was attached to the 1st Battalion, 1st Marines as the situation settled down to the so called 'trench warfare' phase we would go on line with an infantry outfit, and when they were relieved we would stay up with the new company. We would then go to reserve with this company and then repeat the cycle. We did therefore support a number of infantry companies until the 1st Division moved west when 2/11 stayed with 1/7 for the rest of my tour. In most instances the infantry pretty much left us alone until either we were involved in one of their operations or if they were in trouble. We always wanted to remain with our infantry units when we went in reserve instead of detaching back to Fox Battery. They left us alone, Fox saw us as a prime working party to improve the position, haul trash, etc. This only happened once, we learned quickly. We did not support any ROK units and only had contact with them once. On the last night we spent on line on the eastern sector, Item Company 3/7 was relieved by a ROK company and we were to spend a night with them to point out our defensive concentrations, H&I missions and to bring the ROK FO up to speed. It was I believe on Hill 884 which was very steep. The departing Marines had their packs out of their bunkers laying by the trail. Some of the ROK's would kick the packs which went downhill further than most of the Marines wanted to chase them so the ROK's went after them the next morning. I was not unhappy to leave the hill when we were released. In the east we were most often opposed by North Koreans, there were some North Koreans opposite us on the western portion of the line but the majority of the enemy forces were Chinese. The North Koreans fought more fiercely and were difficult to dislodge from ground they had fortified and defended tenaciously. The Chinese fought well but not as determined as the Koreans, often using the force of sheer numbers to influence their actions. Both used mortar and artillery support very well.

The only reference we made to OP's up until the previously mentioned Reno, Carson et al was to specify our position on the portion of the MLR that we occupied within our company front. They usually were bunkers, open to the front with an observation slot. Each team had a tripod mounted scope equipped with a mil scale etched on the lens. I don't recall the magnification but it was excellent. These bunkers are where we would stand our watches or form our center of defense if we were attacked. They usually were in a prominent position within the company front. The term OP was also used, but not named anything specific, for positions we would occasionally man while we were in reserve. On the eastern portion of the MLR it covered a valley near the Punchbowl, and in the west it was on high ground overlooking the confluence of the Han and Imjin Rivers. In both cases the terrain was very lightly defended because of natural obstacles but did require that an eye be kept on it. The Hills we served on were, in the east, 749, 812, 854, and 884 and in the west the only thing I remember is that it fronted Hill 104. Life in the trenches settled into a tedious routine. Watches were maintained 24/7, usually four on and eight off. Comm gear had to be maintained also and then the opportunity would arise to accompany a patrol or to fire a mission. There was however, a sameness to the routine day after day with only an occasional blip to relieve the monotony. On Hill 812 revetments had been bulldozed into the ridgeline and a rudimentary road constructed so that tanks could be moved up and emplaced to provide direct fire from their 90mm cannon on enemy positions on Hill 1052 on the far side of the Soyang River Valley. A 6x6 truck bringing ammo up to the tanks took a mortar round right on top of the ammo cases in the bed of the truck. Both the driver and assistant bailed out unhurt and took cover while the truck burned down to the chassis. The load of 90mm ammo, HE and WP cooked off for several hours. The display of smoke and explosions must've made the NKs think that they had hit an ammo dump. The action would result in no casualties except to the truck and my telephone lines which had the misfortune to he alongside the road. We had to replace a couple hundred feet of comm wire and did it I'm sure in record time. One does not linger long in an area where 90mn shells are lying in ashes that haven't turned cold yet. Because of the success achieved with the tanks, and probably the lack of a violent reaction by the enemy, someone decided to up the ante by bringing up a self-propelled 8" howitzer to the ridgeline. The road gas improved, a revetment was prepared and a large bunker was constructed to house the FO crew and to serve as an OP. I do not know what Army outfit the howitzer and the crew came from, I don't think I ever did know to tell the truth, but they moved the weapon into position and made the necessary preparations to fire it. A request was made to the nearest Marine FO team for assistance in orientation of the Army observation team in acquiring possible targets and familiarization with the enemy front. The FO officer from Fox-2 went to the OP along with his scout/observer and radioman. They were in the bunker along with about 8-10 others when a 120mm mortar round came through the roof. The results were devastating, in more ways that one. Not only were most of the occupants of OP killed or badly wounded, the howitzer crew was sent back and after a couple of days the gun itself was removed without firing one shot to validate the effort made to utilize it. One other Operation occurred which made me very glad to be in reserve at the time of its inception. It was called Operation Clam-up and it was designed to make the enemy think we had pulled out of the MLR for new positions. Much overt activity was undertaken to kick off the operation and then, under cover of darkness, the troops on the MLR at the time went into their bunkers or reverse slope foxholes and remained there to give the impression that the lines were not longer occupied, there were some limited successes in conning the enemy patrols sent to investigate but no major ambushes took place. Life in the trenches was tedious but livable, when you could move around, but it certainly was not when those people had to live like rats for the length of Operation Clam-up. It was short-lived, to no ones dismay, and it was a good time to be in the rear.

The one Fire Mission that I will always recall was a precision destruction mission on an enemy bunker located on the crest of the previously mentioned Hill 104. It was a fairly large bunker and we were sure that it was being used as an OP and a source of sniper fire. We had fired missions on it several times with limited success and they had just as often repaired and improved it. On the day I fired my mission there was even a Chinese soldier in the bunker throwing filled sandbags out of the embrasure and arranging them to narrow the opening. There was a labor strike in the steel industry back in the States at the time so I was told beforehand that there would be a limited number of shells available for me to fire. It took about four rounds to register on the target close enough to fire for effect. The bunker was situated almost exactly on the ridge line with the larger portion of it dug right down into the hill, making it a very small target. The gun firing the mission, one of Fox Battery's 105mm howitzers, put out six three-round salvoes close on target but no hits and I was told that only one more salvo would be fired. The first round was short of the target but directly on line, the second was also directly on line but over it, and the third went right in the embrasure! When the dirt and smoke cleared all that was left of the bunker was a large crater on the ridge line and that is the way it remained, some small payback for the OP bunker that had destroyed on Hill 812 at the 8" howitzer position. We even used the crater as the Able Company command post when the raid on 104 took part. This is best example of a fire mission I could give. This was a known target whose removal would deprive the Chinese of a position from which they could observe, harass, and cause us casualties. Because of its location a precision destruction mission would offer the best chance of neutralizing the position. One gun of whatever caliber, 105, 155 or 8" would be used dependant on the nature of the target. The initial rounds would be used to register the gun on the target and then upon the 'Fire for effect' command, three round salvoes would be fired. The FO would spot the rounds using the target as the point of reference the hits would be called as short or over, right, left, or line, Small corrections would be made in the plot after each salvo and another would be fired, narrowing the impact zone until the destruction of the target was accomplished. As best as I can remember after all these years a fire mission would go as follows 'Fox-24 this is Fox-1, fire mission. Fox-1 this is Fox-24, send your mission. This is Fox-1, fire mission, enemy bunker, precision destruction' and here you would identify the target and type of mission requested, you'd request initial Smoke or Willie Peter if other that HE for spotting purposes, Willie Peter referring to White Phosphorous, give the coordinates, eight digits locating target within a grid square on the map. Coordinates would be encoded and authenticated using a one time pad, then you'd say 'Will observe. This is Fox-24, understand fire mission' and then FDC would repeat the mission, 'This is Fox-1, affirmative. This is Fox-24, will inform On the way, wait one. Fox-1 this Fox-24, On the way. Fox-1, Roger your OTW. This is Fox-24, Splash'. 'Splash' was usually about five seconds before impact. The hit is spotted and a correction made. 'This is Fox-1, left 50, drop 50 acknowledged by Fox-24' and same procedure followed until the target acquisition is close enough to fire for effect. Three round salvoes are fired and spotted, either Short right, Over right, Over right, Short line, Short line, Over line, and finally, Short line, Over line, On target. Then the last thing said was 'Cease Fire, end of mission, Target destroyed'."

**Sergeant Walter Auran**
**64th Field Artillery Battalion 1950-51**

*Author's note: The life, wounding, or death of a Forward Observer and his team sometimes is only recorded out of necessity on a command report, after action report, or even sometimes just a letter home from someone. The author received a letter from Mr. WD Auran concerning his brother, Sergeant Walter Auran, who was a wounded FO team member. Mr. Auran wanted to learn more about his brother's service in Korea, and received information from the 35th Infantry Regiment Association of the 25th Infantry Division. He also provided a copy of the 35th Infantry Regiment Command Report #10 for September 1951, and a copy of a Stars & Stripes article that first appeared after the hill battles near Tangwon-ni in September 1951. This is the odyssey of discovery that many families have gone through to find out just what happened to their son, husband, father, or uncle, other than a letter received by the U.S. Government saying that they had been killed or wounded in action. Below is the letter and excerpts from the documents he sent. Sgt Auran passed away in 1995, leaving his family little information about his service in Korea.*

"Tony – As promised in my recent e-mail, I'm sending on the enclosed material. I hope it might be helpful. My brother Walter passed away in 1995 and divulged little to his family regarding the battle where he was wounded. I am still in the process of gathering data – from his letters, newspaper articles, etc. Woodruff and Gibbons, who I contacted through the 35th Infantry Regiment Association, have been very helpful and provided the three versions of the Sept 6-8 battle enclosed. Both were with Company L, 35th Regiment. My brother identified the personnel (in his letters) who made up the 3-man FO teams from the 64th Field Artillery Battalion that supported Company's I&L on Hills 682 and 717. Those personnel were as follows:

| | |
|---|---|
| FO Officer 2nd Lt Verdun E. Headley, Belmont County, OH | K.I.A. 9-8-51 |
| FO Officer 2nd Lt. Chauncey E. Shick, Clarion County, PA | K.I.A. 9-8-51 |
| ReCon Sergeant Walter A. Auran, Burke County, ND | W.I.A. 9-7-51 |
| ReCon Sergeant Beverly T. Haskell, Blue Earth County, MN | M.I.A. 9-8-51 (dead) |
| Wireman PFC Leonard L. Wilde, Wayne County, MI | W.I.A. 9-8-51 |
| Wireman PFC Charles Ogatu, Hawaii | Unknown |

I am still attempting to locate 'Chuck' Ogatu but so far have been unsuccessful. If this information is of help, let me know and I'll send further data as I receive it. Sincerely, W.D. Auran"

The Battle For Hill 717 and Hill 682 *(Stars & Stripes article)* The Undefeated – Near the village of Tangwon-ni, Korea September 6-8, 1951 – (*Excerpt*) "This is the afternoon of September 6, 1951. Company I from the 35th Infantry Regiment is relieving another company on hill 717, five miles in front of the main line. The Reds have thrown two battalions against the company on 717. For six hours the battle continues without letup. The Communists keep a steady stream of fresh supplies and replacements. The object is to exhaust the defenders until they are unable to fight. Ammunition is running low; soldiers are breaking up belted ammo for their M-1s. Attempts to obtain artillery support fail when the Forward Observer's radio breaks down."

35th Infantry Regiment Association *(reply from Mr. Woodruff) (Excerpt)* "During the 12 hours or so of fighting on the ridge, the experience has been a defining one for all of the survivors. Suffice it to say, it was a case that everything which could go wrong, did go wrong. Early on the Artillery FO team with L Company, and its radio, were destroyed by enemy fire with all personnel killed."

**1st Lt. Harold S. Snow**
**213th Armored Field Artillery Battalion 1951**

"My assignment in the 213th Field Artillery Battalion was Forward Observer for Able Battery. Our orders were to move north to a position near Hwachon to provide added artillery support for the 1st Marine Division. I remember moving into position late in the afternoon of April 22nd. We could hear the small arms fire just in front of us and could see the Marine infantry moving about. We were informed that an intense firefight was taking place but that the Marines were in control. Not long after we moved into position, a column of Koreans came up the road. We were very nervous and thinking they may be North Koreans trying to surprise us. We ordered them to sit in a circle and we assigned men to guard them with rifles for the rest of the night. Between the firefight going on in front of us, and the Koreans we were guarding, no one got any sleep. When morning came, we were told that the Koreans were packers going to carry supplies to the Korean infantry dug in along side the Marines we were supporting. I felt like I'd been kicked in the stomach when a little later the Marines carried out a number of dead and wounded past our position. It was also at this time that we were told that the Chinese had started an offensive. That afternoon we were ordered to move further west where we could deliver more effective artillery fire. We arrived in our position late in the afternoon, and we were to support the 19th ROK Regiment.

I had hardly gotten out of my jeep when Major Max Dalley came running up to me and said, 'Go make contact with the enemy, then report back'. My first impulse was to say, 'Oh, the hell you say'. I was on a B-17 bomber crew in the Air Corps. No one had every told me how to make contact with the enemy. I got in my jeep and turned north on the road going past our position. There were a number of civilians coming down the road as well as some ROK soldiers headed south. I don't know how far I went north, maybe a mile, and I was past the people on the road and pretty much alone. I went maybe another mile and spotted a small tent over in the trees. I stopped and walked over to it. I could hear some rustling inside. I opened the flap and said, 'Hello'. A man spun around, and the next thing I knew I was looking down the barrel of his .45 caliber pistol! He was a captain, I think a Marine. He cursed me and said, 'You God damned near scared me to death'. He thought I was a North Korean, and he said they were all around us. He was gathering up some papers and then was going south. I still hadn't made contact with the enemy, so I got in the jeep and started up the road again. I went only a few hundred yards when the road petered out. I parked the jeep and decided to hike up on a small knoll nearby. From there I could see a small valley and it was alive with movement as well as to the north of me. They were all over the place. Why they never saw me, I'll never know. Maybe they thought I was one of theirs. The light was pretty dim by then. I sneaked off the hill, got in the jeep, and was still gaining speed when I got back to our position. By then the road was jammed with Koreans headed south. I think Colonel Dalley was the one I reported to saying, 'They are coming, we need to bug out!'

When we got our orders to move south down that steep dug away of a road, Captain Ray Cox, my battery commander, asked me to stand by the road leaving our area and direct traffic. There was a rice paddy wall close by and he didn't want any vehicles going over it. It was a lights-out drive. As each vehicle came by, they came a little faster and got a little closer, and I kept stepping back so they would miss me. As the last halftrack came toward me, I stepped back and fell about six feet over the paddy wall. It knocked me unconscious. In a minute I came to and was sure I had a broken shoulder, the pain was intense. I slowly made my way up the wall, got in my jeep, and hurried to catch up with the halftrack. The road was jammed with Korean soldiers and they would not move. I could hear those ahead of me tell them to move and then the screams as I know some of them either got hit or run over. To my knowledge, my jeep was the last one out. I don't know how far we came down that steep road. It seemed like all night. As it started to get light, I saw an infantry command tent to the side of the road. The Koreans had thinned out a little, so I pulled over and stopped. A medic examined my shoulder and told me it was not broken, just badly bruised. He put me in a sling. As I started to leave, I noticed a machine gun nest and three infantrymen manning it. What a relief to know we were in friendly territory. A few weeks later as we advanced back into the same territory, I had a chance to walk up to where the machine gun had been. You could see where three bodies had lain and likely recovered by our infantry who had moved back up a few days before us. Across the road there was a clearing and at least a hundred markers where the Chinese had buried their own. Those three men gave a good account of themselves.

After getting a sling for my shoulder, I proceeded on down the road a little farther and saw the first familiar face I had seen all night. Little Lloyd Baker of B Battery and my neighbor in St. George was standing by the road and jerking the rifles from the terror-stricken Korean soldiers and saying to them, 'If you won't use this, I know somebody that will'. The 213th was camped in a small valley with Aussie infantry dug in close by. I got out of the jeep and laid on a camp cot for a few hours, the first sleep I had had in three days and two nights. That afternoon we were ordered to move further south. I urged one of the Aussie officers to move with us. His reply, with his accent, was, 'We've come a long ways for this, and we don't plan to leave now'. As we moved along the road south, I could see the Chinese coming over the hills to the north. They had nearly caught up with us. There was a loud explosion off to the side and close to where the Aussies were dug in. It was a mortar round. Two Aussie soldiers slowly rolled over. To this day I've always wondered whether they were hit or just getting better cover! Some weeks after all this, I was manning a Forward Observer post where we were supporting the same ROK regiment who had retreated in April. I had become acquainted with one Major who spoke broken English. I asked him why they retreated the way they did, why they hadn't stayed and fought. His reply was that they could see from their high ground when we changed positions. They thought that we were in full retreat and they were left with no artillery support. Hence their infamous bug out. I guess we'll never know!"

**2nd Lt Walton Tully**
**1st Field Artillery Observation Battalion 1951-52**

"I entered the military in Philadelphia, that was my hometown and I entered active service from there with the 235th Field Artillery Observation Battalion on 11 September 1950. We went to Camp McCoy Wisconsin for basic and to indoctrinate draftees into the unit. In September 1951 I went to Korea and served in the Sound Ranging Platoon of the 1st Field Artillery Observation Battalion. I was part of about 25 to 30 personnel from my unit sent to Korea and, I believe, the only one who was actually placed in an Artillery Observation Battalion upon arrival there! The 1st served all over the front in Korea as we were the only unit of our kind there until 1952 or 1953 when the 235th went over to relieve us. I was part of 'A' Battery and was stationed on the west side of Korea near Munsan and Mago-ri, where I was an observer on three different hill tops in this area. My first thought was how cold it was, especially sitting in the bunker during my time on watch. Then I was concerned about being overrun by the Chinese and possibly being killed. It was a lonely life with just a few friends with me. Life as an FO was what seemed to be boring, except when we had an artillery battle being waged and we were able to pin-point the enemy weapons. Our OP's were not in the trenches but were rather dug in on hilltops. We supported the 1st Marines who tolerated us. They were not really happy we were on a hill with them as we had a tendency to draw enemy fire. We also supported the 1st British Commonwealth who were very friendly and seemed to accept us and what we were doing for them. Our battery manned two OP's for Sound Ranging and the same on different hills for Flash Ranging.

The Battalion's code name was Nathan Hale, and the battery I was with served as observers for I Corps first, then 8th Army. We had two other batteries spread across the main line from west to east. When we made an enemy gun location we would call it in to 8th Army and, if they had any shells left that day, they would assign an artillery unit to fire. I do remember getting so frustrated with 8th Army that I ran a commo wire to the 1st British Commonwealth Division where the Sergeant Major said he would fire on anything 8th Army rejected. This was all very hush-hush as I did not wish to be court-Marshaled! Life on the OP wasn't too bad most of the time. One of the worst things I remember is when my best friend was killed on Thanksgiving Eve, 1951 standing the tour I would have handled had he not wished to spend an additional week on the OP. An enemy shell came through the observation hole of the bunker and killed him. I do remember the extreme cold where we would sit on the observation bunker wrapped up in our sleeping bags just to try to keep warm. I also remember Christmas Day when we woke to snow on the ground and cold temperatures. By noon it was raining and about 38 degrees. From slogging through snow to slogging through mud in a matter of hours!"

**1st Lt Thomas Perry**
**69th Field Artillery Battalion 1951-52**

"I got into the service via LSU ROTC, and was called to active duty on November 15th 1950 after graduation in June. I graduated the Ft. Sill Battery Officers Course and was sent to FECOM, where I trained at Camp Fuji, Japan, then on to the 25th Infantry Division and 69th Field Artillery Battalion, a 105mm battalion that was in direct support of the 25th. The 69th at that time was located around the Iron Triangle, Heartbreak Ridge, and Punch Bowl areas at any given time. I greatly appreciated and was treated with respect by the infantry. I felt confident I was doing the job I was trained for. Most of my time was with 'E' Company 14th Infantry Regiment, which had replaced the 24th Infantry Regiment, the old 24th was a black unit which was retired. Lots of discussion about their capability, but I had no experience with them. The infantry troops were very glad to have us there. My FO section wondered why the infantry got a CIB badge and the FO's didn't get anything. Good question! Life was 'dug out' living, and became boring later when the situation became static but good that there more action later in '52. I really wasn't concerned about who I was fighting, the North Koreans or the Chinese, I didn't give it much thought. They were the enemy. I was always impressed by the adaptability of the young troops, mostly 18, and their competence. Almost all the FO's were ROTC recent graduates of class of '50, and also most of the infantry platoon leaders."

*Author's note: The following is a letter written home by Lt Perry in September 1951*

With E Company 14th Inf. Reg.
B Battery 69th F.A. Bn.
S.W. Kumhwa, Korea
September 21, 1951

I hope that by now those heat waves which have been causing so much discomfort to the Shreveport population have given way to hose of a cooler nature. By all reports which I've seen in my trusty Stars and Stripes, your low for the 18th was around the 60's, a state of pleasant atmosphere in almost anyone's almanac. Without doubt, it won't be too long before the same said population will wish to have a few of those heat giving waves return- ah, so. I haven't mentioned it, but I didn't quite understand those war stories that Byer's sis was telling you about her brother's actions on the front. So many things are tangled in translation, etc. and especially items of tactics. I regretted that you had to listen to those tales and all you could say was "He uses ivory in the mountain streams," so behold a tale! A "war story" is a tradition anyone going near the front carries back and harasses those in safer areas with. Therefore, attempting to use as much restraint as possible in my narrative, I shall give you the nearest thing to a war story E company and it's attached elements have run into lately.

The front which I'm sitting on now in this warm sunlight is part of the base of the so called "Iron Triangle" which consists of Kumhwa, Chorwon, and Pyongyang (the apex). The area from Kumhwa to Chorwon is a valley running largely east and west and at this point, is the MLR an infantry term meaning Main Line of Resistance. Now, across this valley the mountains begin again in a "no man's land" if you will (as Doc Choppin used to say) and extends some two miles before you come to prominent peaks on which Joe Chink is located, out of range of most everything except artillery. On the mountains directly across the valley, we are manning company patrol bases from which infantry patrols are sent during the day to probe these stronger Chinese defenses. These patrols return to the company patrol base (or outpost, perhaps) at night and settle down to meet the Chink night patrols which patrol them (that's a lot of "patrol" in just one sentence). Our battalion (infantry) is responsible for one of these bases across the valley about two miles in front of the main line. The three rifle companies of our battalion each stay out there three days and are then relieved by one of the remaining ones on line- a small scale rotation plan-and one I'm vitally interested in.

On the 18th, E Company moved out to this hill and replaced a Turk company which had been there for several days. They, in turn, moved farther west to consolidate their positions as our 14th Inf. Reg. came on line in this area. I had a big time talking to the Turkish observer getting the situation. He would point on the map and say definitely about a low spot of ground well covered by our base and ones on our right, "NO Chinese." About a hill a little farther north, "Uh, one company" with a shrug of the shoulder as if to say "don't worry about it." About that prominent peak referred to previously that was more northerly he grinned broadly and said "many, many." He showed me where his concentrations of prearranged fires were and where their night patrols came to probe this hill (and he was damn correct). All of them were very gracious and were eager to help us anyway they could. Since there was only one Turk that could speak English, you could hear "childish" American being spoken all around, e.g., "where Chinese?", "Shoot much, boom." Also gesturing was more prevalent than at a woman's bridge club. They soon picked up their gear and bid us farewell, leaving us with hill on which they had laid no barbed wire and had placed few, if any, trip flares on the approaches. Fortunately, the first night passed without incident and my three man FO section split the night in three shifts, getting several hours sleep.

The next day's patrol (platoon size) was sent out and met fire after a while and returned back to the company safely. The rest of the day was put in on digging, setting out flares, and barbed wire. I slept on the 9-12 shift that night and about 12:15 one of our flares was tripped off and we had a fire fight going from a hill across the way to our company area around the top of the hill. Since this was E Company's first encounter they threw out a terrific mount of fire, the mortars hit the narrow draw between this hill and us and I hit the hill (about five hundred yds to the west) with artillery. The firing ceased and the remainder of the night was tense but without further actions. I imagine there were no more than ten Chinese on this patrol, no one knows, but they found two the next morning that didn't go back. One of these two they planted a trip flare on which set off the action the third and last night there about 9:30 p.m. During the day we had watched out patrol go out and directed fire on the "uh, a company" peak when it came (the patrol) under fire from positions thereon. All returned safely. When the flare on the body was set off, the mortars with us blasted the area and a small exchange of fire took place. I hit the same hill again. Again about 3 a.m. the boys started popping away and I again shot at this hill that they (our Chinese friends) use as an approach to this particular hill patrol base. About this time, the company communication went out and one platoon got a little excited over the fact and moved their machine gun section back from a key point, however, they returned to the original positions soon thereafter. It was lucky we didn't receive any fire during this slight reorganization. We didn't get any sleep that night and anxiously counted the hours till 5:30 a.m. and the revealing light of the early dawn. They found one that had been hit while coming up the draw to our rear. This, I think, was the most disquieting situation. You can appreciate our relief when the other company came up to relieve us.

Today is the fourth of our six days in the rest on the front MLR, which is a contradiction in itself! Going back to the front line to take a break - funny, yet true. Day after tomorrow we go back on the hill to take G Company's place who relieved F Company yesterday who had relieved us. As long as you caution Sterling and Rudy about not letting the folks know, you can give them this account because it is rather lengthy to write more than once and I don't want to appear to be showing "how rough it is." Actually, it isn't nearly as bad as it sounds on paper. When you find out a person I might know, try to get his battalion if in the artillery or his company and regiment if in an infantry unit. The 64th F.A. that Byers is in is part of our division (25th) artillery along with our 69th, the 159th and the 90th battalions. We support the 14th Inf. Reg., the 24th (being deactivated....colored) and the 27th Infantry regiments. Also the 8th F.A. Bn is in our division artillery (referred to as "div-arty"). As soon as you said Byers was in the 4th, I knew immediately he was in the "Iron Triangle" sector. In relation to Christmas, honestly, there isn't a thing I can think of that would be practical to send. We carry up on these hills just what we need and that's flat all- I didn't shave at all up there...no razor. Some good pocket book, candy, and cake to lend the proper atmosphere is about all my simple wants can wish. I hope by Christmas we can be some other place besides around here. We've been encouraged the past couple of days by news that the peace talks might be resumed. Naturally, I sincerely hope this comes about, but those affairs operate strictly on an AC current. I retrieved a prized possession yesterday when my jeep happened to pass Tim's near my OP here on the MLR. I'd lent this item to him about two weeks ago and then left it. He came to a gravel-spraying halt, backed up, exchanged greetings and gave me back my beer can opener! Tell mom to include a spare in the next package she sends as I believe one is pending.

**1st Lt Joseph McClendon**
**49th Field Artillery Battalion 1951- 52**

"I was a Forward Observer with 'C' Battery, 49th Field Artillery Battalion, 7th Infantry Division from September 1951 through January 1952 when I was reassigned as battery executive officer of the HQ Battery of the 49th. I landed at Pusan on September 9th, hopped a train to the 7th Replacement Company, arriving at Chunchon the next day and was assigned to Charlie Battery on September 1st. As I boarded the train at Pusan for the ride north, I was given a copy of the *Stars & Stripes* newspaper.

On the front page of that issue was a cartoon depicting a Forward Observer lying on his stomach, looking through a pair of binoculars at the distant mountains with his helmet covering his buttocks! The story with the cartoon stated that three Forward Observers from this one battery had been shot in their butts. I thought at the time how funny this was, and low and behold, I was assigned from the 7th Division Replacement Company to that battery. And as you might surmise, I was very aware of this story when I went on the hill three days after arriving at the battery. My first combat patrol was on the 16th moving along the ridgeline from Hill 820 to Hill 851. There was a firefight but no casualties on our side.

'C' Battery was in support of the 3rd Battalion, 17th 'Buffalo' Regiment. As a Forward Observer, I was attached at various times to Item, King and Love Companies. On November 24th, I was working with 'K' company on Hill 1052. The air that night was very heavy and I could hear 155mm shells coming in very close of our bunkers. I immediately radioed back to our fire direction center to notify whoever was firing over our position to stop. Before this could be done, four or five rounds came into the south side of the hill, killing 15 of our soldiers. The next morning was very mournful as the body bags were carried off the hill. On January 18th, I took part in an interesting experiment. With a gun crew we moved a Self-Propelled 8-inch howitzer up to the top of Hill 1243, and I manned the observation post for a direct fire experiment to knock out bunkers dug deep into the hillside. The Self-Propelled 8-inch howitzer was brought to the top of one of Korea's highest front-line mountains to provide assault fire in a unique use of artillery. The experiment was to determine the practicability and effectiveness of artillery 'assault fire' in Korea. In one day we destroyed 40 enemy bunkers. The howitzer and 11-man volunteer crew were from the 780th Field Artillery Battalion, and we and other members of the 49th assisted in fire control and observing. The howitzer effectively destroyed 40 enemy positions across a valley from the 32nd Infantry Regiment's Ethiopian Kagnew Battalion."

### Sergeant Donald Cole
### 3rd Battalion, 5th Marine Regiment ANGLICO 1951

"I originally got into the military by enlisting in 1943 at age 16 and entered as soon as I turned 17. I was in three years during WWII and enlisted in the reserves in 1948, then called back in and served three years active duty. My purpose for being in Korea was vague to say the least. I had joined the reserves at home, in Sunnyside Washington, in 1948. I was on the 'mailing list' as was most men who had served in the regular Marine Corps. I remember getting a letter telling me I could attend some kind of school, if I re-joined. Well, I did not think I would be back in war and would be plenty safe I thought! Along comes a war and immediately I found myself heading back down to Camp Pendleton, California as a Marine Reserve in September 1950. Upon arrival there I was assigned to Camp San Onefrey (Tent Camp #2). I was one of the few men who were retreads, that is, had served before. So naturally, we were looked upon as experienced and as teachers! We spent the rest of the year and into the first 1½ months into the next year training men about machine guns, fighting methods, radio, survival and the whole mess. Even going up to the Big Bear Mountains in the snow to prepare for Korea. Then, we were transferred to a ship and headed back overseas. Well, here I am, a married man with a small daughter going back over to a combat zone. I never bargained for that but did not retreat! I had served in WWII and had been discharged as a Sergeant. My overseas tour had been mainly in Okinawa. I had been there on the invasion, April 1, Easter Sunday, 1945. A Kamikaze plane hit our ship, we limped to a little island off the southern tip of Okinawa, Ei-Shima and 'dumped' onto the southern tip of Okinawa and met the Japanese forces coming head long from the north! This proved to be the bloodiest and most ferocious battle of the Pacific. I was assigned with

JASCO, a spotter for Air/Naval fire support, and when not doing that, I was a foot soldier like the rest and fought every inch of the way.

In Korea I served with ANGLICO (Air, Naval Gunfire Liaison Company), I was assigned to several units, but I was in the 3rd Battalion, 5th Marine Regiment. I served in Korea from February 1951 to October 1951, they had a rotation set up for called in reservists that we had to be home by date we were called into active duty. They missed me by a few weeks because I was called up in August, reported for duty in September, and then were held in reserves after discharge until 1953. In ANGLICO, we were normally assigned FO duty by rotation. I don't recall specific battles I fought in, but know I was in the Iron Triangle area, lots of skirmishes, and sometimes I see names of locations on the History Channel that I fought at. I was scared as hell most of the time and always looking for a hole to crawl into if needed! How else can you explain it? It's your job. The time that I was there, we fired support for the Marines and the ROKs, and we fought only against the North Koreans, not the Chinese. It was rough living on most of the men. Those that survived were lucky. A lot of the support we called in was air strikes and they were successful! We also spent a lot of time stringing telephone wire and had to stay under cover to avoid enemy contact. I spent almost 9 months see-sawing back and forth. When we got there, it was miserably cold, this was the middle of February 1951. We landed at Pohang after Japan, on the eastern side of the peninsula. We took trucks down the coast to Masan and disembarked there and set up a camp and tried to get things straightened out. A perimeter of defense and other defensive measures were initiated. We were finally put on a small narrow gauge train and was taken about 150 miles north where we spent several months in the 'Combat Zone' making camp, going out on patrol, spotting for artillery and combat planes. We would be called to a small hill or high ground and set up 'spotter' situations, and tell the plane, naval gunfire or artillery how they were doing and what adjustments to make to further perfect their field of fire. We were finally stationed in the 'Iron Triangle', which was the last position we were to be stationed in before we came back to the states. They saw fit to give me another stripe and made me Staff Sergeant while doing that kind of duty.

Well, I came back to the states on a converted aircraft carrier, the Roi Namur. It took us three weeks and there were two thousand men on that ship, but no airplanes. Upon reaching the U.S. we were greeted by a broken down truck with a loud speaker and a record on the USMC song. The Marine Corps Band finally got there late...it kinda set the scene for what the public thought of our efforts. We were stationed at San Diego Marine Depot for discharge a short time later. But, I never got my discharge for about two years, although I wrote repeatedly. Things were unsettled yet and they held us in reserves for two more years. It finally came and that was that."

# Chapter Four

## *1952 – Tour of Duty*

During the year 1952, the Korean conflict was considered by some to be in a 'stalemated' or 'stagnated' time of the war, with truce talks ongoing and the front lines solidifying. The crazy and end over end advances and withdrawals, constant moving, attacks and defenses from attacks of 1950 and 1951 were almost gone. As positions and the Main Line of Resistance became more permanent, movement by either side was at a minimum. By mid 1952, the war had the appearance of reverting back to the trench warfare days of World War I. All of this did not mean though, by any stretch of the imagination, that this was not a 'shooting war'. It was quite evident to those who were on the front lines that the war was not stagnated. Fighting was still going on, but those in the rear just didn't want to admit it. The Aerial and Forward Observers were still calling for fire, and the gun crews were still shooting fire missions. Despite what the rear echelon thought throughout this time, it definitely was still a 'shooting war'...

**1st Lt Howard Walrath**
**1st Field Artillery Observation Battalion 1952-53**

"I was a member of the 1st Field Artillery Observation Battalion in Korea from early 1952 until early 1953. I served as a Forward Observer, but the terrain normally prevented our use of Flash, Sound and Radar to locate enemy artillery. While serving in S-3 of Battalion Headquarters in I Corps, I was dispatched to host a Marine FO whose assignment was to direct the fire of the battleship USS Iowa's 16-inch guns on major targets of opportunity in the X Corps area Northeast of the Punchbowl. Our 'B' Battery was responsible for the X Corps area and we visited several of our OP's where we directed the Iowa's guns, primarily on any bunker openings that had shown evidence of artillery emplacements in the past or were suspect. One round on target from the Iowa's guns not only resulted in closing the opening, it often removed that part of the hill! It was a unique experience to see shells crossing from right to left that were very visible during the latter stages of their trajectory. Another time, through my contacts within X Corps Artillery Headquarters, I was dispatched for several weeks to direct artillery fire on targets of opportunity from the rear seat of an Army L-19 observation aircraft. That was even more fun."

**2nd Lt Kenneth Cook**
**38th Field Artillery Battalion 1952**

"I had completed three years of high school at a military prep school, Culver Military Academy, and had received an alternate appointment to the US Naval Academy, which I did not pursue at the time. By then I had then enrolled in ROTC at Stanford University, and upon graduation in 1950, was proud to be a Reserve Officer in Field Artillery. I liked the experience of my military training, and was not disappointed to be called to active duty although I was married, age 23, and had begun my civilian career In our family's department store. When called to active duty in March 1951 as a 2nd Lt, I was assigned as Assistant S-3 to the 7th Field Artillery Group, Ft. Sill, Oklahoma. My duties were to request the battalions in the Group to send their personnel to various schools at Ft. Sill and Ft. Chaffee so that they would be properly trained in their MOS's. After a few months

I was assigned to Associate Field Artillery Battery Officer Course #26. Upon completion I went on leave prior to transfer to FECOM. Going through the replacement depots I ended up in January 1952, assigned to the 2nd Infantry Division, 38th Field Artillery Battalion, 'C' Battery, as a Forward Observer for an infantry Company of the 3rd Battalion, 38th Infantry Regiment. When I arrived in Korea I knew that the usual first combat assignment for a Field Artillery officer was as Forward Observer, and frankly would have later regretted not having served my initiation in that assignment.

So when I reached my battalion, after a few days of orientation, the driver of my FO party put me and my duffel hag in the jeep and drove me up to 'the hill'. By January of 1952, the MLR was fairly stable in the 2nd Division area, and trenches and bunkers were well established by then. The FO sleeping hunker was built just below the crest of the hill, on the reverse slope, on the trench line, and within a few yards of the observation bunker on the trench line on the crest of the hill. The sleeping bunker had a platform made of ammo boxes as I recall, large enough for three sleeping bags side by side. I believe we used inflatable air mattresses under the sleeping bags. Depth of the bunker and the sleeping area was about four feet. At the foot of the sleeping platform at the open entry to the bunker the depth was about six feet. The roof was made up of several layers of sandbags, and there was a small gasoline stove used for heating our C rations. As for eating, our crew of three preferred to eat C rations furnished by our battery rather than eating the B rations served by the infantry company, although we were welcome to join them had we wanted to. Each of the three of us on the FO team had one C ration carton per day containing three meals. No need to go into detail on the C rations for those in both WWII and Korea who knew them so well. Suffice it to say that as for me, I found the variety and quality to be fine, and it did not take long to adjust to eating spaghetti and meatballs, for instance, for breakfast. I got to the point where I did not even look at the can before picking it out, knowing that there were three meals that day and three cans to be eaten. As I recall there were about nine different 'entrees'. In addition there was a can of fruit, a can of crackers or cookies, and a can containing toilet paper, jam, two or four cigarettes, a book of matches, and a can opener. That was the provision for one man for one day.

As to clothing and equipment, by 1952 there seemed to be plenty of seasonal clothing, equipment, and ammunition. At least on the front lines we had winter sleeping bags that were warm as toast. The infantry and FO teams had the new 'Mickey Mouse' boots rather than regular combat boots or shoepacs. The Mickey Mouse boots were for extreme cold, were rubber, and your feet were always wet from perspiration, but warm. The infantry troops in the trenches had mandatory daily foot inspections for trench toot. As I recall, I shaved nearly every day using my steel helmet as a basin and water in my canteen cup heated on our little gas stove. In civilian life I had used an electric razor hut did not think I would he able to use it in combat, so I took only my blade razor with my favorite Barbasol shaving cream. The always-ingenious GI, especially in the field artillery with radio batteries available, knew how to hook up batteries to power an electric razor, and some used them. I was envious. All of the water and gasoline for the stove for our FO team had to be carried up the hill to the OP in five-gallon jerry cans. I soon learned that five gallons of water weighs more than five gallons of gasoline! For latrine facilities, there were heavy open-ended cardboard tubes from artillery shells stuck into the ground for urination. These were placed in the open on the reverse side of the hill as needed. The infantry company had a latrine I am sure, but I do not recall using it. Instead I would take my entrenching tool, go a ways down the reverse slope of the hill, dig a hole, do my business, and shovel the dirt back in the hole.

By January of 1952 the front lines were fairly stable. The infantry company sent out small patrols, usually at night, but they were less than full company size so the FO party did not accompany them. I do not recall that any of them ever required supporting fire during my time with this company. We did routinely order H&I fires during the night. These were preplanned concentrations of fire, randomly fired during the night, on known or suspected enemy routes of approach to the infantry company area. The enemy in that area was well dug in several hundred yards away. They would seldom show themselves, and when they did it was usually only one or a few individuals. Generally they were too far away to engage with effective rifle fire, and too few in numbers to profitably fire on with artillery. Although we were always on alert, particularly at night for enemy ground attack, our main danger was from enemy artillery. It was sporadic, not a daily occurrence, and apparently from single guns rather than from batteries of guns. When we were fired upon it was up to the FO to determine the location of the enemy guns. This was difficult because they were always in defilade behind the hills, but we would usually call for the Air Observer in the spotter planes to look for the guns along an azimuth that we would furnish based on the sound, or occasionally on a 'shell rep'. The shell rep was a rather crude way of determining the azimuth to the gun based on the characteristics of the shell crater. We were told that the enemy guns were carefully concealed, often in caves, and were brought out to fire momentarily then immediately concealed once more. We could sometimes see what we thought was their FO, but seldom fired on him as he would appear only for a moment then duck back into the trench or bunker.

In the spring, probably in March 1952, the 38th Infantry went into reserve in a rear area. Unlike the infantry, the artillery is never in reserve. Our artillery battalion was then assigned to a ROK infantry unit in the mountainous area closer to the east coast of Korea. My FO team supported a company of ROK troops. What a difference there was in the living conditions between US and Korean troops. We were occupying positions previously held by a US Marine outfit. The Korean troops would dig into the garbage dumps left by the marines looking for unopened or partially used C ration cans or anything else they could scavenge! We could not communicate well with them but they were friendly and seemed glad we were there. Some of the officers could speak English so that we could order fire missions. I remember being invited to the company commander's bunker for a meal. I do not recall what the food was, or whether or not I ate any, but we used to think that the Koreans ate fish heads and rice! The fire missions in support of that company were tricky because the front lines were on top of an escarpment or high ridge with a steep drop in front facing the enemy. That necessitated 'high angle fire' if the fire was to be in close to the front lines. In other words, to use regular trajectory fire, the shells could have hit our friendly troops. So we had to have the fire in a very high arc to clear the friendly troops but still impact close enough to their front to be effective against enemy troops so close. High angle fire is subject to a long and high trajectory and to the winds aloft and to the inherently less accurate control of the trajectory.

I do not recall that my area received much enemy fire during that period, however the adjoining ROK company had a heavy shelling that killed Scotty McKenna, a member of the FO team from my battalion. Scotty was a good guy and well liked by all who worked with him. Like all of the enlisted men and NCOs that I knew, he knew his job well and went about it in a professional way. Unlike the officer in an FO team, who would eventually be relieved from the front lines by another new 2nd Lt., the enlisted and NCO members of the team were there for the duration. At least I was not aware that the enlisted men in the FO parties were replaced before their rotation back to the US. The sergeant in my FO team was on the team before I arrived and remained on the team after I was replaced, and I heard that later on he had some sort of nervous breakdown and had to he relieved.

The other member of my team, the corporal, had been with the team longer than any of us and was rotated back to the US during the summer, he was a strapping big Texan who could and did carry the heavy backpack radio up and down the hills as though it were nothing. Both of those men had been on a patrol a month before I became FO of that team. They ran into a heavy firelight and they told me that the FO, my predecessor, was recommended for a Silver Star for valor on that patrol. It was that patrol, consisting of less than company strength, that caused the change in policy that the FO would not accompany a patrol of less than full company strength.

One regret in combat that I had, I had been on the OP with the infantry for days or weeks and had not seen more than one or two enemy at a time, and those were not worth calling in an artillery lire mission. One day I saw in the distant valley below at long range some people, maybe eight to twelve, in the fields. I called in a fire mission. As soon as the first rounds went out, they scattered and hid. I did not observe any casualties, and to this day I regret that they may have been simply workers or farmers. After fifty years I still think of that and regret it. Is all fair in love and war? I don't think so."

**SFC John Engel**
**987th Armored Field Artillery Battalion 1952**

"Operation 'Clam-Up' took place a few months into the year 1952. It was still cold then, and Lt. Sharp, Cpl. Treaske and myself were the Forward Observer team for Battery 'B' of the 987th Armored Field Artillery Battalion. We took supplies and ammo with us for a one-week stay. We traveled by jeep to the MLR, unloaded, and walked a path through a mine field the 2nd Infantry Division had set up. I joked along the way with 2nd Infantry Division men in their fox holes, and was glad I was not one of them. Cold as it was, there were no fires, they must have had one hell of a time keeping warm. Little did I know I would find out what these grunts were going through. We finally arrived at this hill that was held by the South Korean forces. I believe it was the 6th ROK Division. We had to stay on a path up the hill because the hill was mined. It got to be pretty steep, and about half way up laid two dead Chinese. It looked like they had been dead quite awhile. We had to step over them to stay on the path. We finally reached the top and had to crouch walk to our home for a week, our bunker. We were instructed our mission of Operation Clam-Up, we were told to stay low and to not expose ourselves or fire on any targets. The only thing that moved, I was told, was our mail trucks. We were to use the BC scope to search for enemy positions, and observe what they were wearing and what equipment they had. A BC scope is something like a double-headed periscope. You can stay down in the trenches and still look over the sand bag on top of the trenches. After the first day, the Chinese and North Korean forces started to get very nervous and started to act up.

At night they would wind up their tanks and move up and down the low flat land. The sound of their tracks made me very uneasy. At night they could be a way out, but at night sound also travels a long way. Still, it made me very uneasy. We had about a hundred plus Koreans with three Americans, and only small arms and grenades for protection. We ate C-rations and drank water from a well below the hill. I always dropped two iodine tablets in my canteen. We heated with charcoal in two gallon coffee cans and wrapped ourselves in sleeping bags. The Chinese started sending out two men using binoculars. I guess they figured if we opened up on them, they wouldn't lose too much. I never saw a weapon on them. This one day while I was searching the area with the BC scope, I swung out over the top of a ridge about three hundred yards out and to my surprise, there were two Chinese looking right at my position with binoculars. I called Lieutenant Sharp over to look at what I had found. He just grinned. I asked him if I could take a shot at them and told him that if he spotted for me we might drop one of them. He told me, 'No, lay low'. A South Korean, however, took one shot and the two Chinese took off. The Chinese and North Koreans started getting a little brave. To our left down in the valley was a little village. They would dart in and out of the houses trying to get us to fire. I noticed that their uniforms were different, more green and new. Some even wore helmets and carried small arms. This is what we were trying to find out. We had to call in about every fifteen minutes after that. They kept getting braver and started digging trenches around their area and setting up machine gun emplacements. Other observers from 'A' and 'C' Batteries of the 987th also saw this and plotted down these targets.

A lot of crazy little things happened to us during that week. A Korean crawled in our bunker at night while we were sleeping and stole some of our C-rations. I heard the rumble and called to Corporal Treashe, 'Someone is in here'. About that time this figure darted out the bunker door. The lieutenant and a Korean officer heard the noise and asked us what was going on. We told them. When daylight broke, the Korean officer brought the Korean over to us and said he was the one who stole some of our rations. Then he took him over to the far end of the trench and blew his head off. We really felt bad about that, because he was only hungry. From then on, only one would sleep for a period of time and the other would stay awake.

The Chinese kept probing our area, but we just stood fast and waited. For one week we didn't change clothes, except our socks. I never left my boots off too long, because we all had a gut feeling all hell was going to break loose. Now I knew how the men I joked with on the way up felt, cold, hungry, and bushed. Heating with charcoal in the bunkers left our faces black. My nose, eyes, and ears were full of soot. And I sure needed a bath because I started to stink. On the second to the last day, it got so foggy you couldn't see your hand in front of your face. I needed to relieve myself and our only place to do that was on the front down side of our hill. I figured with all this fog nobody would see me. I asked Cpl. Treashe to cover me, telling him that I was going down the hill a little way to relieve myself. I was crouched down by a tree stump when a Chinese patrol came by. I froze still. The first five or so didn't see me, I guess the fog was too bad. The last one looked at my direction. I will never forget the Red Star on his cap. He looked like he had a grin on. Maybe he was as scared as I was. He looked away and walked off in the fog. I got to the top of the hill and got on to Treashe and asked him if he had seen the patrol. He said no, he had lost sight of me in the fog. The last day before we were relieved, our battalion opened up. The targets we had seen were wiped out. I don't know if we did any good in Operation Clam-Up or not. I believe the Chinese used that time to re-supply."

**Sergeant Ralph Collins**
**58th Field Artillery Battalion 1952**

"I was drafted and sent to Fort Knox and took driving school of heavy trucks and tanks and prime movers. I was then sent to Korea and assigned to Baker Battery, 58th Field Artillery Battalion, we were a direct support artillery battalion and fired the 105mm howitzer. My time in Korea, we spent mostly in the Chorwon Valley, I arrived around the first of March 1952 and departed January 3rd, 1953. I remember our OP's serving on or near Hill 409, 'Dagmar', 'Jane Russell', 'Old Baldy', and a few others. As part of an FO team, I was scared but someone had to do the job. We were direct support for the 3rd Infantry Division, and also the Greeks, Turks, Belgian, and several other non-US units. For a while we also supported the 1st ROK Division too, I was with KMAC for a while. We had simple names for the OP's, like OP #1 and OP #2, and there were three for every battery I think. It always seemed scary all the time. We would stay for days and then returned to the Battery for rest, then go back up. It was something a little different from day to day. Our FO team usually was three men, I was the jeep driver, the officer was the FO, and the other enlisted man was a spotter. I have bits of specific memories from my time in Korea, like when the 9th Field Artillery Battalion, which fired a 155mm howitzer, misfired and fired on our outpost bunkers and trenches."

**1st Lt. Francis G. Boehm**
**160th Field Artillery Battalion 1951-52**

"In Tokyo, we were greeted at the airport by the familiar sound of Rosemary Clooney's 'Come On 'A My House' blaring over loudspeakers, as we were bussed to Camp Drake, to receive our orders. While a few men were assigned duty in Japan, the bulk of the arrivals were ordered to Korea. I was assigned to the 45th Infantry Division, which was an Oklahoma National Guard unit that was being filled with reservists and draftees as the National Guard returned to Oklahoma. After only one night in Tokyo, we boarded a train headed south to the Ashiya Air Base on the island of Kyushu. From here, we were flown to the city of Pusan on the southern coast of Korea, and boarded a train that traveled north via Taegu to Seoul, and the 45th Division Headquarters at Yong Dong Po. The train trip was marked by fears that communist guerillas that had been spotted in the area might attack, and we had not yet received our weapons. This problem was remedied in Yong Dong Po, where we received our final assignment and were armed. My unit would be the 160th Field Artillery Battalion, and like most 'shavetails' in the artillery, my assignment was as a Forward Observer with an infantry company, Company A, 279th Infantry Regiment. The forward units of the 45th Division were located in the Chorwon Valley, a vital corridor the defense of which was essential to protecting Seoul from attack.

As we debarked from the train at the Chorwon railhead, and prepared to join our units, we were still not aware of any combat. To orient the new replacements to the 'real world', the 45th Division had devised a simple solution. One-by-one the incoming officers were allowed to climb into a tank, which had been dug-in on top of a hill near the railhead, and fire the tank's cannon. We were told that our target was an enemy position, although we saw nothing. After several officers had performed this duty, the air was filled with incoming artillery rounds from our invisible enemy which flew over our heads and exploded in the valley behind us. We knew now that we were at war. As a Forward Observer, it was my job to direct the fire of the artillery for maximum effectiveness in support of the infantry. Assigned to 'A' Company of the 279th Infantry Regiment, I occupied a bunker on Hill 324, which overlooked a large land mass in the shape of the letter 'T'... appropriately designated 'T-Bone Hill'. Hill 324 was at the juncture of two ridges, which had the appearance of 'Alligator Jaws', and were so-named. It was the ideal observation point, and consequently I was called upon each morning to register the battalion's howitzers. Through registration, the weapons could be expected to fire accurately, whenever called upon. My bunker included a space for me and the commander of 'A' Company, with whom I coordinated artillery support.

During the month of June, the battle for control of T-Bone Hill and nearby Old Baldy intensified. Able Company sent nightly patrols to make contact with the enemy along the Alligator Jaw's ridges, to determine the extent of enemy penetration. Several nights a week, the Chinese troops with whom we were in contact would mount an attack, complete with bugles blaring and rockets being exploded for effect, but we pummeled them with artillery concentrations that had been registered during the daylight hours to assure accuracy when called upon in the dark of night. The Chinese Air Force was not a factor, with dogfights being confined to the northern part of the Korean Peninsula referred to as MIG Alley. Nevertheless, American pilots carried out bombing missions in close support of the infantry. The Chinese artillery was difficult to reach with air strikes, since it was located in caves, and then rolled out to fire. While primitive, the Chinese air defenses were sometimes effective, and I had the misfortune to witness an American jet crash, after hitting a cable, which had been strung across two hills by the Chinese.

One evening, a platoon from Able Company was to move along the ridge towards T-Bone Hill to make enemy contact. In preparation for this mission, I had zeroed in a half dozen artillery concentrations during the daylight hours, to be available if called upon by the patrol should they be attacked. As the mission progressed, the platoon leader radioed his position to me, so that I would know which concentrations to fire for the platoon's protection in case of ambush. As expected, the platoon came under fire, and I fired several pre-registered concentrations to form a protective horseshoe around the platoon, and allow a safe retreat back to their positions. The VT (variable time) shells fell all around our troops, cutting down the Chinese and allowing the platoon to escape without casualties. However, there is a sad footnote to this story. At the height of the conflict, the Company Commander, panicking, insisted on personally going to the aid of his men. This, despite the fact that the bulk of his company was not on patrol. Taking a radioman with him, he headed down the ridge towards his beleaguered platoon. Unfortunately, the Commander's decision resulted in the only death that evening, the radioman who was hit by shrapnel. Diagnosed as suffering from combat fatigue, the commander was relieved of his command. I saw him a week later, and he expressed his heartfelt gratitude for the effectiveness our artillery had had in protecting his men.

It was mid-June now, and the battle for T-Bone and Old Baldy, a nearby hill, had intensified. General Ruffner was determined to seize territory, which would be useful for bargaining, during the anticipated peace talks. I had just returned from a night patrol with an infantry platoon, whose mission was to get as close to T-Bone as possible via the ridges, and wait until dawn before returning to Hill 324. This would protect against any Chinese surprise attack on our positions. The mission was thankfully uneventful, and we returned safely. I was given a day off and my driver and I drove to the British PX for some refreshments. After imbibing for several hours, I received a call from my Battalion Commander (Lt Col. Watters) who offered a proposition. I was to call Lt. Stokes, another FO, and flip a coin to see who would go again with the infantry on patrol the next day. I did, we flipped, and I won. Stokes would go on patrol. My joy, however, was interrupted a few minutes later, when Lt Col. Watters called again to inform me that since Stokes would go with the Infantry, I would have to go with a tank platoon. Sobering up quickly, I listened as the colonel told me where to rendezvous the next morning. The 45th Division was planning an assault on 'Shanghai Heights' at the base of T-Bone Hill, using a Filipino Combat Team in a direct assault, while the tanks would provide a diversionary attack deep into enemy territory via the valley adjacent to T-Bone Hill. We were assured that the Army Engineers had swept the valley of anti-tank mines.

The next morning I felt like a stranger among the tank platoon crews awaiting a 'go'. Having never ridden in a tank, I was confused as to what good an artillery Forward Observer could provide the tanks when I had never seen the area we were attacking, except from a hilltop, and I was totally confused by the tank's communication system which combined an intercom with the crew, and a radio to my fire direction center. Add to this, the fact that our tank carried an overload of artillery shells, strewn on the floor of the turret. As we started out, I stood looking out the hatch to try to determine where we were. I tried to contact my direction center on the radio but got no response. At this point, I realized I was just going along for the ride. Suddenly, the platoon commander in the tank ahead went into a ditch, and waved for us to pass him and take the lead. As we did, the tanks to our rear formed a line alongside us and we started up the valley towards T-Bone Hill. Realizing that we could not revolve our turret, until we expended the overload of ammo lying on the turret floor I ordered the gun to be fired. The trigger was pulled and the gun jammed, and we were now stuck with loose ammo, no firepower, and a stationary turret.

Until now, there had been no 'incoming mail' from the enemy, so I had not shut my hatch. Looking down the line of advancing tanks, I suddenly saw an explosion, and the tread come off one tank. I realized that the engineers had not done their mine-clearing job very well. Then, the air was filled with the whine of incoming artillery. I closed my hatch. Soon I heard someone yelling from outside the tank, 'Is everyone O.K. in there?' Lifting the hatch, I saw a GI who informed me that a shell had exploded under our tank. I pressed the button on my tank radio to switch from radio to intercom with the crew, and asked whether everyone was o.k. Their answer was the last straw for me. Apparently the shell had burst a fuel line, and the tankers were sitting in oil up to their knees. What to do now? We could not turn the tank, and leave the area, because the rules of Armor permit a tank to point its gun only at the enemy. We could not revolve the turret to keep the gun pointed at the enemy, while we turned the tank around. The only solution was to back out of the area, with the gun remaining pointed at the enemy. Thus we dis-engaged, and in a humanitarian act, helped tow another disabled tank out with us. Fortunately, we lost only one tank. Unfortunately, we were able to provide no diversion to assist the Filipino Combat Team as they inched their way up the base of T-Bone Hill.

T-Bone Hill represented 'home' for at least one Chinese Division. From the base of the 'T' the terrain rose rapidly to the crossbar. In the June battles, the American forces were able only to occupy the small hills referred to as Shanghai Heights at its base. This area was barren of all foliage or shelter, and the troops not able to conceal their presence were picked off by snipers. It was here that I was destined to spend two very long nights. During the daylight hours, an infantry squad occupied Shanghai Heights, having been transported there by armored personnel carriers racing down from the adjacent hills, and across an open valley, that were vulnerable to observation and enemy fire. In the evening, the squad was replaced by an infantry platoon, recognizing that the enemy normally attacked during darkness, and these small hills were considered valuable territory. I have no idea what purpose it served to have an Artillery FO, with no visibility or means of communication hunkering down with the infantry for two nights, other than to somehow let the infantrymen see that the Artillery was willing to put their men in jeopardy to somehow boost morale. The hills from which we traveled to the Heights was far better situated for forward observation than the shallow hillocks called Shanghai Heights."

**SFC James Bartoo**
**8th Field Artillery Battalion, 1951-52**

"I was a volunteer in March of 1951, and after finishing basic training and artillery survey school at Fort Campbell, Kentucky, I was sent to Korea. I was assigned to the 8th Field Artillery Battalion, and we supported the 27th Regimental Combat Team of the 25th Division with 105mm towed howitzers. I was there from October 1951 until November of '52, and was with the Headquarters Battery, being used off and on for an observer and OP Sergeant. I started out as a driver and radio man 'C-2', but there were a couple of times I was left in charge of an OP when the FO officer was absent. I fired several missions during that time and they used me more and more as a FO after that. They were short of officers at the time so I was chosen. During my time there we were usually in support of a regiment of infantry, most of the time the 27th Regiment, the 'Wolfhounds', of the 25th Division. I was online with 'E' Company, and also in the battalion OP most of the time. Also I was on line with the Turkish Brigade. I always felt I was one of the men in the company. The only kidding I got was about not having to participate in patrols, of which I was very thankful. We were always up against the Chinese by that part of the war. During most of my stay there it was a stalemate because peace negotiations were going on. The majority of the time was spent in trying to figure out the configurations and depth of the enemy defenses. The war settled into a WWI type of conflict with trenches, bunkers, barbed wire, etc. On a personal level it was boring, dirty, uncomfortable, and dangerous because of mortars and small arms fire. I spent about 2/3rd's of my time as a FO and about 1/3rd as the C-2 Sergeant for the battalion. The food supply was usually adequate as was mail. We rotated on a regular basis for rest, meals, and showers. As I remember the battalion OP was usually called 'Lifeguard 3' and the line company ones were named 'Lion', plus the phonetic word for the company's letter. So the OP, depending on the company it was assigned to, was referred to as say, 'Lion Easy' for Easy Company. The battalion usually had four total, three line OP's and an overall Battalion OP The ones I remember were near Kumhwa, we had an OP on Hill 431 and we fired at positions on Hill 1062 and in the valley to its west. The others were around the Punchbowl and Heartbreak Ridge areas.

I remember one fire mission against an area which had small arms and machine gun emplacements that had a patrol pinned down. We silenced them so the patrol could withdraw. Calling a fire mission was like all training is, it became so automatic that I wasn't aware of anything except the next command or corrections while doing it. I remember firing missions for the Turkish brigade and being observed by a Turkish light colonel and when I had finished he congratulated me and asked why a PFC was firing missions. I said I didn't really know! He said he'd see what he could do, and from then on I got a boost in rank every 90 days and left Korea a Sergeant First Class! Serving with the infantry, you also had to be ready for anything, I remember helping a machine gun squad evacuate a hill because we were being outflanked I carried a box of 30 cal. machine gun ammo in each hand down one hill and up the next. I'm not strong enough to do that!"

**Sergeant Robert Walsh**
**300th Armored Field Artillery Battalion 1952-53**

"I was a poor student at Texas A&M, and suffered from a severe grade point deficiency, so I was invited to leave the school. I tried another college, but didn't like it. My family is a military family and I had always wanted to be in the Army, so I decided to notify my draft board and they called me up immediately. I took Basic Training at Ft. Chaffee Arkansas, infantry MOS. After eight weeks I was sent to Ft. Sill Oklahoma where I took Fire Direction Center technique, and was assigned as cadre after completing my training. I taught at the Field Artillery Replacement Training Center for several months, and then was selected to attend the Army Leadership School back at Camp Chaffee Arkansas. I was the best thing that ever happened to me. I came back to Ft. Sill, was promoted to corporal, and received orders for FECOM. I was actually relieved to get these orders. I felt that I should be in Korea, although I did not volunteer to go. I was just recently married, and was a bit nervous about going, but again I knew I should go.

I left the states from Seattle and arrived in Korea in May of 1952. I did not know where I was going, or what I would be doing. I did not know this until I was loaded up into a two and a half ton truck with many other scared soldiers and shipped northward. Going north that night we could hear the artillery in the distance and even see flashes from the muzzles. This is the honest truth, and I have not said this many times, but my big fear was that I would not be able to stand up to what was in store for me. I knew what my dad had been through in France in 1918, and I didn't want to let him down. I just wonder how many other guys felt as I did. The 300th Armored Field Artillery Battalion was receiving a severe shelling the night I was to report to 'B' Battery. They left me in Service Battery that night, as it was not a good idea to go it the 'B' Battery area. The people in 'B' Battery didn't seem to know what to do with me. For a day or so I was a loader on one of the M7 armored field artillery pieces, 105mm's. We were firing high angle fire and I was having difficulty in loading at these elevations. Shortly after this I went to the Battery FDC where I should have been in the first place. I did not stay there long as we lost our recon sergeant on the FO team. The 1st Sgt said that he needed someone to take his place, and he was looking for a volunteer. He promised me another stripe so I volunteered to go with the FO team. This was all right as I was trained in FDC so could observe artillery fire as well. At this time the 300th was assigned to IX Corps and was located in the East Central area. We were near the Iron Triangle, and the Punchbowl. We were south of Kumsong and were the farthest north of any U.N. units.

The forward observation posts we manned were generally several hundred yards in front of the MLR. The Chinese roamed around them at night, cutting wire and setting up ambush patrols. There seemed to be activity each day and night although not all actions could be called battles. We were involved in the Capitol Hill fight, which was a pretty severe action. I seem to remember Sniper Ridge for some reason or another, probably because this was a time when small actions were the norm. They could be bloody, and severe, but little real estate changed hands. When we got into a fight our job was to call down artillery fire. Since most of the actions involving company sized units or larger took place at night we generally fired at concentrations we had previously fired in. We could shift those fires if necessary, but needed illumination to do so. These concentrations might be avenues of approach for the Chinese or withdrawal routes as well. What was it like being an FO in action? I do not suppose I have ever told anyone this, but during one tight on OP #23 I was so momentarily scared that I actually caught myself shaking. That was not very brave of me, but I shook it off and continued on calling down fire on the attacking Chinese. I was second in command on the FO team. A 1st or 2nd lieutenant headed the team. We also had a radiotelephone operator. I am not bragging, but I could adjust artillery fire very well. It was just something that came naturally to me. I had one lieutenant who had me fire all the missions. He was a former Marine who had fought on Saipan in WWII. He told me this was my war and he was going to keep his head low. He did. He had gotten into an Army reserve unit to make a little extra money, and got recalled. The real problems on the hill came about not because of major fights, or so it seems to me. The main problem was Chinese mortar fire and harassing artillery tire that could hit you at any time. Other people might disagree, but I really believe this. I remember on certain hills you just could not get out of your bunker without drawing fire. We had good support from air too, be it Air Force, Navy or Marine, although I think the Marines supported their own troops mostly. These napalm strikes were impressive to say the least. I was less impressed with the bombing, as it did not seem too accurate to me.

We lived by our radio and our telephone. The radios needed batteries, and the phones need wire. One time, we had to have batteries on one hill. I crawled out of the bunker making my way down hill when the Chinese dropped five mortar rounds around me. I do not know how they missed me, but they did. They did put one round though right in our little slit trench latrine which caused a mess. I felt my chances of getting back home were pretty good. A lot of folks were killed and wounded on these hills, but I do not remember worrying too much unless it got pretty hot. A Chinese machine gunner put a burst right over my head when I stupidly stood up in a shallow trench. That sure awakened me! I know of one American soldier who came on the OP for the first time. Nobody told him not to look out the observation window. He looked out and took a rifle bullet in the head. We used a BC Scope, which is like a periscope to look out these windows. I guess just like every GI over there I prayed a bit. I guess I got some help that way, but we didn't talk of such things and I cannot say what others might have done along this line. We were supposed to be on the hill seven days and down seven. It seldom worked out that way. I left one hill and my replacement was hit before I got to the firing battery position. I had to turn around and go back up the bill. I was there thirty days. We were filthy, and from time to time hungry, and our clothing was in pretty ragged condition. I had a pair of the old tanker boots and the sole was flopping on one boot. The other did not have a heel as I remember it. I do not wish to leave the impression the filth was widespread. It was just that way on the hill when you were up there a long time. On one hill we couldn't get rations because of the river to our rear being in flood. Usually rations were no problem except the guys back in the firing battery, or Service Battery, would take the 'Beanie Weenies' out of the 'C' rations and substitute something like ham and Lima beans. I lived with an infantry unit on the hill we happened to be on. I think it was usually about company sized. We supported the 6th ROK Infantry Division all the six months I served on the hill. You can believe the infantry troops were happy to have us with them. There were usually ROK artillery observers on the hill as well. We got along great with them, and I left Korea with a great respect for the ROK Army, even though they had some pretty had times. We fought the Chinese mostly. We had occasional North Korean Infiltrators around the rear positions, but I think by this time they were on the west coast and pretty well whipped. I had a great deal of respect for the Chinese soldier. He was good and licked us more than once, he did know when he was beaten though and would surrender. There were lots of them, I have seen the mountains when units would exchange positions. It looked from a distance like an ant nest had been stepped on. And their equipment was good, especially their mortars.

I served on three different OP locations. One was #15, one was #19, and the other was #23. We were told that #19 was the farthest north of any allied position. I believe #15 might have been a bit farther, but cannot say for sure. Each firing battery in the battalion manned a different OP, and there are three firing batteries in the battalion. Life as a FO was exciting, and sometimes even boring. It was like most infantry combat situations. Your team was close and everyone did their job, and you took turns observing to see what the Chinese might be up to. You were under a considerable amount of fire and certainly earned the $45.00 a month combat pay, and your four rotation points as well. I remember a very amusing incident that happened to me. There was a Chinese observer about for or five hundred yards from one OP. You could see him from time to time but he did not stay up long. My lieutenant asked me if I thought I could get him. I had a carbine and knew better than to even try with it so I got an M-1, put a tracer round it and shot at a rock out about the same distance the observer was located. The Lt. got the spotting scope and we got settled down behind some sandbags and waited. The observer popped up and I let loose around. The Lt. said 'you got him'. About that time a bayonet with a white rag tied to it could be seen waving over the trench the observer was in. I guess he had a sense of humor. I tried again later that day and think I got him for real.

When I called a fire mission I would alert battalion or battery FDC by radio or phone that I had a mission. It could be anything such as a recoilless rifle firing on us, or maybe a machine gun firing. Many times it would be Chinese troops we could see doing something or another. We could locate the target by coordinates, or we could give a shift from some previously fired concentrations, or we could locate the target along a certain azimuth at a distance we would estimate. We usually used coordinates. We would send the information to FDC and we would request the type fire we wished such as fuse-quick, fuse-delay or fuse VT. FDC would do the plotting, and send the information to the guns. We would receive a notification the rounds were on the way. Sometimes we would get a

'Splash' notification a short time before the rounds should arrive. That helped us knowing when to expect the explosion. If we were in adjustment and would make a correction for the next round so that it would hit closer to the target. These adjustments would be to either add so many yards, drop so many yards, move left so many yards, or right so many yards. This gets complicated, but when we got a line shot that is an imaginary line from the observer to the target we would drop or add and then if possible split the bracket and call for 'fire for effect'. We would then get the type fire we requested with the proper number of pieces firing. Most of the time we adjusted fire with only two or sometimes one gun. Firing for effect utilized the entire battery, or it could be even more than one battery. I was privileged to be allowed to observe eight inch artillery fire on two or three occasions. There is nothing like it. There was one bunker we had tried to get with 105 fire, but this just didn't work. Using the eight inchers, I hit it with my third round in adjustment and the whole bunker rose up and settled down. I could actually see the round go through the window opening through the BC scope. This is the truth. We loved that eight inch because it is the most accurate artillery piece ever designed. I also remember one Time on Target mission. I just observed it, but it was impressive. We could call I was told nineteen battalions of artillery on a target if the need arose. I do not know how many units were involved in the ToT but it was a bunch, and most of the rounds went off right on time, and at the proper altitude.

It depended on the target and the ammo supply. Another mission I remember almost saw my demise. I was not observing, but was on the phone relaying corrections from the lieutenant. We had a rain falling and lightning struck the land line, came up the line into the bunker and absolutely fused the phone. It knocked me up against the top of the bunker, and burned the soles of my boots. I thought the flash was a recoilless rifle round that had hit the bunker. I was not much good the rest of the day I would imagine. We sometimes would receive Chinese tank gunfire. This was not often and just happened to me once. I vacated my location pretty quickly as those tank guns were accurate. I observed direct fire from 155mm howitzers against well dug in bunkers. I also watched M-26 tanks in direct fire on bunkers. That was a real sight. One thing that I have not mentioned yet was that it was horribly cold. I cannot describe it adequately. We honestly were not dressed for it in my battalion. I never saw a thermal boot. At night we would have to man the observation window. When that horrible cold wind came down out of Siberia it did not warm much on the way south. You could just barely stand it. This is not something to brag about but I have wished for a slight wound that would send me to a hospital tent where it would be warm. I mentioned harassing fire the Chinese would put the OP through. I remember one round that killed five men. That is pretty good harassing. My first experience with a combat death happened on the first day I went to an OP. I had been involved with overhead artillery fire in training, but when it is no longer overhead, but aimed at you it is somehow different. My FO party was climbing this extremely high OP, #23 it was called. I heard a shell coming and fortunately as near a large rock mass. I hit the ground, as did the other members of the party. The round hit about fifteen feet from us. A Korean 6th Division Officer was behind me and slightly up hill, He was almost blown in two, but was still alive. I could see his kidneys as most of his backbone had been blown away. He died naturally, but it was a terrible introduction to this new way of life. I mentioned that I was slightly wounded. The artillery piece that was responsible for many casualties on one OP could not be located. I watched by the hour for a sign of smoke when the piece would fire, but never could see anything. It got so bad the lieutenant told me to take a shell report. This was a procedure where you examine the point where the round hit on the ground. You were supposed to be able to plot a back azimuth by examining where the fuse hit. You could then plot on your map a line that would show at least the direction the gun was located in. Somewhere on or near that line the gun would he found. If two different OP locations got good usable shell reports you could draw the lines on a map and where they intersected the gun should be. This is good theory, and it was usable. The gun fired, the round hit and I went out to take the shell report. I was not comfortable doing this as I was exposed, and a bit scared to be honest. I found the location where the round hit about the same time that the gun fired gain. I was young then and had the best hearing of anyone on the hill I believe. I knew that round had my name on it. I made a run for a trench and as I was airborne, it hit. I do not remember the explosion at all. All I remember was that something had entered my, to be polite, anal orifice and I was bleeding, but not hurting. It must have been a piece of rock and all it did was to tear the blood vessels. I thought I was in bad shape, but fortunately this was not the case. I was a bloody mess and very, very sore eventually. I was needed on the hill and so I stayed. I did not get a Purple Heart, but I sure had a purple butt. This was just another part of life on the OP.

Light mortar rounds are on you before you know it. They make a swishing sound as they come in. I could hear them in time to hit the ground. Artillery rounds make a sound I cannot adequately describe. To me they moaned in a fashion somewhat like a low pitch scream. You could hear them coming and you could pretty well know if they would hit near you. I remember another time my wireman and myself were checking wire or something when a round came in on us. There was no place to go that we could reach. It landed twenty or so feet from us, but was a dud. It landed in an anti-personnel mine field we had set up. I never thought about the minefield as I thought I really had an opportunity to get a good shell report. I was going over to where it hit when the Korean soldiers started shouting at me. I then realized where I was. I retraced my steps out of the field very carefully. The Chinese would place artillery pieces in caves on hillsides. They would roll them out by hand, fire them, then run them hack in. I remember one that was causing some real problems. We tried to get it with 155mm fire, but just could not get a round in the opening. We called for an air strike and an A-26 bomber tried with 500lb bombs. That did not work either, but the P-51 Mustang dropping napalm did the job. Air Force Forward Air Control controlled this strike. I marveled at the looseness of their radio procedure. We were required to use absolute proper procedure, but the Air Force folks had a little better approach I thought. No one who was there can ever forget what air power did during that war.

The last fight I took part in happened in late November, or early December 1952. I was on OP #23, which I mentioned was a very high mountain or hill. It was well protected, and we considered it to be one of the easier hills to live on. Late one evening the infantry company was relieved with a new company. These were green troops with new uniforms, and wearing old WWII issue high top shoes. I remember that looked odd on these Koreans as they usually wore a soft tennis style shoe. This was their first combat chance. About 0100hrs the Chinese hit them pretty hard. They shelled the OP to keep us down I suppose, and there were green tracers going everywhere it appeared to me. These new Korean soldiers were down slope from us, and did beautifully. It was a rough night for all of us, but about 0300hrs the Chinese put up their green flares and pulled off the hill. We killed forty-four of them, our losses were much lighter. We fired VT concentrations on them as they pulled hack off the hill and I would imagine caused many more casualties. Of interest might be what caused most casualties on the battlefield. I believe it was mostly from mortar fire, artillery fire, hand grenades, and then small arms fire. You can protect yourself fairly well from small arms fire, but these other things seek you out. The FO had the reputation of being in one of the most dangerous lines of business. This was true, but I believe our wiremen were equally at risk. They had to lay that wire regardless of the danger involved. They were always on the go, and they were very likely to be under observation while doing their work. I had one of my friends severely wounded while he was attempting to put an overhead wire crossing across a road. He was in a shot up tree pulling wire up when the Chinese dropped an artillery round under the tree. You had to have these overhead crossings across roads or the tanks and other vehicles would run over the wire and break it.

I have never been the least bit bitter about Korea. I was in a bastard outfit that was pretty well ignored by the Army. This may be because we were not in direct support of an American unit, although we did support the Marines and the 2nd Infantry Division at one time. Our equipment was not in good shape. The first time I fired my carbine the rear sight fell off. That is real encouraging. Our self-propelled howitzers were pretty well worn out, but when the aircraft radial engines were changed out with Ford V8 engines in 1952 their performance was certainly improved."

### Lt Roy Dittamo
### 37th Field Artillery Battalion 1952-53

"I was an FO with the 37th Field Artillery Battalion of the 2nd Infantry Division in 1952 and 53. We were in direct support of the 23rd Infantry Regiment. I normally was with Charlie Company of the 23rd, but often I had to relieve other FO's supporting other companies. We lost some FO's and, for a while, we were a scarce commodity. I would have to think about the OP's I was on, but the most stressful was the attack on Old Baldy when Able and Charlie Companies of the 23rd executed an envelopment to retake the hill from the Chinese. I was with Charlie Company. I remember a destruction mission I adjusted on Baldy against a machine gun emplacement. He knew I was there, and he tried to take me out. To his misfortune, I took him out first.

It was nearly the end of July 1952 when the 1st Battalion, 23rd Infantry Regiment was called upon to retake Old Baldy, a prominent hilltop near the Chorwon Valley. I was a member of A Battery, 37th Field Artillery Battalion, assigned as the Forward Observer with Charlie Company of the 23rd. A short time before, the 2nd Infantry Division had relieved the 45th Infantry Division in that sector. The Chinese opposing us took advantage of the relief activities and captured Old Baldy. After some give and take, Able and Charlie Companies were given the job of taking it back. My friend Joe Hagan was the FO with A Company. In a double envelopment the two companies swept up the hill and took it back. At the conclusion of the assault, I was huddled in the company CP with the company commander when a platoon sergeant from another part of the hill approached me and said they were taking fire from a machine gun. I accompanied him back to his side of the hill, and he pointed out the area where the fire might be coming from. I observed for a while and ultimately I saw fire coming from a well dug-in, tunnel-like position several hundred yards away. I called in a destruction mission trying to hit the machine gun position. After a few rounds of adjustment, the machine gunner understood he was being fired upon and would cease-fire as the round screamed in. As this happened I would stick my head up above the trench, observe the round hitting, and sent back my adjustment to the fire direction center. This continued for a while with the machine gunner firing at our trench line, ceasing fire when the round came in, and my observing the round's impact. I became concerned over the repetitive nature of my observations and moved down the trench away from where I had been observing. As the next round came in, I peered above the trench to see where it impacted and to my surprise the machine gunner did not duck. Instead he fired a burst at the spot from where I had previously been adjusting fire. If I had not moved, he would have had me dead to rights. The next round struck his hole dead on and that was the end of that machine gunner. Charlie Company did a hell of a job on that hill. Able Company did as well but caught heavy mortar fire. My buddy, Joe Hagan was badly wounded and evacuated. Of the four FO's in A Battery, 37th Field Artillery originally participating in the relief of the 45th Infantry Division, one, Luke LeFevre was killed, Ron Turner and Joe Hagan were badly wounded and evacuated. Only one wasn't scratched, me. I spent my tour as a FO and later as a Liaison Officer with the 23rd and returned home unharmed. To this day I can't explain it."

**2nd Lt Kent Arnold**
**1st Field Artillery Observation Battalion 1952**

"I put in nine months as an artillery Forward Observer on the front line of X Corps in Korea in 1952 after having completed 'Flash' training at Fort Sill Oklahoma. We were located approximately fifteen miles above the 38th parallel, eight miles from the east coast and just northeast of the 'Punch Bowl'. We used flash angulation methods to locate enemy artillery positions and the closest of the OP's that participated in locating the enemy location would direct the fires of either 105mm or 155mm howitzers or sometimes 8-inch guns that we had in the area. Our closest OP to the enemy was OP #1, which was less than one hundred yards away from 'Luke's Castle' or better known as 'the Rock'. We were overrun by the enemy in September of 1952 and for a short two week period we were sent to the Chorwon Valley in central Korea to set up a 'hasty base' and conduct FO duties in that area."

**Sergeant Allen Hatley**
**145th Field Artillery Battalion 1951-52**

"I was in my second year in college when the Korean War began. I had grown up during WWII, and because the war ended before I was old enough to join the Army, I was determined not to miss this war. I had also gone through three years of Junior ROTC, two summer camps, and 2 years of College ROTC and knew more than most about the military. I especially knew that I did not want to join the Army and have no control over where I went and what I did, so I joined an Army Reserve unit in the summer of 1950. I assumed the entire Army Reserve unit would be called up and I would go with them to active duty within a few months. A year later, except for summer exercises at Camp Chaffee, we were still there, so I requested a call to active duty. On August 27, 1951, I arrived at Ft. Sill and was assigned to a unit making up the Artillery School Aggressor Force, an Armored Infantry Battalion. About a month after I arrived at Ft. Sill, I was told that the 145th Field Artillery Battalion, a Utah National Guard unit that was 155mm Gun 'tracker drawn' unit also assigned to the Artillery School was being brought up to strength to go to Korea. Over 50% of their National Guard people had already been discharged and they were searching for warm bodies. I visited with the First Sergeant in Battery 'B', 145th, a Regular Army Noncom whose name was Master Sergeant Sullivan, and he said he would put in a request for me, as I was older than most of those he was getting and he wanted some 'older men'. I was all of 21-years old. Within a week, I had been reassigned to the 145th Field Artillery and within a few more weeks we were loaded, along with all of our equipment, including all vehicles and weapons on a train and moved to Oakland, California. During the next two days we were loaded on a large troop ship and then sailed for Japan. Twenty-seven days later we arrived at Yokohama and 36-hours later left for Pusan, arriving there on December 5, 1951.

In Pusan we unpacked and made ready to be moved in two LST's, with Japanese crews, and land on the east coast of Korea. In Pusan we found out that we were to be assigned to the X Corps, not the 8th Army. I also soon found out one reason why Master Sgt Sullivan wanted an 'older man' in Baker Battery, when he sent me out with three others in a jeep to liberate two .50 cal. machine guns for perimeter defense. The Army did not issue any such weapons to artillery units. I found two and also traded some of the equipment we were leaving in Pusan for several boxes of .50 cal ammo. On or about December 15th, we landed at Sokch'o-ri, on the east coast of Korea near the 38th Parallel. As we left the LST's we started out in two columns, the first with HQ, Able and Charlie Batteries going to Kong Gong, in support of the 7th Infantry Division. Baker Battery turned north first, and we drove over a very narrow ice covered road up to Sugong-ni, and went into support of the 11th Marine Regiment, 1st Marine Division. Service Battery went to Chukkong-ni, further to the rear. It was snowing when we arrived in December, 1951 and would snow much of the time until sometime in April, 1952. The ground was frozen when we got to Korea and not until early April could we dig more than a few slit trenches with dynamite from the engineers. Baker was the first battery to fire our guns in Korea, at grid reference 200890 in December, 1951.

Baker Battery would be detached from the rest of the 145th for all of 1951 and 52, and initially be attached for operational control to the 196th Field Artillery Battalion, a 155mm howitzer unit. In April of 1952 we were attached to the 955th Field Artillery, in July attached to the 623rd, and in October attached directly to X Corps Artillery. The only exception was for one week in November 1951, when all three firing batteries came back together at Kumhwa in the IX Corps area. That was during the attack on and defense of Triangle Hill-Sniper Ridge. Following that week together, we went back to our previously separate firing positions in the X Corps sector. Two days after Christmas 1951, I went with a group from our battery to see how the other batteries were set up in their Fire Direction Center, which was my original first assignment in Baker Battery, and also to look at the Observation Post being built on Hill 932, called 'Heartbreak Ridge'. Another reason we were there was to lay the first wire telephone lines to our OP, although it would take the Korean Service Corp the better part of a month to complete building for the ground was frozen. It turned out to be a good lesson for all of us for one of the people who passed us going up the hill as we laid wire, later stepped no more than a foot off the tape marked path and was seriously wounded when he set off an anti-personnel mine. The OP on Hill 932 was where personnel from Able, Baker and Charlie Batteries in the 145th would provide OP personnel and I was to be rotated among those given OP duty in the future. While on the OP we would direct fire of Able and Charlie Batteries. Baker Battery's firing missions in support of the 11th Marine Regiment and others were directed by aircraft or occasionally by the FO's from the 196th Field Artillery Battalion. This was because visibility directly to our front was limited and most of our fire missions in support of the Marines came from aircraft.

In April 1952, when the 1st Marine Division came off-line and were replaced by the 8th ROK Division, we moved our firing battery and camp approximately one-quarter mile south and onto an open slope next to the road leading to our Service Battery. This was important because the first battery firing positions we occupied in December 1951 was a trap. We had been placed in a cul-de-sac, where we could never have gotten out if the North Korean's had even broken through the Marines and come south just a few hundred yards. Our road out went through a Marine tank company, and toward the Main Line of Resistance for over a quarter mile, before turning south onto the main road. When we arrived at the new positions, the ground was thawing so we immediately began building bunkers for FDC, living quarters, officers quarters and placed all guns in revetments. We also set up better perimeter defense and emplaced the .50 and .30 cal machine guns in bunkers, set mines and trip flares on the flanks. While moving we had lost two men to serious wounds from anti-personnel mines they ran into while laying telephone wire between each battery position. We had laid a wire line so we could conduct fire missions even if FDC was not yet set up in the new camp.

I had initially been assigned to the Fire Direction Center in Baker Battery and also worked in the communications section. Within a couple of months as all National Guard personnel were shipped home, I was moved out of the FDC and made Communications Chief in Baker Battery. I was a Corporal doing the job of a SFC, but wholesale promotions as had happened in Korea that first year, had been stopped. A few months later I was promoted to Staff Sergeant. In the spring of 1951, I began going on rotation as a Forward Observer to Hill 932. Our OP on Heartbreak was just west of the high point along the crest. We had a sleeping bunker on the reverse slope. The observation bunker had its entrance on the reverse slope and the observation port, just below the crest on the forward slope. A trench ran part of the way from the OP to the sleeping bunker. We were very aware of our movements being seen and the possibility of incoming artillery lire, for the Main Line of Resistance was maybe 100 yards in front and below our OP. We had an excellent OP, on the highest point on our side of the MLR, so we could be seen by anyone and we could also see in some areas for maybe ten miles to the north. We received incoming fire hitting close to the OP only once while I was there. I was looking through a spotters scope, when a mortar round hit in front of the OP and gravel hit me in the forehead as I looked through the spotters scope which had protected my eyes. I did not go down to the aid-station for help, as it soon stopped bleeding, and it was a very steep climb back in the dark.

The 145th had arrived in Korea just when operations to capture ground were ended and operations to kill more enemy troops went into effect. We had been told this in Pusan and that moving more artillery units to Korea was the way the UN was going to bleed the enemy. As a result of that change in objective and our location along the east coast, in what was the roughest terrain in Korea, we did not get involved in any named outpost battles. The only exception was in November 1952, when we briefly moved to Kumhwa in the IX Corps sector to support the attack on and then the defense of the Triangle Hill-Sniper Ridge Area. While there, the 145th delivered more artillery fire on the 4 and 5 of November than during any other two day period since coming to Korea. A very large number of artillery units had been assembled in that sector. We were all set up in a broad valley with other artillery units, 155mm guns, 8-inch howitzers, 105mm guns and 155mm howitzers, spread out around us. None were dug-in and we had occasional incoming rounds, but there was never a time day or night when there was not some of our or nearby batteries firing their guns. Another area we were involved in was the Punchbowl, which was just to the left front of Baker Battery and in our sector of the X Corp. In addition to the division troops manning the Punchbowl, there were usually other UN troops there. I remember that for a long period of time the Turkish Battalion was stationed there. The Punchbowl consisted of a nearly circular valley surrounded on all sides by steep but relatively low-lying mountains. At one time, one of the roads into the Punchbowl was under observation by the enemy and they often fired at vehicles on certain parts of the road. During much of the time I was in Korea, the north rim of the Punchbowl was the MLR in that area. It was just east of Heartbreak Ridge, but visibility from the OP on 932 was poor. It was in the Punchbowl where in addition to firing missions from Baker Battery, we also manned a self-propelled 155 mm gun.

Baker Battery took more incoming rounds due to counter battery fire than the other firing batteries in the 145th, at least according to the Command Report narratives I have seen for our battalion. Baker Battery drew counter battery fire from 76mm and 122mm North Korean guns in February, March, June, July, August, September, and November. In September 1952, when the 45th Division replaced the 8th ROK on line, Baker Battery counted 185 incoming rounds during that period. Even though that was a high number, this kind of enemy action always occurred when divisions came off line. The enemy thought more men were exposed moving around and could be hit or increasing their artillery fire at that time would disrupt our freedom of movement. Our 155mm guns, called the 'Long Tom' performed different fire missions than those fired by 105mm guns, or even the 155mm Howitzer. The effective range of our guns was up to 12 miles, although few fire missions were at that long a distance. Based on my experience in FDC and at the OP, most of our fire missions were called 'Harassing and Interdiction' fire. These were either fired at specific targets that continuously drew the attention of our observers, or were some type of fire mission to stop an enemy action, like counter battery or firing at the enemy during an attack, or at strong paints. Counter battery fire would be directed at our 155mm guns more often that you think. This was because of the huge muzzle blasts from our guns at each shot. At night they could be seen for miles. You could not hide that flash and our battery location. A second type of popular fire mission was called, 'Time on Target'. One good example of this type of fire mission was when we fired at certain targets like cross roads or locations on roads that could be seen at night by watching for truck headlights. These targets were 6 or 10 miles behind enemy lines and no matter how often we fired such missions, within a few hours we were likely to see the enemy trucks again turning on their lights. They seemed unable to understand that we shot at the lights and could not see the vehicles in the dark if they turned off their lights. These fire missions were only effective if we knew how many seconds it would take for our shells to reach the target once those in the OP had given the order to fire. It was a game of cat and mouse, which when secondary explosions were seen after calling a ToT mission, you knew you had hit something, giving gunners and FO people a good feeling. 'Time on Target' fire missions were to me the most fun. About half the time we fired White Phosphorous on ToT's, at least after the first registration rounds landed. A couple of times large secondary explosions, obviously larger and delayed after our rounds hit the target were very satisfying. You knew you had hit something and it had exploded causing even more damage. It has been fifty years since I called my last fire mission, but if memory serves, it went something like this. Ring FDC and call, 'Fire mission'. If the fire mission is at a pre-registered target give them its number or simply give type of target and coordinates of target. Give type of shell desired, HE, WP, smoke, etc and fuse setting if an air-burst is desired. FDC calls back, 'one round on the way' and gives the FO the time on target. The FO corrects the aim and FDC again says, 'one round on the way'. If a hit or very near miss, the FO calls, 'Fire for effect', and all the guns in the battery fire. We also fired observed and unobserved fire missions on targets of opportunity, which were called in by air or ground observers. Several times we were also called on to help direct naval gunfire from a U.S. Battleship off the Korean coast. Usually an aircraft directed the fire, but several times our OP on Hill 932 was used to direct that fire. As a Forward Observer I made sure I knew exactly what was going on in the FDC and at the gun positions during a fire mission. That way when I was in the OP I knew about how long it would take to arm and lay the guns for a fire mission. I did not want any surprises. I also watched for things that appeared different each morning through the spotters' scope that might be evidence of building a new enemy gun emplacement or bunker or wire had been strung or moved. I felt that being a Forward Observer was a great chance to make a difference conducting the fire missions and do a better job killing the enemy.

For FO's of 155mm guns, with one exception, no artillery FO was in any trench along the MLR that I ever heard of. We would normally be on a high point where our FO could best direct effective fire missions that might call for weapons like ours with such a long range. There was one exception to this general comment I know about, which was when a self-propelled 155mm gun was used for close support. Several times Baker Battery also had a 155mm Self-Propelled gun attached for use in the Punchbowl. I have no idea which X Corp junior staff officer decided to move a 155mm SP to the MLR, but no one who had actually seen a self-propelled 155mm gun in action would have made that mistake in the war we were then fighting. This misuse of a 155mm SP gun would never have happened at the Artillery School. But, X Corp decided to use the 155mm SP to fire directly at close-in targets on the MLR like enemy bunkers, a job usually assigned to tanks. It was a never-ending disaster for the gun and crews every time it was used. If the gun was not immediately moved after the first shot was fired, it always brought down immediate counter battery-gunfire and heavy mortar fire, often killing or wounding several cannoneers and damaging the gun itself. It would then be pulled out of line for several weeks to be repaired. It was a terrible use of the weapon and people in my opinion, and I lost friends killed or wounded there. I had no special hardships as a Forward Observer, except for an occasional heart attack, when the poncho hung to cover the back entrance to our observation bunker would suddenly be swept open night with no warning. When that happened, I always expected to hear a grenade bounce off the wall or a burp gun go off. It took, however, very few times throwing an entrenching tool at the entrance to change the habits of a lifetime to those who scared me death. I never got bored on the OP. There was always something to see out front, or on the reverse slope. Anti-personnel mines had been swept off Heartbreak and as the ground thawed out that first spring, there were always new things to find on the reverse slope after such a pounding by artillery when the 2nd Division took Heartbreak. In the chewed up ground of the Ridge as it thawed out, two enemy dead bodies popped-up, old mess kits, a couple of grenades but never an unexploded shell. Hot meals were not served on the OP as at the battery kitchen, but C rations, if you were selective, were not that bad and my home was in an underground bunker at both the OP and at Baker battery. I got about the same amount of sleep, though in shorter segments, and it was colder on the OP, plus no lights in the OP at night.

Baker Battery supported the 8th ROK Division from April 1952 to September 1952. I do not believe the remainder of the battalion was ever in direct support of a ROK Division. In September of 1952, just short of nine months after arriving in Korea the 145th Field Artillery Battalion fired its 100,000th round in Korea. That was an average of 123 rounds fired every day by each one of the three firing batteries, or an average of just over 11,000 rounds fired each month by the 145th at enemy targets, and that is considering limits on ammunition. During the entire time in Korea, Baker Battery was facing North Korean Divisions, which was pretty much the history of the X Corp on the east coast. I was always told that North Korean soldiers were more cruel and clever than the Chinese, but have no way to know the truth. In Baker Battery few Utah National Guard personnel made it to Korea, and most that did were very clannish NCOs and a few officers. Within the first four months almost all were gone. I went on R & R with buddies from Baker battery. By the time I left Korea, most that I knew well had already rotated. Fifty years later I can still see the faces, but can not recall many names in the 145th except a few I really liked Worthington, Grice, Pickering, Razz, Weeks and others I just can not put a name to in Baker battery. The rest are like ghosts and that probably accounts for the reason I have never been to a 145th Field Artillery reunion. I arrived in Korea on December 5, 1951 and left about December 10, 1952. I had the points for rotation prior to that, but was delayed because there were very few NCOs arriving in Korea at that time to replace those up for rotation. Delays in rotation were common throughout most units in Korea. When I finally left in December 1952, the 145th was at only 69% of authorized strength."

### Sergeant Jerry Sax
### 213th Field Artillery Battalion 1952-53

"I had arrived in Korea in August of 1952, went through the usual Repo Depot route and was shipped to the 213th Field Artillery Battalion, a 155mm towed unit in IX Corps general support. At Service Battery we were assigned to the various batteries, and I went to Battery 'A'. There I was in the wire section and had had all sorts of jobs, like driving a ¾ ton truck, hauling the water trailer and twice a day I would drive over to the reservoir and pick up drinking water for the battery. I also was a wireman, even though my MOS and my basic training was that of a cannoneer, a member of a gun crew. In a short while I learned how to climb poles, run telephone wire, and make splices, including what we called the Korean splice, a misnomer since I later learned it was a Japanese Army splice. Like the other fellows in the section, I also picked up some radio skills. When the first opportunity came about, I volunteered to go up on the hill with Lt. William Corbett, a Forward Observer from Able Battery. It was an experience that I enjoyed. I was really on the front and what I did as an individual had a real impact on the war. I had sharp eyes and was able to spot targets in a way better than most. Lt. Corbett, a real, real gentleman and I and the other enlisted man got on very well. The lieutenant let me shoot a disproportionate amount of the missions, which truthfully was fulfilling, because if I had to be in Korea, I might as well make a real contribution. I was pretty good at that also. Before the Battle of White Horse Mountain ammunition was rationed. We could shoot about eighteen rounds a day, for the whole battalion. That's one round per day per gun. We could go over the ration against active enemy artillery. If there were men in the open, we had to count how many there were. If there were over say fifteen, we were allowed to shoot. I remember, a few times, seeing enemy soldiers in the open and counting perhaps a dozen and abandoning the mission. By early October, I had been on the hill, always on OP 'Love' on Hill 395, White Horse, for a few of the five or so day periods that each FO team stayed. I was pretty familiar with the area in front of us, which was dominated by the Chinese occupied Hill 396, which was one meter higher than the ridge-like Hill 395, and the 600 ridgeline beyond it. I remember the stream coming from the east from what was, or once was, a small reservoir. I can still see the nighttime firefight off in the distance between the South Korean patrol and the Chinese. Spark-like flashes, single ones and bursts from automatic weapons. To me it was unreality. I was a detached observer, since we couldn't fire in support.

We were supporting the 9th ROK Division, which was subsequently called the 'White Horse Division' and we generally had little contact with them, even if we were in their midst. Language and cultural differences were huge separators. There were some Korean officers who spoke some English. Our communication vehicle was the Japanese-Korean pidgin that all the GI's quickly picked up. Even if the Koreans understood this pidgin, hands and facial expressions were the main way of communicating since the pidgin vocabulary was very limited. The Koreans were poorly fed and poorly clothed. We had our GI boots, they wore high sneakers. Their uniforms were in pretty poor condition and their equipment was generally inferior to what we had. They were primarily draftees, not highly motivated and were cruelly treated by their superiors. The 9th ROK Division had been on the line for a while but it had not really proved itself. At that point there were only two Korean Divisions that we felt were battle hardened and dependable, the 2nd ROK Division and the Capital ROK Division. There were two incidents that occurred on OP Love about this time that I remember before White Horse. The first was a deflation of my ego by a Korean soldier. The line had been static awhile and the Chinese were very well aware where the artillery OP's were. Every morning at a specific time they would shell us. Well one morning a shell landed on the reverse slope near the little wooden box that the OP members used as a latrine. The thing was covered with slivers of shrapnel and it was impossible to use. Lt. Corbett asked me how good my carpentry skills were and when I told him that I was pretty good at it he asked me to build another one. We got some wood somewhere and borrowed some tools from the Koreans. I measured the wood and started sawing away. It was a terrible saw. It was as dull as hell and I was having a hell of a time sawing that board. Suddenly I felt a tap on my shoulder and a Korean soldier with a mixed look of disgust and compassion mimed that he would saw the wood for me. Somehow that terribly dull saw worked for him and in no time he finished all the cutting. This moment was preserved for posterity by one of the other members of the FO party with two photographs.

The other incident was the first time that I was under fire. It was my second day on the hill. The OP was shelled by mortars. Let me tell you, I was scared. I had just come up from the reverse slop of the hill where I met a ¾ ton truck which brought us mail, some water, and a small stove to cook on. The stove was mighty dirty, so I decided to clean it with some gasoline. I took the stove outside and cleaned it in the communication trench outside the bunker which was on top of the hill. Just as I finished, I heard a whine which got louder and louder. Now up until then I didn't have experience in hearing incoming mail that was coming nearby. But you can't mistake the sound. Well I listened another second and went down as low as I could get in this commo trench. In a couple of seconds the whine became a screech. Then, boom! The shell landed somewhere in front of me. In no time flat, I moved the ten or fifteen feet and was inside the bunker. The Lieutenant got on the B.C. scope and started combing the hill for the mortar. He asked another OP to do the same and requested FDC for an Air Observer to join in. A few more rounds landed and even when I heard the outgoing rounds whistle by I said, 'Oh oh, here it comes'. The lieutenant told me to calm down. After awhile it got monotonous so I started washing my dirty hands which were full of soot. A total of fifteen rounds landed in this general area, a few of them on the hill nearby. About forty five minutes elapsed from the first to the last round. We spotted the mortar and asked for artillery. Since there is a shortage of ammo they allotted only two rounds, both of which missed the target. After the shelling, I was told to keep the B.C. scope trained on the mortar position. After awhile, I saw a couple of Chinese moving around. Finally a ROK 105mm outfit, which has an Observer on this hill too, hit the mortar position. The fourth adjustment hit right where the mortar was, but there was no secondary explosion. They probably damaged the position, but didn't knock it out."

**Sergeant Robert Taylor**
**937th Field Artillery Battalion 1951-1953**

"I was drafted into the army in early 1951. I took my basic training in Ft. Riley, Kansas where I was unfortunate enough to be caught in the Kansas flood. From there I went to Seattle, Washington for a month and then shipped to Japan where I went to school for a month. I then shipped to Pusan, Korea. I was assigned to 'B' Battery of the 937th Field Artillery Battalion. Our battery had four 155mm 'Long-toms', which ordinance could switch to 8-inch tubes. Our weapons were the largest ones in Korea at the time. We backed the 25th Infantry Division in the Chorwon Valley. I was in Korea from November of 1951 to January of 1953. Our weapons were so large that they had to be surveyed in for accuracy. We sat back from the front line approximately two miles, and my job was to direct the artillery fire by talking to spotter planes and relaying the data to the gun crews. Whenever the spotter planes were out of service, the battalion would order me to the front to fire direct on any targets I spotted. I don't recall any major battles because in 1952 the front line was pretty well established on the 38th parallel, and we spent most of our time firing at the North Koreans with them firing back at us or at any moving objects. When you are in the artillery you are only allowed to carry a carbine rifle or a .45, which has very little distance, it would have been nice to have a M-1 rifle for distance. I had no trouble with the infantry units in the trenches, when you are at the front line you had better all be comrades! Out of our three batteries, Able, Baker, and Charlie, each one had a man to work OP duty. Life as a Forward Observer was just waiting until you could spot something worth calling in on. Being in the trenches was not good. When I tried to get some sleep at night the rats would come out and crawl all over my shoulder and sometimes I would roll over on them and they would squeal. Due to the fact that the front line had been in the same position for so long and the infantry had buried their remnants of food and trash in the ground, the rats would come out at night, I never saw them in the daytime. The rats and being very cold, I think that best describes things.

We had one fire mission where we were directed to move one of our guns to the front line and fire direct. I had an uneasy feeling about that because of the large size of the gun. But orders are orders! I was calling the fire direction from the bunker, and we had a colonel observing with us, but the gun crews were exposed to the outside with the gun. We spotted a North Korean mortar team firing at us from a distance and there was a wide slot to see out of the bunker and one shell landed outside of the bunker slot and the impact threw the colonel and myself against the back of the bunker wall, it stunned us for a minute. One shell landed on our gun causing a fire, but luckily the gun crew didn't get hurt. That was the end of that mission. I still remember going down the hill looking back and seeing the smoke rolling from the gun. They knew they had us. Back in my battery area at another time I was firing a mission when an artillery shell came in right outside my tent and exploded. Luckily for me a lot of the shrapnel shredded my tent and I only got one piece in my leg. It could have been worse. They took me back to the rear medics and they sewed up my leg with stitches. My thoughts were, 'This is how I am going to get out of this hell hole.' I asked the doctor, 'Am I going to get to go home?' He said, 'No, I do good work, that will heal, get back up there.'"

**2nd Lt Hugh Hunt**
**1st Battalion, 11th Marine Regiment 1951-52**

"I joined the Marine Corps' Platoon Leaders Course program as a sophomore at the University of Southern Mississippi. I attended summer training for two years, was commissioned upon graduation in May 1951 and went to The Basic School at Marine Corps Schools at Quantico, Virginia for basic officer training. Following completion of Basic School in November 1951, I requested Korean duty and was sent over with a special replacement draft of platoon leaders in December. When I got to Korea, I was assigned to 'C' Battery, 1st Battalion, 11th Marine Regiment, 1st Marine Division. We fired 105mm howitzers, and were in X Corps on the East Central front at the Punchbowl and in I Corps on the West Coast after mid-March 1952. I served with 'C' Battery from December 1951 to September 1952. I arrived in Korea as an infantry platoon leader but because of a shortage of artillery officers was assigned to the 11th Marines, the artillery regiment. After a week's intensive training as a Forward Observer I went on line as an FO supporting the 1st Korean Marine Regiment at the Punchbowl in east central Korea. We were in defensive positions on the north rim of the Punchbowl supporting patrols and raids by Korean Marine infantry units. After moving to the west coast in March we manned Combat Outposts, called COP's, in front of the MLR supporting 2nd Battalion, 5th Marine Regiment patrols and defending the COP's against attacks by Chinese forces. When the Outpost Line of Resistance, the OPLR, was abandoned in May 1952, we returned to OP's on the MLR. Some of the firefights at the Cop's were fairly large scale. The heaviest fighting while I was there was at and around Bunker Hill in August.

I was fortunate to have a short grace period for on-the-job training with the Korean Marines in early 1952. It gave me time to develop and improve my skills as an FO. The experience was valuable when we moved to the west coast in March to face the Chinese. FO duties at the Punchbowl were almost entirely comprised of firing on daily targets of opportunity from my OP on the MLR. Action on the west coast at the COP's was both offensive and defensive. In late July 1952, the Imjin River flooded behind us and washed out our two supply bridges. For two days we faced the Chinese without resupply of ammunition, food and other materials. They didn't know it but we did. The fighting at Bunker Hill and nearby outposts in August was probably as intense as any in our sector in 1952. We directly supported the 1st Korean Marine Regiment at the Punchbowl and the 5th Marine Regiment on the west coast. I think they both recognized and appreciated the value of artillery fire support and accepted us as fellow Marines who shared the same conditions and could fight as riflemen if needed. We directly supported the 181st Korean Marine Regiment, and at the Punchbowl we faced the North Koreans, and in the west we faced the Chinese. The North Koreans were tough, well-trained troops and good fighters. The Chinese were good, too, especially their artillery, but their infantry seemed to depend more on numerical superiority than tactical skill. Our battery FOs normally manned three OP's. I was on 'Nan I', 'COP I', 'COP 2', and Hills 229 and 111. Nan I was the OP at the Punchbowl on Hill 1026. The COP's on the west coast were on low-elevation hills. When we pulled back to the MLR my OP was on Hill 229. In mid-August I went back on line at Hill 111 as an FO to support the 5th Marines at 'Elmer', 'Hilda' and 'Irene'. Along with serving on Hills 1026, 229, and 111, Hill 924 was another hill that I remember also. My life was probably no different than thousands of others online. We manned the OP's twenty four hours a day with four or six hour watches. Between watches we slept, ate, improved our positions and living quarters, trained new troops and coordinated operations with infantry unit commanders and forward air controllers. By stateside standards our living conditions probably would have been condemned. By Korean standards we lived pretty well. By the winter of 1951-1952 we had the best clothing and equipment, thermal boots, armored vests, double down sleeping bags, parkas, etc. We ate C-Rations. When we were with the Korean Marines we ate what they ate and didn't ask questions. Cleanliness was a rumor. I went from January to Mid-March of 1952 without a bath or shower. Fortunately for others, they did too.

The most memorable fire mission was the morning the regimental commander visited my OP on Hill 229. After adjusting fire on troops in the open I was ready to call for fire for effect. The colonel ordered me to mass the regiment for a 'Triple Ripple'. Fifty-four 105s and eighteen 155s fired two hundred and sixteen rounds of HE within about a minute and a half. We didn't know the term then, but it was truly 'Shock and Awe'. I've never seen anything like it. A typical fire mission began with a radio or telephone alert to the battalion Fire Direction Center. After identifying the OP, the fire mission message was transmitted, something like this, 'This is Woodduck Charlie One, Fire Mission. Troops in the open. Coordinates such and such, Fuse VT, Shell HE'. Fire was adjusted by establishing a hundred-yard bracket on line with the target, splitting that bracket and calling for fire for effect. For example, 'Right 100, add 200... Drop 100... add 50, Fire For Effect'. When the mission was completed, a surveillance report was sent, 'Cease fire, end of mission. Ten KIA, ten WIA, ten ran away.' In February 1951 X Corps ordered its divisions to fake a withdrawal, it was called 'Operation Clam-up' to lure the North Koreans into a large-scale ambush. Line units made a show of daytime withdrawals with covering artillery fire, returning to concealed line positions at night. The North Koreans probed but didn't bite. For two days I sat waiting in sub-zero temperatures in a hidden OP on the forward slope of the MLR. A North Korean squad-size patrol came close but left before they got to my OP or the MLR trenches. X Corps gave up after a couple of days and we went back to work in our regular positions."

**1st Lt Robert Bush**
**555th Field Artillery Battalion 1952**

"I got an ROTC commission, and when I finished Battery Officer training at Fort Sill I was put on orders to FECOM. I was then assigned to the 555th Field Artillery Battalion, 'C' Battery. We fired the 105mm howitzer, and were assigned to I Corps at the time, around Chin Chun, Panmunjom, and the Punchbowl. I served from January 1952 through November 1952, and as soon as I reported to the battery I was assigned by the battery commander as a Forward Observer. I served with the 40th, 45th, 1st ROK, and 3rd ROK Infantry Divisions, we were usually in direct support, and usually had two or three OP's manned at any given time. I was scared and lonely serving with the Korean infantry, only one person spoke English, my recon sergeant! That was not a fun experience and very lonely living with the Koreans, it was hard to communicate. We ate C rations every day, and when supporting Koreans, I thought I would never get out alive. From what I recollect, we fought mostly the Chinese, too. After July '52, I became assigned as an Aerial Observer till I left in November of '52. While on the ground we were pretty good at identifying and wiping out artillery or incoming mortar fire, by getting a compass reading or shell hole. But it was difficult finding targets as the enemy was very well dug in, we had to respond only to muzzle flashes. I can remember being accidentally attacked by U.S. Air Force aircraft, twice with napalm and once being strafed. My most frightening experience was as an Air Observer, when over enemy territory we were caught in the back wash of a dive bomber and blown all over. I can still see the bomber pilot's face as he flew by, we thought he took off our wing. My pilot, Dennis Whelan, told me to jump first, opened the door, and I was almost ready to jump and he pulled me back. This one memory is with me every day."

**1st Lt Howard Farmer**
**160th Field Artillery Battalion 1951-52**

"I enrolled in college in 1947 and was a student at Cornell. My parents were not capable of financially assisting me through college so I worked at the snack bar three nights a week during my college time, and when it came time when I was a Junior to take advanced ROTC I did so because they paid $27 dollars a month. I graduated in January of 1951, and of course the Korean War was going so I didn't even try to get a job, I knew I was going to be called to active duty. I entered the active military around April of '51 and was in Korea by December. I was assigned to the 160th Field Artillery Battalion, 45th Infantry Division, I think they were the National Guard division out of Oklahoma. The 160th fired 105mm howitzers, and while I was there we fought at such places as T-Bone Hill and Old Baldy. What was life like as a Forward Observer? Well, basically speaking, I am not the type of person who enjoys killing. Unfortunately if someone is shooting at you, you just kind of react and say 'oh well, I guess I'd better shoot back'. My most horrible time was on T-Bone Hill when the infantry captain thought his patrol was on one side of the 'T' and in reality they were on the other. He asked me to provide fire on the other side that he thought his men were, and as it turns out they were where he directed me to fire, and killed eight Americans and wounded quite a bunch of them. When the remainder of the patrol came back they would've liked to hang me from a tree, however the captain admitted that he had made the mistake and it wasn't my fault. I was also with the 1st ROK Division for a while, and they were kind enough to leave me on my outpost and retreat without telling me. I found myself behind North Korean lines, and I had a sergeant and a corporal at that point in time, and we decided to just sit tight and wait and eventually the South Koreans returned to where they had left. That wasn't what I'd call a fun time. We supported 45th Division and the 1st ROK Division, although I couldn't tell you which exact units. The problem was, when the infantry rotated out, I stayed behind on the front lines because we didn't have enough FO's. So, my recollection was, we were supposed to have two weeks on and a week off, but we didn't have FO's to support the three companies we were supposed to support, we only had two. There were no people to take our place when the infantry went to reserves, so every time the infantry went into reserves I ended up being the FO for a different company. We fought mostly the North Koreans when I was there. I didn't think much of it, I wanted to be home. I don't have any thoughts on it, just tried to put it out of my mind.

When I established my OP, which is generally at the highest point of visibility, the infantry made sure they stayed a good ways away. One OP I was on, I had a North Korean tank zeroed in on me and if you put your head up above at daylight hours they'd just try to shoot it off. The first New Years eve I was in Korea, I was with the 1st ROK division, and an airplane flew overhead playing Olde Lang Sine. I thought 'Oh that's nice. New Years Eve and they're playing Olde Lang Sine'. Well it turned out that ended up being the South Koreans national anthem or somebody's. And then on a loud speaker in the airplane it says 'Lt. Farmer. We have a letter from your mother', and referred to my mother's name, 'And she wants to know how you're doing'. Then they said 'As a matter of fact we have other mail from other people if you wish to surrender. We'd be glad to feed you well and provide you with this, that, and the other'. And I thought 'Oh this is nice. I've only been here a couple weeks and they already know I live here!' On Thanksgiving of 1952 the general commanded that every man in the unit would have a thanksgiving dinner so after dark I sent my jeep driver back to the battery to get our thanksgiving dinner and they put it in one of those insulated things. And I think they had turkey and gravy and mashed potatoes and some kind of vegetable and ice cream all in the same thing. If you use your mind, that doesn't generally work. You can't put hot and cold together but that's what they did! And the jeep driver on the way back ran into some kind of hole and the jeep went on its side. And being alone, he did all he could do to get the damn thing back on its wheels, and he finally arrived back at the outpost about six or seven hours later, and we opened the thing that had the three containers in it and my recon sergeant, Sgt Ralph DeBoise said 'Give me a hand Lt. I found the meat'. We didn't have any eating utensils because they were pointless when we were eating C rations. What's the point of having a mess kit? So I would grab a potato or turkey flavored with vanilla ice-cream, it was really joyful."

**1st Lt. Jack G. Callaway**
**213th Field Artillery Battalion 1952**

"On the OP on three occasions I went out on patrol with the South Koreans at night. That was a very frightening thing. This was with the ROK's. I spoke no Korean, but I stayed very close to their leader, who spoke a little English, and we did a lot of sign language. We thought we were going to be able to get close enough to a concentration of Chinese to where I could call in fire on them. But it never happened, we never were engaged at all and we never were engaged by them, although we could hear Chinese, we weren't, the situation was such we couldn't pin point their location. We had no instructions to raid or seize prisoners, so when we couldn't locate them, we backed off and waited to see if they would reveal themselves, and they never did. That was before the Battle of White Horse, Hill 395. Before the attack started in full fury the first night, I got a coded message from battalion. They said 'A green flare means this, a red flare means that'. And I got on the radio with them and said 'Look, these guys are getting close enough that I'm going to be able to let you talk to one of them in a few minutes, I don't have time to go through this translation routine, tell me what it is'. So, they gave me the rest of the message in the clear, and that saved us a lot, because they did make heavy use of flares and when a flare went up I knew what it meant.

At about eleven o'clock the barrage started, and it was heavy enough to tell me something big was in the wind, so I got out in the trench. I never observed out of the bunker, ever. And that barrage continued all night, off and on, I mean maybe there would be a five, ten minute pause and then it would start up again, and it was fairly heavy, and it lasted as well as I can remember, till five o'clock Monday afternoon, that would have been the 6th, and about six or seven o'clock, it was still light enough to see, the Chinese started coming after us, and going toward White Horse. Lt. Joseph Adams called me, he was on the OP located right on the front of White Horse Mountain, and I was already out in the trench watching, and the nickname I had with my unit was 'Cabot'. He called, and at that time we had a landline, and he said 'Cabot, look at the foot of my hill'. I looked and I said it looked like wheat, but it can't be wheat. And he said, 'No, I got reports that the Chinese are moving there'. And I said 'Well, just a minute', so I got my BC scope, which was twenty power, and you could see Chinese moving abreast and what they were doing was flanking the outposts and coming up and attacking the flanks where he was. The hill runs north and south, and what they were doing was they were running down the east flank of that hill and cutting up the base or the end of that hill, in their efforts to make penetration and outflank the outposts and a large portion of the defenses. And at the same time, another group appeared and started heading towards my position, on Hill 284. His hill was convex and Joe couldn't see them, but I could, so I began shooting the mission on the troops and I told him, 'This is where the assembly area is I think, can you see that?' And he began shooting at that, but of course he couldn't see what the effect was. But I could see what my effect was, and I would see the rounds impact. There would be a very low order explosion, after the round had skipped, in other words it hit the soldiers, knock them up in the air like bowling pins, and then hit a second time and then go off, but it was very low order. The shells were being fired without fuses. They had run out of fuses. It was just the impact that was making it go off like that. I kept calling the battalion and telling them we kept getting low order explosions, 'What's wrong? What's wrong? What's wrong?' And it was only after the battle that I found out they had run out of fuses.

The first night we began firing flares, and at some part of that fight, because it was so hard to see, there was so much dust in the air, but I do remember seeing people on top of Joe Adam's bunker. And Joe called and said that he was being overrun, there were people on top of his bunker, and I said 'I'll dust you off with Victor Tare', VT fuses, variable time fuses. And he said 'Alright', and I did that. By this time, his radio operator had taken one or two rounds into the radio, so it was dead, and that's the reason I couldn't hear from him, and I was just really torn up because I was sure that I had screwed up and killed him. It wasn't until I came off the hill that I realized he was alive. And I think I slept about four hours between Sunday night and the following Friday night, so I was a little delusional. I went down to the battery, and was in the tent and was taking off the rags that I had been wearing, and a medic was there to clean me up and stuff, and Joe walks in with this bottle of whiskey. And he said 'Hello Cabot', and I just ignored him because I was convinced this was another one of my delusions, and I took the whiskey, I think one shot, and then I discovered that I had worms because my stomach began to hurt, and then I passed out. I think they said I slept for about eighteen hours. They didn't come close to me that first night, they had got to the base of the hill, and they had put a sniper down at the base of the hill. And as I said I never went into the OP bunker, I was always crawling around on the hill, and if they started shooting I'd go into the nearest bunker. But this sniper, every time I would move, he would nail me, and you could just, you could really hear it crack. And I finally decided that if I don't get him, we're all going to get killed, because I can't direct the artillery fire. So I got to where I was sure that he would be able to see me, and I started to rise, and then I dropped, just enough time for him to take aim and get off a shot. He hit the left lip of the bill of my helmet, coming across my right cheek, up across the bridge of my nose. I lay there, and figured this sucker has to be in these ruins down there, some farm houses and some structures there at the base of Hill 284. He was probably two hundred to three hundred yards, no more than that. So I called Battalion and told them what my problem was. And I said to them 'I want one battery with VT, one battery with Fuse Quick', a contact fuse, 'I want one battery White Phosphorous Fuse Quick, and I want a ToT'. Well I got it, and I lay there for a few minutes, and decided to do the same thing again from new location, and I did that. I did that twice from that location, and I never heard anything, and I thought that that sucker could be faking out, and waiting for another good shot. So, I made another move, and didn't hear anything, and it was then that I was sure I got him, and I didn't hear from him again through the rest of the fight.

The fight got quiet except on White Horse, it was still going on there, but not the intensity it had, obviously from the first wave, and now they were preparing the second. Flare ships began to arrive, and they would kick their flares out, parachute flares, but the damn things had failed to arm somehow. And I'm running down the trench and look up, and I see this white parachute coming down, and I thought 'Oh we're cooked, they're throwing in airborne'. All I had in my hand was a pistol, that's all I ever carried up on the hill. I saw this parachute coming down with this dark object beneath it, and I opened fire with my pistol, and hit it, and it was close, and it sounded like metal. The minute it hit, I jumped out of the trench and went running over to it, because if it wasn't dead I was going to make it dead. And I discovered it was a flare and I called back to the 213th FDC and said 'Your flare ship is about a thousand meters off target, to the south, he needs to go further to the north and he needs to activate his flares'. So they called that in, so finally when the flares started activating, that whole opposite front, there was about three columns of Chinese, and all of them was heading towards White Horse. I put everything I had on it, because it was just our battalion, and they kept the flares going, and the one column that was coming towards me earlier in the day was not making good progress at all. There was a river, it was maybe six hundred yards from the base of our hill. It had a steep gorge, both walls of the stream were sheer walls, and they had to get across that to get at me. And when they would get down in that ditch, that's when I put some fire on them. I couldn't tell you how many guns, but I put fire in that ditch, continuous fire, and continuous fire means you just keep firing at those co-ordinates until I tell you to stop. I don't know how long that went on, but I didn't see that many people coming out. Eventually they did, and they then got around us, at least, they had a semi-circle around us. I wasn't completely cut off, but they had us surrounded to the extent that you couldn't get re-enforcements into us without them coming under heavy fire. That went on all evening, and I was still feeling bad about having, what I thought, killed Lt. Joe Adams, and asking the battalion if we were going to get more guns in here, and it was our battalion, the 213th, and the Koreans that took them on, and I said 'Can you control the Korean 105's?', and they said 'Yes, if you've got missions for them, give them to us', so I gave them missions for the 105's, so we had about two more Korean battalions with 105mm's helping us.

I was on the OP from Sunday night to Friday afternoon. By the second week, it was obvious that it was over. The partial encirclement of our hill was gone, they had pulled back, there was no movement anywhere out there. After the first night, we had inflicted a lot of casualties, we inflicted a lot, an awful lot. The Chinese were wearing Red Cross bands, and would come out, and they would police up maybe one of two dead soldiers. But when they would police up they would stack weapons on, they would have one dead Chinese soldier on the stretcher, completely covered with Tommy guns and other stuff like that. They were really out to salvage weapons and ammunition, and I spotted that very quickly. I knew the lay of the land very well by that time. I saw where they would come out of their trenches and I would see where they would go back in. I called the guns, give them the co-ordinates, put them on stand-by, to fire at my command, and wait until those suckers were just about to go back into their trenches, and then I would drop all of them. They continued to do that for two more days, then finally decided that this wasn't paying off, they were losing people and weren't getting any weapons back. I figured they were going to do this at night, too. They normally started early in the evening, and go all night if they can. I mapped it out and put a little sketch together, and called it back to battalion and told them this is the way I wanted to play this thing out. I want you to keep H&I fires going in there all night and at random intervals. The next morning when the sun came up first thing I did was put the glasses on it and yah, you could see Red Cross arm bands out there, not moving.

At one point, I was very familiar with the terrain, and I was the senior Observer in the battalion. At one point I went to sleep standing up in the trenches. This was daylight, and this was near the end of the fight for White Horse, and my radio operator, Sergeant Quinterro, he shook me awake. But my eyes wouldn't open, and they say that's perfectly normal, once your body gets so fatigued you go on automatic shutdown, and that's what I had done, but my mind was going and I said to Quinterro, 'Tell me where they are', and he told me. And I said 'Take an azimuth to where you see them and he did that and we called that into battalion. That's what was called a polar plot, that's where you give them an azimuth and distance from your position, which they know and that's where they fire. And I would ask where did the rounds hit, did they fall behind, in front, to the right of, to the left of them, and he told me and I corrected it. We fired several volleys like that and finally I began to see dimly, I could see what I was shooting at. I told him that he can't let me go to sleep again, until this thing is all over, because I may not be able to see at all, and that would be critical. Direct fire hit our bunker, our living quarters twice, I think it was a 76mm cannon. They had a direct fire gun on the hill opposite us, and I called in air strike after air strike on that thing and we couldn't get it. I called in an awful lot of air strikes, and what they would do is they would make their runs from south to north, and I would tell them the minute you start your pull out, the minute your over the target let me know. I could see tracers coming up, and we would fire flak suppression. When the guys came out of their holes to man the guns they were greeted by a whole flock of air bursts of 155mm, and that was very effective. We had a lot of good air support from the Navy, and it always looked like they would crash into their target, when they would come to it before they would let go, but they didn't. This allowed us to breathe a little bit. And then I got word that there were some 8-inchers, and there was a code name for them, and I said 'O.K. I need them. I want all four guns Converge Sheef', which is all rounds converge on the same point, and that's very unusual for 8-inch. We had one gun fire the adjust, and when the Chinese fired, I counted eighteen layers of sandbags above the aperture of where the gun was firing from. That's when I told them I want the full battery Converge Sheef. They fired several volleys, and an Air Observer said he saw the trails of the gun go out the opposite end of the tunnel it was in. When the direct fire initially hit us, we had our sleeping set-up on the wall closest to the line, where the enemy was, so all the fragmentations hit the other wall and didn't hurt us. When the fight started I transferred every critical item that we had to the front wall of the trench, the bunker. This was on Monday before the attack. They were still shelling us, and I had to have a bowel movement so bad, that my eyes were beginning to turn blue. Before I had went up the hill, I was whittling a stool because the Korean's field sanitation was absolutely awful. So Monday night when the shelling was relatively light, I dug my own hole and put my throne up there, and I figured things are pretty quiet, so if I going to take a bowel movement, now's the time to do it! I started out in the trench and I could hear this screech, and I knew it was incoming, high velocity. So I just dropped back down on the floor of the trench, heard this loud explosion close, right up to the trench, and I looked up and my throne was gone. It had been a direct hit right on my throne. You've heard about people being scared stuffless, I didn't have to have a bowel movement again until five days later when I got back."

**1st Lt David Nimocks**
**424th Field Artillery Battalion 1951-52**

"I got my commission via ROTC when I was graduated from Georgia Tech in 1949 and was placed in the Army Reserves. I went to work in Danville, VA and transferred to the Virginia

National Guard so I could make $25 per month attending drills, etc. I quit my job at Dan River Mills and went to Basic Officers Course at Ft. Sill. While at Sill my Virginia National Guard was federalized, I think we were the last unit to be federalized in the Korean War, and upon graduation from Basic Officers Course I rejoined my Virginia National Guard unit that was now at Camp Polk, LA. Per Army regulations an officer could not go overseas until he had been to Basic Officers Course. Needless to say, I was immediately transferred to the 424th Field Artillery Battalion that was shipping out to Korea, filling a warrant officers slot in the 424th's Table of Organization. And that is how I got to Korea in November 1951. The 424th was an 8-inch howitzer unit, tracker drawn. We were in general support of IX Corps during my entire tour and the battalion located in the Iron Triangle Area. I was with the 424th in Korea from November '51 to November 1952. Corps or someone decided that the battalion needed Forward Observers on a battalion level, and you got an extra rotation home point a month as an FO, so I volunteered along with Ashby Gibbs. We were FO's for 8-inch howitzers in general support, and while the unit fired continuously, our FO position was not with any infantry troops. We just had our outpost on a high hill facing 'Mt Papasan' in the Iron Triangle. If my memory serves me correctly, I think our battalion OP was a temporary setup and was moved from time to time and was manned only when the circumstances warranted. However after I shipped home our 'A' Battery was overrun and received a presidential citation for their gallant actions. We never were really with any specific infantry units, and yes there were ROK units on the front lines in the IX Corps area, but I'm not sure of which ones. I wasn't really sure if we were fighting against Chinese or North Koreans, we just fired the shells at targets assigned by IX Corps."

**PFC Doug Whitham**
**HQ Battery, 11th Marine Regiment 1952-53**

*Author Note: The following letter was written by PFC Doug Whitham. It is a letter that was mailed home by Doug after he was wounded. The events that he writes about occurred during the Battle for 'The Hook' in late October 1952.*

Dear Dad,
You've been wanting to hear just what is going on, well I guess it's about time I told you, I wish you wouldn't let Mom or Leona read this along with you because I know they will worry. I'll start off like this: Last Saturday the 25th we started off at 'O' 3:00 in the morning for OP # 3. There were five of us as the OP teams go, 'Woody', our OP Chief, Vance Worster and myself were regular hill men and two wire men, a fellow named 'Roy' from Manchester, N. H. and the other fellow 'Truman' from upstate N. Y. We got all our gear squared away and the watches set up. We were getting 'incoming' pretty regular, what we call 'harassing fire'. I'd better tell you a little how the hill is situated first though. From our pit looking out into brother Joe's Territory, the hill we are on runs to the right and left of us and forms a kind of ridge, on the right it curves something like a hook and most of the fellows call it 'the hook'; but I think the last official name on the books is 'Warsaw', on the left it is called 'Ronson' and another notorious hill called 'Vegas' and where we are it is called 'Hill One Niner'.

The whole ridge is about nine hundred yards long and on each end it slopes gradually to sea level, better known as the rice paddies. All five of us volunteered to go up on the hill that time so we can't blame anyone but ourselves for what happened. The day ended with a minimum total of 11,000 rounds landing on the hill that was some kind of record because we only used to get about a thousand and they usually came all at once. Maybe I'd better tell you Dad, you can fight a gook but there is nothing you can do about an artillery round or a mortar but sit and wait and pray. Usually when they shell us on one day, the next day they knock it off and we were expecting a day of rest Sunday.

Saturday night they threw in a few rounds now and then to keep us on our toes, but they didn't have to worry we already were. Sunday morning started off real quiet and all our lines were in and every once in awhile they would drop in a round or two. About a quarter to four in the afternoon they started to open up again and Vance was in the Pit then and Truman went up to relieve him at four. The rounds started dropping so fast you couldn't count them if you wanted to, you would have had to count about 20 every second. Truman wasn't gone twenty minutes when he came running into the Bunker with the instrument that we get the azimuths to the guns with. The pit took a direct hit with a 122 round and blew it all to hell, with him in it. All he got was a scratch on the cheek and covered with dirt. All this time they were still dropping 60mm and 120mm mortars, 75's, 105's, 122's and 152mm artillery pieces, all we could do then was sit in our bunker and wait. All five of us were sitting around it, I was facing the door, sitting on the lower bunk in the rear, Vance was standing over to the right of me, Truman to the left and Woody and Roy were standing near the doorway. It was about 45 minutes after Truman got out of the pit and we were discussing whether a 122mm round would go through the bunker when out of nowhere, it felt like someone hit me with a sledge hammer.

The whole damn bunker came down on top of me, I thought for a minute my neck was broken and my shoulder hurt a little. Vance grabbed hold of the lower bunk and lifted all the logs and sand bags and dirt off me at once and pulled me out from under it. Woody yelled and asked if I was alright, Vance laughed a little and said "Hell yes, Can't you hear him swearing?" That round blew Woody and Roy right out the doorway and did a hell of a job on the bunker. Not one of us got hurt or hit with a piece of shrapnel (a 120mm hit the bunker) from that, I think that was pretty lucky. There was a CP bunker about forty feet from our bunker and Woody told me to go down and see if there was any more room for us. I yelled for them to come on down and I didn't have to yell twice. There were a bunch of other guys in there, about 17 in all and we had to sit and wait. Two guys were standing near the doorway and a round landed right next to it and got them both. One fellow lost half of his face and his chest was full of holes, the other guy was just full of shrapnel.

It was about eight o'clock when a guy came running in and said the chinks had Ronson and Warsaw and they were coming still. We had to run out to our bunker and dig out our weapons and ammunition. The artillery fire seemed to increase so it was hitting as fast as you could pound a drum. Vance and Roy went in the CP bunker because they needed someone to guard the fellows in it, there were quite a few wounded in there. That was the last time I saw Vance and Roy. Woody, Truman and I were lying in a trench between our bunker and the CP Bunker. We laid there for about a half hour and in that half hour about 800 or a 1000 rounds hit the hill. All I did was eat dirt and pray and I didn't stop praying. While we were there Woody got hit in the back and the leg. Truman got hit in the leg and the arm, a piece went right thru just in back of his wrist, a tailfin from a 120 landed on my back-side and Woody pulled it off and through it out of the trench. Just about then the Gooks covered the area with Willie Peter (White Phosphorous) and Truman yelled if we didn't get out of this trench then we'd never get out so we took off thru all the incoming and the W.P. burning on the ground and in the trenches. The trenches were pretty well leveled and we had to go in the open. We met about five more fellows that got off of Ronson and we set up a defense along another ridge that's right next to '1-9er' its about a hundred yards running parallel with it and there's a little dip between them. Woody's back was bothering him pretty bad and he had to go down to an Aid Station at the bottom of the hill. I didn't see any of those guys after that, I ran along that whole ridge line looking for them. The Chinks started coming and the incoming stopped a little. There couldn't have been very many because I don't think I saw any.

It got to be about ten o'clock and I didn't have any ammo for my M1 so I left it and picked up a carbine from a guy that didn't have any use for it anymore. We had one machine gunner set on top of the ridge where we were and he covered Vegas, Ronson and One Niner. About three or four more who should have been there bugged out. I could have kissed that guy because he really stopped the chinks. He was all by himself, from evening till midnight when we left. I left the hill and went down to the Aid Station to look for Woody or Truman. All I found was Woody, they evacuated him to C. Med. He had quite a chunk taken out of his back and he's all right now. Truman was evacuated but I didn't know it at the time. I went down a little further to a couple more bunkers and ran smack into my C.O> Lt. Phillips. I was never so glad to see anyone in my life, he brought another Lt. and a truck driver name Harry Kohler, (I think you have a picture of him), and another man named Calberg. In the meantime the Gooks took all of '1-9er' and as far as I knew Vance and Roy were still there, there wasn't much to do but hope for the best.

We went inside the bunker and tried to set for a while, there were about 12 infantry guys with us in there shaking like a leaf. I was really disgusted with them. Just about then a fellow came running in and wanted some one to volunteer to move four dead Gooks, they were about twenty feet from the bunker, laying in a trench. Not one of those guys would move, so me, like an idiot, said I'd go. Harry, Calberg, and I had to lift them out of the trench, got one most of the way out sad he fell in two pieces. I swore and told those infantry guys off and walked down the trench toward another bunker and just about then, a round came and landed next to Harry and Carlberg and lifted them up and dropped them on the deck, I know just how they felt cause when I was laying in the trenches with Woody and Truman, I was lifted and dropped quite a few times. It stove up Harry's leg and he got concussion out of it, but he ran into the bunker with a busted leg, Carlberg was a little shook up but OK. There weren't any corpsmen around so we put Harry on a stretcher, bound up his leg and Lt. Phillips and I on one end and Lt. Reed and Carlberg on the other end we picked up Harry and started for the Aid Station at HQ three miles back. We ran with him for five hundred yards through the impact area and got to the road. Our truck was supposed to have been demolished but we got down the road a little further and there it was, big as life. We set Harry down and I ran and pulled a radio out of the front seat where someone had put it, cranked up the truck, put Harry on the back and we took off, no lights and I never drove a six-by before. We met a tank almost head on, the right side of the truck scrapped the bank around the left side scrapped the tank. I didn't bother to stop. We got back to central eventually with only two men out of the five OP men accounted for, Woody and myself. We didn't know at that time Truman had been evacuated.

Roy and Vance were still at the CP bunker; a gook came in and sprayed the bunker with a burp gun, then threw in nine grenades. There were six dead two wounded and Vance and Roy left. Vance got both legs pretty well blown up and some in the neck and other places but was still going He got seven gooks with his carbine coming over the hill. They came in the bunker and Roy was still OK, he had a piece in his hand and a little piece in his lip. He would have been dead but a wounded GI rolled on top of him and saved him from one of the grenades. One of the Gooks sat on top of Roy, stuck a match on his hand and Roy didn't move. It got about day break on Monday morning and Roy decided had better take his chance getting off the hill rather than dying there. He shot three gooks with his .45 and used case of grenades getting off the hill, they shot at him all the way down and his helmet was full of dents where the slugs bounded off. When he left he said Vance was still alive and couldn't walk and two more guys were alive. Woody, Truman, and Roy are down to the Medical Company now getting fixed. I prayed for Vance last night and today, he was a swell guy. I'm still hoping he is OK but they held an air strike on the hill all day, dropping Napalm and all kinds of gear. I think I was the luckiest guy there because I got out with only a few scratches and a little concussion and shock, all of them had that. Our whole team got purple hearts and Harry and Carlberg got them to. The minimum artillery that landed on '1-9er' was 5000 rounds and you could add 2000 more and not be far from the right number. Well Dad that was the worst two days and nights I have ever spent in my life and I hope it never happens again. Dad don't worry about me, if I got out all right last night I can go through anything. They also took Bunker Hill that night, I don't know what happened, I was too busy.

Love, Doug
p.s. That is the straight scoop, there's a lot of officers who don't know as much yet.

*At the bottom of the typed letter is a note, handwritten, that says; "Lt Phillips was killed in action the next day. Vance was found two days later, Doug had to identify him. Roy, Truman, and Woody are all back. Eddie, in case you don't know, Doug is a Forward Observer for artillery. He directs the fire for the big guns behind the lines. The OP's are usually on a hill out in front of the Main Line of Resistance."*

**2nd Lt Wally Woods**
**37th Field Artillery Battalion 1952-53**

"I do not recall anything out of the ordinary while enroute to report for my assignment held at the 2nd Infantry Division HQ. We went by a midget Korean troop train this time from Pusan to Uijongbu, a railhead a few miles to the north of Seoul, where all the new players were picked up by truck for transport to their respectively assigned units. Along the way, the ravages of war were quite apparent. Wrecked locomotives here and there, burned out villages, and the cities we passed through, Taegu, Taejon, Osan, and Seoul were nothing but piles of rubble in a dismal, colorless and drab winter setting. Upon arriving at 2nd Division HQ Rear, we were given welcome and greetings by a General Hayden Boatner, assistant Division Commander, who told all present to forget about the Army's rotation policy and any other thoughts we had about going home. The only way we could ever hope to get out of Korea was by medical evacuation or in a mattress cover, which was the same as the high tech term used during the Vietnam War, Body Bag. This was the same Boatner, a crusty old SOB from WWII who gave the exact same speech to Al Woods, my uncle, when he arrived as a medic in the China-Burma-India theater in 1943.

Upon arrival to the 2nd Infantry Division my MOS was that of a tank platoon leader. I had had a lot of good armored training and experience at Fort Knox the previous year. Naturally, I'm thinking that my assignment would be to one of the tank companies in the 9th, or 23rd, or 38th Infantry Regiments, or to the 72nd Tank Battalion of the 2nd Division. How wrong can you get? Boatner pointed out that the Division had had so many Forward Observer casualties in their artillery battalions that we were now officially considered to be FO replacements. HQ was gracious enough to tell us there would be indoctrination for us newly knighted FO's shortly in the form of a small class to be held slightly behind the front lines where we could learn to ply our new trade. During the indoctrination class, each of us new replacements were given the chance to call, adjust, and direct artillery fire on assorted enemy targets out front. While the school was in session, the class did experience some incoming fire as we were evidently too bunched up and presented ourselves as a good target. Being a rookie, I couldn't tell the difference between the sounds of outgoing and incoming tire but this was the first and last time that this would happen. The next time I heard fire either going in or out, I knew without a doubt which kind it was. Our little class lasted two or three days, at which time I then reported to my new assignment, Battery 'C', 37th Field Artillery Battalion as a full fledged and qualified Forward Observer in the eyes of our dearly beloved HQ troops.

It was sometime in mid March that I reported to the Battery. The 37th Field Artillery Battalion was the supporting artillery unit for the 23rd Infantry Regiment of the 2nd Division. In particular, Battery 'C' of the 37th was assigned to provide its FO's to the line Companies of the 3rd Battalion, 23rd Infantry. Fortunately for me, my services as an FO were not required immediately and were not assigned to a line company for approximately a week. The only recollections I can recall from that period are trying to sleep at night while the firing battery was providing friendly patrol support or furnishing H&I fire, and on a Sunday afternoon of that first week, the Battery took some small arms fire from somewhere off to one of its flanks. I asked for, and was granted permission, to take a small patrol up one of the suspect hills to flush out the culprits who were responsible for this enfilading fire. After climbing and searching for about an hour with no results, the game of playing infantry was concluded and we returned. Sometime after that first week, my FO team did get its first combat assignment and I began my new career. My team consisted of a recon sergeant, a radio/telephone operator, a jeep driver, and me. We went to an OP on a relatively quiet area on a moderately high hill that looked out over a rather flat and wide valley floor. I don't remember to which company we were assigned but the sector remained very quiet with little action over a period of a couple of weeks. Shooting up some bunkers off in the distance was about the only major activity in which we became involved. Also during this period, I fired at a live target for the first time, an enemy work party out on the valley floor. Immediately after shooting at them, I physically shook for at least ten minutes until my nerves calmed down. Shooting at people is a totally foreign and incomprehensible undertaking until the necessary realization sinks in that it is all part of a 'you or me' proposition. My shaking experience was a one-time occurrence and it never happened again. This rather sluggish pace of the war lasted until our company, along with the rest of the 23rd Infantry, was rotated off the lines. We came down with our unit and went back to 'C' Battery, not for a respite, but for an immediate reassignment to some other area on the lines. Such is the life of an FO. If you are not required to be with your 'regular' infantry company, you are expected to function in a backup role and provide artillery support in other areas along the Division front, if required. I suppose that if you are not an FO, this is a solid concept of providing maximum firepower to wherever and whenever it is needed. However, we would have liked some of that relief time for ourselves.

I guess we stayed on line through the month of May with a South Korean outfit. These were deceptive folks, our allies who couldn't be trusted beyond your nose. It was always a question of whether or not they would hang around to fight when required or whether they would bug out at the first sign of trouble. All our personal gear had to be watched like a hawk as these 'friendlies' would steal your eyeballs and everything else that wasn't nailed down. This included our carbines, binoculars, .45 pistol, spotter scope, phones, radio, fart sacks, and anything else worth mentioning. Near the end of the month we were finally relieved by elements of the 2nd Infantry Division. We came back to the 37th where everybody in the Battery went through additional training but, in general, we took it easy for the month of June. All was right with the world at this point, three hot meals a day, if you wanted them, PT every morning, weapons cleaning, straightening out ammo supplies for the guns, building new ammo pits and latrines, etc. Although in a reserve roll, the battery was always on constant call for fire missions and we did our fair share around the clock. In mid-July, the Regiment was alerted that they were going back on line. The 2nd Infantry Division was going to relieve the 45th in the Chorwon area and the relief was to be effected around the 16th of July. As such, we FO's who went up in advance of the 23rd to become familiar with the terrain and existing fire patterns, had to strip our 2nd Division patches from our sleeves and replace them with those of the 45th Division before joining the 179th Infantry Regiment. This is done as a precaution in the event of our being captured, the enemy is not supposed to learn that a relief unit is coming on line. I never did hear the complete story of how the Chinese found out about this operation, but during the actual man for man relief on the appointed night, they caught our infantry in the change out and we paid a heavy price especially in the area of hill 266, which later became known as Old Baldy. The 2nd Battalion of the 23rd Infantry was the first of our troops to try to get in place on Baldy and while successful for a night or two, they were finally pushed off after suffering considerable casualties. The 3rd Battalion of the 23rd, Companies I, K, and L were then ordered to take Baldy. I was assigned to 'I' Company. After a few more futile attacks to take and hold the hill, our efforts were also deemed unsuccessful only because we couldn't hold it in the face of the terrific artillery bombardment by the enemy and we had to withdraw. For the next week or two each side pounded the shit out of this hill until it seemed nothing would be left except a mound of soft dirt full of shrapnel. The hill had a saddle that effectively allowed, at times, the good guys on one side and the bad guys on the other.

Pork Chop Hill was about 1000 yards to the east of Baldy. I had been out there on two occasions to reconnoiter the terrain to its front. Our guys out there were not taking the brunt of the fury that was expended on Baldy for most of this period, but just prior to one of the night assaults on Baldy, I think over 3000 rounds of big stuff plastered Pork Chop in a one half hour period. The CO of the 37th Field Artillery said he never before witnessed such a concentration of firepower, even in WWII. It turned out that this bombardment was only a feint to distract from the real assault that followed on Baldy. These events proved that the USAF was completely wrong in their 'tut-tut' statements that claimed that nothing, ammunition, supplies, or anything was getting through to the Chinese because they were bombing and shooting anything that moved on the forward side of our bomb lines. Without a doubt, we were facing a tough, determined, and skillful enemy regardless of what the flyboys said. During this tour for the contested ownership of Baldy and while I was attached to Company 'I', Tommy Miller was assigned as my recon sergeant and we effectively remained an FO team until late October that year. Our RTO's and drivers were constantly being changed and it was my standing decision that the jeep and our driver were to return to the Battery area after making an almost daily run to our OP, if it was accessible, to bring mail, rations, and any special supplies we may have needed.

In late July our FO team was reassigned to our old pals in Company 'I' on hill 347. This hill was located to the right rear of Baldy and to the left rear of Pork Chop. If you think of the letter V, hill 347 would be at the apex with Baldy at the top left and Pork Chop at the top right of the letter. The height of all these hills on military maps is given in meters above sea level so it's easy to see that we were about 90 meters higher than Baldy and 140 meters higher than Pork Chop. We had a commanding view of all the terrain for a few miles around. We were fortunate enough to remain apart from the close in fighting for Baldy at this location but we continued to provide supporting fires wherever and whenever needed. During this period, I remember seeing men from the 1st or 2nd Battalion attacking up the slope toward the crest of Baldy. The attack was bogging down due to a Chinese machine gun that was spraying the slope with grazing fire. This machine gun was on a small four-wheeled carriage and was located in a fairly well camouflaged and protected hole that was dug into the same slope that our troops were attacking. The Chink gunner would periodically push this machine gun out of the hole, spray the slope, and then pull back to safety. On 347, our guys from Item Company were firing their 57mm recoilless rifle, Mike Company guys were there also firing their 75mm recoilless rifle, and I was calling in precision destruction missions from the 105's of the 37th. Not one of us hit that SOB or his bunker with all our high-powered ordnance. During this time I was informed of an Air Force flight of two F-80's that was in the area and that they were available to support us. Battalion agreed to use these planes and requested me to mark the Chinese machine gun location with smoke rounds so the planes could attack with their bombs and/or napalm. We had red smoke fired at the location and the smoke canisters landed within 10-15 yards of the target. We then waited for the coming air show. The planes flew in and went into their attack mode. This routine meant that they would fly a figure eight over the target area and drop their ordnance while diving on the down legs of the figure eight. What a waste! These guys were pulling out of their dives so high up that when they let their ordnance go, all this stuff tumbled to the right, left, and to the rear. An explosion from a 100 or 500 pounder is a major happening when you are close by. You can actually see the shock wave coming at you, it looks like a huge bubble expanding at a fantastic rate of speed and you are in its path. If you aren't in a prone position at this time, it will knock you over. Additionally napalm is a nifty piece of ordnance to have in your bag of tricks if it is used on your enemies. Fortunately, this stuff didn't land directly on us to cause burns or suffocation, but it came close enough for us to feel the heat and the rush of air being sucked into the fireball. Were we scared? You bet! Grenades finally took out the machine gun from the attacking troops. Many, many dollars were expended for the same purpose, but in the end, the infantry did its time-honored job without fanfare.

While providing supporting fires for other friendly attacks up the slopes of Baldy, I remember watching a Chink carrying a satchel charge run out of his bunker near the crest. He ran right up to one of our buttoned-up tanks advancing just in front of the infantry and tossed this charge at one of the tank's tracks and then zipped back inside his bunker. How he managed to get through the hail of small arms fire directed at him and disable that Sherman M4 tank was some kind of Chinese miracle. During one of these episodes in a Baldy support role, a second FO from Battery 'B' of the 37th came up to our OP, why he came I don't remember. What I do remember is that during one of the 23rd's attacks to retake Baldy, both of us were watching out the bunker aperture when a round of high velocity gunfire hit close by. After the crunch of the explosion, I heard the familiar pulsating whizzing sound of the shards coming at us followed by a 'thok' just off my right shoulder. It sounded exactly like a ripe grapefruit being smacked. This visiting FO was hit by a piece of shrapnel in the forehead. Fortunately, the shard's violent energy was spent by the time it hit him, and although it did not penetrate his skull, he did bleed profusely. I patched his head with the bandage from his first aid pouch and sent him on his way down to the medics. The whole campaign for Baldy is somewhat hazy but a few happenings do standout. During the fighting I was winged in the hand and arm but it was of such minor consequence, I did not consider it reportable. What I vividly remember is that while on an advanced OP at a place called Checkpoint Easy for three or four days after we had been pushed off Baldy, the bunker I occupied took a wallop that was unbelievable. Checkpoint Easy was a moderate lump of earth on a small ridgeline or finger that ran straight to Baldy. It was the most forward point that the 23rd held when the Chinese were in control of Baldy some 300-400 yards to the front of us. When this particular round landed, we lost all our radio and phone communication back to the battery. It was a round of really large caliber and it landed just in front of the slit aperture of the bunker. The horrendous noise of the explosion and concussion were unlike anything I had experienced before or since, and I was hurled to the rear of the bunker and I was dazed or quite possibly unconscious for a short period. When my senses finally began to return and I could begin to see again, everything was red and remained so for a quite a number of minutes until all cleared and left me with a king-sized headache and a loud ringing in my ears. We stayed for about three or four days on Checkpoint Easy and due to its location and activity, there was no re-supply. While living there and in consideration for your own safety, a wise choice was to urinate in your canteen cup and toss the contents out through the aperture at night, and any other normal bodily functions were ignored for the duration. Constipation was acceptable.

During this time on 347, we had a small bunker for our OP that was located approximately 25 yards from the crest of the hill. The forward half of the bunker was for FO business and the rear half was to function as our sleeping quarters. I suspect the Chinks must have known this OP because we seemed to take an inordinate amount of incoming day after day. Perhaps they spotted our radio antenna poking over the ridgeline. In any case, the sleeping quarters were such that if it was your turn to get some sleep, you had to literally slither into a dugout and totally claustrophobic space that was just long enough and wide enough for one body. Your head protruded into the OP or fighting portion of the bunker but when you looked up, all you could see was this huge load of dirt ready to collapse if any incoming came too close and dislodged it. Sleeping under these circumstances for about a week or so inspired me to want to build a new bunker further up the slope and nearer to the crest. This we did, however, my memories of those dugout-sleeping quarters still bothers me to this day. We built our new bunker near the crest of 347, just barely on the forward slope. We had a lot of help from the 37th who sent a lot of men who were willing to help us as long as they got the chance to 'get up on the front lines to see for themselves what it was all about.' We did not get the same crew everyday and I'm, sure if they had the chance, they would have declined. Being in a work party which was a perfect sitting target, squelched their further curiosity about life at the front. For about three days while the construction was in progress, we would take sonic daily high-powered gunfire, rather than the high-angled stuff, as the Chinese attempted to discourage our project. On one occasion of shelling, I do remember leaping from just outside the perimeter of the hole being dug directly onto the back of one of the guys who was digging about six feet below. Luck was with us as neither of us suffered any broken bones, although whoever that was at the bottom of the pit surely had some aches and pains to nurse for the next couple of days! When the bunker was completed, we were much more comfortable for the duration of our stay on 347. The bunker was at least six feet deep at the front end where the aperture was and about five feet across the front and four feet back to the start of our living quarters. We had plenty of room to move about with our scopes, weapons, phones, radio, wire reels, and other assorted FO equipment. The living quarters were about six feet long and were as wide as the front end five feet. In these quarters, we rigged up a double deck bunk arrangement made from approximately six-foot poles that were strung with commo wire to support our bedrolls. The lower space was used as our 'sofa' and a place to stow our personal gear while the upper portion was for sleeping. The roof was made of logs laid in two directions perpendicular to each other and then lined with ponchos for weatherproofing before piling on about five or six layers of sandbags. It is interesting to note that it only took a matter of days before the rats could be heard scurrying around all throughout the overhead. And when the smell of rat excrement became too bad, our option was to sprinkle Mennen's aftershave lotion sent up from the Battalion PX to mask the stink.

Cooking was done over a candle on the floor, or if we were lucky, we had sterno cans sent up from the Battery. Our meals that were brought to us by our Jeep driver were the famous or infamous C-Rations, never had so many variations of beans in my life before or since. There were beans with, tomatoes, beans with hot dogs, beans with pork, beans with, ham, arid on and on. There was also a cruddy can of sausage patties that were absolutely gross, tasteless, lumpy, and dripping in grease. It was not until many years later, well into the 1970's, that I could or would eat beef and noodles. For some reason at the time, We had no provisions for cooking or heating the beef and noodles, so when you devoured this tasty mess with your canteen spoon, it came out of the can as cold, solid, jellied white grease carrying some stringy meat and grease coated noodles. You didn't have to chew, it slipped down your throat with lightning speed. We also had our fair share of Spam and there were some number 10 cans of shredded pork that the kitchen sent up that weren't too bad. Care packages would arrive from my Ma and Grandma on a fairly regular basis. These packages would contain salamis, cookies, cheese, bouillon cubes, and other dry soups. I lived on those little bouillon cubes for days on end.

After moving into our new home, we received a daily 5:00pm visit from some Chinese gunners who would drive a self-propelled gun from behind a hill mass that was a couple of thousand yards to our left front. These were probably the same guys who were taking pot shots at us while the bunker was under construction. They would quickly fire off three or four rounds and then disappear back behind the hill before any counter battery fire could be brought to bear. Because this became a routine each afternoon, we would start getting jumpy in anticipation. Calls to the 37th Battalion S-2 intelligence section were a joke. The only time they showed any interest in our status was when we kept them on the phone while we were being shelled. When they heard the near misses and explosions, they acknowledged that perhaps some of the FO's in adjacent line companies should try to bring this Chink gun under fire. Obviously, battalion S-2 HQ types did not endear themselves to us. The shelling routine lasted about a week. We and our adjacent FO buddies never did get him, always too little and too late.

Throughout the month of August, I didn't participate in any new major battles. All action in the 3rd Battalion 23rd Infantry was patrolling, raiding, ambushing, and reconnaissance. The summer had been approaching its peak hot weather in the latter weeks of July and by the time August rolled around, temperatures was in the 100-degree range. The monsoon season was beginning and boy, it rained! These were hard driving soakers on a daily basis and they turned everything into a sea of mud, literally. If you weren't careful, stepping in the wrong place could mean having your boots sucked right off your feet. It would be knee-deep in places and when trucks and jeeps got mired down, it was a major effort to get the vehicles moving again. Over in the French Battalion area to our right, particularly around T-Bone hill and the Alligator Jaws, they were having a catastrophic time with their bunkers which were collapsing and killing the occupants. It was bad enough to fight the Chinese without having to worry about your immediate environment. Depending where you were at any given time, it may have meant that you had to hay in the shallowest part of the puddles in order to get some sleep. This happened on numerous occasions when we had to move to other bunkers in the company area so we could see and have direct communications with the nightly patrolling activities. There were some nights when all patrol activity was canceled because of the mud and/or swollen streams that were not fordable. Dry out time did not arrive until hate August and early September. Korea is a land of stark contrasts, monsoons in the summer with temperatures that can get to 120 and in the winter, it takes on the howling winds and snows out of Manchuria that drop the temperatures to 30 below zero. Firing weapons in this frigid cold poses all kinds of problems, small arms tend to jam and in the case of the 105 howitzers, the guns do not go back into battery for two or so minutes after firing one round due to the temperature-induced highly increased viscosity of the oil in the recoil system. This is a serious condition to occur when a lot of artillery fire is needed to support a critical field operation.

Sometime during this month, I was called by 37th Battalion HQ and was ordered to report to a tank unit that was marshaling in an area off to the right and rear of the 23rd Infantry sector. The division brass had formulated a plan to stage a tank company raid into the valley out front to shoot up Chink bunkers and other targets of opportunity. Division wanted an FO to go along to call in artillery as a supplement to the tank gunnery, so what a natural choice for them to get an FO who had limited 'experience' in armored operation from Fort Knox the year before. At least I was familiar with the M-4 Sherman tanks because that was all we had at Fort Knox, leftovers from WWII. I remember us leaving the assembly area about 10:00am and returning about 6:00pm. My code name for radio communication to 37th fire control was 'MARIGOLD', and after trying for the first two or so hours into this exercise, I found that I could not raise the 37th fire control nor anybody else. So any artillery 'on the spot' support went out the window. In effect, I just went along for the ride. A Piper Cub liaison plane from 37th was flying overhead trying to reach me, which I found out that night, without any success. Everybody could hear me calling but I couldn't receive any radio traffic on the radio I had on board. The tank commander, who was a Sergeant, was not too happy that I took the 76mm gun loader's position which was at the left turret hatch for my OP and I hoped that we wouldn't run into any trouble. We did take some mortar fire but we were pretty well impervious to it as it was small caliber stuff and I recall us buttoning up the hatches for a short period until the mortars stopped. These tank raiders did a lot of shooting and tore up a considerable number of bunkers and installations that had been previously beyond our normal observation. I'm sure it was a complete surprise to the Chinese to see twenty tanks on the move toward their positions. All did go fairly well but we did have two of these tanks break down and they had to be rescued by a tank retriever.

During my tour with the 23rd in August or early September, the 3rd Infantry Division was on line to our immediate left. One particular night, there was a terrific ruckus just beyond the 23rd's left boundary at a place called Kelly Hill. Somebody out there was taking an awesome shellacking and when the pounding ceased and all went quiet, everything apparently returned to normal. However, when talking to Battalion HQ Fire Direction Center later that night, we were informed that the Chinks took the hill, captured the entire infantry company, and disappeared back into their lines leaving only the US casualties behind. While on 347 in August, Item Company was periodically taken under high angle fire from somewhere out to our front. It was large caliber fire, more than likely from their 80mm mortars. We only had an idea where it was coming from because it was high angle ordnance and it was well hidden behind a hill out of our sight. In the time frame that this was happening, 37th HQ asked if we wanted help from some aircraft that were available and in the area. We responded that we did and were told that we would see a couple of Marine aircraft, F4U Corsairs, shortly. These planes were the gull-winged prop driven fighters or fighter bombers that the Navy and Marines had in WWII in the South Pacific. As before, we marked the proximity of the mortars position as well as we could with smoke rounds. The aircraft liaison officer at 37th HQ must have told the pilots that the smoke was only a general area because we, on the line, could not actually see the mortars. The planes made a flyover in the general vicinity of the smoke and then took off out of sight. It must have been a few minutes later when we heard them come screaming in at low level, dodging hills heft and right, and swooping in at the target. The first plane was firing Mickey Mouse rockets, these were highly unsophisticated by today's standards, but they sure tore up whatever they hit and the surrounding area. The second plane that followed by a minute or so, dropped a load of napalm, so much for the Chinese mortars, never heard from them again!

Every night a new password and counter password was given to all the troops on the line. This lets patrols go out, remain on their objective for however long is required, and return through our lines safely. It is also used by the people such as noncoms and officers making their nightly rounds to all positions as they travel through the commo and fighting trenches. In one instance while on 347, a CO was going from his place to another when he was challenged by someone in a bunker built just off one of the trenches on the forward slope. A lesson was well learned by this traveler, who when challenged, was supposed to respond with the password. He cane back with the snappy statement, 'Bullshit!', and was promptly shot in the stomach.

The 23rd Infantry regiment was again pulled off the line to go into reserve for rehab, replenishment of troops, and training sometime in Mid-September and our FO team was sent up to go on line with the 31st Infantry Regiment, 7th Infantry Division. We changed out our patches again and reported to a new OP much further to the right or east of the Old Baldy area. The weather was comfortable and everything remained quiet until the end of the month when activity started picking up. In the area of hill 281 and White Horse Mountain, we were finally joined by our old pals in the 23rd Infantry in late September, when they came on line and swapped out positions with the units of the 31st. This time our FO team was attached to Company 'K' and we occupied a small and quite low hill mass that was slightly east of 281 and south of White Horse. White Horse was held by units of a South Korean Division and this was always cause for my concern as they never really did distinguish themselves to be a reliable and steadfast neighbor. In early October while on our OP in this new sector and when daylight was rapidly failing, we spotted a 90+ man Chinese patrol advancing towards us in a single file. There was absolutely no mistake about this number as we watched them in our spotter scope and binoculars. They were silhouetted one by one as the file came over a ridge line, hence the count was accurate. They were proceeding on a route that would take them through a known and plotted artillery concentration point that we had previously registered approximately 300-400 yards to our front. I called the 37th Fire Control and gave them our fire mission with the stipulation that they would only fire on my command. When the bulk of the Chinese were estimated to he crossing the concentration point, I called for 'Fire for Effect'. The 37th HQ's assessment of the target composition had allocated all three firing batteries with three rounds per gun, 54 total, of VT fused HE. VT is a Variable Time fuse that works on the principle of radar, it sends out its own signal forward of the shell while in flight. When it receives an echo that it is nearing target, it explodes the shell before there is any actual contact with the target. It amounts to an air burst about 20-25 yards over the target. As we did not get probed nor into any firefight that night, we assumed we had discouraged their aggressive plans for the evening. After so many months on the line, we learned that the nature of the Chinese was somewhat predictable so we assumed that they may try the exact same scenario on the following night. We were not disappointed, they came into the same concentration point and got themselves shot up again. We were neither probed nor sucked into a firefight that night either.

Sometimes things come in threes, so we expected a repeat of the first two nights to reoccur for the third night running. For this 3rd night we thought we could make good use of a searchlight truck, which we called 'Moon' that was located to our heft and could he available. We requested through Battalion HQ that the 'Moon' move to a position that would allow them to aim their beam directly on the deadly pre-plotted concentration point that night. The 'Moon' got into position that afternoon and zeroed in on the concentration point. Prior to dusk, I called Fire Control to alert them for repeat performances this coming evening. At dusk, the Chinks were on the move toward us again. I called Fire Control with the fire mission and also told 'Moon' to standby. When this bunch filed into the concentration point, I called for 'Fire for Effect' and the entire Battalion again fired three rounds from all the guns. I immediately called for cease fire to allow the Chinese medics and sweeper-uppers to arrive on the scene and begin their cleanup operations and evacuation of the casualties. In about 15-20 minutes, when their cleanup operations were estimated to be in full swing, I called for the 37th to 'Fire for Effect' again. When the first of the 54 round volley whistled overhead on the way out, I called for 'Moon' to turn on. The Chinese were startled by the brilliant light and just as they hooked up to see what this light was all about, they were clobbered. There were bodies and body parts flying all over the place as they too were caught in the open. When this action took place and we already had blown the Chinese away, I remember calling back to fire control, 'Cease fire, Cease fire!', but Division Artillery must have been so excited and geared up to destroy a crowd like this, the shells kept landing for at least five minutes after the first 'Cease fire.' Again, no personal remorse, it's either me or him and he had been having a good time trying to nail me down. This was the last night that they attempted to do whatever it was they had planned and, of course, no probe or firefight the 3rd night either.

As part of the United Nations effort on Korea, the 2nd Infantry Division was augmented with troops from France, Thailand, and the Netherlands. Other US infantry divisions in Korea were augmented by similar forces from other participating UN nations. These countries sent token forces, usually Battalion-sized units. In our 2nd Infantry Division, the 9th US Infantry Regiment had the attached Thailanders, the 38th US Infantry Regiment had the attached Netherlands detachment, and the 23rd US Infantry Regiment had as its attached foreign troops, a battalion of French infantry. Because the UN nations were sending only infantry units, the US divisions were providing almost all the rest of the required support functions for these troops and this included artillery Forward Observers. Early in the afternoon of 6 Oct, our FO team received a call from 37th Field Artillery HQ to report to 'N' Company of the French Battalion that was up on hill 281 over on our left. We were being sent up to replace Luke LeFevre and his entire FO party, they had just been hit. We were being replaced in King Company by another FO party that was on its way up to our OP. Hill 281 had been taking a constant and steady pounding all day long and the bombardment was considered to be some kind of a softening up process for a major effort by the Chinese soon to begin. This info had been gleaned by Division Intelligence in the past few' days. The French had reinforced 'N' Company with an assortment of troops from their Battalion staff along with a platoon of US combat engineers. These engineers and HQ personnel were on an outpost which was on a small rise some 300 yards down the forward slope of 281. All totaled, they must have had about 225-250 troops up there on that afternoon. We left to go back to Charley Battery to get what supplies we thought we needed then took off for 281 by jeep. On a map, the contour lines of 281 resemble an arrowhead, it is a hill mass that's eastern, southern, and western perimeters are defined by a river named the Yokkok-Chon. Hill 281 sat across this river isolated from the rest of the 23rd Infantry and was considered a thorn in the side of the Chinese. Upstream, the Yokkok-Chon is fed by the Pongnoe Reservoir which the Chinks fully opened on the night of 6 Oct in an effort to flood the area and cut off all reinforcements to the troops on 281. The small pontoon bridge that we crossed at the rear base of 281 that afternoon was washed out later and really isolated us but we didn't know it at the time. After dismounting and sending the jeep back to the Battery, we began our climb up the hill to report in as the replacement team. The ascent was a difficult, scary, and arduous exercise. For about every ten steps taken, it was hit the dirt because if incoming. The hill was under constant and intensive bombardment all day and many of those incoming shells were just missing the crest and falling on the reverse slope that we were climbing. For the whole journey to the top, we were pelted, showered, and blasted with dirt, rocks, and shrapnel. Upon reaching the top, we reported in to the major who was in command and were dispatched to the right side of the crest where we set up shop. On our way to the right side of the crest, I only remember running past a 75mm recoilless rifle that was blasting away to the front from just behind the crest.

Believe it or not, the intensity of the incoming shelling kept increasing until darkness set in and at that point, it really went wild. The Chinese assaults began using their infamous human wave tactics and they sent about seven waves at us that night. We were fortunate enough to get the magic words, 'final barrage', back to the 37th Fire Control before our phones went dead. Once again, the radio, our backup, took a crunch and was of no use to us. This had to have been near 8:00pm and until well into the morning hours, about 3:00 or 4:00am, our artillery pounded the forward slopes with everything in the book. When the word 'barrage' is sent back, it is the signal for the batteries to fire continuously until a notified by a cease fire command. They will fire HE, white phosphorus, smoke, illumination, and anything else they have left in the ammo pits. We had reestablished communication with the 37th by relaying messages through the Infantry via their commo nets that were working. I am incapable of describing the scene as the Chinese assaults were carried out. The enemy is pounding your defenses and trenches at the top of the hill and we are blasting the forward slopes with all the fire power we can muster. The combined bombardment of this area for hours at a time is a continuous series of flashes, explosions, reports, concussions, inconceivable noise, earthen upheavals, dust, and showers of dust, rocks, and shards. And the small arms fire is snapping all about. To communicate with someone almost standing by your side, you had to shout and even this was no guarantee that you would be understood. When crawling around in these commo trenches which were dug about waist deep, in the darkness when flares were not being fired, it was almost a given that you would bump into bodies, some of which, would moan while others would be silent.

From our position on that first night, we could see the attackers coming en masse after they had overrun the outpost manned by the Engineers and HQ troops. Beginning with the first enemy human wave assault and all the assaults that followed, both Army Air and supporting artillery and mortars were giving us illumination. The Army Air was using a Piper Cub type plane circling overhead to drop flares and the 155mm Divisional Artillery guns were shooting illumination rounds. These illumination rounds would 'pop' and ignite about 100 yards in the air on a parachute and provide brilliant intense light over the whole area until either the flare went out or the chute drifted away. From where we were when the 'pop' was heard, we had to duck down immediately because the canister that carried the chute and flare would go screaming by and plow into the hill a few yards away. It sounded as though the canister was going to take your head off. Our infantry and artillery were chewing up the Chinese pretty badly throughout these attacks but the effort was only 99% effective, some Chinks who managed to survive our firepower were getting close. Personally, we were firing our carbines and tossing grenades until the grenade supply ran out. The word was sent back for more grenades and a couple of wooden boxes were finally brought up. Unfortunately, neither of these boxes contained any fuses. We had grenades but couldn't use then. Talk about loose bowels! A couple of boxes of fuses were brought up later and then we could start assembling the grenades that were so badly needed. Some of these Chinese were getting so close that we were pulling the pins on the grenades, letting the handle pop off, and then counting for three or four seconds before pushing or rolling it over the edges of the trenches. We had to trust these fuses absolutely, they were supposed to have a seven second burn time. One single, solitary, battered, and bleeding engineer escaped from the outpost slaughter and worked his way back to our main positions. He was fortunate enough to survive the Chinese assault and the small arms fire from our main position. Tommy Miller still remembers shooting at this poor guy. This bewildered and bespectacled engineer finally did make it to safety and went to the rear. Sometime hater that night, William Harmon, our RTO, went over to a nearby machine gun emplacement, the crew of which all had been killed or wounded. He took over as gunner and stayed on for the rest of the night. Initially, Tommy Miller and I helped re-supply the gun with ammo. Tommy then stayed on with Harmon as both assistant gunner and ammo re-supplier for the remainder of the night throughout the rest of the assaults. By daylight the next morning on 7 Oct, the attacks had subsided and I headed back to the Command Post on the heft side of the hill taking the reverse of the route as the night before. I passed the 75 recoilless rifle I had seen the previous night, it was abandoned at the edge of the defensive position and the front half of its barrel was peeled back just like a fresh banana, except the banana was missing. The rifle had either taken a shot right up the muzzle or it had a premature round go off while it was on us way out of the tube.

As mentioned before elsewhere, some of the Chinese actions were predictable. So it was that their attacking human wave tactics were employed for the next three nights through 10 Oct. All of these nights in this period were duplicates of the initial effort of 6 Oct. What a nightmare, it felt like our luck had run out and our chances of survival were slim or none. It was a standard Chinese practice in their night attacks to throw seven waves of infantry rushing directly behind their own artillery and mortar barrages. Of these seven waves, only the first three waves were given weapons, the succeeding waves were to pick up the weapons laying in the field that were dropped by their fallen comrades en route to their objective. So if you had been a Chinaman and were give a rifle or some other weapon just prior to an assault, you may have realized that something quite bad was in the works. The 7th and last wave of attackers was usually committed to the assault by 3:00 or 4:00am.

On about the third day, at sometime in the afternoon when action was in a lull, one of the French lieutenants took a patrol to the 281 outpost on the forward slope. The patrol was to bring back the weapons and some of the other gear that our men had with them when they were KIA and overrun on the night of 6 Oct. They left armed to the teeth along with surgical masks to be saturated with spirits of cloves to hide the powerful death odor. The whole area we occupied on 281 was engulfed in this overwhelming sickening and sweet smell from all the dismembered and bloated dead bodies lying around. In support of this patrol activity, we provided smoke rounds fired on approximately ten or fifteen suspected Chinese OP's in order to hide the patrol's maneuvers. On the night of 6 Oct, reinforcements were sent upon 281. King Company had been ordered to send up two platoons to reinforce 'N' Company and it was a welcome sight to see additional troops arrive at the top of 281. They had just made it to the top when a friend of mine, Walt McKellar, was killed. He was a platoon leader in Company 'K' when a tiny fragment of a mortar round got him in the head and he probably lived about five minutes after going down. He and I became friends back in May or June when, just by chance, we sat next to each other at one of the 3rd Battalion outdoor church services, the kind where the altar is the hood of a jeep. He was single and his family lived in Abbeville, SC. He also had a sister who lived in Chicago. I have no idea how I got his address but after I returned to the states, I wrote to the family and attempted to explain what happened to Mac along with how I felt from my own personal loss. I didn't trust the CO of 'K' Company to do the same as he didn't like Mac at all and was forever giving him a hard time.

The holding of 281 was not accomplished without considerable casualties to that reinforced 'N' company. Tommy Miller said he recalls hearing that there were only 60+ survivors, but the figure I remember hearing was 80+. It doesn't really matter which figure is correct, both of us survived and walked off. Here again, Tommy and I were carried as MIA's until we surprised our replacement team on or about 10 Oct. The ending of the battle for 281 was my last intense combat assignment as a Forward Observer. The 37th Field Artillery was getting replacement FO's from the states and I was recalled to Charley Battery to take over as Exec Officer. That was really the first good news I received in a long, long time. Tommy Miller stayed on as a Recon Sergeant and was assigned to Phil Snyder, one of the new FO rookies, who sure benefited from Tom's hard earned lessons of the immediate past. About a week after the heavy fighting for Baldy ceased, I was reading accounts of this battle in the Stars and Stripes when it dawned on me that this was the place known to us as hill 266. The press must have given it the name of Baldy and it certainly was a picturesque description as there wasn't a stick of vegetation left on its slopes after the first few days of the heavy fighting."

**2nd Lt Gerald Wilcomb**
**58th Field Artillery Battalion 1952**

"The most exciting day of my life covered the short period of association I had with 1st Lt Willis Cronkite, 65th Infantry Regiment, on or roughly between 0700 to 1900 hours, 28 October 1952. About twelve hours out of my life, most of which I consider as borrowed time. Also, our entire association that day was also spent between our Outpost Line of Resistance and that of the Chinese... pure 'NO Man's Land. I arrived in country somewhere around the second week of September, and was assigned as a Forward Observer with Battery 'B', 58th Field Artillery Battalion, 3rd Infantry Division. My battalion provided direct support artillery fire for the 65th Infantry Regiment. The night before I arrived at the 3rd Infantry Division, Company B, 65th Infantry Regiment had been overrun on 'Kelly' Hill in the Imjin River sector. I do know that the 58th Field Artillery Battalion Forward Observers, Lts. Hanby and Smith, were captured along with many B Company troops. This put a crimp in the battalion's FO resources and because of this I did not benefit from the battalion's policy of putting a new guy with an old guy for a couple of weeks to break him in. I was assigned the next day as FO for the 3rd Reconnaissance Company. They anchored the division's left flank between the 65th Regiment and the British Commonwealth Division. This company had extraordinary organic fire support capabilities. Every man had an automatic weapon of the some kind and there were many ground mounted .30 and .50 cal machine guns that had been removed from their light tanks that they had cached in the rear somewhere. Attached twin .50 sections from the 3rd AAA Battalion and a fifteen man British artillery liaison party headed by a captain were also in the company area. When the company fired final protective fires it was really something to see. The Chinks didn't mess with them too often. It was a good place to figure out what a FO's job was all about. We had a good overview of Kelly Hill to the east and were able to provide some good supporting fire for the 65th Infantry during their trying times at Kelly. I recall the Greek Battalion marched up to the rest of Kelly and our Air Force dumped a load of bombs on them. They then marched off saying, I'm sure, the Greek equivalent of screw it'.

These salad days ended towards the end of September when the 3rd Division went into reserve and was replaced on line by the Republic of Korea 'ROK' 2nd Infantry Division. I remained in this same position because the artillery was never placed in reserve. I was then sent closer to the Imjin River to a battalion OP across from Big Nori and Little Nori in what had previously been the 3rd Division's eastern sector. For some reason the Greek battalion was also there although it was 2nd ROK Division country. I got to witness a whole raft of small battles, in relative safety, on the likes of Kelly, Cavite, Nick , Tessie, Betty and Big and Little Nori... a great enfilade view and I got in some great fire missions. After a week or so of this, the 3rd Division Artillery moved overnight about forty miles east to the Chorwon Valley. It was still dark when I got to Chorwon Valley. My assignment was to establish a 58th Field Artillery Battalion Observation post on Hill 300 which sat dead center in the valley. This was the 9th ROK Division sector and they were up to their ears in taking and retaking White Horse Mountain. The French Battalion was hanging on at the adjoining Arrowhead Ridge. The valley was almost deserted of friendly infantry and my F O team was the only unit in residence on Hill 300. About mid October, right after the battle for White Horse Mountain died down, the 9th ROK began to fight to regain Hill 391 on their eastern flank. Where Whitehorse had been three miles to my left, Hill 391 was three miles to my right. As I was soon to become painfully aware, Jackson Heights was the southern promontory of 391. I don't know where the 3rd Infantry Division Regiments were at this time. The 9th ROK had quite a 'dust up' going on at Hill 391 for about five days. The Chinks finally ran the ROK battalion off the hill and that battalion then moved to my location on Hill 300 to lick its wounds. I asked the battalion commander, a major, where they'd come from and he pointed at Hill 391, drew his finger across his throat and promptly went on a two day drunk where he did nothing but sit on a wooden case of .45 ammo and fire his pistol at C Ration cans until the ammo box ran dry.

About the 24th or so of October, the 65th Infantry came on line and I joined 'E' Company as Forward Observer. After five weeks on line I had finally married up with the 65th for the first time. I'm not really sure exactly where we were, but it was closer to hill 391 than I had been before. For the next three days we could sort of observe the flap the 65th Infantry was having on Hill 391. I know now this was 'G' Company and Captain Jackson going at it. We could follow part of it on our FM radio. Sometime after dark on the 27th I was told to report to my battalion headquarters, where I'd never slept, pick up a different reconnaissance sergeant and radio man, draw a radio and some wire, and join Company 'F', 65th Infantry in time to jump off at dawn the 28th to retake a hill. I spent the entire night finding my battalion headquarters, drawing equipment, meeting my team, and finding Company 'F' which was commanded by Lt. Cronkite. My jeep had no starter so I kept it running all night. My watch had gotten dirty and had been plugged up for a long while so I didn't know exactly, except by guessing at the sun, when I was where. I was dog tired, and had no sleep. My plan was to accompany him with my radio man and for my Reconnaissance Sergeant to carry a pack board with which he could pay out two MX/306 donut rolls of telephone wire. The radio was a backbreaking SCR 610 that could be carried in two loads (battery pack and radio) or in one load in operating mode strapped to a pack board. The load tipped a man over backwards because it rode low on the back. It was a two preset crystal channel affair with a rigid antenna, and not even as remotely easy to carry as the infantry's SCR300. I carried my map, which consisted of four loose map sheets, binoculars, one EE8 telephone, and two carbines, mine and the radioman's. The Recon Sergeant had a carbine, the wire and another EE8. The radioman also carried our SOI code book, I might add.

I think I found Lt Cronkite just south of Outpost Tom, about 0630 in the morning and Company F were just about to hit for the line of departure. He greeted me very civilly, said to stay with him, and off we went down the 'primrose path' through the minefields and wire. Supposedly preparation fires had already been laid on by the 58th Field Artillery, I guess they were fired, I don't remember looking for them. As we approached OP Tom I observed Lt. Smith, a black officer from my battery, coming towards us. His face was covered with band aids and he looked like hell. He wished me good luck and continued on. It was a very sobering moment. Within minutes 82mm and 120mm mortar rounds were dropping all around us. I suspect 76mm direct fire artillery as well. I remember doggedly trying to keep up, and periodically diving behind a boulder or paddy dike or anything. It was terrifying in that mortar blasts are so loud and you couldn't tell when they were coming in. I then remember heavy automatic weapons fire coming at us. I swear to this day I could see bullets in the air and I don't mean just the tracers. A man ahead of me went down and was yelling like hell. The Lt asked a sergeant to check him out and he motioned he'd been grazed on the thigh. We hugged a dike for a few minutes. I could not see my radio man, but the recon sergeant indicated he may have gotten hung up in the wire. We took off towards the base of the hill and I recall I took refuge behind a rock wall in what might have been an orchard at one time. The wire line was being chewed up by the mortars so the recon sergeant started back, policing and splicing the line. I grabbed what was left of the remaining donut roll and continued laying it as we went. I looked up and saw the assault platoon running up the hill. As I started running up the hill machine gun bullets started hitting around me, and I hit the dirt on the hillside and both carbines I was carrying crossed underneath my chest forming sort of a bipod keeping me in a nearly erect position. I really felt stupid and hoped no one was watching, and promptly chucked my radioman's carbine at that point and continued up the hill. It was rather quiet except for some rifle fire to the north east. I recall the Lt was walking around, looking over the crest and generally taking in the situation. Somewhere along the line he pointed to a small bunker and said I could have it. A nice gesture I thought. It was about two feet deep and had been pretty much hacked out of solid rock. It also contained the body of a 'G' Company staff sergeant, who had apparently been killed the night before. I could only get half way in. It was useless as on OP because it faced the wrong way, or to even fight from for that matter, so I left it. I guess about 10 or 11 o'clock things quieted down a bit. I recall Lt. Gibbs, carrying a M1 rifle, checking in with Lt. Cronkite and mentioned he had shot a Chink during the assault. I mentioned the OP bunker had a body in it and he apologized. I thought 'Hey, he's alright'. About this time I had begun to lose my second wind. Lack of sleep was making me see spots and I was mad because I had no communications, just an unconnected telephone. I was dog tired, the sun seemed to be hot as hell although it was the end of October, and I was hungry. The dead sergeant in the bunker had a can of spaghetti and meat balls in his jacket next to the wound that had killed him, I thought the wound had probably contaminated the can thus making it inedible, so I didn't take it. That shows the way a tired man thinks.

Around noon or so I was sitting on a small ledge about two feet square, just trying to keep from sliding off the mountain. Jackson Heights was a steep uplifted slab of granite with no dirt to dig in. A squad of troops was sitting around me. Suddenly I think 61mm mortar or rifle grenade hit about three feet below me. It lifted me a few feet up the hill, but the small ledge had kept shrapnel from hitting me. It started my ears ringing and they rang for days. I dusted myself off and looked at my watch. It was running after being clogged all the time. Three or four of the troops received small flecks of shrapnel in the face and started leaving the hill. Some unwounded troops started helping them down which sort of gave them a legal ticket off the hill. One soldier, the only one carrying a carbine, looked at me, gave me the magazine out of his carbine, and took off after the others. I walked around in a daze for a bit and I looked down and saw a helmet lying on the ground. It had my battalion's crest on one side, the 3rd Division patch on the other and a second lieutenant's bar in the middle. I figured this was Lt. Smith's helmet that he must have lost the night before. I picked it up planning to take it back to him, because I recall it cost about five bucks to have all that art work applied. Sometime later someone suggest I put my steel pot on top of the helmet liner I was wearing. Again, the way a tired man operates.

Sometime in the early afternoon I recall Lt. Porterfield, 'A' Company Commander, and Lt. Glasgow 'A' Company FO coming up the hill. I wasn't aware 'A' Company was even included in this 'dust up' until I saw them. Porterfield was wearing the first armored vest I had ever seen. He apparently had enough points to rotate but volunteered for one more shot at glory. I wondered what his troops thought of the 'old man' wearing the only vest in the outfit. Lt. Glasgow had brought with him a SCR-619 radio, similar to the infantry SCR 300 in size and much more portable than the clunker I had been given. About this time I also recall the weapons platoon leader, a Lt. Doan, or Doane, came up the hill to check out the situation. He seemed to be a frisky 'Teddy Roosevelt' sort of guy. Meanwhile, 'F' Company troop strength seemed to be dwindling away. I presume 'A' Company had arrived with two platoons, but I couldn't say for sure I ever saw them. Every wounded man seemed to be getting more and more help getting back. The hill was solid rock so every incoming round detonated above the surface. There was no soil to absorb any of it, so each round maximized blast, shrapnel, and noise. Plus, they threw rocks around which was just as bad.

I sat down on a ledge next to Lt. Glasgow who was next to Lt. Porterfield. Lt. Gibbs sat on the other side of Porterfield. There appeared to be some confusion from the battalion as to which company would stay over night and which would return to the line. Initially 'A' Company was told it would remain and I thought that was one great decision. I gave Lt. Glasgow most of my cigarettes, my telephone (which I kept on my lap for protection), and whatever else I might have had that he could use. Then the word came that 'F' Company was to stay and 'A' Company would go back. I took back all favorable thoughts I may have had about the infantry's decision making process. I really did believe that if I ever went to sleep on that hill, I'd never see the light of day again or quite possibly be captured. I was too tired to be frightened, I took back all the stuff I had given Glasgow and walked over about 20 feet to where the SCR 619 was lying to make a communications check with my battalion. I bent over to pick up the microphone handset and at that instant occurred the loudest, shrieking scream and blast I had ever heard before since. A tremendous force threw me down onto the radio. I just lay there stunned for a time. The air smelled burned and acrid. I stood up, put on my helmet and turned toward the ledge where a moment before we four lieutenants had sat shoulder to shoulder. The first thing I saw was a charred and blackened head with a portion of a shoulder still attached (Lt. Porterfield). I then looked to the right and there slumped Lt. Glasgow, still in one piece, but his head had been pushed sideways into the rock and flattened, thus doubling the size of his profile. His prematurely gray salt and pepper hair stood out clearly. Lt. Gibbs appeared dead also, but I recall seeing no apparent wound. I really kind of lost it for a while at this point and sat down by the radio. I didn't want to look at the ledge again. I noticed troops now going down the hill in small groups and some singly. I could see some strung out in the valley below heading south. This all took place towards mid afternoon. I recall Lt Cronkite calling his battalion requesting permission to withdraw as there were just the five of us, all officers, left on the hill, Cronkite, Doan, Barker, Atterbury, and me. I asked if I should call for fire on the hill after we had gone to keep the Chinks at bay. I believe he said 'OK', but I couldn't find any code book and I wasn't about to go through Lt. Glasgow's pockets looking for one. I tried to explain to my gunnery people, in code, that we were leaving. I asked what the code word for 65$^{th}$ Infantry for withdrawing was, and I recall the answer was 'gallows'. I remember what a bad sound that had. Anyway my battalion didn't know what 'gallows' was and I guess didn't care. It was stupid on my part to worry about code at the time. This wasn't a classroom situation. I asked for some defensive fires to be fired 15 minutes after I said 'go', and they said 'OK'.

When it came time to leave, I recall meeting Lt. Atterbury and Lt. Barker for the first time. They were with Cronkite and Doan, were going to carry Lt. Gibb's body back on a stretcher. I called for fire from the battalion, either shot up the radio, or dreamed I had or wished I had, and off I went down the southwest slope of the hill to catch up with them. I remember worrying that Chinks would come around the west side of the hill where it joined the valley and capture us. I therefore guarded that approach diligently with my carbine which by this time must have had six inches of dirt in the barrel. To this day I don't know if the battalion ever fired the defensive fires but I never thought to ask. I spelled off various officers on the litter detail. I vividly recall the Chinks incessant sniping at us with direct fire 76mm cannon. We'd run, hit the dirt, put Lt. Gibbs back on the litter, and take off again. In one instance, as I lay on the ground, I observed a 76mm round making a ricochet crater and exploding maybe 50 yards down range. Part way back we ran into a group of Korean Service Corps 'Choogie' bearers carrying supplies to Jackson Heights. We turned them around and made litter bearers out of them. As we approached OP Tom I fell and simultaneously sprained both ankles. Some willing hands came out and helped me drag myself in. I vaguely remember Lieutenant Colonel Betances, the Battalion Commander, separating troops into groups. He was taking rifles and bayonets from some and trying, I guess, to get another bunch together that would go back. I don't remember leaving, my driver, recon sergeant and radio man met me, as did the 2nd Battalion Artillery Liaison Officer. I remember going to my battalion headquarters, debriefing to the battalion commander, executive officer and operations officer, none of whom I'd ever met, getting chewed out for having a round in the chamber of my carbine, and then, I guess, going to sleep somewhere. I never did see my recon sergeant, radio man or driver again.

After piddling around the 'B' Battery area for about then days I was assigned to be an artillery Air Observer with the 3rd Infantry Division Light Air Section. Where before I had worried about being fired at me from above, I now had to worry about things coming from below. We were fired at daily but unless the Chinks were using 85mm 'ack-ack', it never really came very close. If they did use their better stuff or used tracers we'd call in counter fire on them. This pretty much leveled our playing field. All in all I flew 194 missions and fired hundreds of fire missions over the next six months, many over Jackson Heights. I'd look down and remember our 'salad days'. In mid May I returned to the 85th Field Artillery Battalion, and they allowed me, at my suggestion, to piddle around with the 65th Infantry Battalion. I felt I had detailed knowledge of the area 'over the next ridge' that might be of some use to them having flown over it for six months. I don't expect my help was all that enormous but it made me feel like a big shot...sort of an artillery liaison officer without portfolio if you will. As I walked around Outpost Harry and its bunker of 12" square timber, I'd think of the 'G' Company sergeant's puny bunker on Jackson Heights. It turned out that 'Harry' needed those bunkers when the 15th Infantry occupied them during the 1-14 June great fight that ground up a company and a Chink regiment per day. The 3rd Division Artillery fired over 120,000 rounds or final protective fires on and around Harry. There was not a single land or groove left in any howitzer in the 58th Field Artillery. They ended up purely smooth bore from the heat and rate of fire. I was in Charlie Battery at the time and reveled in the volley of fire, night and day, of hundreds and hundreds of rounds in defense of 'Harry'. Sometime in July I made it to the troopship home, just ahead of the Chink final push that shoved things back to the Line Wyoming area. I had been in country ten months and had 40 rotation points. Except for a five day R and R, everyday had been in a four point area, in range of something the Chinks had, from 7.62 PPSH burp gun to 152mm cannon. The 3rd Division Light Air Section had provided me a great tool to exact vengeance for our fight on Jackson Heights."

### Sergeant Lucian Mascarella
### 3rd Battalion, 11th Marine Regiment 1951-52

"I entered the military after graduation from high school. Two of my older brothers and a first cousin had served in the U.S. Navy, and I thought that was the service to join. I changed services in 1951 after my brother-in-law was killed in the Korean War. I was discharged from the U.S. Naval Reserves to join the Marines in April of 1951. After completing Marine Boot Camp, advanced training including artillery Forward Observer and two weeks of cold weather training, the group of Marines I trained with was sent to Korea. We departed on November 14th 1951, aboard a troopship the General John Pope to Kobe, Japan. Two days later we arrived in Korea. I was assigned to 'Item' Battery, 3rd Battalion, 11th Marines, 1st Marine Division. Item Battery was a 105mm howitzer unit, but the 11th Marines had 155mm howitzers and gun batteries also. I was in Korea from mid November 1951 to early December of 1952.

The 1st Marine Division was assigned to the US X Corps in the Punch Bowl area until March 23, 1952. Then the Marines were moved about 180 miles west near Panmunjon on the US I Corps line to help guard the Pyongyang-Seoul corridor. To the right of the Marines was the British Commonwealth Division. I was trained in artillery school as a FO, but after arriving in Korea and being assigned to Item Battery, I was then assigned to gun #6 of the battery because at the time I was needed more on the gun crew than as a FO, but I did eventually get to be a FO, the MOS I was specifically trained to do. My records show I am credited with three battle stars, but that is not the way I saw it. After the lines became nearly static, there were many Chinese and North Korean attacks that evidently were not considered big enough to be classified as battles. I believe the Marine Corps gave me credit for the Battle of Bunker Hill 122 Bunker Hill, on August 12th thru the 16th of 1952, Outpost Bruce on hill 148, September 6-8 a fifty-one hour siege, and the Battle of the Hook, October 26-28 1952.

The Bunker Hill action that took place in August of 1952, I was on the hill as an FO. The only thing I can state about this action it was another one of those crazy attacks by the Chinese and North Koreans to overrun a specific part of the line. In this particular action, there had been an episode that morning in which another FO and I were in an OP bunker looking for targets of opportunity. Since we had telephone lines at that bunker and the radio was at the bunker we lived in, the FO officer was in his bunker and there was only one of the communications men with us. It was early in the morning, and I do not believe the enemy was ready for what was going to happen. At first we thought that the target was to far for our guns and it did not look like a target for an air strike. After looking at the map very close, we decided to call the target in for a fire mission, and let fire control decide if the guns could reach the area. The problem with the mission was it was only a few troops moving around and appeared to be a cave they were working at. We called in the mission, and the fire control people accepted it without question. We had lied just a bit about the target, but after the shells started landing it proved to be a worthwhile target. Evidently, the enemy was storing a lot of ammo around that cave for use later. There were secondary explosions at the target area, and it was not but a few minutes that we received incoming fire. Their FO's had us well under observation and were retaliating. A shell landed just below the OP bunker and one went over it. I told the other FO to get down, and he said 'get down shit, let's get out of this bunker!' He was a bit more experienced than I was, and it was good he was. We ran down the trench line down the hill to our good bunker and waited awhile. Another FO for another battery had watched were the fire was coming from and they got some of their own medicine. We went back to that OP bunker, and I was damned happy we had gotten out of it. The bunker had a long open area we used to look out of about six feet long and about one foot high. One round had hit near the opening spraying the inside of the bunker with shrapnel, the BC scope we used was hit, and the sandbags on parts of the wall were cut. The small tree we were using as a place to tie our communication lines to was just about gone, and telephone lines were scattered about the area. The other FO just looked at me, and did not say one thing. I know what he was thinking though, and was glad he had the sense to get us out of that bunker. Well that night the North Koreans did attack. They first used artillery and mortar fire on our positions, and tried to get through. It did not work, but we did sustain a few wounded men. The bunker we lived in was hit and we had to help get a wounded man down the hill to a chopper. We had to use the radio to call in fire missions, but that was not a problem. We had firing reference points marked on our map that we had called in and used to adjust fire from these. Once a frontline, MLR, becomes static, fire missions are easier to call in.

I did not really give the actions I was in too much thought at the time. However, there was one action were I did become a bit concerned about the enemy's attack. With all the ammo we were firing, and that some of the battery was being sent up to the lines did make me think of a serious breakthrough. Sometimes it was necessary to fall back instead of being overrun or killed. I believe every fighting man thinks about that. I was never concerned about having to destroy things or killing or wounding the enemy. Being an FO is really different from other actions. In the Marine Corps the FO team was attached to an infantry company, and there was coordination with those units. Sometimes the infantry units you were with were really friendly, but some did not exactly appreciate the artillery until there was one of those mass enemy attacks. The 11th Marines usually supported the Marine Regiments on the line, 1st, 5th, and 7th. I remember being in reserve for about a month and did fire some missions from a new position. We were near Panmunjon, and that was an odd shaped area. It is also possible that our regiment could have fired missions for the British Commonwealth units on our right flank. As I remember our sector of the line on the East Coast at the Punch Bowl area there were Chinese troops. The Marines were moved to the West Coast in March of 1952 and in that area of the MLR there were mostly North Koreans troops. I could not tell the difference from the Koreans or Chinese, and frankly, to me an enemy was an enemy. Some military people believed that the Chinese were better fighters, but I did not accept that.

Our OP's were usually identified as OP '1', '2', etc. or there were some units using the name of the battery and a number such as 'OP Item One'. Some FO teams just announced this is the FO. Marines units used an authentication code, and that could be used to check if fire control thought the fire mission was by an enemy trying to call fire on a friendly position. Our unit was not at all very strict about the OP names. Item Battery had two , but not in use at all times. I remember specifically one on the East Coast on Hill 812, and on the West Coast Hills 122 and 148. Life as a Forward Observer was a rather good assignment, and as dangerous as any frontline duty. FO's were like infantry troops, and were usually considered kind of different by the Marines on the gun crews. As any small unit there was a real feeling of comradeship by the FO team. The team usually took care of their day to day food and other needs, but could get the hot meals when the infantry received any. Life in the trenches for the FO's was somewhat better than for the infantry. The FO's did not have to be in the frontline trenches, the OP was usually located away from the MLR, and at times I did not actually see the infantry I was with on the line. We had telephones to the Company leader, and usually our officer coordinated fire for the infantry unless it was just a separate fire mission that we called ourselves.

The one mission that I called, that caused quite a bit of damage to the enemy. It had to have been an ammunition depot. I was also in the OP on numerous occasions for fire missions, but I believe it was a target that a mission was not called that bothers me the most. I had not been on the hill very long, and was looking for something to fire at. I was using the BC scope and gradually worked my way out further from our lines. I had gone quite a distance out, and suddenly saw a large group of enemy walking around in a wooded area. I told the senior FO and he viewed the target, but stated they are too far for our guns. I accepted that, but realized later he was incorrect. It was too late the troops were gone. Why the enemy was out in the open was and remains a puzzle to me because the Chinese and the Koreans seldom moved much in the daylight hours. The fact was they were within the range of the Marine 155mm guns and Army 8-inch guns, and those guns were available to the FO's because we had used these guns on other fire missions. We could have wounded or killed those enemy troops, and probably saved one or more of our peoples lives by doing so.

The fire missions for the Marines and I believe the Army were about the same. An FO is constantly looking for targets to fire on, if it is in an enemy assault that is evident. Once the target is identified, the FO or someone on the team gets on the radio or the telephone, our telephone was a EE-8, and contacts the fire control unit. The mission usually starts with 'This is OP 1, fire mission', and we'd identify the target such as troops in open, vehicles, etc. We usually gave the number of troops or a good estimation of same, map location or other type of location of target, type of shell, HE, WP, Al, and type of fuse such as quick, VT, or time and then a request for the number of guns believed needed to destroy target. If the FO believed he had the target viewed to the point there was no doubt of the area of impact. He asked for 'fire for effect' with more than one gun. That kind of mission was possible after lines were static as in Korea after late 1951. A mission could then be called 'This is FO One, Fire Mission, 100 troops in open, at location, shell HE, fuse quick, give me one gun for adjustment'. Some experienced FO's seldom used any adjusting and simply called fire for effect. The fire control people could change the shell or fuse but they did not do that often. Some missions were made very brief and were called in as 'FO One, Fire Mission, 100 troops in open; at location, give me an adjusting round', and fire control planned the distance and other firing procedures then called the battery and gave the information needed to fire the mission. The shell type was usually HE with either a VT or quick fuse. The maps we used after the lines became static had firing points that we had called in and marked on the maps. The FO's then used these points as control points to fire other missions, it made it faster to get a fire for effect."

**1st Lt. Joseph C. Adams Jr.**
**213th Field Artillery Battalion 1952**

"I obtained a commission as a 2nd Lt. in the Coast Artillery in June of 1950, via ROTC at Utah State. Sometime shortly after this date the Field Artillery and the Coast Artillery were combined. I was called into active duty in June of 1951 and received orders to report to the armed artillery group at Fort Hood Texas. After serving about three months at Fort Hood, I managed to get assigned to the Artillery School at Fort Sill Oklahoma. Shortly after arriving at Fort Sill, I received orders to Korea, which I had deferred until I finished the school in December, 1951. I reported to Camp Stoneman on New Years Eve and was sent to Japan, processed, and sailed to Korea a few days later. I was assigned directly to the 213th Field Artillery Battalion, and arrived there about the middle of January, 1952. We were the northern most field artillery battalion in Korea, and I got there on a Saturday and on Sunday we got the shit shelled out of us. I was assigned to Headquarters and Headquarters Battery, then Service Battery, and then about May 1st, to 'B' Battery. I had the privilege of serving under Captain Harper in Service Battery and Captain Helm in Baker Battery, both outstanding commanders. The 213th was a 155mm howitzer battalion situated behind Kumhwa on my arrival, and moved behind Chorwon in March, where it stayed until after my departure in December 1952. It was a 9th Corps artillery and was in support of the ROK 9th Division most of the time at Chorwon. Sometime in April '52, the battalion decided that all junior officers would take turns manning two OP's in the Chorwon Valley area. If my memory is correct, I was sent to OP 'Love' while in Service Battery shortly before I was assigned to 'B' Battery. After that, we took regular turns on the OP about once per month for a week at a time. I served as FO only with the ROK and once with the French Battalion. The only problem with the ROK's was communication. I arm wrestled with them, I was helping one of their choggy boys with English, but mainly we did not have too much exchange. They never missed a chance to steal from us. I even had one come in at night and steal my shaving kit and a box of C-rations. I never saw North Koreans. We were always against the Chinese. They even called me by my name on our radio prior to White Horse. Most of the time on the OP, it was calm, although it seems that we received incoming each time we were up there, mostly mortars, until the battle for White Horse Mountain in October 1952, when things got hot.

Anthony J. Sobieski

I was on White Horse for the big battle in October of '52. Lt. Miller was manning OP Love and was wounded, and I was sent up to take his place, as I was scheduled next in line for there. I can't recall if it was shrapnel or splinters in the face, but it wasn't that serious, and he was to have been up there until Friday or Saturday, and I was the next in line to go up there to the OP, so when he got wounded they sent me on up. I was there about two or three days before things started. The brass was expecting an assault on the hill and we were all anticipating the assault. The evening before it actually started the ROK's, just after dark, opened up and fired over into the valley. There were so many tracers and explosions that I didn't think anything could get through, so I was very confident that the ROK's could hold their own with the Chinese. The day that the Chinese actually attacked, we were shelled all day. I remember someone in FDC told me to go out and get a reading on where the shells were fired from, they already had us counting and reporting the number of incoming. We were over 100 in our count, and I told him if he wanted that info he would have to come get it himself. That afternoon, the Gooks had a recoilless rifle shooting at our bunker from across the valley. We timed it and would duck down about the time the round would hit. You could see it was recoilless, probably a captured one of ours. We would see it fire, and it got so that we would count before it got there at the bunker, and we'd duck, playing little games, you know. They were supposed to hit us it seems like it was a Friday, but they were a day late, but they were hitting us with artillery for about three days before then. They shelled the shit out of me. At first there was a mountain with a ridge, Arrowhead, sticking out not more than a half mile away. It was just an old barren dirt hill. Pretty soon that thing opened up. It was nothing but a large trench, and that's where the first ones came from, and they were shooting right at our bunker. Pretty soon, as far as you could see coming across the valley, were a line of Chinese coming at us. There was a line about every fifty feet, and they were just marching. There was one line behind another, far as you could see, it never ended. They were just walking across. We were shooting at them with everything we had. Marine Corsairs were dropping napalm and phosphorous across the whole valley, but they kept coming. We were firing everything we could. 1st Lt Jack Callaway, another 213th FO who was on the Hill 284 manning OP 'Roger', I could hardly get on the radio because he had so many fire missions going! The Chinese were all over there, as far as you could see. The ROKs were shooting everything they had, too. The ROKs had air support, plus artillery support, but they just kept coming.

That was just before dark. Next thing I know, things got kinda quite. I didn't know what was going on where! So I went out of the bunker and walked up the trench line a little ways, looking for a place to turn around so I could see down into the valley a little better. I was looking down there to see what the hell was going on, and that's when I got hit in the helmet, I got shot right through the back of the helmet. Evidently I had dropped down, I know I was standing on my toes stretching to look, and I must have just dropped as he shot me. The bullet hit me right in the back of the helmet, and it went in and up and around, and it chipped out a furrow through the helmet liner and came out the front. You could stick three fingers through the hole in the front. I didn't even see any Chinese around me till then. The shot knocked me down, and I had a mouth full of dirt, and I'm sure I was knocked out for a second or two. I got up, my helmet was lying in front of my head, so I picked that up and broke all kinds of fifty yard dashes through the trench line to get back to the bunker. That's when I knew the Chinese were all over us. I turned around as I was running and I saw the guy with the rifle, he was maybe fifty yards up. We were out on a ridge near the top. The crest of the mountain was higher than we were. I could see him, and I broke the fifty or hundred yard dash in the crouched position, I'm sure. I was looking north and he hit me from behind. They came up from the northwest, and our ridge went out a little bit to the northeast. The ROK's only manned White Horse from only half way up to the top. There was this finger that went out to the west, but it was more like a ridge and went toward the east up to the peak and went back down again. Until White Horse was over the ROK's only manned the top of it. That's where they had their defensive line, set across the top of it. So the Chinese came up that other ridge first and got behind us. We were literally right out in front, with no place left to go to get out of there by then because they were behind us. That's when I called artillery fire in on us, on our bunker. I told the FDC that if they didn't hear from me or us in ten, maybe fifteen minutes, to do it again, because the damn radio was outside. There was a little bunker right outside the main bunker, where the radio was in for some protection. The initial artillery on top of us knocked the radio out.

I called in for artillery on us, and I went back inside the main bunker and by then the Chinese were all over the place. They came up and threw grenades in and shot in there, but they couldn't see because it was dark back in there. It was moonlight out, and we could see them. They rushed us probably four or five times, and each time they rushed in there they could only get one in through the doorway at a time, and we were back in there and I was shooting around the corner with the carbine left handed. You know, you could pull off a lot of bullets one at a time, and I don't know how many of those Chinese we got because there was none left in the bunker. They would throw a grenade in and they would rush it, rush in right behind the grenade and we'd shoot back at them, and they'd get their ass out of there. This was while we were waiting for the artillery to come in, to get there. Normally it took eight minutes, but I think it took longer than that because of some fuck-ups down at Fire Direction Center. When I called FDC, I think I called some stupid fire mission. I said something like 'The fucking Chinese are all over the place start shooting at my bunker!' or something like that. It wasn't what you would call a regulation fire mission! The amazing part is we got out of there. This bunker must have been the best bunker the 9th ROK's ever built because it had ten by ten foot timbers going up and across and after the Chinese popped grenades, well there were Chinese grenades and American grenades going off in there with the beams going across with sandbags and weight on them, they shifted three inches. I couldn't believe it. But where we were the concussion was pretty great, but it wasn't overpowering because we were back in, and like a muffler, there was an exit hole, the observation port, it wasn't doing all that much damage to us. Partly the concussion would knock you out of it, I would think. The 213th were firing VT fuses. They said they shot everything they had, and they said they were going to put rocks in the barrels and shoot that! I think the FDC called Lt. Callaway on OP Roger to adjust fire because he said that when those first rounds came in it was like someone took a sickle and just wiped them off, they were all over. They were lowering a guy down in from the top trying to look in, to see what was in there, you know. Of course every time they tried to get in we pushed them out. We could see this head come down, and I'd take a bead on him, left handed with my carbine, and they'd haul him back up, I never did shoot at him. They were lowering him down from on top, to the doorway. About three times they lowered him down.

It's kind of funny, that afternoon before all the shit started, I'm sitting there looking out the BC scope and I hear somebody behind me, and I turn around and there's this full bird colonel. He was about six-six, and his shoes are shiny, his helmet liner shined, he's got all his ribbons on, and seams sewed into his fatigues. He introduced himself. He was Colonel so-and-so from IX Corps Artillery. He wanted to see my defensive fire plan. Well, our defensive fire plan was about five pre-fired spots right down at the bottom of the hill there, right under us. I couldn't call a defensive fire plan, and I said to him 'what the hell is a defensive fire plan?', and patiently he explained it to me. And I says 'Oh! you mean this?', and we had a aerial photograph of the hill and it was sitting right behind me, and there were these things marked on it, you know. And I said 'this is what you mean? I don't know if I could call that a defensive fire plan' and he looked at it and said 'I can't either!' So he had me call the FDC, and he called down and he got a hold of Major House and he just chewed ass and he said 'you have a God-damned defensive fire plan up here by six o'clock or you'll be a corporal!'. And then he turned around to me, and he looked out there, out of the observation slit, and he says 'you see right there?' and there was this ridge and this mountain that was right across from us coming down Arrowhead. And he says 'There's twenty thousand Chinese massed right behind that ridge there and they're ready to attack, I want you to adjust on it and call in for division artillery, one round ToT, Time on Target', so I got on the phone with FDC, and of course they already knew he was there, and I said 'Division Artillery, one round' and I give them the base point, 'Left twenty degrees, one round Division Artillery, fire for effect'. And the colonel looked at me and he said 'Your kind of a smart little son of a bitch, arn'tcha?' And I said 'Colonel, there's twenty thousand Chinese coming' down at me from that God-damn thing I'm not taking' time to adjust!' And eight minutes later here it comes, you know, and they just covered that area. This was either the day of or the day before the battle, I think it was the day before. I'd been there, it was mid October, I'd been there since January, and was a little salty by then, so I figured I sure wasn't going to adjust in on that.

The Chinese hit just before dark, and we got back to the outfit probably four o'clock in the morning. I reported in to Captain Helm. Every place I looked there was dirt, they were digging holes. The dirt was coming out, they were getting the shit shelled out of them at the battery. I walked around for quite awhile, and then I went up to Battalion HQ and reported in to the battalion commander, Lt Col. Humphrey. Then I came back, and it was probably nine thirty in the morning, something like that, and I went in and laid down on my bunk, and the captain sent this guy in and he said to go sleep in his tent, it had sandbags all around it, to go to sleep in that. So I went over there, and it couldn't have been more than a half an hour, and the shells started coming in, and I took off for one of our personnel bunkers, and about half way there one came in and landed about ten feet from me. You don't hear them when they're that close, you don't get that much warning, and I was in the air and diving when it went off. Evidently the shrapnel went over the top of me, and it rolled me over in the air, and I didn't get a nick at all. I made it into the personnel bunker and it was only made for about four people, and there was already six in it, and I made room for one more. The guy in the doorway there was yelling 'We're full up! We're full up!' but I said 'We are now!' and I put my shoulder into him and pushed the rest further back in. I think the first one hit my tent and that was the second or third one when I got to the bunker. Our outfit was out in the open, we weren't up against a hill like most, we were out in the open, and we had only one guy get hit with shrapnel, I think it was a nick on the wrist, that's pretty unbelievable in itself.

After I left White Horse, Colonel Humphrey sent me over to the French Battalion. They were in the thick of things, as they were located just west of White Horse. We got shelled on our way there, and we were surrounded for the first three nights there. I participated in a 2nd Infantry Division Time On Target shoot while there. Every gun in the 2nd Division plus our battalion participated. The French, they had a tank out, and it came back in and reported there was about five thousand Chinamen coming down this draw, towards Arrowhead. The French Company Commander asked me if I could, he told me he wanted to bring in division artillery, can I get my battalion in on it? I said I would find out. I called up and FDC said yes. So we called in 2nd DIVARTY, Time on Target, three rounds from the 155's and eight rounds from the 105's. And by that time the 213th got in on it, we lit up that hillside there, for what seemed like twenty minutes. There was nothing that could walk through it, it was quite a sight. That was the second or third night I was with the French, nothing came through and the location was lit up for ten minutes just from the shells exploding. After things quieted down, the French Company CO invited me to lunch. We had French Wine cut with water, fresh French bread, and C-ration hamburgers, sautéed in wine. It was the 1st time I ever liked the C-ration burger. The French had to have their wine and bread. In fact one night their bread truck got hit with a mortar, and got rolled over, and you could see it from where we were. The French Company Commander got a hold of battalion and told them to get another truck, and they did! I hadn't had any sleep at this time since I went up on White Horse. The French CO told me when he saw me he wondered why they sent an old man up to help him. I guess I even looked worse after ten days up there! From where we were on Arrowhead Mountain, from where I was with the French Battalion, I could see the battle for White Horse. I could see the top of the mountain right across from me. I watched during the daytime the Chinese and the Koreans fighting. The Koreans couldn't throw a hand grenade more than 50 feet, they would run half way and then throw it, or they would get three of them and throw them, and sometimes when they would do that they would get one of them back! One time they got napalmed, the ROK's, so next day they had their plastic markers out to show the planes where to go. I remember The ROK's attacking up the side of White Horse, maybe a platoons' worth, and it was pretty steep, and they got pinned down by a machine gun bunker about half way up. And then mortar fire was coming in from a ways off, but you could see the puffs of smoke from where I was out in the valley. They kind of bunched up like sheep when the mortars started to come in. That was probably a week into the battle. I was with the French for ten or eleven days."

# Chapter Five

## *1952 – 1953 Carrying on the Mission*

During the pivotal time of late 1952 going into the winter and 1953, the United States and the UN were entering into the fourth year of the war, and many thought that there would be a continuation of the 'stalemate' that was considered to be the prevalent description for most of 1952. The Main Line of Resistance, Outposts, secondary lines such as the Kansas Line, all became more solidified than ever. Regular rotations of units were the norm to the Outposts positioned in front of the MLR. Forward Observer teams continued to do their jobs and manned their Observation Posts into the winter months, where infantry movement slowly became minimal and the weather grew worse. FO's became the watchdogs of the battlefield, and what artillery fire that was delivered was either on pre-designated Harassing & Interdiction missions or what the FO was able to observe over the cold harsh landscape. This was an extremely harsh winter in Korea, but slowly, with the winter thaw, there was the inevitable increase of infantry action and ultimately, a large and stead growth in artillery use. Many FO's who went to Korea during this time would eventually unknowingly see the last battles of the war, and some would even be on the front lines on the last day…

**Sergeant Victor Reynolds**
**143rd Field Artillery Battalion 1952-53**

"Growing up in the 1930's and 40's reading and hearing about war's seemingly everywhere, I thought I would like to go into the service someday. While my family was not in favor and wanted me to go to school, the Korean War afforded me the opportunity to join the service and as corny as it may sound, to serve my country which I dearly love to this day. So I enlisted in the Army, a true RA, 'Regular Army' as we were called. I did basic for fourteen weeks infantry at Ft. Dix, and then was told I was eligible for O.C.S. What were my first three choices? This seemed like a slam dunk with my infantry training so I selected Ft Benning, then just to fill out the list I selected Ft. Monmouth and Coast Artillery. I was shipped to Field Artillery O.C.S. in Ft. Sill Oklahoma. I completed sixteen weeks of the twenty-two required but I was weak in math, trig, calculus, and the like. The commandant suggested I take a two week set back and go on from there. He told me I was probably the youngest to even enter the school and that was hurting me some. I decided not to take the set back in school and dropped out. I was told I would probably end up in Korea which was ok. Little did I realize what lie ahead. This took place in 1952. I was sent to Seattle and sailed on the Gen. Nelson, I think. Sailing out of Seattle the silence was deafening. I remember watching the city slowly get smaller and smaller and wondering If I would ever see home again, half convinced that I probably wouldn't. We landed in Japan in Yokahama, were put on a train headed to Camp Drake. Very strange sensation looking out the train windows and seeing all kinds of electrical signs and advertisements but there was nothing in English, kind of like landing on another planet. Once in Camp Drake we were given unit assignments. My MOS was rifleman so I was assigned to a rifle company in the 7th Infantry Division. However, a warrant officer looked at my file from some reason, and he noticed the artillery OCS information and spoke to me telling me I was reassigned to the 143rd Field Artillery Battalion, 40th Infantry Division. The 143rd was a light artillery unit firing 105's. However during my tour as an FO I had access to and called fire for 155's and on two occasion's 8-inch guns from division. I also had occasion to work with and direct tank fire.

I was in Korea from about March '52 till January or February of '53. I reported to 'B' Battery 143rd and the Battery Commander. I remember he asked what area I'd like to be assigned to. I'm sure this was a setup. I hadn't though about it so I was hesitant. He asked if I could direct fire and I said yes. He said they desperately needed another FO but he couldn't force me into it. I remember telling him firing in Ft. Sill was easy because nobody was shooting back but what the heck I'll do it. He told me to be ready in two hours as the team I'd be with was going up that afternoon. I went up and never really came down for any time, to the extent that I did not know any of the gun crews. I knew a few of the others in FO parties but that was it. That was kind of unfortunate because I owed a lot of thanks to those gun crews, certainly a lot more than they ever knew. Much of the action we were in was repulsing probes and large size patrols perhaps company size up to battalion size. I believe they knew the war was over for them, they couldn't win. They had no air support and were almost incapable of massing artillery. We were able to pick up on their artillery, mortars, etc and we put them out of action very quickly. Only time I can remember they fired a ToT and caught us somewhat off guard but we recovered quickly and put them out of commission. The incident happened when we were up on Heartbreak Ridge. I had gone to another OP to assist the team in removing their radio which they didn't know how to do. That done, they pulled out three fresh eggs they had gotten from somewhere and we scrambled them as my reward I guess. Great dinner! The FO team when we finished went to the OP up and over the ridge crest. I was a couple of minutes behind them intending to get near the ridge top and going back to my OP. As I reached the ridge it seemed like the world blew up. A ToT had hit us. I believe the country jumped six inches out of the ocean from the concussion. I remember they were sweeping the ridge top with heavy machine gun fire, and I watched tracers ricochet off the ridge and stayed put until there was a let-up. Then I went up over and down to the OP where we began directing fire and in a few hours it was over. Curiously, we never saw infantry or troops. It was strictly weapon fire with no attempt to advance. It would be impossible for me to describe the many, many probing actions and fire fights. I know we always won and never gave up an inch of ground.

One of, if not the most significant fire mission, I directed was during the last major action that I was in around Heartbreak area. I directed fire in many, many situations but for me this one was the most significant. There's a humorous story that goes with this action. A story that I was ordered to never repeat but fifty years later I guess it's okay. Besides, I found it funny in one sense and an act of God's protection. I was in the OP with my radio operator trying to keep warm as usual. The field phone buzzed so I answered it and heard a lot of people laughing and it sounded like partying. Our lieutenant, who was almost never in the OP, I don't think he could find it, was on the phone laughing and calling from the infantry CP. He asked me if we saw any activity or movement all the time laughing. I thought 'if you want to clown around fine. I'll play' so I said yes. I saw three enemy soldiers hiding behind a rock. The conversation ended and the next thing I saw was the Lt. in the OP asking where I saw these people. I told him I never saw anyone. I thought it was a big joke and he was clowning. I said 'I can't believe you're serious when you're laughing so hard you can hardly talk'. He of course was panicked and said our report had put the division front on 100% alert. So say nothing. Thank God for the error because within an hour we were hit and it was a full blown attack intended to drive us back and give up territory. I called the fire mission, gave FDC coordinates from one end of the valley to the other using both VT and HE rounds and told them to sweep the valley then drop fifty yards and sweep again. I instructed FDC to bring the sweeping fire right in on top of us as the advanced units were penetrating the wire and getting to the ridge top. FDC said they would not bring fire in on top of us because of our own people. I tried to assure them that I could and would advise the infantry to pull in their heads, but they still wouldn't come in on us. The result was a number of enemy troops were able to penetrate our lines but we or the infantry finally succeeded in driving them back. Air recon the following day told us that there were so many dead that it looked like a snow storm had hit, the dead enemy on the hill were numerous. I remember looking at the bodies and thinking some looked so young. What of their families who they would never go home to and I was a major cause. That feeling has never left me. I don't know one day since then that I haven't though of Korea and the parents of those dead soldiers who ended up in mass graves and never went home.

The feeling during these actions was for me an adrenalin rush. Intense concentration to ensure accuracy of fire. Being in an OP you saw no one else except members of your team possibly. For me it was a feeling of being very much alone in the situation and knowing I had to do everything on my own. Yet I never sensed panic, fear yes, but never panic. I was still young enough to have a since of invincibility. I thought of being captured and imprisonment, but it was really after the action that I though about what happened. Who was hit and who was okay were things I was concerned with after the action was over. As I said earlier, when the action was going on, there was a job I had to do and that was my concern, and focused my thoughts and actions. The infantry units we were supporting were various units of the 40th. We had virtually no contact with the infantry units we were supporting. Some of our OP's were in advance of the MLR so we were not often physically near them. OP's were usually manned by artillery FOs with protection from a rifle squad. I think they knew our OP's were targets so it was prudent not to stay too close to us. I never had any sense that they reacted to FO's in any particular manner. I believe they thought we were a little crazy for volunteering to do what we did. This was probably reinforced by our action on Christmas Eve 1952 when we inadvertently started a fire inside our bunker and went outside while it burned in the night and sang Christmas carols. I guess we were a little crazy and I'm sure we confused the hell out of the Chinese. The CO of the infantry company was upset to say the least and gave us strict orders to put out the fire but we could continue caroling. Afterwards we all shed some tears as we compared notes on what was going on in our homes on Christmas Ever. The Chinese who were facing told us via loudspeaker that they had left gifts in the wire and we would not be harmed if we went and picked them up. I still have a piece of the propaganda leaflets and some other things that they left in the wire and true to their word they never harmed any of us. What a weird situation, granted it was done for propaganda purposes but I would have called fire on them if I had seen them.

I was in support of ROK units whenever my units went into reserve and were replaced by ROK troops. We stayed on the hill. After all I was earning four rotation points by staying on the line so that was the quickest way home. As for the ROK units, I believe they were elements of the 2nd and 6th ROK Divisions, but I'm not sure. I am sure that we fought the Chinese. My thoughts were fairly basic. They were on the other side so they were the enemy. I did feel I'd rather face the Chinese because I don't believe the average Chinese soldier truly wanted to be there or die there, and they were more civilized than the Koreans. The North Koreans on the other hand were much more barbaric, fanatic and desperate as they had been beaten when on their own and couldn't survive without the Chinese support. We normally manned two or three OP's per battery I believe. They were on various hills around Heartbreak Ridge and Bloody Ridge, the others were just hills with no significant names that I remember. There were several hills where we engaged and were in some serious fire fights but many were fire fights to chase off the probing patrol action and became almost routine.

Life as an FO was bearable. You developed close friendships during your stay but they faded away when you came home. Food was 'C' Rations primarily. I learned to trade with ROK troops when I was with them. So I got rice and a hot soup made with things I didn't want to know about. It smelled so bad the rest of the FO team wouldn't let me in the OP or even get near me. But it tasted great with the rice and it was a break from 'C' rations. Staying clean was impossible. I remember two or three showers in a year. It wasn't always safe to wash in streams due to the bacteria from bodies or human waste products. We had drinking water which we used sparingly to shave and clean up a little. In winter we melted snow for water. Funny incident, I remember using my steep pot to melt some snow and shave in. Shortly thereafter I got a cocoa powder so I put snow in my helmet and melted it and added the cocoa powder, mixed and heated it and poured it into my canteen cup. Then I lit a cigarette and sad down to drink my cocoa. Have you ever had a drink of cocoa mixed with shaving soap and whiskers? Believe me. It's awful! A good portion of the days were quiet as the Chinese and Koreans couldn't move freely in daylight. We did borrow an infantry sniper rifle on occasion and take shots at any movements we saw.

The only fire mission that could come close to the big one I fired during the Heartbreak action was one that took place in July or August at the height of the rainy season. Looking out from the OP, I detected six Chinese digging out a trench, probably to establish an OP or gun position that would look directly at us fairly close in. Unfortunately the rain clouds were low and at times completely obscured vision. I called the mission, gave FDC the azimuth and coordinates, described the target and requested a battery round mixed VT and HE fuses and asked for a fire at my command only. While I was concerned with VT fuses in such rain and cloud cover I felt it would work. When I noted the clouds breaking a little I requested fire. I literally watched as the people dove for cover in the trench and the full battery went in on top of them. I could see the dead and again that feeling that due to me they would never again go home to their families. Calling a fire mission required a decision regarding a target. Troops in the open, gun or mortar positions, vehicles moving or stopped. The accuracy of your azimuth reading was super critical and the coordinates from your map designating where the target was. Classically you would attempt to get a bracket on the target then close it down so you could go from the single adjusting round to a battery fire for effect. Unfortunately there were times where a moving target or some other factor required you to take your best shot the first time. Not necessarily recommended but that was a decision you had to make on the spot. You were oblivious to anything around you when you received 'on the way' and responded with your 'on the way wait'. Your eyes and brain were focused on the target and anticipating how you would adjust for your second shot if you got one. No one and nothing existed except you and the target. Then it was over and you advised FDC of the results.

When I think of significant events I think of the day I was told to report to the battery commander immediately as I was going home. We were in an OP on the eastern coast in an area I knew as 'Smokey Valley' which up to that point I had heard was a 'hot spot' but it was relatively quiet up to the time I left. While it was sad to say goodbye to the team especially 'Murph' who I had spent so much time with, it was exciting to know I had made it through and was going home a little older and wiser I thought."

**Sergeant Seymour Podbers**
**90th Field Artillery Battalion 1952-53**

"I was drafted into the U.S. Army in November 1951. I was sent to Fort Sill for training, and then was on a ship that left Seattle, we dropped off troops in Alaska then sailed to Japan where we were outfitted and landed in Inchon, Korea. My assignment was with the 90th Field Artillery Battalion, Baker Battery, and I was assigned to the Fire Direction Center. We supported the 25th Infantry Division, and were a 155mm howitzer unit. I arrived in Korea in April 1952 and was there until August of 1953 and rotated with forty-four points because the so called police action was coming to a close and I was extended beyond my tour. I was assigned as a Forward Observer because everyone in Fire Direction took turns at the OP. When I first was assigned to the 90th we were at Heart Break Ridge. After that there many small battles or locations that didn't have names. Being an FO, at first it was interesting and exciting but after the second time when you saw the death and destruction that was caused and that your own guys were getting killed really changed that. I remember one morning all three men on the OP had been killed with their throats slit. Hello! Certainly was a wake up call so as not to let your guard down.

We supported the 25th Infantry Division, but I remember when they were in reserve we supported the Turks. It was difficult communicating so every once a while one of us would go on a recon patrol with them. I don't recall supporting any ROK units while I was there. We never got into close encounters to tell the difference if we were fighting North Koreans or the Chinese. To the best of my knowledge we only had one OP to man, and even though we worked four hours and off four hours, one did not get really restful sleep. We slept with our clothes and boots on and also slept with our weapon very close by. Next, think about the food we had, it was either C or K rations. And not to be gross, but when had to use the bathroom, it usually was where ever worked. After three days we were smelly, dirty, and tired, and would look forward to a shower even though it would be a cold running stream. On top of all that, the weather was always a big problem. All of our fire missions were special to us, and especially when on a few occasions we used direct fire on some targets. After identifying a target it was called into FDC with coordinates. After the first volley we would close in. Determining what the target was would determine the type of fuse to be used. We were once staffed by our own Air Force planes. It was our own fault, there were different flags to be placed in different directions each day and someone forgot to change the flags. Thank God no one got hurt."

**2nd Lt William Verkler**
**999th Armored Field Artillery Battalion 1952-53**

"In the fall of 1947, I enrolled at Arkansas State at Jonesboro and began the ROTC program. I also joined Company 'I', 153rd Infantry, Arkansas National Guard. When I graduated in May of 1951, I was commissioned a 2nd Lieutenant, and after serving at the ROTC summer camp at Ft. Sill, I went on extended active duty in August. When I went on active duty I was sent to the Battery Officer's course at Ft. Sill, and while there I received my orders to Korea. I spent two or three months with a training division at Camp Chaffee and then went overseas in March of '52, and was there till April of 1953. I was assigned to the 999th Armored Field Artillery Battalion, we were an I Corps Artillery unit located in the Chorwon Valley not far from the Imjim River. Our unit fired a 155mm self-propelled howitzer commonly known as a 'Long-tom'.

I was first assigned to our HQ Battery as Assistant Communications Officer, and about half of the time I served as an FO. After about one month I was assigned to 'B' Battery as an Assistant Exec, and again I served as an FO about half the time. About five months later, I was assigned as Executive Officer. We supported troops fighting on Kelly Hill, Big and Little Nori, Old Baldy, Pork Chop and the 'T' Bone to name a few, and as FO I directed fire in support of our troops and attempted to destroy enemy artillery and mortar positions. Since most of the action took place at night, I couldn't see much of what was going on and felt rather helpless. We would fire on pre-registered points and occasionally flares were used. There was only one large scale attack that they made during the day in our area and it was in a heavy fog. Usually the fogs lifted in a few seconds, but this one just rolled back north and the Chinese went with it. I remember being highly frustrated. The Chinese made very good use of their artillery and mortars, digging through ridges and hills from the reverse slope and then covering the opening facing us. They used several types of artillery, the most common being the 76mm mountain gun. Their most effective heavy weapon, in my opinion, was the 120 mm mortar. Frequently, they would zero in on a target, with several guns spread out over some distance, thus making it more difficult to locate any one by sound. They would also light several fires before they started a mission so that the smoke would confuse us. I probably blasted a number of bonfires before I caught on to that. There was a period when we were always short of artillery shells. On one occasion I located a 76mm and couldn't get anything to fire on it. I watched all afternoon while it worked us over. I also remember cussing out a major. Fortunately, he was very understanding. An article appeared in the *Stars & Stripes* claiming that a decision was made to limit artillery shells in order to prevent us from making a major push and possibly disrupting the peace talks. Although this was denied, after the article came out we had all the shells we needed. In fact, we received an order to fire at least a certain number of shells a day. At times it was almost like a game. I tried to locate them before they located us. I felt very detached. In the incident involving the battle in the fog, however, I had what might be described as a blood lust as I anticipated the fog suddenly lifting and the enemy troops being out in the open.

We supported a number of infantry units, including the 1st ROK Division, 1st Marines, 1st Calvary, 2nd Division, the Commonwealth Contingent, the Philipinos, the French and the Turks. Much of the time our OP would be in an isolated position. When we were in the trenches, the infantry always treated us very well and fed us the best they had when they could. I might note that the French had the best army chow! When we supported the 1st ROK, which was considered one of the two best divisions the South Koreans had, the battalion commander of our battalion was a personal friend to the DIVARTY Commander of the 1stb ROK, and wherever they went, they would call for us. We fought mostly against the Chinese while I was there. The three firing batteries of our battalion each manned one OP and the HQ Battery also manned an OP. We had an OP on hill 347 for a while, and there were a number of others along a rather wide stretch of the MLR that we would man when called. As I recall, all told I used about five different OP's since we were in a bulge in the lines and could fire over 180 degrees. When I was an assistant exec, I preferred to be up on the hill because you are much less likely to be bothered by the brass. Much of the time we sat in our bunker and looked. The saying that life on the front is 90% boredom and 10% terror seems to fit pretty well. I had two men as a part of my OP team. We would divide the day up into watches. Usually I would take the 2 a.m. to 5 a.m. watch and toward the end of that time fire up the burner, make some coffee or hot chocolate, eat a can of C-rations and then go to bed at 5 a.m. and get back up at 8 a.m. At the end of the day I would try to clean up a little before I went to bed, and then be rousted out at 2 a.m. for another stretch. Life got a lot better when they started bringing up hot food after dark, along with the mail, if we had any. We looked forward to this time all day long.

One of the most satisfying fire missions I had occurred about two weeks after I got to Korea. The OP was on a narrow, chewed up ridge to the left flank of Old Baldy. There were body parts sticking out of the ground and I discovered two or three skeletons in an abandoned bunker. It was not the most pleasant introduction to Korea. Three or four days after we manned the OP, a lieutenant from the 1st FA Observation Battalion, who had an OP nearby, came by with a photograph of a recoilless rifle position directly in front of us that had been taken from one of their planes. He asked if I could locate it and knock it out. It was almost dark, but I managed to locate the position. I trained my BC scope on it and switched on the light. This put the position in the lighted circle. By this time it was dark, but I was able to adjust onto the position from the light from our exploding shells. The next afternoon the lieutenant was back with more photographs showing the position completely destroyed. He was very complimentary and I felt very proud of myself for being able to knock it out in the dark. Another specific mission I remember involved a dug in 76 in the Big Nori/Little Nori area. They would run the weapon to the front of their cave, pump out several rounds, and then pull it back. I would adjust on their position, and, although I was able to hit the entrance, was never able to put the weapon out of action. Other FO's who relieved me had the same problem. One day I heard that they had an 8 inch howitzer far forward on what was called a sniping mission. When it was over, I asked if I could use the 8 incher. I adjusted in on the cave and apparently hit their ammo dump. The whole front of the ridge blew out and fires burned for some time. Some months later when I was ready to leave Korea, I went up to that OP to say good-bye to a friend of mine. That hillside was still blasted open and my buddy said there had never been any further action from that spot. When we called in a fire mission, we first identified ourselves and gave the azimuth to the target. We then gave the coordinates or distance from a check point and identified the target. When they fired the first round we adjusted from that point to the target. When we could drop 50 yards, we then fired for effect. Sometimes the first round would land in a narrow valley and we couldn't see the smoke. We would then call for a white phosphorous round so we could locate it and adjusted from that point. After the mission was over, we would describe the damage and either repeat fire for effect or cease fire.

The specific actions that I was involved in as an FO were fights for the hills I was on. One night we lost an entire company less one platoon on Kelly Hill. There was quite a bit of action then. We were involved several times supporting fire fights on the T-Bone and Pork Chop. Our OP was on a narrow ridge overlooking those hills. The Chinese knew where we were and fired on us several times with their 76's. However, their trajectory was very flat and they would either bit on the ridge down below us or pass over us and land a quarter of a mile in the valley behind us. One day, however, they adjusted in with the 120mm mortar and just walked it down the top of the ridge. This was somewhat disconcerting because we didn't have a bunker constructed at that time. Fortunately, we were between two blasts. That night the bunker was well on its way to being finished. One of the events that has bothered me since that time occurred was when two of our Air Force pilots apparently got lost and dropped their ordinance on our service battery. Over twenty of our guys were killed. This included three who were waiting to rotate home and one of our battery's drivers who was there getting some work done on his track vehicle. One other event occurred when I was Battery Exec. Corps called in a mission early one evening and we fired as fast as we could all night long. We were ordered to disregard restrictions on rapid fire and by morning, four out of our six tubes were burned out. I think that action involved Pork Chop, but I'm not sure. I've often wondered about the carnage we must have created during that night."

**Sergeant Conard Blevins**
**11th Marine Regiment, HQ Flash & Sound section 1952-53**

"I enlisted in the Marines on 1 Aug 1951 at Joplin, Missouri, and was sent to Korea as part of the 20th replacement draft in the latter part of May 1952. I took the usual boat ride and went ashore at Inchon. Initially I was assigned to a firing battalion in the 11th Marines, but I was an 0846 MOS, Field Artillery Scout Observer. But before much transpired, I was assigned to the Flash/Sound unit which was part of HQs 11th Marines. This unit had their 'central area' up close to the infantry's so called rest area. It was known as the Flash/Bang unit. Since the flash/sound unit was counter battery, we shot all types of artillery, even the Army's 8 inch howitzers. We were in support of the 1st Marine Division on the western front. I arrived in Korea about end of May, 1952 and was there until June, 1953. When I arrived, it seemed the division had only recently moved to the western front from the east. The thing I recall is that there were lots of uncharted land mines and the division suffered many casualties because of them. I worked as a flash/bang FO trying to suppress enemy artillery and mortar fire. We were able to shoot fire missions on targets of opportunity in addition to those to close caves or destroy possible gun or mortar emplacements. I know I did a lot of fire missions with all kinds of guns.

I always just tried to do my job and make sure my team members were OK and that we didn't loose any equipment. As I recall, the time was always 'right now.' And yes, many times I was so scared it was a wonder I still functioned. In counter-battery work, you have to be looking while the stuff is coming in. Since I was counter-battery, I was usually involved more on a company or battalion defense area. We got along well with the infantry, they liked what we were trying to do. Also, they found we could shoot those targets of opportunity. Further, the Forward Air Controllers always like to visit. We had some good optical equipment and had no problem getting a 105mm smoke round to the proper place. Flash/bang OP's were numbered 1, 2, and 3. Locations changed in late 1952. OP#3 was on the Hook, I think #2 became Boulder City in 1953. I remember being on COP 1, which was 'Nan' I think, on the west side of the Panmunjom corridor. There was also COP 2 on the east side of the corridor. And I never forget COP Vegas. We never supported any ROK units accept for one for when I did deal with the Korean Marine Corps west of the Panmunjom corridor. It was hard to function there because of the restrictions about firing close to the corridor. Being an FO was tiring, you never had enough sleep, you lived in a bunker dug into the ground, and the C rations weren't the best cuisine. You were somewhat clean when you went to the OP but after two or three weeks, filthy. I went six weeks one time without a shower. It seemed a rare day when there was no incoming fire, plus the Chinese did have snipers. Those Chinese snipers weren't too good, but they could drop an 82mm mortar round in your hip pocket.

I remember lots of fire missions, how important they were, I don't know. I had a little duel with a Chinese mortar crew one day and I prevailed because I was using 105mm howitzer with VT fusing. Calling a mission, basically, you contact Fire Direction Control, request a fire mission, justify your target, give them the coordinates or azimuth and range, then use one gun to adjust. After getting on target, you fire for effect. A lot of our fire missions were 'precision missions' using only one gun. The 8 inch howitzers were the most accurate. The duel with the mortar was interesting. I was in a fairly substantial OP bunker and the Chinese mortar crew was in an open dugout. They were putting those rounds right around the OP and I was adjusting that 105. After about three or four rounds I got a battery one round of Variable Time fuse and that took out the mortar crew. One ran out of my sight and the other two didn't move. The battle of the Hook in October 1952 probably had more affect than anything else during my tour. In about three days our unit had two KIA's and four or four or five WIA's. I was lucky to have survived. I recall being involved in some probe attacks and other skirmishes, but that battle I recall best. I was on that OP for three weeks prior to the Chinese overrunning it, my team was relieved the night before it happened. About three days later, after the infantry took it back, I went up with the lieutenant to see what, if anything we had left. A mortar round got both of us, and we were evacuated to the forward aid station. He died, I survived."

**Sergeant Warren Rehfeldt**
**1st Field Artillery Observation Battalion 1952-53**

"I enlisted in the Army, a family tradition, in September 1951, after completing my first year of college. I was sent to the Field Artillery Replacement Training Center at Fort Sill, Oklahoma, as a flash ranging specialist and was shipped out to Korea in March 1952, and was assigned to Battery 'A' 1st Field Artillery Observation Battalion. I served as a Forward Observer on front line OP's in the Chorwon and Kumhwa sectors of North Korea. I was with a great bunch of guys and we worked and got along well together. The mission and operation of the battalion was to locate enemy artillery and mortars by flash, sound, and radar ranging, provide survey control for friendly artillery, perform surveillance along the front to collect intelligence information, and provide meteorological data for friendly artillery. I served with the 1st FAOB from April 1952 to January 1953. My entire tour was spent on the OP's, and was involved in battles for Old Baldy, Pork Chop Hill, and White Horse Mountain. I called numerous fire missions, mostly on enemy mortar and artillery positions, and often on enemy troops in the open.

When I first got to Korea, I went ashore at Inchon in a landing craft. From there, I was transported by train to Yongdungpo, and from there by truck to Headquarters Battery of the 1st. The sound of not too far-off artillery fire highlighted my first night in Korea. In the morning I was transported to Battery 'A' which was located about 1,000 meters from the front line in the I Corps sector near Chorwon. I was assigned to Battery 'A' Flash Platoon as a Forward Observer and immediately was sent to OP #2 on Hill 347. I was regular army and 'gung ho', but I wondered how I would do in combat. Hill 347 was located on the Main Line of Resistance, and overlooked Pork Chop Hill, Old Baldy, and Chinese held Hasakkol and Pokkae hills. Operations along the front at that time, April 1952, were confined to small-scale actions characterized by patrols, probes, raids, and limited objective attacks. The 179th Infantry Regiment of the 45th Infantry Division controlled this part of the I Corps Sector.

Five to six Flash Platoon OP's occupied accurately surveyed positions along the I Corps front. To be effective, Forward Observers had to look into enemy territory, therefore, the Flash Platoon OP's were located on most of the strategic and dominating hilts along the front, and the Flash OP crews worked together to locate flashes from enemy artillery by intersection. Since our primary mission was to locate and destroy enemy artillery, observers on at least three of our OP's had to get a bearing on the flash from the same enemy gun to locate the gun by triangulation. The azimuths to the gun's flash would enable the Flash Plotting crew at the OP to accurately plot the location of the gun and direct neutralization fire on the enemy gun. By the time I got to Korea, the battle lines had stabilized, partly because of the truce talks in Panmunjon. Operations along the front were characterized by assaults on isolated positions, sieges of outposts, and especially heavy artillery bombardments. During the spring of 1952, Hill 347 was often the target for enemy mortar and artillery fire. I conducted numerous fire missions, using 105mm, 155mm, and 8-inch howitzers, using Corps artillery units like the 17th, 955th, and 999th Field Artillery Battalions and, at times, Division artillery units. During my tour, the Flash OP's were manned by four observers, all enlisted personnel, According to the book, observation battalion OP personnel should be mostly NCOs, but the guys I served with were privates and PFC's. Because of the new rotation policy, the NCOs rotated back to the states and were mostly replaced by Privates and PFC's! The guys I served with on OP #2 were all guys I trained with at Fort Sill, Jack Potter from Peoria Illinois, Virgil Sachs from Iowa and Larry Towne from a place called Fond du Lac Wisconsin. We each would take a three hour watch scanning the terrain for enemy targets, three hours observing through the BC scope, then time off to sleep, eat, read, or whatever, until our next watch. Contact with other members of the platoon was mostly voice contact by field phone and radio. The only times I met other guys in the platoon was when I left the OP and went to the rear area to get a shower and a change of clean clothes.

That happened about every three weeks. I'd spend the night at the Flash CP, usually played cards and drank beer before hitting the sack, then returned to the OP early the next morning. I remember seeing a USO show during the summer, actor Jon Hall was the featured entertainer. The only officers that I remember were Platoon Officers Lt Blair Ross, who was a West Point graduate from Tennessee and Lt Gene Nuovo, a Reserve Officer from New York. Our Battery Officers didn't visit OP #2 very often! Our bunker was an elaborate one, dug in on the crest of Hill 347. It consisted of a sleeping bunker with an adjoining instrument room for the spotting BC scope. The bunker was constructed of heavy logs and sandbags, with tarpaper and old tarps on the roof for rain. There was about six feet of headroom. A gasoline-fueled 'Yukon' stove provided heat and candles provided light. There were two camp beds and two litters suspended from the overhead logs for sleeping. Along one side of the sleeping bunker was an opening to a narrow tunnel that led down to the forward trench, which we sealed off. The tunnel, constructed by the CCF, was called the 'Chink Bunker'. It had a small cave dug on one side, with room enough for three people, and we would huddle in there during heavy artillery barrages. The cave was also used to store our beer ration! Our hill was overrun with rats, so our medic, 'Doc' Engleman provided us with several rattraps. Late one night a triggered trap awakened us, but nobody wanted to check it. In the morning we looked and found a rats tail, but no rat. Another time, late at night, a huge rat walked across the sandbags in front of my BC scope. I shouted at it, and the surprised rat jumped and struck the overhead logs and hit the ground running. I also remember when an infantry guy caught a rat, doused it with gasoline and set it on fire, it took off down the bill like a flaming rocket.

Our spotting scope was set up to sight through a narrow port, looking northwest, with about a 180-degree view of the front. To our left we could see Old Baldy, to our front, Pork Chop Hill, Hasakkol and Pokkae, and to our right, T-Bone, Arsenal, and Eerie. Flash OP #1 was located to our far right and Flash OP #3 was located to our far left. I was standing watch one night when I noticed moving lights a long way off, beyond Pokkae Valley toward the Yokkok-chon River. Looking through the spotting scope, I could see what appeared to be vehicle lights. They were out of artillery range, but I reported what I had seen to the Flash Plotting crew at the CP, and they confirmed that the vehicles were out of range, but would pass the information on to The Air Force. One summer day, a Marine F-4U Corsair was providing close support for the Infantry in the area of Chink Baldy. The aircraft made several passes, dropped napalm, fired rockets, and strafed. I observed an enemy machine gunner firing at the aircraft from a well dug in cave on a low ridge. I reported the coordinates of the cave and called for a fire mission. I requested 'delayed fuse', which would explode seconds after penetrating the ground. The artillery rounds were on target and effective. On another occasion, as I observed a close-support air strike on T-Bone Hill, one low-flying aircraft was hit by CCF ground fire. The pilot bailed out but, as his chute opened, he drifted into the ball of flames rising from the crashed aircraft. One afternoon there were some huge explosions, pretty close but down the hill behind our position. We assumed it was 'incoming mail', but saw US aircraft overhead, friendly aircraft bombed us!

The Chinese usually remained hidden in their caves and bunkers during the day and came out at night to fight. We all became more alert and uneasy when the sun went down. On moonless cloudy nights, huge searchlights located in the rear would reflect their beams off the clouds to light up 'no mans land' between the lines. Often, flares would light up the area in front of our position. On some nights, we could hear music played over CCF loudspeakers located in the vicinity of Hasakkol hill. Old Baldy, one of several outposts established by the infantry, was the scene of heavy fighting and was overrun by both sides many times, Pork Chop Hill was another outpost that changed hands often. 'Operation Counter', a series of attacks by the 45th Division to establish patrol bases around Old Baldy, was launched early in June. The CCF troops countered with a series of attacks against outposts on Snook Hill, Pork Chop, and Old Baldy, all defended by the 179th Infantry. During this period, CCF artillery and mortars heavily bombarded Hill 347. One night I contacted our CP to report that enemy artillery and mortars were pounding us, and that the division artillery FO told us that Chinese soldiers were seen on the hill. Our Platoon Leader, Lt. Ross, ordered us to 'stay in yoah bunka'. Soon after talking with Lt. Ross, our phone lines were cut. A little later, in all the excitement, the antenna for our radio broke off. By dawn, the Chinese had left Hill 347 and the infantry returned. During the night, shrapnel hit our BC scope and several nearby bunkers were destroyed. During one of my daytime watches on the BC scope, I spotted a CCF guy on a trail near Hasakkol and heading toward Chink Baldy. He was carrying a basket-type backpack. About a half minute later another CCF guy appeared, also with a backpack. Several more guys followed at spaced intervals. I figured they were packing supplies like grenades or ammo, and called for a fire mission behind Chink Baldy. Soon, our guns opened up and that area was swept with VT rounds, which explode and spread shrapnel before hilling the ground. The next day I was told that a CCF attack was delayed because of that fire mission. On another occasion, enemy mortars hit an infantry outpost on Hill 200, located southeast of Pork Chop Hill and in front of Hill 347. I could hear the mortars firing from the area behind Hasakkol and Chink Baldy. As I searched with the BC scope, I spotted the smoke from the firing mortars. It was in a location where I had conducted previous fire missions and our artillery was registered to hit that area I called for a fire mission that silenced the mortars.

On about July 18th, the 2nd Infantry Division was supposed to come on line and replace the 45th Division. On the night of the 18th, at about 2200 hours, the Divisional FO on our hill entered our bunker and said he could hear chink voices on his phone line. He thought some commo wires got mixed up, and thought The CCF was going to attack. He said when he left his bunker, he couldn't find anyone in the trenches or infantry bunkers. No one told us that the infantry defending our position was going to withdraw. Larry Towne left our bunker to check if the four-man crew in the Sound Platoon's bunker was still there. They were OK and hadn't heard anything about a pull out. Larry returned to our bunker and called the Flash CP. He was told that we should stay where we were. I set up the BAR in the passageway of the bunker, determined that no one would come in unless I knew them. About that time, all four of the guys from the division artillery bunker joined us, they thought the chinks were coming up the hill, and they called their CP and were told to move in with us. We couldn't see or hear anything from our observation port. As far as we know, the CCF never made it up the hill that night and we were happy to see the sun rise in the morning. At dawn, we saw the troops from the 2nd Division come up the hill to occupy the positions vacated by the 45th Division the night before. Apparently there was a mix-tip on the time that the 2nd was to relieve the 45th. The new 2nd Division infantry guys on our hill were green, jumpy, and trigger-happy. At times during the night, some soldier would hear something down the forward slope and start shooting in the direction of the sound. One night, a soldier was killed and three wounded by our own infantry. The one that was killed and one that was wounded were shot at daybreak, about twenty feet in front of our observation port. One of the wounded was an artillery officer from my Fort Sill training battery, he was returning from a visit to a listening post when he got shot. A few days later, a startled soldier killed an infantry officer when he jumped down into the trench. I was afraid to leave the bunker at night to relieve myself for fear of getting shot! During daylight air strikes on CCF forward positions, the new guys would watch from the top of the hill, some wearing white t-shirts, which was almost always drawing enemy mortar or artillery fire.

From mid-July to the first week in August, during The battle for Old Baldy, enemy artillery and mortars again heavily pounded the OP #2 area. One night during this battle, a small force of Chinese overran Hill 347 but was driven off by morning. Communist forces repeatedly assaulted Old Baldy, which was then held by the 23rd Infantry Regiment. I remember watching, through my spotting scope, one of our tanks move up the hill firing into bunkers. A Chinese soldier ran toward the tank and placed a satchel charge on the tank track, and as he ran back, the explosion disabled the tank. The battle for Old Baldy raged for several days. Our Flash observers located numerous enemy mortar and artillery positions, and provided extensive battlefield intelligence coverage. One afternoon, while I was on watch, the Chinese began firing at our position with a flat trajectory weapon, probably a recoilless rifle. I saw the flashes from the gun, but before I could call for a fire mission, three or four rounds hit below the observation port and sent splinters flying off the overhead logs. By the time our artillery was ready to return the fire, the Chinese had stopped shooting and withdrew into their cave. Our bunker began to cave in near the end of July, and we had to rebuild it. Korean Service Corps laborers helped by carrying materials and logs up the hill. The logs were eight or nine inches in diameter and twelve feet long. We covered the roof with two layers of logs, several layers of sandbags, and three feet of dirt. At that time, Dutch troops attached to the 38th Infantry Regiment occupied the defenses on Hill 347. One problem we had with the Dutch, they took whatever they could carry from our supply of materials, sandbags, tarpaper, etc. and at night we would try to take back whatever they took from us. The Dutch CO accused us of taking their stuff! Then the bunker they built next to ours, using our sandbags of course, got a direct hit. We retrieved most of our sandbags.

The Dutch soldiers were a good group to be with, although we didn't always know what they were talking about. They seemed to be more professional than US soldiers - - - they came to fight a war and didn't worry about 'spit and polish' stuff. As with the US infantry, the Dutch drew food rations from Corps Supply for our crew on the OP. When the US troops were on the hill, we seldom ate with them. It was a hassle, not enough to eat, the mess lines were long with at least five yards between each man because one round could get you all, and it took forever to get served. So we ate C-rations in our bunker. The Dutch weren't so fussy. The food was brought up the hill in big containers to the back of our bunker, out of sight of the CCF, three times a day. The guys would gather around in a group, were served quickly, and went back to their positions to eat. The food tasted great, seconds for everyone, and once in a while they even served ice cream! We always ate with the Dutch!

The rainy season began towards the end of July. Late one morning, after a torrential downpour, the sky cleared and the sun shone warm and bright. I observed some activity on low-lying Pokkae Hill, several Chinese soldiers, taking advantage of the sun, had spread their wet clothes on the ground to dry. I immediately called for a fire mission and requested VT fuse, which would explode in the air and spread shrapnel in all directions. The fire mission was successful, the soldiers were caught in the open and the clothing on the ground was shredded. One morning, early in September, several news photographers with cameras and a movie camera visited our OP to take pictures of Pork Chop and Pokkae hills. They said they took pictures on Old Baldy, and their films will be seen on TV in the states in October. CCF artillery was increasingly active in September, and we located and conducted numerous counter-battery missions. In mid-September, the CCF tried to take Old Baldy again and overran Pork Chop Hill. Hill 347 was hit by a heavy artillery barrage. As in past episodes, our communication lines were cut but were quickly restored by our battery wire crew. A few days later, US troops arrived to replace the Dutch infantry. In October and November 1952, troops from Thailand, attached to the 2nd Division, took over the defense of Hill 347 and the outposts. The Thai soldiers were friendly, 'gung ho' and spirited. For amusement, they often held kickboxing contests in the area behind our bunker. With the Thai troops on line with us, I felt safe and secure. As with the other infantry units that came on line with us, the Thai would draw food rations for us from Corps Supply. The Thai cooks prepared almost everything as a stew and served it all on rice. I learned to like the food they prepared, but I usually ate C-rations.

Early in October, General Van Fleet attached the battalion and elements of I Corps artillery to the IX Corps artillery to conduct counter-battery fire in the Triangle Hill and Sniper Ridge sectors. We pulled off of Hill 347 and, with the rest of Battery 'A', moved east near Kumhwa, to support operations during the battle for White Horse Hill. My OP #2 crew moved into a makeshift bunker on a high hill near White Horse. Our position was not surveyed in, so we couldn't call in fire missions. We spent our watches reporting intelligence information and enemy movements. I don't remember seeing infantrymen on the hill with us. I celebrated my 21st birthday on that hill. We moved back to Hill 347, in the Pork Chop and Old Baldy area, in early November, and again occupied our old OP #2 bunker, As fall turned to winter, there was a decline in front line activity, and we spent more time improving our OP #2 position. Toward the end of November the 7th Infantry Division came on line to replace the 2nd, and the Thai troops left Hill 347. On Thanks-giving Day, the OP crews were invited to Battery headquarters for Thanksgiving dinner. Only one guy at a time was allowed to leave The OP. Later, on my way back up the hill to the OP, a few enemy mortar rounds came in. In my haste to seek cover, I managed to sprain my ankle. It took nearly a month before I could walk without a limp. December 1952 was very cold on the hill. Some nights the temperature dropped well below zero. Our sleeping bunker was usually warm, but the instrument room was unheated. When on watch, I wore my winter parka and wrapped myself in a sleeping bag to stay warm. It snowed a lot, and when the wind swept the ridges and valleys, there seemed to be little action along the front line. I rotated back to the states in January 1953, shipping out from Inchon aboard the USNS Marine Adder. The ship landed at Sasebo, Japan, where we transferred to the USNS General W. H. Gordon and headed for San Francisco."

**1st Lt Robert Sherwood**
**143rd Field Artillery Battalion 1952-53**

"I was drafted and took basic and leaders school at Fort Dix. From there, I was sent to OCS at the Artillery School, Ft. Sill, OK. I started in the new class #1, but was held back to graduate class #2, my MOS was 1189. The class was then split into various battalion assignments and then sent to Korea. The 143rd Field Artillery Battalion was a 105mm direct support unit for the 40th Infantry Division of California fame. Most of the Ops that I served on were on terrain or around names given generally to terrain or action, such as the 'Chorwon Valley', 'Iron Triangle', 'Heartbreak Ridge', and 'Commies Nose'. These were all locations along the established MLR. I served from February 1952 to March 1953. I was awarded two battle stars during 1952 and 1953 with three ribbons including the UN medal. I was an FO at all times, with occasional relief back to the battery for a short period of time to rest. The MLR was stable, but was regularly active with action, mostly probes, patrols, bombardment, all needing twenty-four hour observation. As a Forward Observer, we were on constant vigil on the B.C. scope with the commo sergeant and the wire corporal. It was constant observation to keep track of physical activity of enemy and reaction by 105s to suppress that activity. We also observed and monitored time-on targets by augmented, combined artillery of battalion and division. This entailed 105mm, 155mm, and 8-inch guns when notified of impending bombardment of the observable sector. Being north of the 38th parallel, it was as cold as hell is warm. All posts were in sand bagged bunkers with ports of observation and fire. A savior in the cold was the 'Mickey Mouse' boots, when your feet are warm you can cope with anything. We had a good relationship with the infantry. They were happy we were suppressing sightings and fire from enemy. We know they wanted and appreciated our support. Due to the ridgeline OP's, supporting artillery had to often fire at high angle resulting in an infrequent dose of 'friendly fire' around our positions. I am no war hero though. When asked to take aerial observation, I refused as L-19 spotter planes were regularly being shot down. I decided to take my chances on the ground. Night observation as you can imagine was particularly stressful as one tried to see and hear any activity in front of observation posts, and occasionally, infrequent night flares were used."

**Sergeant James Settlemire**
**92nd Armored Field Artillery Battalion 1952-53**

"In 1951 I knew my draft number would be coming up shortly so my fiancé and I decided to get married on July 14th, 1951. On August 27th, 1951 I was drafted into the Army and took my basic training at Fort Dix N.J. When I finished with basic training and field wiremen's school at Fort Dix in January 1952 I traveled by troop train from N.J. to Seattle Washington and waited for a month on pier #91 for the troop transport S.S. Marine Adder. As it turned out the Marine Adder was the transport that took the unit I would be assigned to in Korea in September 1950. We arrived in Korea via Japan in March 1952 and unloaded down the landing nets in Inchon since there was still no docking to unload. From Inchon we traveled by train to Chunchon south of the central front which was a replacement depot. I was assigned to the 92nd Armored Field Artillery Battalion, known as the 'Red Devils', and was taken by truck to the unit which was positioned on the MLR near Kumhwa on the central front. The 92nd AFA had self-propelled 155mm howitzers mounted on M41 tank chassis, and while I was assigned to the 92nd the unit was assigned to the IX Corps Artillery on the central front near Kumhwa above the 38th Parallel. I arrived in the 92nd on March 23rd, 1952 and rotated home February 23rd, 1953. When I arrived in the 92nd, they needed someone to work in the S-2 intelligence section in HQ Battery. This duty also included spending time on the OP as an enlisted man helping the various officers who were in charge. Eventually I was assigned regular duty on the OP team serving one week on, and one off, twenty-four hours a day. We were positioned with various infantry units who happened to be on the IX Corps front line at the time. We supported the U.S. 3rd and 7th Infantry Divisions, the ROK 2nd Infantry Division, the Turkish Brigade and the Greek Brigade, and we fought almost exclusively the Chinese. I recall we usually had one OP for each firing battery, Able, Baker, and Charley, and two OP's for HQ Battery.

While I was there the main battle during October 1952 was the struggle for Triangle Hill which was positioned right in front of the Chinese held Hill 1062 which was called 'Papa San' because of its size and view of the entire Kumhwa Valley. Our OP was right in front of Triangle Hill. The 2nd ROK Division tried to take the hill several times but failed. The Chinese were dug down in deep pits and survived our battalions pounding time after time. As the ROK infantry squads reached near the top of the hills the Chinese would open up with mortars and would pop up throwing hand grenades which drove the ROK troops back. Finally it was decided to turn the assault over to the U.S. 7th Infantry Division who finally captured the hill after suffering heavy losses. When I was there the MLR was engaged in trench warfare. Each side was a well dug in network of bunkers and connecting trenches. Most of the action was at night when the infantry would send out patrols into 'no mans land' hoping to engage an enemy patrol and kill or capture the enemy. During these patrols there would be calls for supporting fire from the artillery units along the line. Before I reached my unit I pictured the front lines as a mass of army units a mile deep on the main line of resistance with a lot of back up forces behind the front line units. In reality the thinly positioned infantry in the front line trenches were the extent of the friendly forces with some artillery battalions scattered behind the MLR at various distances. There would be reserve blocking divisions behind our positions but they would be several miles back. It was very apparent that as a FO sitting on top of a hill you were vulnerable to a mass enemy attack which could very easily sweep through the infantry positions in the valleys below and leave our position surrounded on top of the hill. Many nights when intelligence reports indicated the probability of such an attack we considered it a 'boots on' night and slept fully dressed ready to evacuate if necessary. Another concern we had when we were supporting the ROK infantry was they were prone to 'bug out' under such an attack and leave their positions without communicating this to the FOs.

The most memorable fire missions were the 'Time on Target' missions. These were missions were we would locate specific Chinese positions in advance such as a location were they were building new fortifications for emplacements on the top of a mountain. We could see the position during the daytime where they had been working during the night when they couldn't be seen. The ToT would be planned during the night when it was assumed they would be again working on the fortification. IX Corps Artillery would coordinate every artillery battalion within range to fire at the appropriate time so that all rounds would reach the target at the same time. Needless to say it provided a very impressive barrage that eliminated the target effectively. Along with the actual fire missions, some other things you never forget. I remember during the attack on Triangle Hill I had my 20-power spotting scope focused on the lead ROK squad as they approached the top of the hill where the Chinese were dug in. The Chinese opened up with mortar fire and stood up in the trenches and started throwing hand grenades. A mortar round landed in the middle of the lead squad and lifted a ROK infantryman up off his feet and threw him down the hillside mortally wounded. As he rolled down and down the hill I followed him with my scope until he rolled out of sight, wondering if he had survived the blast."

### Sergeant Carl Bennett
### 49th Field Artillery Battalion 1952-53

"I was drafted at the age of 19 and was sent to Korea from Camp Stoneman California, by an army transport ship called Meigs in May 1952, and was then transported through Japan overnight and landed at Inchon, Korea. I was assigned to the 49th Field Artillery Battalion, Battery 'A'. We were a part of the 7th Infantry Division, and we were in direct support of the 17th Infantry Regiment and the 31st Infantry Regiment. The 49th was a 105 mm outfit, and we supported actions in I Corps in the Chorwon and Kumhwa valley or in the Iron Triangle area. I was an FO Sergeant for my battery, and we had the honor of shooting the first divisional fire mission that included the U.S. Navy battleship New Jersey with her 16 inch guns. A real sight to see! The 49th Field Artillery Battalion had the honor of being the only field artillery battalion to reach the Yalu River, with the 7th Infantry Division. Our last place of battle was the 'Chop' in 1953.

I was there from June 1952 thru July 1953. I volunteered to be a FO but was a machine gun sergeant for my gun battery first. Our OP's were 15 and 17, we fired on hill 200, Pork Chop Hill, Old Baldy, T-Bone, Pokeye, to name a few, all in the Chorwon area. We participated in battles on Old

Baldy, Pork Chop, T-bone, Hassakol, 3 Sisters, Pokeye, Alligator Jaws, we covered a lot of hills from this area around hill 200. we had OP's on the 'Chop' , 200, and Baldy, and could attain very effective fire on these areas. Sometimes the battalion had a number of different OP's like 15, 17, 20, but mostly 15 and 17 on hill 200 and the 'Chop', but we did switch back and forth with others. My Lieutenant and myself were mostly alone on these OP's to send supporting fire when needed. Most of the time things were normal as could be but it got very scary with the fire fights at night, they were the worst. But, you soon learned to live and look out for your buddies and they would be there for you. The infantry took good care of us FO's because they needed us to knock 'old Joe' off their backs, so it was all a team effort. With the 17th and 31st Infantry Regiments, we all were a family in the trenches. I have to take my hat off to the riflemen they were a great bunch of guys and we all looked after each other, we were welcomed to their outfits with open arms.

I think we were up against mostly North Koreans. As a FO you felt good about your job, you was a big helping hand to your buddies ,and you felt like the job you did was very important and you felt good about what you were doing for bringing the war to a end. The trenches were pure hell just, ask any infantrymen and you will get the same answer. I wonder sometimes how we made it through some of the battles, and why some had to loose it all. The most memorable fire mission I had was when we had a DIVARTY fire mission, I had the job of calling it in, we fired all of DIVARTY that we could muster and the USS New Jersey fired with us, it must have been pure hell on the enemy. He had just overran Pork Chop, and we gave him it all, we were able to take it back but with a great cost of lives on both sides. All fire missions were important, we walked several squads and platoons of men back thru our lines and kept 'Joe' away from them, it was very rewarding. The infantry was always sending out patrols so we just helped them get back. I think Pork Chop Hill was the most significant fight we had at the end of the war, we tried to keep it for the high ground and 'old Joe' wanted it real bad, we called fire mission after fire mission, and lost a lot of good men for a piece of worthless ground to this day sits alone in the DMZ. What a waste. There were lots of proud moments but knowing that our Division went to the Yalu, that's quite a pure pride of your outfit."

**Sergeant Thomas Hannon**
**955th Field Artillery Battalion 1952-53**

"I was drafted into the United States Army by the Selective Service # 25 of Bronx New York. On October 10, 1951, I was inducted at Whitehall Street in Manhattan, New York City. After completing basic training at Camp Chaffee Arkansas, where I had both infantry and artillery training, I flew to Fort Lewis Washington, and from there I was taken by troop ship to Japan, then on to Korea. I arrived in Korea about April 15, 1952 were I was assigned to Able Battery of the 955th Field Artillery Battalion. The 955th had three firing batteries each with three 155mm howitzers which were towed by a tracked vehicle known as a 'Cat'. There was also Headquarters Battery and Service Battery. The 955 was known as a bastard battalion since we were not attached to any division. We were under the control of the 8th Army attached to various Corps at various times such as I Corps and X Corps. Since there was a rotation system, based on 36 points, I spent from approximately April 15, 1952 to May 15th 1953. When I first arrived I was assigned to #3 gun section as cannoneer. After about three months since I had FDC training in basic I was asked if I wanted to go into the detail section, consisting of radio and wiremen and FDC people. The fact that Lieutenant Levy and Lieutenant Collins were both New Yorkers was a factor in my being chosen to get into that, what I thought, was a prestigious section. After humping 98lb. artillery shells, powder canisters and other very manual type work, I thought that working the in the detail section would be a better job. Since Lt. Frank Collins was Reconnaissance Officer he asked if I would want to be his R.O. driver but that would involve working the OP's. This seemed like adventurous work so I said 'O.K.'. This job also had the perk of not having to pull regular perimeter or gun guard duty.

My first venture to the OP was on a summer night in July with Lt. Frank Collins as the FO and a guy name Lee as wireman. I was the team radioman. We were driven up to the OP area via an open ¾ ton truck in the eerie light of some large floodlights that were set up on trucks located near our main battery. The purpose of the floodlights focused on the enemy hills was obviously to hinder their vision and facilitate our night moves. This first encounter was the only time I saw the floodlights in use. When we got to the base of OP hill and disembarked from our vehicle, we managed to get a few ROK infantrymen to 'choggie' some of our supplies consisting of cases of C-rations, 5 gallon cans of water and a variety of supplies up the long hill. These infantry guy, as was the custom were paid by us in a few cans of C-rations and cigarettes. We carried our own personal effects, such as the B.C. scope, our sleeping bags, some extra clothes and of course our carbines. We were huffing and puffing by the time we reached the top of the hill and the OP living bunker. On the way up the trail which was partially in trenches and partially atop the edge of the trenches since at that point in time we did not receive any enemy fire. As we strained up the hill we could hear some small arms fire in the distance and the occasional rumble of artillery. Some of the ROK infantry grinned at us as we passed, but most were understandably glum. Lt. Collins relieved the other officer and the team who had been there for about ten days went down the hill and was taken back on the same truck that brought us up. I believe that they were from another battery.

Our living bunker built of stones, some logs and stacks of sandbags seemed reasonably sturdy. The living bunker was only about ten yards from the crew of the hill where the actual OP bunker was located. It took us a while to get ourselves oriented and we were all anxious. It was now very dark and a bit scary. We had some candles and a small Coleman type lamp. A poncho was hung over the bunker opening so very little light could escape. Of course there was no light at al in the OP bunker which was on the top of the hill with only a narrow slit aperture toward the enemy lines. The first night was not eventful, other than the sound of distant occasional small arms fire. However the three of us slept very little. In the brightness of early daylight we became a bit more up-beat. We came out of the living bunker and cased out the OP bunker. We set up the B.C. scope and took turns looking over the territory which was typical of Korea's rolling hills and valleys. It was our duty, among other things, to register the battery each day by firing the center piece, #3 gun at a pre determined target such as an enemy bunker. Due to atmospheric conditions it was necessary to reregister almost every day. Unfortunately on this first day on the OP we found that our wire phone was not working properly, so the wireman Lee and I went out on a wire patrol. A myriad of wire were strung along the back of the trench, so we slowly walked along looking for possible breaks in the wires. Since we were somewhat engrossed we did not notice that the front side of the trench towards the enemy lines had slowly dropped down so that our heads were clearly exposed above the trench rim. I heard a very loud crack and a bullet smacked into the rear side of the trench only a few inches between my head and my partner Lee's. It shocked the crap out of us and we both dropped down to the floor of the trench. We crawled for a short distance then ran back towards our bunkers. I was more angry than scared, so when I returned to our living bunker I asked Lt. Collins if we could have our ROK infantry pump some automatic fire into the valley and hill in front of the trench where the sniper was located. There was the obvious language barrier, but we found a guy who was manning a 50 cal. out of a hole not far from our OP bunker. We tried to make him understand that a sniper had just fired upon us from a certain nearby location. Our guy was not about to fire his machine gun thus exposing his position without actually being confronted by an obvious enemy. I then learned the lesson that in this World War I type of static trench warfare, it was best to stay inconspicuous, in your bunker or holes.

A few days later we spotted a few enemy infantry known to all of us simply as 'Joe Chink', since we fought against Chinese troops because in 1952 the North Korean army was mostly decimated. We called for some V.T. fuse rounds on them. Since this was more or less on-the-job training we were embarrassed that our first rounds were far off target. After a few more corrections we managed to make them disappear off of the hill. During my thirteen month tour of duty I manned either five or six separate OP's and since I drove a ¾ ton tuck as well as a jeep I was called upon to drive other OP teams sometimes from other batteries to and from the OP's since I was quite familiar with the territory. Our OP's did not have names that I recall. We knew them only by numbers; OP's #1, #2, #3, and #4. Our battalion moved a few times so of course the OP locations moved also. Most of my OP tours were with Lt. Frank Collins and the wireman, Lee. Since Lee and I worked as a team and had begun to amass a lot of experience, some new green observers asked us to accompany them to the OP's. Understandably these young lieutenants, only about 23 years of age felt more comfortable having someone with them who at least knew which direction the enemy was located. Of course it was a little more involved than that. We also worked with a Lt. Jones and a Lt. Cannonico. The living quarters of the bunkers were very cramped so we got to know each other very well. We would eat together and sleep in our sleeping bags known as fart sacks, only a foot or two apart. Night time was the worst, since it was very dark and claustrophobic. We tried to keep some type of light available either a candle or partially screened flashlights, behind the poncho at the bunker opening. It was terribly cold in the winter but we had pretty good heavy sleeping bags. That was the only time we could feel reasonably warm, but I remember having my breath form ice crust on the opening of the bag. Each Observer had a different personality. I got along the best with Lt. Collins. He was a fellow New Yorker, had a rather dry Irish sense of humor and was quite bright. Lt. Jones was a nice quiet guy, I believe from Texas. Lt. Cannonico was also a fellow New Yorker, always looking for a little more excitement, in fact on one of his first nights on the OP he and I chucked some hand grenades down the hill 'just to wake up the gooks'.

Each OP was an adventure in a different way. Most of the OP's were in the general area of the Iron Triangle consisting of Chorwon, Kumhwa and Pyongyang. We had OP's at Snipers Ridge and Whitehorse Mountain and other numbered hills. During the very cold winters, Collins, Lee and I were sent to an OP facing Snipers Ridge. On the ride up we received some machine gun and other small arms fire from the ridge. We got a respite after rounding the base of a hill. While unloading the truck we found ROKs to carry our equipment up the long hill. Some of the poor bastards wore only sneakers in the snow. One guy was shivering in the cold and asked to have his C-ration pay before 'choggying' up the hill. This delay probably saved our lives because Joe Chink had it timed so that they thought we were on our way up the trail and left loose with a barrage of mortar fire. Fortunately we were still at the protected base of the hill. While at another OP Lt. Collins was called back to the battery location overnight while Lee and I remained at the OP Even though we had some protection from the ROK infantry we still took turns staying awake for our own peace of mind. On this particular night while Lee was asleep, I got out of the bunker to take a leak. While doing so, I observed some flashes of enemy artillery being fired. I phoned back to the battery and they confirmed that they were receiving some rounds right on the battery position. I then contacted two other OP's and we were able to triangulate the artillery flashes. I then called for fire at the proper position and after a few moments the enemy fire ceased. I never knew for certain whether or not I knocked out their guns or simply silenced them, but I felt some pride in knowing that I personally spotted the position and called some very accurate fire. At another OP Frank Collins and myself were in our OP bunker calling for some fire on a nearby enemy bunker to register the battery on a nice sunny day. Suddenly a recoilless rifle or bazooka type weapon landed a round against our bunker with an ungodly bang that caused dirt and pebbles to rain on us from inside of the bunker. We could not see who was firing at us but after a moment we knew that they were very close, because we could hear the metallic clank of the round being loaded into the tube and another round slammed into the front of our bunker. It was about then that we thought it would be best to get the hell out of there and back into our living bunker just on the reverse side of the hill where our partner Lee was located. Collins cut out, crawling through the slit trench out of our bunker just as another round smacked into the front of the bunker. I was going to follow Collins, but I thought, sure as shit that they were timing us and I would catch the next round as I came out of the bunker. I waited alone for a few seconds which seemed like an eternity for the next round t hit. As soon as it hit, I took off crawling, stumbling, running down the slit trench, jumping over black combo wire, as I heard another round hit the trench behind me. I fell into the living bunker where Collins and Lee were waiting, huffing and puffing. The adrenaline was really pumping and Collins and I were half laughing, half crying. A common term we used to use in the living bunker was, 'Woe, misery and unhappiness.' That made us laugh even harder. A sad and tragic epilog to the bazooka incident took place that same night when a ROK soldier took a position in our OP bunker. Obviously the gooks had gotten the proper range while practicing on Collins and me, because they put one right through the opening and killed the poor guy instantly.

The worst OP nightmare, in the wee hours of a dark and cold night I was sound asleep in my fart sack when Frank Collins began roughly shaking me awake. In a stupor I cursed at him. But in a frantic whisper he said 'Can't you hear that?' Of course by then I did hear it, the rapid small arms fire that sounded just a few feet from our living bunker. Collins took my carbine and scurried out through the poncho at the opening and out into the trench. I grabbed his .45 pistol out of its holster and cowered in the corner. Poor Lee had been suffering for a day or so with what turned out to pneumonia. I told Collins to give a yell before he came back through the poncho because I was prepared to shoot anyone coming through the opening. Within a minute or less he was back in the bunker informing us that we were being completely overrun. I took a look and saw dark shadows jumping over the trenches and flashes from burp guns and rifles all around. Collins said to get our battery for help. I called and the guy on FDC could obviously tell the urgency in my voice. I told him that we were being overrun and we needed some Victor Tear right in front of us. After a long moment the FDC guy said that our position was in the red or no fire zone and he was going to refer the mission minutes later as we huddled in the dark living bunker the rounds came screaming in exploding as designed above us. Unfortunately they went off directly above us while our ROKs were battling off the Chinks. The attack subsided and when morning came we found several dead, not all Joe Chinks but some of our own ROK guys. The ROK infantry lieutenant verbally abused us indicating that some of our rounds killed some of his troops. I don't know who killed whom, but I did feel bad that I was the one who actually called the mission and may have unintentionally killed some of our own troops. A sad day. These events are the most vivid in my memory. Interesting thing was, even though I was fired at on the OP's by all types of weapons, rifles, mortars, bazookas, machine guns and artillery, it was in the battery that I was wounded by artillery shrapnel and awarded the Purple Heart."

## Sergeant Peter McHugh
## 176th Armored Field Artillery Battalion 1952-53

"I enlisted in the Army, and after training was sent to Korea aboard the troopship USS General H.B. Freeman in June 1952. I was with IX Corps Artillery from July of 1952 to July of 1953. I worked out of Headquarters Battery of the 176th Armored Field Artillery Battalion, which was a Pennsylvania National Guard 105mm outfit. In IX Corps at the time, the 176th was in the eastern central front at the time. I spent about all of my time on Hill 949 and OP 121. We generally supported the 18th, 22nd and 23rd Infantry Regiments of the 3rd ROK Division, and we worked together just fine I thought. It was during the stalemate, so there was not too much infantry action, but lots of artillery though. Some infantry action did kick in the last few months of the war. I liked it, being an FO We did a lot of calls for fire on all types of targets every day. I, a capitalist grunt, was calling fire on communist grunts. I had no stocks or bonds and they didn't qualify to join the party. That is exactly how I thought at 17. Except for the incoming artillery, it was like camping out. Unlike others, calling a mission was no big deal to me, I didn't get any sort of adrenaline rush. I volunteered for Forward Observer duty because I was intrigued by the combat pay. I could have come home in April of '53 but I kept extending myself a month at a time until my battalion commander ordered me home in July with 45 points. Some things do stand out as memorable to me, such as the time I spotted a Chinese company of infantry was walking through a valley and I called for a lot of VT on them, and in the spring of 1953 when the Chinese pushed us off of Hill 949."

## 2nd Lt Leonard De Bord
## 39th Field Artillery Battalion 1952-53

"The 40th Infantry Division began assembling at Camp Cook, California in September. We cleaned up this old WWII camp and began intensive basic and advanced training, and I mean intensive. I had started as a rifleman but ended up in the mortar section of the weapons platoon. Ever try carrying a backpack, with a strapped-on mortar base plate, on 15 and 25-mile forced marches. At any rate, along about March or April of 1951, my company commander told me I was eligible for OCS and that there were vacancies in the infantry, artillery, or engineer branches, so I choose artillery. In April, the 40th Division started shipping out to Japan enroute, eventually, to Korea. In late May or early April I was sent to NCO leadership school at Camp Roberts, CA, near Paso Robles. As part of the school curriculum we cadre'd with the basic training companies of the 7th Armored Division at Camp Roberts. More road marches! In August I was ordered to Ft Sill Oklahoma to commence training as part of OCS class 7. What a screw up. Class 7 had already started and 28 of us new arrivals had the delightful tasks, for the next 5-6 weeks, of preparing the barracks and grounds for the September class, Class 8, of which we would become members. We graduated 96 of a starting class of about 150 on 26 February 1952. I was then sent on my first duty assignment as a 2nd Lt to the 720th Field Artillery Battalion, Ft Lewis, Washington. The trip to Korea started at Ft Lawton, Washington in July 1952. Originally, a group of us prospective FO's were to go by ship from Seattle, but we were told there was an urgent requirement for FO's in Korea and we were to be flown over there. Another 'good grief'. We left Seattle by train, arrived Victoria, B.C., enplaned on Canadian Pacific Airlines and arrived in Tokyo. We went thru a whole lot of Mickey Mouse processing culminating in a stay at Gifu and eventual embarkation at Sasebo for the harbor at Pusan.

Approximately 48 hours after landing at Pusan I was the sole, proud occupant/temporary owner of a 3rd Division, 39th Field Artillery Battalion OP in the vicinity of Outpost Kelly. I was soon to learn that the 65th Infantry Regiment had been kicked off Outpost Kelly and that the 15th Infantry

Regiment, whose motto was 'CAN DO', was going to try to get it back. I was shortly taken off the Battalion OP and assigned to 'A' Battery of the 39th where I joined an FO team comprised of a recon sergeant and a driver/radio operator/wireman with a WWII Jeep and 1/4 ton trailer filled with all sorts of gear and soon to be our sort of mobile household for many months. Our call sign was 'KANE ABLE 9er' and our FO team was sent to the 1st Battalion, 15th Infantry Regiment and awaited assignment to an infantry company while the Division and Regiment finalized their plans for attacking and taking Outpost Kelly. For whatever reason, and there may have been several, the attack did not take place and we eventually returned to our battery to await reassignment. It was not long in coming. We were given an FO team assignment to a ROK company for a short stint on Outpost Queen. That was quite an experience! While we were there the sector was pretty quiet. Just after we left all hell broke loose and the Chinese hit Queen, Big Nod and Little Nod hard. The ROKs and the 2nd Infantry Division had their hands full. This was the second time our team just missed being involved in a major engagement and as time wore on it seemed that we continued to live a charmed existence.

Later, the 3rd Division, part of the IX Corps, moved to the Chorwon sector and for the next six months I was in and out of observation posts on Alligator Jaws, Whitehorse, Hill 284, a rice paddy OP in the middle of Chorwon Valley which I can't remember its name or number, and OP's Tom and Dick. The 3rd Division inherited Whitehorse just after the ROKS had finished repulsing numerous Chinese attacks aimed at taking the mountain. Chinese dead were still tying in the concertina wire barriers and, in places, stacked up like cordwood for eventual burial. The stench was memorable. We got there late, again, but we weren't complaining!

The life of this FO and my team pretty much paralleled that of the infantry. Although I was somewhat of a free agent when with the infantry units, with few exceptions, my team and I were subjected to most of the difficulties and problems experienced by company personnel. The team was in the dirt with them, sometimes on a little higher ground and, sometimes, in a somewhat less fragile position than the rifleman. The recon sergeant and I usually took turns at observation duties, but the radioman, assisted at times by the recon sergeant, had most of the down-and-dirty work to do, maintaining the vehicle, obtaining supplies, keeping EE4s, PRC-6s and a damned unreliable radio, which I forgot its number, but it was a plain metal, 00 box with one knob and an antenna, working and supplied with fresh batteries, a major problem, and, most of all, laying and maintaining land-lines of communication, a major, major problem. A Herculean set of tasks in many situations, Upon gaining a deliberate observation position, the team attempted to improve the position, but my first and immediate priority was to commence observation in my assigned sector, company, platoon, or whatever, front. The initial occupation of the OP involved a flurry of activity, laying wire to the field artillery liaison officer and to the infantry company commander, establishing radio contact, orienting the map to the terrain, setting up and orienting the B.C. scope, if the position allowed its employment, otherwise, setting out markers or otherwise establishing azimuth reference points, obtaining the commander's plan for defense of the position and advising on the integration of artillery fires with the infantry's fire plan, plotting concentration points and final protective fires, such as barrage locations, establishing artillery registration points in the sector if not already there, conducting or verifying registration fire in the sector, identifying and plotting enemy avenues of approach and assigning concentration numbers to those areas, firing in selected concentrations, identifying possible or probable enemy OP's, gun positions, etc, drawing sketches which identified the terrain in front of the OP and delineated visual dead zones, key terrain features, and any other distinctive feature, such as a ruin, large tree, pile of rocks, tank or railroad car hulk, etc, and establishing and marking the azimuth to each, establishing a plan for illumination of the unit's front, making a plan of final defensive fires, and protective fires for any forthcoming company patrol or listening post activities, creating map overlays of all proposed concentrations or fires and sending them back to the PA LNO, moving equipment and supplies into a sleeping bunker or hole, if there was one, otherwise, set up a small tent to the rear of the company and in defilade, and last but not least, dig foxholes or find some!

Now, I'm not trying to make more of a deal of this than it is, and certainly not attempting to equate our actions or problems with those of the infantry, but the FO teams do face some large responsibilities and a fair range of challenges. Even though Korea was, during my time there, more or less trench warfare we did our share of backpacking up those damn hills and mountains. We may have had more shelter from the elements than some of our predecessors but we still got soaking wet in the monsoon season, hot as hell in the summer, got frostbite, and froze our gonads off in the most damnable cold weather in the world. Also, because at the time there was a shortage of artillery shells due to a steel strike in the U.S., this amounted to a rationing of ammunition for fire missions and restricted routine firing on targets identified by the FOs. I was personally subjected to such restrictions. However, if all hell had broken out in a particular sector the ammunition would have been provided, but at the cost of other restrictions in other vulnerable areas. We had a mountain in the 3rd Division sector we called Papasan which was in the Chinese's area and overlooked some of the main line of resistance, most of the main supply route and other trails leading to the front and, some of the rear areas. Camouflage nets were erected over and along the main supply route to cover vehicle traffic and for added good measure all windshields were removed from their vehicles so there was no sunlight reflection, and were stored someplace. That was all well and good until winter came along and windshields were still verboten. Ever traveled, day or night, in an open vehicle when temperatures are hovering at -60 degrees Fahrenheit? Talk about frostbite! There were a lot of jobs worse than an FO's, but like most others on the leading edge of any conflict it can be a miserable, uncomfortable, lonely and frequently unsettling existence. My biggest concern, prior to my first assignment as a FO, was wondering if I would overcome certain apprehensions and survive the war.

Upon my arrival at that first infantry company this concern rapidly gave way to the immediate realization and awareness that a tremendous responsibility resided in my hands. The company commander, of course, had the responsibility for his unit and was deeply concerned about the performance, care and welfare of his men. By virtue of my position, I was tacitly handed a large share of the responsibility for the security and protection of this unit of 120-150 individuals, an awesome position for any young and relatively new 2nd Lt to contemplate. Can I do the job was a gnawing question. At this point, disciplines learned in training came to the fore, and the routine, and not so routine, of daily business stiffened my spine and strengthened my confidence. I even began to enjoy the C-rations...and I didn't duck so often. My obsession from then on was one of doing my best to make sure that I always kept up my end during any operation, regardless of conditions or situation.

From the top of Alligator Jaws east to Outpost Harry was about eight miles, around 14,000 yards, and that was the domain of the 3rd Division during my days as a FO. Better known as the Chorwon Valley, the area between the rugged terrain of Whitehorse, on the west, and Harry, on the east, was rice paddy flat and virtually devoid of trees. It was marshy in the summer and ice solid in the winter. The valley began at about the destroyed city of Chorwon and appeared to run about fifteen miles north toward high ground. A railroad line connecting North and South Korea had run through Chorwon but nothing was left but twisted railroad tracks and hulks of railroad cars and engines. The nearby and higher rugged ground to the northwest and northeast constituted the Chinese line. During this period, my time was spent mostly with 'A' Company and some with 'B' Company. Usually, the infantry treat their FOs with high regard. My case was no exception. Although I had a somewhat more comfortable position in my OP and spent a good deal of time with the company commander, when I was among the men of the squads and platoons there was a general atmosphere of appreciation for having the service of the artillery close at hand. Having been an enlisted man previously I would have been naive to believe that there was no grumbling about my position as an officer. I personally felt a great deal of empathy with these men who lived in the trenches, and stood at alert in the mud, rain and snow. At the infantry company and platoon levels, in general, there was very little difference in the ambient living conditions among the ranks on the front line, however, conditions on the outposts were spartan for all.

With all having so little, a significant change in perception might occur should an extra sandbag, blanket, poncho or other small amenity be showered on some and not on all. Most of the Chinese attacks in our area were at night so, little, if any, sleep was obtained until daylight, but only after dawn stand-to. I always figured the Chinese got more sleep than we did. During the course of most quiet nights there were the usual sounds and visual fireworks provided by both sides in harassing and interdiction fires. The sky would be lit up by tracers, most spectacularly by the anti-aircraft artillery guys and their quad-50's, parachute flares provided by the USAF, parachute flares provided by ours as well as Chicom artillery, and on cloudy or overcast nights by 60-inch searchlights aimed at the clouds to provide artificial moonlight illumination. Some of the friendly illumination was a bit disturbing at times because on occasion we thought that it aided the Chinese more than us. For entertainment, the Chinese would broadcast music and verbal propaganda, frequently by a sexy voiced female, over the loudspeakers they had scattered among the hills. There was always a special message for the 15th Infantry Regiment. The 15th had served in China during the Boxer Rebellion and was also stationed there from 1912-1938, so the voices on the loudspeakers threatened 'agonizing death and total destruction of the white devils who had pillaged and raped China' during that period in history'. For additional thrills they would broadcast bugle calls, or fire signal flares of varying colors, which were bogus, but meant to create the impression of an impending attack and thereby cause anxiety among our troops. Got to be pretty much 'old hat' but you had to guard against complacency... sometimes they weren't kidding. To break up the monotony, they frequently used their version of the WWII Japanese 'Washing Machine Charlie', an old radial engine biplane to fly up and down our front lines at low level and draw fire. I don't remember them dropping any grenades or small bombs from the aircraft as the Japs did, but they sure drew fire. It became obvious that this was their intent so, after a while it was directed that firing at the aircraft was to cease. Trouble was that no firing element could accurately pinpoint 'Charlie' in the darkness and, as far as I know, he always flew away unharmed. Following these forays, we would sometimes receive mortar or artillery fire probing our positions.

There were as many casualties during the so-called 'stabilized front' portion of the war, 1952 and 53, but it seemed there were fewer highlighted or publicized battle zones or sites. Although there were major dust-ups on Jackson Heights, involving the 65th Regiment, some heavy action to the west in the 2nd Division and east in the 7th Division area during my tour as an FO, most of the action in the 15th Infantry area was on a relative small scale involving squads and platoons on ambush and patrol tasks, and relatively small unit Chinese attacks on our outposts. Chinese mortar and artillery fire on our outposts was frequent and their attacks on our patrols were relentless. Regardless, those involved in these skirmishes felt just as battle-involved as any of those who were in the much press-heralded Yalu River, Pusan Perimeter, and Chosin Reservoir, actions. The TO & E of the 39th Field Artillery

Battalion allowed for three FOs per firing battery. In several instances, however, with the exception of the admin WO and the battery CO, all of the officers in some batteries were sent out as FOs. The three firing batteries then, in normal circumstances, could have nine FOs out supporting an equal number of infantry line companies. In reality, since infantry units were rotated between line and reserve duty, some of the nine FOs were employed in other battery or field artillery battalion positions when their assigned infantry units were off line. There was always plenty to do to keep one busy! I and my team were sent to the ROK 17th Field Artillery Battalion in IX Corps to monitor and attempt to control their ammunition expenditures. It seemed they were reluctant to abide by our ammunition rationing procedures, and I was supposed to review all of their fire mission requests for reasonable validity prior to them being fired. However, I would hear a lot of artillery firing during the night, for which I had seen no requests, and was told it was another unit firing!

The shooting of a fire mission is, usually, a textbook procedure, and followed to the letter to insure clarity, proper response and speed of delivery. There are a number of ways to call for fire, to include simply calling for a specifically numbered, previously plotted concentration. Another simple way is a call to 'mark center of sector', which allows the FO to get an immediate round from which he can adjust fire onto his target. Once a target is spotted, there is an adrenaline rush and an urgency to get the rounds 'on the way'. As I remember, my first fire mission in Korea was directed at a number of Chinese digging in a trench line on the forward slope of one of their hills. That mission could have, or at least should have, gone mostly like this as a discussion between the FO and the FDC. 'Jumbo, this is Fox Oboe 9, fire mission, over! Fox Oboe 9, this is Jumbo, send your mission, over. Coordinates XXX-YYY, ten personnel digging trench line, fuse HE, will adjust, over. Coordinates XXX-YYY, fuse HE, will adjust, wait, on the way, over. On the way, wait... right 50, add 200, over. Right 50, Add 200, wait, on the way, over. On the way, wait, drop 50, fuse VT, fire for effect, over. Drop 50, fire VT, fire for effect, wait, on the way, over. On the way, wait, end of mission, ten casualties, good shooting, over. End of mission, out.' Now, this one is probably a bit exaggerated, although I did have a mission or two like this, because a new FO, in a new area, is seldom, if ever, this accurate. Believe me, I've thrown 'em out of the ballpark, but I never threw a short round. Some infantry that might read this would probably say, 'Oh yah, we've heard that before'. Admittedly, the artillery does occasionally and tragically dump on the infantry. We're sorry as hell, but the fault usually lies with the FDC, the data put on the guns, or the infantry position being miss-plotted or misidentified.

The extent of my emotion upon the conclusion of a fire mission was elation and satisfaction that I had put some of the enemy out of action, dead or not. One major mission that I fired will always stay in my mind because of the uncommon target that was presented. The time was Jan or Feb of '53 and I was with 'A' Company of the 15th Regiment, located on Hill 284 just to the east and at the base of Whitehorse. It was a sunny, early afternoon, a light snow was on the ground and I was doing my usual routine of scanning the front with the BC scope when I noticed, in the Chorwon Valley approximately 4000 yards to the east, a large number of black spots in a symmetrical arrangement. As I watched it became apparent that this was a group of about 100 Chinese troops, arraigned in ranks eight to ten men wide with ten to twelve men to a column, walking toward a group of saplings just forward of a ground level OP on the MLR that I had previously occupied for a time. I was struck dumb for a moment. What the hell were they doing so exposed in open terrain? I checked the azimuth, timed their speed of march, consulted my map, and called for a ToT fire mission on coordinates the group was approaching. The mission was accepted with some incredulity, even though I gave assurances that I wasn't seeing things. I had expected that maybe my entire battalion might fire the mission, but I was informed that I was to get an entire division artillery ToT with a two round

HE volley per gun! That amounted to approximately 144 rounds. I kept watching the formation's progress and it was still moving when the ToT burst on the valley floor. There was a virtual volcano of dirty snow, flash and smoke 'dead-on' target. I waited for the air to clear and watched the area for some time trying to determine casualties so that I could report results to an impatient FDC. There was absolutely no movement to be seen in the area where the Chinese had been when the ToT impacted. I reported 'many casualties' and explained that I could see some of what appeared to be bodies, but no movement. I searched with my scope the next day and was unable to locate the bodies I had seen the day before. To this day I still wonder what the actual situation was. That formation had to be decimated. Many would have been wounded, but those who might have escaped death or serious injury could have just lain there until dark and awaited pickup by their comrades. The Chinese went to great lengths to remove their dead and wounded from the battle area. As to why that group was there, it was assumed that it must have been a green group on their way to occupy some infrequently used positions in the vicinity of our MLR.

One other very memorable mission was a bit unusual. To the west, between Hill 284 and Whitehorse was a flat, open space, slightly behind the MLR which was routinely used by a platoon of tanks from the division's tank battalion, I think it was the 64th, as a firing position. Several times a week, on an irregular schedule, two to four tanks would roll up next to the perimeter wire of 'A' Company, and blast away with their 90mm's at the Chinese hill across from us and Whitehorse. That terrain feature was my target area and I knew most of the active targets there. The tanks just sprayed the area and didn't do much good that I could see, but they kept their hand in. Sometimes the Chinese would throw a mortar round or two at them and they would rapidly return from whence they came. Anyway, these were the days of rationed artillery rounds and there was a Chicom position in the middle of the summit of that terrain that frequently held a mobile, light field piece in a multiple embrasure bunker that occasionally sniped at positions along our front. There was also a trench line just forward of the crest that the enemy kept digging and repairing. Although they dug mostly at night, morning light exposed fresh dirt, sometimes I could see the tips of shovels throwing dirt during the daylight. I kept asking my LNO to allow me to fire on these targets, but because of the ammo rationing in effect at the time these targets were not deemed to be lucrative enough relative to the ammo expenditure required. It was an irritating situation. The next time the tanks rolled up, I crawled under the company perimeter wire on the side near the tanks, ran to the back of the nearest tank, got on the telephone on the rear of the tank and asked the tank commander, who just so happened to be the platoon leader, if he wanted a fire mission, and he readily accepted. I climbed onto the deck of the tank, stood behind the turret, the platoon leader opened the hatch, popped up, and I pointed out to him the 'irritating' targets on the hill. He asked as how he would destroy them for me, if I would adjust his fire. He disappeared, dropped the hatch, I ducked behind the turret, and a second or two, later the main gun fired. I observed the impact, the hatch opened, his head appeared and asked me how that was. I gave him a small correction, and then these procedures continued for about 7-8 minutes until both of my targets had been destroyed to my satisfaction. The embrasure bunker and a stretch of the trench line had been collapsed. I gave the platoon leader my sincere thanks, returned to my OP with a deep sense of gratification, and promptly called my LNO to tell him what a good boy I was. I had attacked my targets without using rationed artillery ammunition! Well, I was informed that I had placed myself in unnecessary jeopardy by standing exposed on the exterior of a favorite Chinese target, invited fire which could have hit the infantry of my company as well, and could have deprived my company of a live FO for a period of time until another could arrive. At any rate, I was threatened that, should I attempt this again, a courts-martial would be in my future. To rub salt in the wound, in a day or two the Chinese had, more or less, rebuilt what the tanks had demolished. I didn't see anymore digging in the daylight though!

Another very unusual situation occurred when I was acting as the 39th LNO at the 1st Battalion, 15th Infantry Regiment. As I remember, 'B' and 'C' Companies were online. One afternoon the battalion was making preparations to send out a squad size night ambush patrol of ten to twelve infantry. The patrol leader was a sergeant who met with the Battalion S-3, S-2 and myself to perform routine planning for the mission, to include the timing, designation of routes to and from the ambush site, and the location of artillery concentrations, should fire support be needed. Once the map overlays had been produced, copies were sent to front line and fire support units as necessary for coordination and information. The ambush location was just north and west of raggedy old Outpost Tom. I say raggedy, because Tom bad been shelled and traded back and forth so often that it was a beaten zone akin to a shell pocked garbage dump. Old c-ration cans, commo wire, concertina, broken sand bags and other debris of war littered the place. Usually, I monitored the infantry radio net during all patrol activities. This night was no exception. The patrol was to return to the MLR before daylight the next day, but an hour or so before dawn the patrol got caught up in a firefight as they were returning to the MLR and the patrol leader called for artillery fire support. I relayed the request to the artillery FDC and the concentrations the platoon leader called for were fired. He was satisfied with the effects and indicated he was slowly continuing to move his squad toward the MLR. Dawn was rapidly approaching and it became apparent that the squad would be caught in the open during daylight, a tempting target for Chicom mortars. A request was received for smoke to cover the squad's movement. For the moment they were hugging the ground. The situation presented a bit of a firing problem since fire would have to be continually adjusted around the squad. There was no front line FO in position to observe this fire and the squad leader had his own set of problems, to include being somewhat off course from the preplanned route. I borrowed an M-l 0 plotting board from the infantry, radioed the patrol leader to give me his estimate of range and azimuth to OP Tom, with back plot this provided his approximate location, and made a plot of the supporting artillery's position relative to the position of the patrol, which this provided range and the gun-target line. With this information I could now, with some degree of assurance, use the M-l 0 to blindly fire a protective screen of smoke between the enemy and our patrol. I had the FDC fire one round of red smoke at a safe distance from the patrol, asked the patrol for the location of impact, and then switched to white smoke to be fired on a continuous volley basis as I directed. With the combined efforts of all, we kept the screen adjusted around the squad until they were safely within our lines. Several in the squad had been wounded in the fire fight, but not severely. More importantly, the patrol was not subjected to enemy indirect fire. A well done was received by all and some of us proceeded to get some sleep.

As with all wars, there is generally a lot of activity some places and a lot of dullsville in others. In Korea, my activities were interesting most of the time, busy a lot of the time, exciting at times, downright scary on occasion, and less than comfortable all the time. I was one of the lucky ones. Many of my friends and classmates were not so fortunate. In hindsight, had I gotten to Korea earlier or later than I did, I'm sure my prospects for coming out whole would have been severely diminished. When it was decided that the truce would occur on 27 July 1953 we were informed that all firing would cease at 2200 hours. By this time I was the Charlie Battery Commander of the 39th, and I guess the Chinese figured they would rather shoot up their ammo stores rather than carry them away so, it was a bit like the Fourth of July up until around 2100 hours. We ducked, but replied in kind. Once again we were fortunate because of our proximity to the hill, most of the artillery coming in over the hill impacted to our rear in the rice paddies. From about 2130 hours on, the entire area was deathly quiet. It was one of the most astonishing experiences I ever had, complete and total darkness and silence for hours. Everyone was holding their breath. Well, it was over. We soon left the Kumhwa Valley and moved into blocking positions in the Chorwon area, and were soon replaced by the, believe it or not, artillery of the 40th Infantry Division! Talk about completing the circle. To this day in my mind's eye, I recall it all very clearly, the sounds of incoming and outgoing, the little albino rat that kept sticking his head out from behind the newspaper that covered the inside walls of one of my OP bunkers, the EE-8 telephone that occasionally crawled out of our team tent during the night when someone wanted our commo wire and would wind it up at a distance, the only way to stop it was to cut the wire, although we eventually staked the phone and wire. The FO who refused to return to OP duty, heating C-rations on the Jeep's engine, trying to keep the radio batteries warm, the mud, the knife-edge cold, the latrines, running after a man who panicked during heavy incoming, seeing a dead acquaintance or friend, the pitiful little tree or twig that was supposed to be the OP Christmas tree, and wet feet in Mickey Mouse boots to name just a few."

**Sergeant James Butcher**
**Fox Company, 17th Infantry Regiment 1952-53**

"When I was a sergeant in an infantry platoon I was given a brief course in observing and calling fire missions. On several occasions I led patrols to call in artillery barrages, mostly against the T-bone. I volunteered and entered the army the day after high school graduation. After jump school I was assigned to the 82nd Airborne. I volunteered for Korea several times in 1952 but the 82nd would not release me. I wrote my senator, Harley Kilgore, and he wrangled an overseas assignment. I was assigned to Fox Company of the 17th Infantry as a rifleman. We had about 30 ROK infantrymen assigned to the unit, too. I was in Korea from October 1952 to July 1953. When I was promoted to assistant platoon Sgt my company commander sent me and another Sgt to an FO school for a week because we were running a lot of patrols and fire missions and did not typically have an artillery FO with us. We fought at places like 'Jane Russell' Hill and 'Pork Chop' Hill, which were two of the biggies. At first, it was like a field placement in a geometry class, I enjoyed the 'intellectual' exercise. I did not particularly like it when we drew fire from Chink Baldy and had to make a rapid and uncoordinated exit under both mortar fire and machine gun fire. My buddy, Bill Estes, and I still laugh about that event when we get together. One day we were ordered to go down the ridge on a two-man patrol only about 300 yards toward Hassakol to serve as Forward Observers on a fire mission against some suspected artillery observers that the Chinese had posted to fire against us. The company commander instructed us to fire only a couple of mortar rounds because he was afraid that we would be found out and would draw fire from the Chinese. He was right! In spite of the fact that we had found ourselves a pretty good position to avoid detection as soon as we called in our fire mission with our rounds against the suspected targets, we came under searing machine gun fire from two different positions on the enemy hill. The Chinese also were zeroing in their mortars against our hideout as well. Bill and I decided that it was time to clear out. As we headed back along the trail back up to the MLR after our duel with the Chink observers, the machine gun bullets were kicking up dirt around our feet. Our actions might have appeared a bit humorous to someone observing because we were running clumsily at a crouch, stumbling, and falling here and there as we headed for safety. We, however, held our own laughter until we got back through our wire and into the safety of our emplacements. When we got back we wondered out loud 'What are two peace loving West Virginia boys doing playing such a dangerous game in this far away land!"

**Corporal Kenneth Cole**
**424th Field Artillery Battalion 1952-53**

"I joined the Illinois National Guard in March of 1947 at 18 years of age. In 1952 President Truman activated the 44th Illinois National Guard for active service and was sent to Camp Cooke California for training. After six months of training our 44th Division members started getting orders for over seas duty, most were sent to Korea. After a fifteen day leave most of us were to report to Camp Stoneman, California. I was with a group that boarded the USS Hase troop ship for a thirteen day trip to Japan. After two days at Camp Drake in Japan, we left on another troop ship for Korea. On the third day we arrived in Inchon Harbor, and we were put ashore by landing craft. We were then put on a train to Seoul, where we were picked up by the units that we had been assigned to, and taken up north where our unit was. I found out that I was assigned to Charlie Battery of the 424th Field Artillery Battalion, 8th Army, but attached to the IX Corps. The 424th served the entire central sector of Korea. I found out that we were an 8-inch howitzer battery with two guns up just behind the infantry and two guns about two miles back. I was assigned to spend half my time in Fire Direction Center and half in the OP as an FO.

I arrived in Korea in September 1952, & left in October of 1953. During the first eight months we stayed in the same area and used the same OP over looking Papasan Mountain. The infantry was in trenches in front of us, and we would fire on targets we saw and other targets that were spotted by airplane. We also had a quad .50 machine gun beside us that would fire at targets or just for harassment. During October 1952 we fired 4,300 rounds at enemy targets, which was a lot for one month. When we found a target we called FDC and gave them the mission, they would fire one round, then we would have them adjust the range and deflection for the next round, and by the third round we would be ready for them to 'fire for effect'. All of the guns would fire several rounds then. Each projectile weighted two hundred pounds and could be fired about thirteen miles. Our front gun position got shelled a few times, and on April 11th 1953 incoming rounds killed one, wounded six, and destroyed one howitzer. We had a road up to this OP, so the cooks brought one hot meal up to us each day. Another thing I remembered about the OP, when they sent me up there the first time, they said take a 'grease gun' with you. This was basically a .45 caliber machine gun. Well I took it and several magazines of ammunition. But I had never fired a 'grease gun' so I practiced with it up on the OP.

On June 13th we were given orders to move to the west in I Corps sector to support a U.S. Marine outfit. We were given an OP already built on top of a mountain, but no road to it so we carried every thing up to the top. We not only fired long range but some times short range with in 2,000 yards of our troops. We got shelled several times on this OP, and in several cases we could see them rolling out heavy artillery from caves and firing on us. We would call in fire on them each time, and they pulled their gun back in the cave. After each shelling of our infantry in front of us, they would bring in helicopters to evacuate the wounded. We never had direct contact with the infantry, but I am sure they were aware when we silenced the enemy gunners. The back side of this mountain had no cover so some times we were shelled trying to carrying equipment back up the bare side of the mountain. There would be three of us in the OP at a time, one lieutenant, and two other men. During July the enemy increased there shelling on us by what seemed four hundred percent and they also put more men on their front line. Two of our 424th OP's were overrun, and the 'A' Battery gun position was overrun. They were defending themselves with rifles and machine guns, when the order came to lower their 8-inch howitzers and fire directly into the enemy on the hill side.

On July 27th the war ended, I was never wounded, but I sure did dive for cover several times. I invented what I called the portable fox hole, when we would move to a new position I would load up some sandbags and build a fox hole on top of the ground. When we found an unexploded round of artillery stuck in the ground, we could use the angle in the ground to determine where the round was fired from. So some fire missions were at targets we could see, some were just for harassment, and some were unobserved fire missions on suspected target areas. Life in an OP was lonely at times, but during fire missions it was a very exciting time. One member in the OP was observing over the valley at all times. We had two beds made with rope stretched between two 2x4's, and a stove that burned charcoal for heat. Our bathroom was outside down the path. Our communications was by telephone most of the time, but we did use our radio sometimes. After the war ended, we were sent up on a mountain to build a new OP. We used explosives to blast out the rocks, and then build a structure with sand bags around it and on top. We had a ROK OP beside us, so we did see them quite often. When we were back in our gun areas it was back to army life again, everyone up every morning for inspection. I left Korea in September 1953 out of Pusan by ship for the United States."

**1st Lt Phillip Finley**
**57th Field Artillery Battalion 1952-53**

"I enrolled as a freshman in September 1947 at Kansas State University in Manhattan, Kansas. At the time, the draft from World War II still continued, and ROTC was mandatory for two years at land grant universities. In 1949 I was interviewed for advanced ROTC and offered artillery and was commissioned in May of 1951 a 2nd Lieutenant of Artillery. After commissioning in May of 1951 I joined the 504th A.A.A Battalion, which was a 90mm towed unit. By April 1952 I was ordered to attend basic artillery officer's course at Fort Bliss Texas. The artillery instruction had become one, field artillery and anti-aircraft artillery combined instruction at Fort Sill, Oklahoma, and at Fort Bliss, Texas, they combined surface gunnery and aerial gunnery. By state side orders to Far East Command, I reached the 7th Infantry Division seven days after departing Travis Air Base, Washington and was interviewed by the acting Div-Arty Commander as the colonel who was Div-Arty Commander had been killed in the Triangle Hill action.

I was assigned to the 57th Field Artillery Battalion. The 57th was a 105mm towed unit, which we adjusted fire in direct support. When general support artillery preceded an infantry probe, we sometimes adjusted 155mm towed. The first time I was assigned as an FO, I was tasked with another lieutenant who was with 'B' or 'C' Battery and reported to Lt. Butcher, he was from Iowa, and was my liaison officer. I was further ordered to join the 31st Infantry Regiment which had high casualties on retaking Triangle Hill near Kumhwa. One infantry platoon was defending eight hundred yards of main line of resistance frontage where I went as a Forward Observer. I recall that enemy positions built up on Papasan Hill, a tall mountain in which a full enemy field hospital had been dug out of the mountain's interior. Enemy field artillery caves near Papasan would wheel out and fire several rounds and pop back in the caves. Suspecting an enemy buildup for an attack after the Triangle Hill fight, I Corps called up eight inch self propelled guns for saturation fires and direct support. FOs and our liaison officers collaborated on what target adjustment was required. Well, Lt Butcher dropped us off at an infantry company 'housing' area and we walked up the trenches to a darkened FO bunker. Lt. Butcher leaned into the bunker and said 'This is Finley, your replacement' a voice said 'McDougal, S.C.' and grabbed my hand and said 'Binoculars and B.C. scope here, telephone here, map and final protective fires here'. And he finally said 'My time is up, I'm gone'. And he and Butcher left. I found my recon sergeant from Alaska taking his sleep break in an infantry bunker nearby and a tall South

Korean who was our driver from the ROK forces so that adjacent ROK land lines could be monitored to prevent North Korean tap-ins on land lines. The tall South Korean had been artillery liaison for language with artillery FOs for three years 1950-1952, had a family, and slept on the bunker floors with his helmet on his head as he slept. I often wonder if he survived and if so where he lives now and did he get to see his kids grow up.

The 57th supported the following units while I was there, the 31st Regiment and 32nd Regiments, of the 7th Division, the Ethiopian Battalion, and the 1st Capital ROK Division. The 1st Capital ROK we supported in the Imjin River Sector, an I Corps task force that went north at Chorwon Valley. We fought Chinese mostly but trench fighting in early October at Triangle Hill near Kumhwa showed North Korean casualties in the majority. We had outposts overrun at Baldy, Westport, Arsenal and the winter padded uniforms had seams horizontal while previous North Korean casualties had uniform seams sewn vertically. One of our OP's was south in line with Jane Russell Hill. I recall Secretary of Labor Anna Rosenberg visited the 7th Division forward command post near our OP south, that was interesting. As I recall each liaison officer commanded three OP's for each battery A, B, C in the battalion in each of the regimental sectors of the division front. The location was on the infantry company sectors point next to an infantry outpost. I remember battles involving Yoke, just behind Triangle Hill, which was Hill 1581 I believe, and just below Baldy and on Imjin River Hill called Caisson. As artillery Forward Observers, we were not infantry but we patrolled with the infantry. The old tube-powered back-pack radios were heavy. We carried our own radio and were responsible for the artillery fire support on call from the infantry patrol leader. Crawling through wire was a hazard with the radio on your back pack. The wire would hook tight as you crawled under unless an infantry soldier held it clear and if they had action or heard a sound they took off and there you were alone trying to get free and catch up in the dark. Life as an FO was we lived, ate, and patrolled with the infantry, supported and also adjusted with 4.2 and 81mm mortar sections when needed. Things could get very mixed up. Patrols leaving, coming back, calls for frenzied final protective fires and flares when problems occurred nightly. When the 31st Infantry Regiment had been shot up at Triangle Hill and the 32nd came in, they started vigorous patrols, and one time I had to adjust 4.2 mortars with smoke to screen a pinned down return patrol. Firing a mission was done simply on command of 'Fire Mission'. You read the polar coordinate, tell what mission was to be fired and request it! Also, you had to make sure to say what type of round you wanted, H.E., V.T. or Incendiary or smoke. Then came from FDC 'One round, on the way...wait, Splash'. You waited and you sensed the splash and adjusted.

When I joined 7th Division and the 57th Field Artillery in late Sept 1952, I Corps was commanded by Lt. General Bruce Clark, located I believe, at Pusan or Maybe Taegu. I was assigned on 25 June 1953 to head a mobile artillery task force and we engaged along with the First Capitol ROK Division, a two division North Korean, Chinese attempt to break though into the Chorwon Valley to Seoul just before the armistice. I mention this because we were given a Korean Military Advisory Group Lt. Colonel as a guide into strange positions at night after a sixty mile road march. The KMAG Colonel was driving and I had put him in front of the mobile artillery column with a sergeant from my task force. The Lt. Colonel KMAG dropped off the sergeant by the side of the main supply route and disappeared. We got into position and burned out tubes and barrels to support a fixed bayonet counter attack by First Capitol ROK troops. The second night, 27 June 1953, in a driving rain we had a mobile M-3 half track command post, and I was lying in water on the floor getting a quick nap when I looked up and stepping in the little back door of the track was I Corps Commander Clark. He asked questions and left and I received a citation but thought I would be court marshaled!

So General Clark, the I Corps Commander, was, on 27 June 1953, on the Imjin River Heights above the Chorwon Valley.

At the close of the Triangle Hill Battle near Kumhwa, the 31st Infantry Regiment had been mauled, but had fulfilled the request 'a deuce and a half load of dog tags or that hill!' The third time they took the hill. The 31st was to leave and the 32nd regiment was passing through their lines when the combination of cold, rain, darkness, and an enemy barrage based on compromised land line communications created havoc. I marched with the 31st Regiment to a regroup area about fifty miles south and then the 7th Division replaced the 2nd Division about the middle of November 1952. I had sixty-seven days of the mandatory ninety days required to be considered for a Battery Officer vacancy. The Div-Arty commander sent verbal orders to turn my FO equipment back to a replacement and become team leader for the 7th Division counter mortar radar team nearby. This team had a Q-15 stationary radar with five operators and a recon sergeant and a lieutenant team leader. I had been trained to operate the 584 radar and its successor the M-33 radar to control a battery of 90mm guns at a specialty school at Fort Bliss, Texas in the fall of 1951. The assignment as Q-15 counter mortar radar team leader lasted eight weeks and then a new Sperry-Rand radar with an accompanying team came from the states and the Q-15's were turned in. The Q-15 radar was located with the infantry and they always wanted us away on a hill because we drew fire each time the electronic signature was transmitted. The radar used up and down trajectories from enemy mortars and with the completion of an alpha angle, could pinpoint enemy mortar locations for artillery counter battery fires. We were close to the Australian brigade of the British Common Wealth Division by Christmas of 1952. The Aussie's set up an ambush by putting up Christmas trees with decorations and small lights and hooked into our radar power supply Christmas music. Then when the Chinese sneaked up to see what was on the tree the Australians ambushed them and took prisoners. We finally were told to relocate our position as the counter mortar radar team was caught one time between opposing forces retaliating for the ambushes and captured prisoners. We were all reassigned when the Sperry-Rand radar arrived. My stateside battalion commander in an automatic weapons battalion while in Texas was a Colonel Brightman, and he had me reassigned to Battery 'C' of the 15th AAA Automatic Weapons Battalion in 7th Division, which he commanded. I was an automatic weapons AAA platoon leader from January through May 1953, and provided harassing and interdiction fires from positions bunkered in the main line of resistance directly adjacent to and interlocked in communications with the mortar platoon and the machine gun sections of the infantry. We were near Old Baldy, Arsenal, and Pork Chop Hill and West Port. The battle for Pork Chop hill is most vivid. The weapons in the AAA Platoons were four M-16's, which were quad .50 caliber machine guns on a half track chassis and four M-19's, which were twin 40mm anti-aircraft guns mounted on a light tank chassis and powered by two synchronized Cadillac engines. I was briefly assigned to the Fire Support Coordination Center for the Ethiopian Expeditionary Force during the counter attack by the Ethiopian forces with U.S. 7th Division artillery support to retake hill Yoke. The Ethiopian Battalion was Haile Selassie's bodyguard as dictator of Ethiopia at Adiss Ababa, the capitol where the palace was located. The Ethiopians were the same height from six feet to six foot three and had no common national language and used Spanish, Portuguese, and Dutch languages. They were each promised a palace and maiden as a wife if they fought well and survived. It was rumored they were caught collecting casualty ear tips to send home to substantiate their claims of courage in combat. The U.S. postal service began to inspect their mail bags en route to Adiss Ababa.

I was in Korea late Sept 1952 through mid August 1953. I was on the MLR the night before the armistice went into effect and witnessed it the next morning. There were three significant events that affected me while I was an FO in Korea. My best friend in college, Jack Lay, who was from Gypsum Kansas near Salina, and is buried there, had been released from FO duty by the Div-Arty commander to be reassigned as a battery officer and was leaving the FO bunker when an enemy mortar round killed him. I arrived at the same area one week later to be an FO. The second was in my home town of Colby Kansas lives Dan Dennler. We were friends and were commissioned in artillery from ROTC at Kansas State University. Once in Korea I was seeking out an M-16 quad .50 caliber machine gun position on the left flank of my platoon to drop off parts and repair a malfunctioning machine gun. I went to an infantry bunker to warm up and there was my K-State friend Danny Dennler lugging machine gun parts to one of his outlying positions. Now we are old Korean veterans at Colby, Kansas having coffee together. And lastly, I became friends with Maj. Gen. Robert Ensslin who was Adjutant General of Florida forty-five years after we served as Forward Observers for artillery in the 7th Division sector near Triangle Hill. Forty-five years following our Korean service at the same locations in the same division we became Adjutants General in Florida and Kansas! We were on nearby outposts during the Triangle Hill battles, and continue our friendship. Two thoughts of casualties to this day continue to cross my mind. I was at Camp Stoneman waiting to air ship to Korea. Lieutenant Jim Piersall, a friend from service at Fort Bliss Texas and I shipped together. Jim, a close relative of the pro-baseball Piersall was daring and flamboyant. He persuaded me to try out for Aerial Observer, adjusting artillery from L-19 bird dog single engine aircrafts. I had a tendency to get air sick and after a trial ride to division rear in an L-19 on a rough weather day returned to the hill as on FO. Well, Jim Piersall was shot down just hundreds of yards in front of where I was positioned as a ground FO and was killed flying as an observer in an L-19. I also have memories of a Kansas man who was killed in Korea in my sight in a bizarre incident. A Korean house boy from the battery I was assigned to stole a ride with an ammunition truck to the main line of resistance. The infantry called to our attention that they had found him getting off the truck but he ran and was hiding for a day. The Kansas soldier from Wichita was taking him to go back on an incoming truck and we talked briefly. The solder and the house boy went into a bunker that was partially destroyed and an incoming enemy round with V.T. fuse grazed a tree, sent shrapnel into the bunker, killed the soldier and wounded the house boy. I saw the explosion and we summoned helicopter evacuation of a casualty, but Virgil Hurst of Wichita Kansas was dead. When I got home I received a call from Hurst's mother because her son had written her saying he had met a Phil Finley from Manhattan, Kansas working as an FO in the area where he was assigned. Combat is unforgiving. If Hurst had ignored the kid he might have lived, but Virgil Hurst was an instrumental and band teacher who had been drafted and cared for kids."

## 1st Lt Gerald Silvester
## 49th Field Artillery Battalion 1952-53

"I was drafted on January 30th, 1951., and after basic training, I went to OCS at Ft. Sill, Oklahoma in September 1951. I was then sent to Ft. Campbell Kentucky until the end of August 1952, and shipped out of California to Korea by the end of September 1952. When I got to Korea, I was assigned to the 7th Infantry Division, 17th Infantry Regiment, 49th Field Artillery Battalion. We were a 105mm direct support unit. When I first got to the 49th, I went up on Hill 1062 on my first FO assignment. I was up there over six weeks, that was around the first week of October '52. After that I was a ground and Air Observer until July 27th 1953, which was a great day, and my time lasted until I rotated home in September 1953. I was first assigned as an Forward Observer by Colonel Robinson, the battalion commander, who ordered me to the OP in front of Hill 1062. I participated in the battles for Little and Big Nori, which I served as a ground observer, and Pork Chop, when I was an Aerial Observer. Being an FO, it was not much fun. I was not involved in the assaults, but called artillery in.

In supporting the 17th Infantry Regiment, we were a part of them and we were very compatible. Our battalion had Observation Posts usually around Hill 1062, which was called Papasan, Alligator Jaws, and Chunchon. We also had two others overlooking the Nori's and the Imjin River. The battalion moved two times while I was with the 7th Division, so the unit covered a lot of OP's. Generally, compared to other jobs, I thought we had it very good. I had a jeep diver and radioman and we were mostly on our own. We lived with Koreans from the middle of December until the end of January in a nice quiet zone. We would move about going from battalion OP to battalion OP, outposts and FOs on different OP's, we worked as instructed or needed, but mostly we were free and on our own. The trenches were very protective but living with the infantry guys was okay, I always felt they had it harder than we did.

One fire mission I recall was when we had to stop support fire on Big Nori because our guns were shooting short and hitting the ROK going up hill. It was a sad affair and the hills would not have helped us if we did take them. Pork Chop was the same way. Pork Chop could not help them, or us, it just seemed like a lot of waste. While as an Air Observer, we had a concentration on a crossroad. A truck and jeep from the north were coming, and I called in a mission to fire at my command. The 105mm rounds and the truck came to the cross road at the same time. Also as Air Observer I took over an H & I mission from a previous FO and was about to call it off and the next two rounds hit the mouth of a North Korean cave as a guy was coming out. The next day the North Koreans had put out the largest Red Cross Flag I have ever seen! The cease-fire came about two weeks later. While on 1062, Papasan, my first OP, we could see the North Koreans coming down the valley and then turn the lights off of the trucks but every night there were trucks coming down from the north. One day while looking north, a jet, one of ours, was coming down the valley lower than me, and the north were trying to catch up with him with anti aircraft fire. We were at the OP on the Alligator Jaws and getting shelled very heavily for about four to five hours. The next morning an infantry guy came into the FO bunker and asked me to come with him. I was the only officer at the OP. We went to his bunker that he shared with five other guys, and showed me a dud 105mm shell that was imbedded in the wall. It was made in the USA, 1941, but it was definitely fired from the North Koreans. Good thing it was a dud! We also had to take another 105mm dud out of the trench. I flew one hundred and twelve air missions, and remember one afternoon the North Koreans moved up an anti aircraft gun and really surprised us. They got one valley off and had the right altitude but the spread was too wide thank goodness, or I would not be writing this. I was flying with an ex WWII pilot and he got us out of there in a hurry!"

**Lt Harold Tomlinson**
**555th Field Artillery Battalion 1952-53**

"I was an FO with the Triple Nickel, the 555th Field Artillery Battalion, a unit of the 5th Regimental Combat Team. When I was there we were in the Punchbowl, across from Hill 795. I was an FO from about November 1952 through about April 1953 when I became a battalion liaison officer and then a regimental liaison officer. I served through and including the 'Kumsong Salient', when the Triple Nickel got overrun by three Chinese divisions. I was drafted, and after OCS at the Artillery School at Ft. Sill, Oklahoma, I was sent back to Ft. Dix, NJ to be an instructor in the M1 rifle and Colt .45 semi-automatic pistol. In November 1952, my orders for Korea came. They flew me to Ft. Lawton, WA, Anchorage, AK, Simya, Aleutian Islands, and finally to Tokyo, Japan. After two weeks in Camp Drake, I attended CBR School in Gifu, Japan then the ferry from Sasebo, Japan to Pusan, Korea. The 555th Field Artillery Battalion was part of the 187th Regimental Combat Team at the time, and we had 105mm howitzers, truck drawn. From the time I was there, the CO of Charlie Battery had a rule, all new officers had to have FO duty, including service battery officers. As a battalion liaison officer after my FO duties were completed, I placed general support FO's for the battle of Outpost Harry, June 1953, an attack by the Chinese 74th Division. As an FO, I frequently provided close-in, high angle fire for groups of 'Tactical Liaison Officers' or TLO's, who were stationed in the Punchbowl and dressed as Chinese soldiers to retrieve Chinese prisoners. During this time I was in an OP on the northern rim of the Punchbowl. Later, in July 1953, I was assigned as regimental liaison officer. The 5th RCT was split up and the 555th was put in support of the ROK Capitol Division. On July 14th, the Chinese sent six divisions into the ROK lines. Our FO radioed immediately that the line was not holding. The Chinese overran the Triple Nickel. We were firing our 105's point blank at them. This was the last offensive of the war and became known as the 'Battle of the Kumsong River Salient'. The Triple Nickel lost thirteen howitzers and had three hundred casualties, KIA and WIA.

There is an inherent fear that hangs over combat, but directing artillery fire requires attention to the fire mission and fear is set aside. During support of the 'TLO's', it was frequently more difficult to get the FDC to fire high angle because of the inaccuracy of that type of fire. The infantry of which I was in support chose our artillery over their own mortars because we were so good. When we were in support of U.S. infantry, it was always the 5th Infantry Regiment. During my tour on the line as an FO, the 5th moved out and we were in support of ROK troops for a time but I don't remember which unit it was. I remember that I was assigned an interpreter named Kim Kil Bai. The infantry company commander was named Lee Moo Bong. We had problems at first with the Korean soldiers using the trench between the OP and our living bunker as a latrine. My FO team members threatened to kill them if they continued the practice. Lee Moo Bong stopped it and had bunks made from commo wire and engineering stakes for my men in our living bunker to make up to us. I have a sketch of me he made while on the hill. We were also in the 'Iron Triangle' in support of the ROK Capitol Division troops during the Kumsong Salient. All the while, we fought mostly against the Chinese. When I first reported to the Triple Nickel, I was assigned to their OP #1, a general support OP. I subsequently moved to a direct support OP for Charlie Battery. It was opposite Hill 795 and looked up to a large mountain we called 'Papasan' which was heavily populated with Chinese soldiers. I believe we manned four OP's. One general support OP and three direct support OP's. I don't remember the specific hills on which we were located, but at first, it was on the northern rim of the Punchbowl. Then we moved west into the Iron Triangle area of Chorwon, Kumhwa and Kumsong.

I had no routine as an FO, as every day brought different activities. We were in a stagnant, trench-type warfare at that time. I called fire missions on targets of opportunities during the day and usually fired support missions for the infantry against probes or attacks on our positions at night. I also supported the TLO operations through my OP because it was the farthest forward on the hill of any of our other OP's. In the mornings, I usually adjusted the battery, Charlie Battery. Then I looked for targets of opportunity. At times, I was required to support for U.S. troops making probes of their own. My OP was opposite Hill 795, and it had an aperture that looked out at our lines. One day, I heard an explosion on the back wall of my OP. It had been caused by a 75mm gun from the aperture on Hill 795. It missed my head by less than eight inches. My artillery had not been effective against that hill, so I had to take alternate methods to neutralize that threat. I went over to one of the tanks of the 5th Tank Company positioned to fire at Hill 795. The tank commander said he didn't have the proper optical equipment to hit accurately but if I could direct his fire, he could put a round into the aperture. I went back to my OP, and sighted the aperture through my BC scope, a two-eyed periscope, asking the tank to fire a round into the side of the hill. He had said that one click on his gun control could move the round about one foot at that range. I moved his 'splash' three clicks and asked for another round. It hit just about one foot below the aperture. I asked him to move it up one click and give me another round. At first, there was no sign that it had hit anything. Thinking that it had gone over the top I asked for another round. Before he could load and fire, I saw smoke coming from behind the hill. His round had gone clean through without moving anything on the face of the hill. I said 'Don't move anything an give me a round of Willie Peter'. A large plume of white smoke billowed up from behind the hill. I never had any trouble from that hill again.

I once saw a large enemy column moving towards Papasan and called for a fire mission. As the target became more visible, I saw that it was larger than our battery alone could damage. I asked for and got the 'Corps'. I remember at Ft. Sill Artillery School to 'fire the corps' was the ultimate for an FO. I got our battalion, 155mm howitzers, 8-inch howitzers, and a real thrill. The mission was a great success, as many vehicles and troops were dispersed and wounded or killed. We always were required to identify the target and report KIA's and WIA's as best we could. One time I identified the target as a platoon sized gathering of troops, some tents and wooden buildings typical of a bivouac area and twenty pair of long johns hanging on a line. As I remember, we were attached to the 45th Division at the time and the commanding general took a great deal of umbrage with that description. He made an unannounced inspection of my OP the very next morning very early before it was cleaned up following an enemy probe that night. He was very nasty and asked if I thought the war was funny. I never liked the guy after that. 'Keep your sense of humor'. I also called for and directed air strikes by Navy planes. That was really fun. On R & R I met up with a pilot from the USS Philippine Sea. We discovered that he was one of the pilots I had directed a short time earlier. Talk about your small worlds!

Almost all fire missions were called according to standard protocol taught at the artillery school. Only infrequently did I have to call for help without the standard protocol. My S3, the operations officer in FDC almost always accommodated me. He was a recalled WWII veteran who was terrified he would be killed after surviving the other war. He and I escaped the overrun by the Chinese in a jeep together during the Kumsong Salient, with my trying to keep him on the road with a flashlight going over a treacherous mountain road at night with Chinese artillery all around us. Outpost Harry was the most vivid recollection. There were many actions that could not be described as notable other than the Kumsong Salient, during which I was the Regimental liaison officer to the CO of the 5th RCT. I was a very lucky FO. There were at least six times I was almost killed, but I never even needed a Band-Aid. The worst thing that happened to me physically was a fourteen day bout of constipation. As I recall, General Dean only had eight days of that problem when he was captured! I tried to keep a sense of humor and tried to overcome loneliness between the times of boredom and terror."

## Sergeant John Devine
## 1st Amphibian Tractor Battalion 1952-53

"On September 13th, 1951 I was drafted and volunteered for the Marine Corps, for a two year commitment. After training in San Diego boot camp and Amphibian Tractor training at Camp Delmar I was sent to Korea on the 19th draft. Then our 1st Amphibian Tractor Battalion was set up at Kumchon Korea, about fifteen miles south of the front lines. I was pulled out of one of the companies and was transferred to Headquarters Company. Then in October of 1952, Colonel William Blatti, the battalion commander, asked me to volunteer to go to the front lines to call fire missions for the artillery. I don't remember training for this, but that I found myself calling artillery fire missions without much difficulty. We had a different 105mm battery each month set up behind us south of the OP Also, when I thought we were firing more important missions, I would call for a 155mm battery, and 90mm tanks fires were also used. The incoming artillery was mostly from 122mm mortars and 76mm artillery, which I am pretty sure were all Russian weapons. I served in Korea from April 1952 to March of 1953. We had three outposts just across form the convergence of the Imjin and Han Rivers. When spotting a column of troops, in an example, I would call the battery on duty and ask for a round to land at preset or prearranged coordinates near the target. Then raise or lower the next round and adjust left or right in order to reach the target. Then fire for effect with white phosphorus or other explosives. Although I did call a lot of artillery fire missions, I was never informed or concerned with particular missions. To me it was just a duty. At night being alone sitting behind a B.C. scope was rather scary, especially if your imagination took hold, but I read books back in the deep bunker where I slept. I also learned how to play harmonica to help with the time."

**1st Lt Rex Wallace**
**10th Field Artillery Battalion 1952-53**

"I joined through the ROTC program at Jocelyn State University. I was with the 10th Field Artillery Battalion, 3rd Infantry Division in Korea. We were a 105mm howitzer towed unit, and the 3rd Division was with IX Corps by the time I got there. I was there from July of 1952 to about May or June of '53. It was a policy of the commander that all lieutenants would be Forward Observers first and have a rear job second. I knew I was probably going to be an FO All lieutenants from the artillery could anticipate that they'd go on duty in combat. I anticipated that and so did the other two men that were with me. We were all assigned Forward Observer duty from unit to unit. The commander told us the policy, and sent us all to the hill. And we come off the hill and the oldest man, the guy who had the most time on the hill, comes off the hill first. That was the rotation off the hill back to the rear area. They were trying to talk peace about the time I got there, and so Truman decided that we'd just stay on the hills and fight in those positions. We could not increase our area very much or decrease it at all. You stayed there and got shot at. So that was kind of irritating to most of us human beings up there.

The 9th Cotton Bell Regiment, 3rd Infantry Division, that was the US troops that I stayed with for a month or so. Then I went with the 1st ROK Division, and I stayed with them about a month I believe. Then the infantry went off the hill back to the rear for rest and recuperation, and they were replaced by the 9th ROK Division, known as the White Horse Division. And I stayed with them for about a month. Then I went from there and stayed with the Marine Corps for about 30 days. While my infantry unit I was with was back in rear resting and recuperating I was down fighting with the Marine Corps! Then I left them and went with the French for about 30 days....the French troops over there in Korea. I was selected to go to the French Battalion because I could shoot a pretty good fire mission. I went over to the French, I got there about dark and the French were right there on the hill. I asked them permission to spend the night with them there in their area, and I went up the next morning to the Observation Post to relieve the officer that was up there. It was someone I had known previously back in the States, and he was just down in the hole and I didn't know what was the matter with him. I told him to get out of the hole and go on and get something, thanksgiving dinner or whatever it was available. And so I get in, and this general comes stomping up there and he had selected me, because they were afraid that the French might get a heavy attack and they needed someone over there to direct American artillery for him. So he and my battalion commander came up there at that time to visit, just as I was getting close to my own Observation Post, and I looked around and here they came. So I was happy to see the general, and I'd seen him before and talked to him. Anyway, he walked up to me and the map the guy had that was on the hill I had given to him some time previously and he had never changed the page on it, never turned it over to read his area. Then the general walked up and said 'Wallace, I've come here to see you shoot today'. I said 'yes sir!' And I reached down to get my map and looked at it. He said 'Wait a minute. That dog gone map doesn't even cover the area.' I said, 'But sir...' and he said 'Well, you can't even shoot'. I didn't have a map showing the covered area by the OP But it was my map they were looking at that I had given to him. And I just asked 'Is my map still in the OP?' And he said 'Yes. Fine. Go home.' Anyway, when he said 'you can't even shoot' that kind of hit me rough. And the fact that he had selected me to go with the French, it was really disappointing to him I guess. So I said 'Yes sir I can shoot with or without a map!' I opened my big mouth, you know. And he said 'Fine let's see.' He reached up and got that periscope. And the artillery officers, they know Ft. Sill quite well and there's a hill out there you shoot at and so on, but when you're shooting across the range there's valleys and hills and it all levels out from where you're seeing. It can be five miles and you'll think its three miles or two miles, you know? Anyway, he put the cross hairs with the B.C. scope or Battery Commander Scope on a spot and he says 'All right, and he told me and my colonel to assume that's a battalion of Chinese attacking, and shoot the artillery accordingly. Period. 'You tell that to the unit' and he told the colonel to tell the unit to shoot whatever I was asking for as if there was an actual battalion attacking and not just for show and tell. So I picked up that scope and I gave him coordinates. I knew where I was, and the unit, the battalion knew where I was on the map, so I just gave him the direction from me to the target and a distance or range, say 5,000 yards or something like that. And my rounds almost hit exactly on the target. And I was just looking out the aperture now and all I had to help me was a pair of eyeballs! I looked out the aperture and guessed the direction and guessed the distance and almost hit directly on the target about five miles away on the first lick! I dropped the rounds fifty meters, I told them to drop back fifty yards then drop five zero, and fire for effect and it made the whole area there explode with I guess 18 artillery cannons and they just blew it to pieces. I looked at the general and said 'Uh, I guess I'll get that map straightened' and he grinned. Well at any rate, I say that because it was an unusual thing, and I had about memorized the locations of things by map now. I could tell the coordinates of something just looking out there without looking at a map. We had just shot them so much and concentrated so heavily on it and so strongly that that was the case.

I went back to the rear as a liaison officer for about a total of two weeks. A liaison officer goes back with another artillery unit and transmits to them information that our artillery need. I had some good officers working with me, two Korean officers that had been to school in Fort Sill, and spoke good English. Smart people the operations and intelligence officers both were. We were working with a ROK artillery battalion for about a week, and my colonel called me and told me he wanted to fire on a certain target and he wanted it done right now. So I told their colonel and their colonel said no it would be wasting ammunition and he wasn't going to fire it. So anyway, I called back my bosses and reported back to my unit that that was the case, and the next thing I hear on the phone is my Lt. Colonel, and he told me in no uncertain terms, 'Wallace I'm giving you a damn direct order. You will make them shoot.' I knew he was desperate. He says 'we're in trouble up here. We're desperate. We need that ammunition fast.' So I told the Lt. Colonel commanding the Korean artillery battalion and his operations officer and intelligence officer, they all spoke English, I told him that they had to shoot. And he said it was wasting ammunition and if he shot the general would shoot him if he did. I said 'take your damn choice' and I pulled out my pistol, and I said 'fire and do it now. Now. Right now. As fast as you can.' And the operations officer's eyes got big and they started shooting, just like I had ordered them too. The first ROK division was outstanding company. I thought they were rascals to start out with but later they had come to be darn good and the name of the captain was Captain

Pat Tae Yung, an ornery little devil, but he was good. He put me in for a medal of some sort. I don't know what. He took care of me well after I go to know him for about three days but I stayed with them. I enjoyed them, they were fighters, and they'd fight like the devil! I spent a month up there on White Horse Mountain, and the other one, Sausage Hill. Some hill names didn't stick with me much, it was just hill something, you know, 200, 800, whatever it was. This was northwest of Yang Chon. We didn't have a name for our OP there, in fact, I think I dug it, me and my troops did. I served on White Horse right after the battle in October 1952, I think I relieved the guy that was up there during the big battle.

There are a lot of fire missions that stick out. There's not particular one. One we got a good shoot on, as a matter of fact, I didn't even discover the target. The infantry sergeant went looking through my scope and in a minute he comes back and says 'Hey, I see something yonder! Way over yonder. It's a bunch of enemy troops!' So I looked through it and said 'Gosh, there are about a hundred of them'. It was quite a bunch. I started counting them walking by into an area. And of course I sent the artillery on that area, all I could get to reach it and let them have it for about five minutes or so. I couldn't give a pretty good evaluation of the results because I couldn't see anything except that we were hitting where they were. And so we really blasted the hell out of them. There were a lot of missions that were very important to me. An infantry patrol went out one time, and the commander arrived and I just talked to him. He was real cocky and he wanted to let me know. And I said 'well if you want me I'll be down the hill in a bunker'. I went and dug a hole and crawled in! Well about two days later I asked him to keep me informed about when he was going to do patrols and I could get with the officers and sergeants leading the patrols and make sure I knew where they were going and what they were doing so I could help them. And he said 'well, if we need you I'll let you know'. And I said 'Well if you need me I'll be down in the hole'. About two days later, he sent out about a 30 man patrol and didn't tell me a darn thing about it, of course he didn't have to tell me anything about it but it had been stupid not to. I didn't know where they were or what they were doing and suddenly he asked me to please come up to where he was at, and as a matter of fact he was at my Observation Post, and he started showing me 'Right here they're getting shot at. They're surrounded. They're going to get slaughtered'. And his finger was poking all over the damn map going at about two miles a minute. He was kind of nervous I guess.

I finally got the lieutenant leading the patrol on the radio, and talked to him and asked him where the enemy was. And you could look down and see the fire. They were shooting at each other so to speak, but them shooting at us mostly. And he said 'They're directly at my front and I'm at checkpoint 4', so I knew where that was. And I said 'Okay, where are they. How far out?' He said about 50-100 yards. So I increased that number by about 100 yards. There was a word we used 'splash' about five seconds before the rounds hit the ground. I told him when I said 'splash' for every man to stick his head in the dirt and hang in there because this was coming in darn close and I asked the artillery to be very careful and make sure everything was just right. And they did. And then they just blasted the hell out of the enemy out there. When they started coming back in I just walked the artillery behind them all the way back to the front line. I just put artillery on the front and sides of them and just brought them in sort of in a half circle there....brought them back to the front line. Not a man was hurt. But it looked like he was going to lose them all. From that date on that infantry lieutenant acted like a human. Their sergeants come by, every one of them that night and shook my hand. Every troop, all 34 of them came by to thank me for saving their butts. So, that was a significant thing. We shot a dozen just like it, maybe even more than that. We had several fights like that when I was on a patrol with the infantry. The company commander, said it was my duty to fire for the company not one squad or one platoon. I wasn't going out with those squads, but if the company commander went then I'd go right along side of him because it was my duty to watch of the whole company. I became very friendly with all of the sergeants that led the patrols and all of the lieutenants that led patrols. And before they went anywhere from then on out they'd come out and show me where they was going. The FO saved their butts so many times they'd never forget it in their life. Once we raided this hill out in no man's land and raised hell and the company was one of the most outstanding companies I served with, lead by 1st Lieutenant Joseph Franklin. We worked together just fine for quite a while, me and the sergeants and the officers were shooting the hell out of enemy and all of the officers eventually got hit but me. I was sitting off to the side where I could observe everything, and all the officers got hit that night but me. That night Lt Franklin got shot in the leg and I got the medics to him immediately. The medics and I grabbed him, and came back across the little path and they said he was shot in the big muscle in his leg, I think he was out for 3 months."

### 2nd Lt Robert Helbling
### 987th Armored Field Artillery Battalion 1952-53

"I was in the National Guard before going to Korea. My MOS was Forward Observer, and when I got to Korea I was assigned to the 987th Armored Field Artillery Battalion, we were direct support for the 2nd Infantry Division, the ROK Capital Division and the Turkish Brigade. The friendliest were the South Korean Capital Division. The 987th fired the 105mm self-propelled howitzer unit, and I was with them as an FO from October 1952 to September 1953. We fought at places such as Capital Hill, Hill 972, and several others. It was a tough situation for us, I lost many friends. I remember that we fought against both Chinese and North Korean units for a while. We had OP's around Capitol Hill, Yellow River, and Hill 1062. We got extra points for being on the front lines as part of an FO team, and I even remember I passed up R&R to Japan hoping I could return to the states sooner! Life was hell at times due to the shelling, and a lot of our fire missions were to knock out an observation post or to assist a patrol in the capture of prisoners to obtain information. I also acted as a liaison Forward Observer to the Air Force for close air support, planes strafing, that sort of thing. Calling in a fire mission was, at first, excitable, but afterward, very sad, when you realized what you just did, maybe killing personnel. In 1953 we had a big 'retreat' when the Chinese advanced, we lost a lot of guys and equipment. After I got home, two years later we found a small piece of shrapnel in back of my rear thigh, which my wife removed. I have never asked for Purple Heart because I always thought it was an ingrown hair!"

### 2nd Lt Pascal L. Hovis
### 424th Field Artillery Battalion 1952-53

"I served as a Forward Observer in Korea with Battery 'A', 424th Field Artillery Battalion, an eight-inch howitzer unit. Arriving in Korea in October 1952, I served as a Forward Observer for a period of time during the winter and spring of 1952-53 and served as Battery Executive Officer during the latter part of my tour. I was there when the conflict ended in July 1953. During my tour of duty in Korea the conflict was at a standstill and Battery A maintained an OP on the front line observing North Korean activity. The two junior officers rotated the duty going up for one week at a time, with two enlisted men accompanying the officer.

I volunteered for the Army after completion of high school in 1948. Among the tests taken during the indoctrination was the one for OCS which I passed but was not of the required age (19 ½) as I recall. Upon reaching the required age I applied and was accepted. I graduated from OCS in July

1951 and was commissioned in the Field Artillery and sent to the battery officer's course at Fort Sill, OK. After serving with the 47th Infantry Division at Fort Rucker, Alabama and participating in an exercise in Texas in the spring of 1952, I was sent to Korea in the fall of 1952. We were in IX Corps, in the vicinity of Kumhwa, Korea, in the central sector of the peninsula. This particular sector was manned by ROK troops with American artillery in support. Our unit was the largest artillery in the sector with the mission of firing on targets reported by the OP. There were other smaller units, 105's and 155's in the area, too. The junior officers in the battery were assigned the duty of Forward Observer. The OP maintained by Able Battery was a fixed position, a bunker on top on a mountain, on the front line. An officer and two enlisted men went to the OP for a week at a time. The area surrounding the OP was maintained by ROK infantry. The two junior officers in the battery rotated this duty. I was assigned the duty for several months until one of the other officers rotated back to the USA and a replacement arrived. The OP was several miles in front of the battery position and did not change the entire time I was in Korea. The battery stayed in the same position also. We were in general support of the particular sector of the ROK infantry. Surrounded by ROK infantry while on the OP, we were not moving with a particular infantry unit in the sense of a FO. I don't recall the exact designation of the ROK units we supported. I did not have the experience of an artilleryman in the trenches with the infantry, being a stationary OP. Not able to speak the Korean language, communication with ROK personnel who did not speak English and surrounded our OP was extremely difficult. Each firing battery maintained one OP and the 424th was spread over the entire IX Corps area. I don't recall any exact names given to the OP's, we just referred to 'the OP' in Battery A.

The three men on the OP alternated 8-hour shifts maintaining watch 24 hours a day reporting any activity observed on the mountains across the valley. The CCF had small artillery weapons dug into caves in their territory. They would move the weapons out, fire a few rounds, and then move them back into the cave. It was our duty to try to knock out the weapon while it was firing or fire into the cave later. The 8-inch howitzer was the most accurate howitzer the army had at that time and perhaps still is. Any troop movement was also a key target. During the still of the night the CCF played oriental music that we could hear. The OP had bunks and air mattresses for sleeping while not observing the enemy. We had a charcoal burner for heating the bunker during the winter and we took enough food to last for the week. The food was mostly C-rations but we also took any fresh food available in the battery and occasionally we would have steak available to cook on the charcoal burner. When not directing fire at a target we would talk with the men back at the battery, by radio or landline. When not on duty and action was at a standstill, naturally your thoughts were about the family and/or girlfriend back home, looking forward to R&R in Japan, reading mail, writing letters, reading whatever material was available, and discussing activity observed by the man on duty.

During my tour in Korea the war was at a stalemate and the front line was somewhat stationery, with only minor skirmishes taking place. That is until 13 July 1953 when the CCF and North Koreans mounted the last major offensive before signing The Military Armistice agreement on 27 July 1953. At this time, I was the Battery Executive Officer. The CCF forces overran the OP and all of the ROK infantry positions in front of our position. Getting into the American artillery units in the area, the CCF told the Americans they were ROK troops and manned vehicles as they pulled out. Our unit was the only one still with contact with IX Corps and was told to stay in position. Most, perhaps all, of the other artillery units pulled out while we, the largest unit, stayed. Fifty caliber machine guns on American vehicles manned by Chinese fired across our battery area. An enemy machine gun fired at us from a hill across the road from the battery area. We fired an 8-inch howitzer point-blank at it and did not hear from it anymore. During this battle the officer on the OP, Lt. Frank Wilkinson, was killed and the two enlisted men were captured and later repatriated. Another enlisted man was killed in the battery area also."

**1st Lt William Hendrickson**
**143rd Field Artillery Battalion 1952-53**

"I entered active duty with the 47th Infantry Division from Minnesota. At the time I arrived in Korea, I was originally assigned to 'A' Battery 143rd Field Artillery Battalion as Recon & Survey Officer on August 16, 1952. I was 1st Lt at that time. All of us, except the battery commander and executive officer, pulled tours as Forward Observer with the Korean infantry units we were supporting at that time. We were in the Kumsong Salient which was later lost to North Korea after our battalion had moved over to support Heartbreak Ridge. Service as a Forward Observer with a Korean rifle company was sometimes a little difficult. The company supported by my battery was commanded by a 2nd lieutenant, about 22 years old, the only surviving officer in the unit. The senior NCO was a staff sergeant. No one spoke English to any extent, but several did have the ability to let us know of targets, patrols, and operational plans. It was fortunate that we were in a static situation at the time, in a mobile attack or withdrawal it would have been almost impossible to coordinate artillery support. Any time that something was planned, someone came out from battalion to help coordinate. All of the ROK infantry units were designated by code numbers at that time, but I cannot even identify the unit.

Our OP was dug through the crest of the ridge we were defending and was well protected overhead. To the north and west was a great area of small hills and the Kumsong River which separated our forces, dominated by the massive mountain called Papa-san. The river formed a 'V' that pointed sharply to the north, outlining the salient. To the west were 'Sniper Ridge' and the Kumhwa Valley. Visibility was fantastic! One time I was able to identify, at about 5,000 meters with my BC Scope, a Chinese Forward Observer team trying to move forward into a better position. We chased them all over the mountainside with 105mm artillery fire until we caught them. Another time, the NKA had an 82mm mortar dug into the reverse slope of a small hill in the valley. At about 6:00pm they would run that mortar out on wooden rails, fire off several rounds, then shove the mortar back into the hill and pick up the rails before we could get any counter battery fire off. Their targets were our outposts and hilltop position. I was finally able to set up some planned fires to forestall their mortar attack, and also to be able to respond almost instantly. I'm sure that we had an effect on the mortar crew, but we never did get that mortar. From the OP it was about 200 feet down the reverse slope to water from a spring, and another couple hundred feet down to a point that a jeep could reach. The team driver would try to bring a hot meal every day. During the October rains he was unable to deliver food or mail because the bridge about two miles back had washed out. The Red Cross representative called me by telephone on the OP to tell me that my daughter was born on October 18, 1952, and after I returned from that FO tour, I was transferred to Headquarters Battery.

The 160th Infantry Regiment went on line at Heartbreak in late October 1952 and probably had been pulled off line in December, even though they had been hit hard. When they first came on line they were greeted with loudspeakers blaring 'Welcome, Killers of Koji-do'. The 160th had been on guard duty at the POW camp on Koji-do. Obviously the relief in place was not a secret from North Korea troops. We faced a strong North Korean attack against our positions on Heartbreak Ridge. There were a number of casualties. That night we were throwing out every kind of ammunition we had. We fired all of our illuminating rounds, and I understand that some guns even fired out propaganda rounds. Major Fred Angel from Mississippi was the S3. He had Service Battery trucks on the road all night searching for ammunition. Our ammo people even high jacked ammunition and trucks from other units. To the best of my recollection, more than 10,000 rounds were fired that night. All of the units received counter-battery fire and sustained wounded or injured. My recon specialist from 'A' Battery, Sgt Woomer, was killed on Heartbreak that night. During the November 3 attack on Heartbreak, the FO on the right of the line called for fire on his position. He verified that his position was overrun. After a battalion volley of air bursts, we were unable to contact him. He survived the attack, but lost all communication. Some of the other positions were also overrun, but the 160th was able to regain control of Heartbreak before daybreak.

Initially I was assigned as Battalion Survey Officer, then as S2, then as Asst S3. Things were happening so fast that I did not receive any paper orders on that. I went to every observation post in January 1953 during a changeover. We moved out of the Heartbreak Ridge area in the dead of night. I made the trip up to the Ridge to orient new FO's from our replacement unit. We left all FO equipment in place, transferred the telephones and radios and maps to new FO's. When we pulled a gun out of position, a gun from the replacement battalion dropped a gun in the same gun pit. Initially I started out from regimental HQ to the first FO position, on the right point of Heartbreak, with the communications officer, Lt Harry Wigness. We came under a mortar bombardment and he rolled off the trail and down the hill into an aid station, so I continued without him. It took from 0700 one morning until after 0100 the next morning for me to finish all seven OP's on both sides of the Mundung-ni River. I ended up with frost bite of the fingers and toes because insulated boots and lined gloves were not authorized for headquarters troops. Then we moved out. I woke up on the ground someplace east of the Punchbowl with snow in my face. We waited there until nightfall and moved almost to the east coast, near Anchor Hill, to again support a Korean infantry unit. The battalion then moved Far East in Korea, near the Japan Sea. There we also had heavy battles with North Korean and Chinese forces. We were in that position when the truce took effect in July 1953. We moved back into central Korea and I was one of the first to leave in August 1953."

**Sergeant Claire Bjorgen**
**69th Field Artillery Battalion 1952-53**

"I volunteered for the draft. My older brother just got married and they were going to draft him so I volunteered in his place. Spent one year in the U.S. and then sent to Korea, and got there on Christmas Eve of 1952. I was assigned to the 69th Field Artillery Battalion, which was a 105mm howitzer battalion in direct support of the 4th Infantry Regiment. I served from December 1952 to October 1953. I started out in one of the gun sections and eventually volunteered as an FO We fought in a number of battles and areas, Carson, Iron Triangle, Pork Chop Hill, Jane Russell, and Outpost Harry. We gave the infantry direct artillery support, adjusted fire on the enemy and their trenches, and I was one of those that directed artillery fire for the battalions. We were on the front lines directing the artillery. My thoughts were to do it right. Because of what we could do with artillery support, the infantry guys liked having us around. I think we fought North Koreans, with the Chinese helping the North Koreans with troops and Mortar fire. The work was very dangerous. We were the first ones they tried to take out. One time we were in an outpost with a B.C. scope and we had a sniper shooting at us through the aperture of our out post. And we had a tank dug in along side our outpost, so I asked him if he would mind doing some landscaping to get rid of him. He said he'd be glad to so he shot down everything the sniper could be hiding in. That did the trick. Calling a fire mission, we basically called in and gave gird coordinates and adjusted from there. There were a number of times that were very harrowing to me. One time when we got over run and we had to shoot our way out with M-2 rifles, another time our battery area got overrun just after I got off the hill and we fought hard and getting out of there, we lost five of our men. Some things stick with you too, such as the time we had a short round fired from one of our guns and it hit one of our own men, so an Army captain and I had to get the shrapnel from his body, so we could find out which gun it came from."

**1st Lt Joseph Reynolds**
**936th Field Artillery Battalion 1952-53**

"Firing my first fire mission, it was early the next morning when I could first see, I was back at the observation port in the OP Could hardly sleep so why not see what was going on. Everything was real quite so I looked through the 20-power scope at the road junction the Lieutenant told me to watch. There were a group of eight or ten enemy soldiers approaching the road junction and were approximately 200 yards from the intersection. The road appeared to be more like two tracks in the dirt but the Chinese were using it regularly. I grabbed the telephone and cranked it rapidly. When fire direction answered I gave the following command. 'Fox Oboe Able, fire mission, azimuth (number), check point (number), enemy troops in open, request ToT'. That was a big mistake. The fire request of ToT is the acronym for Time On Target and is one in which the data is prepared and sent to multiple batteries. All batteries fire so as to have all rounds burst on the target at the same time. Unfortunately, this takes time and the fire direction sets a time for all batteries to fire. On this mission the fire direction center responded with 'ToT six minutes from now, one battalion, one round.' This target really rated no more than one battery to fire but since I requested ToT they gave me a whole battalion or all 18 pieces without questioning me about how many troops were in the open. As green as I was and as excited as I was, they should have asked me to describe the target first.

My first thought was why were they giving me six minutes. The enemy will be well past the road junction before then. Then I realized that I should have said, 'Fire on my command', and only used one battery. That way the guns would have been ready in about one minute and the gunners ready to pull the lanyards to fire the howitzers when I thought it was the correct time to fire. I do not know how in the world I could have requested a ToT. When I realized that I had made a mistake I started guessing which direction the Chinese would take. Go straight ahead, turn left, or turn right. Also, how far would they be down the road after the rounds hit the road junction. I realized that I had really screwed up the mission big time and they would probably get away. While running this guessing game through my head I kept an eye on the road junction and was absolutely amazed that when they reached the road junction they just sat down, possibly wondering which direction to go or maybe to just rest. They sat there for what seemed like an eternity as I watched both the road junction and my watch, all the time expecting them to get up and move on. The whole battalion of eighteen 100-pound rounds burst in the air and on the ground completely obliterating the whole road junction from view. When the smoke and dust finally cleared I could see some bodies lying on and around the road junction. I reported what I saw to fire direction. I had been training for two and one half years for that moment and suddenly I felt really sick as to what just happened. I thought of the British soldier killed the day before and thought of how he looked. I hated to think what those bodies looked like and all day I kept periodically looking at the road junction wondering if someone would pick up the bodies. Apparently they picked them up that night for they were gone in the morning. Since this fire mission occurred on the first morning that I was on the hill I thought this would be a typical everyday situation. Actually, until three days before the war was over I never again saw another group of the enemy in the open. An occasional head bobbing up above a trench, or when we were short of ammunition and could not fire except on large targets I would see two or three together. The enemy always knew when we were low on ammunition.

The 936th was in general support of the British Commonwealth Division and Battery A was in direct and general support, reinforcing the Canadian Brigade. That is why we had to have a Forward Observer. Life is not bad on the observation post, if you don't mind living simply. You have very little to do during the day and night but look out into enemy territory, sleep and eat. But it seems that can become extremely time-consuming. The OP bunker is made up into two compartments. One the observation room and the other the living compartment. The living compartment is about 8 feet square with two bunks. Ours had a wooden floor, but most of them don't have. The walls are made of 1 by 12-inch lumber with a roof of 3 by 12-inch lumber, reinforced with 12 by 12-inch beams and six feet of dirt, rock, and sandbags. It is made to take direct hits with about anything the Chinks have. As long as a man stays in a bunker, he is pretty safe. The viewing compartment is connected to the living quarters by a tunnel. It has a small slit to view through and a 20 power telescope, 10 power BC scope and pair of binoculars are furnished. You can see quite a distance with these. To get to the bunker you start at the bottom of a hill in a six-foot trench, and it goes all the way to the top. Most hills don't have them going all the way from the bottom, but we did because the Chinks could see the rear of the hill from the Hill John, which was to the side and left of the hill which was Hill 355. The chow wasn't so good. We had American C rations, which are canned foods in individual meals, plus a can containing coffee, milk, sugar, cookies, crackers, and jelly. We ate the Canadian meals but the British food, when they are here, is not so good. The Canadians meals usually consisted of, for breakfast, 2 hard-boiled eggs, bacon and bread. For dinner, beans, beef, one hard-boiled egg and bread. For supper, beans, ham, sweet or Irish potatoes and an orange. When someone got hungry he would say he would get dinner. Then, that person would put some water on a small alcohol heater to heat water and drop in some selected cans of C rations. Everybody had their favorites and mine was pork and beans and stew. Some liked the hamburgers best. We would open up a case, take out what we wanted and throw the rest over the side. Additional rations were available from the British and we always had peanut butter and jelly with either C ration crackers or British crackers. Once I thought I would try the British rations but that only lasted for one meal and I was back to C rations and peanut butter and jelly.

About 300 yards to the right was the first ROK division and about 3 to 5 miles to the left was the 1st Marine Division. The observation was done 24 hours a day. I was usually on all hours of the day and four hours at night. There were four of us and only two bunks. If a man goes to sleep outside the bunk, he does it standing up. We made hot coffee 24 hours a day over a small stove. If you would see the stove you would think living conditions were terrible, but actually they are not bad at all. It was damp, and we kept a gasoline lantern going even in daylight to light it up. I kept the two men busy cleaning and scrubbing. One reason was to keep the place clean, but the other reason was to keep the men busy at something. It was seldom that I ever observed more than two Chinks at a time. They would always be 800 to 1000 yards away. We never had a set time to eat. Because our primary function was to provide a constant watch from our OP, two men were awake and on duty at all times with one watching and the other as a backup. Besides, we only had the two bunks. The sergeant and corporal were pretty well trained as observers but the PFC seemed to change every week and so did little more than occasionally watch with some one else. We kept a flack jacket by the entrance to our bunker to be grabbed when running out to try to find the damned mortars. One day I was setting on the edge of a bunk when a damned mortar came in. I grabbed my helmet and made for the exit, grabbing for the flack jacket. It was caught on something and slipped from my grasp but I kept going, running down the trench to our favorite spot for observation. I thought 'This is the time I am going to get it because I did not get the jacket'. But I didn't. As I was walking back to the bunker, a Limey soldier told me, 'You Yanks got it all wrong. When the damned mortars come in we pop in a bunker and you Yanks go flighten down the bloomin' track.' I just laughed and went on.

Forward Observer parties rotated every week, most of the time, in the 936th so after a week on the hill my party and I rotated back to the battery where we could use all the water we wanted. We were real dirty when we got off the hill and smelled the same. A shower would be nice but none were available unless we traveled several miles on very dusty roads in open Jeeps, so we just took a bath in our helmets. We did regular battery duties when we were back and I was both the Communications Officer and Recon - Survey Officer and also worked as the Assistant Exec at times. Our days were full, especially with a bunch of young men always looking for something else to do other than shove bullets in a gun. There had been some heavy fighting on the hill we were on a year or more before and somebody had been buried or covered up in a foxhole. The body had been very near where the trench was dug and over time the dirt had fallen away until the bones of a hand and part of an arm had been exposed. I passed by the arm protruding slightly from the side of the trench several times a day and everybody assumed it was a Chinese or North Korean, but we really did not know. Finally, the bones fell away and were trampled into the mud. I mentioned it at a morning meeting because we really did not know what nationality the arm was but nobody was concerned and Graves Registration was not notified as far as I know.

The British and Canadians did not go on many patrols whereas I understand the American forces had patrols out practically every night. The listening posts were sent out but seldom were formal patrols sent out. I wanted to go on a patrol to see what it would be like and one morning the Captain described a patrol he wanted a lieutenant to make. It would wind across the MLR to a point where the Chinese set up a heavy machine gun if they were going to make a probe. I immediately volunteered to go along to provide artillery fire support if necessary. The captain looked at me kind of funny but the lieutenant immediately accepted my offer. Going on patrol and not knowing what was going to happen was one way to keep your adrenaline up all day. I decided to take a carbine along instead of a pistol because I felt I could shoot the carbine a lot better than I could throw a pistol. I carried the necessary radio and just wore a field jacket so as not to be encumbered as with a parka. It was so cold that night that I would have welcomed a little encumbrance to be a little warmer. The Army field jackets were not the warmest item of clothing. The patrol was made up of the lieutenant, myself, a sergeant, six riflemen, brene gunner, engineer with mine detector and one medic with a stretcher.

We left the hill at about 2330 going through the 'gate', which was a place where the barbed wire could be moved to make an opening in the barbed wire around our perimeter, and proceeded along the top of an old rice paddy dike. This path had been used earlier by the listening post men and so no checking for mines was done at this time. The area in front of our hill, it was very heavily pocketed with small craters from shell bursts and I was surprised at the huge quantity of telephone wire lying along the path. The listening post men quite often laid new wire as they went out and seldom used the existing wire, so after a time the first part of the path was literally covered by telephone wire. There was also a very large quantity of machine gun and rifle ammunition scattered about and much of it was Russian. The Lieutenant and I studied all of the landmarks from my OP for about two hours, tracing every step of the way we intended to go and we discussed contingency plans. Several prominent features were thoroughly identified such as small hills, our listening posts, trees, and gullies. We used our observer glasses and went over the entire patrol route at least six times thoroughly. The Lieutenant brought all of the men going on the patrol to my OP to look at the entire route and discuss the patrol with each man. I also planned numerous checkpoints so I could call fire in easily. I felt we were thoroughly ready for the patrol. The patrol left at the appointed time and after leaving the last listening post the engineer with the mine detector assumed the point with the bren gunner and two riflemen ahead of the Lieutenant and myself. We proceeded rather slowly because of the mine detector but eventually reached the end of our patrol route and traveled over a small rise where the Chinese machine gunner could be. Nobody was there and we proceeded back a little more rapidly. We arrived back at the MLR at about 0230. By that time I had been awake some twenty-one hours but was not the least bit sleepy. And that was a patrol in which nothing happened.

Two days later another patrol was planned into the same area and the same Lieutenant volunteered to take the patrol and I volunteered to go along also. The patrol was much the same as the last patrol and with the same men, but this time the Chinese found out that somebody was out there. Possibly we had disturbed one of their listening posts. A machine gun started firing spraying the area. I thought the guy would never stop firing and we laid by a dyke and a small depression for cover. I wanted to bring artillery fire on it but the Lieutenant though it was too close. I also thought I could take the guy out with my carbine but the Lieutenant was not about to have that. We did not fire a shot at the enemy or take any action because the Lieutenant thought they really did not know where we were or if we were really there. I thought the machine gun brought both arguments into question. After about 30 minutes of lying a little flatter on the ground than I ever thought possible, the Lieutenant crawled about 100 feet away and threw two grenades into a mine field. Immediately, the machine gun started firing into the minefield area and we left as fast as we could crawl out of there. When we arrived back at the MLR and were going through the 'gate' I found that two men had been wounded. One was grazed on the throat and the other had apparently had his foot sticking up when he was lying on the ground behind the dike and was hit in the heel. Two men were helping him and the stretcher was not used. That was the end of my foot patrols but strangely enough I slept soundly when I got back to the bunker. The next morning meeting we discussed the patrol and the Captain thought that we should have brought the artillery fire in but just firing single rounds in adjustment. The rounds could have been walked right down the hill to the machine gun. He said they did that quite often in World War II. One day there was some rifle shooting and I went outside the bunker to see what was going on. Several soldiers were shooting at a deer that had wandered out into the no-mans land area. They were just trying to scare it over toward the Chinese side and when it had run about half way over, they shot it with a machine gun. They knew the Chinese would do anything to get the deer. That night both the British and I had a checkpoint on the deer and periodically dropped artillery fire into the area. No listening posts were set up in that area that night. The next morning the deer was gone. The Chinese had risked their life to pick up the deer for lunch.

Early one morning there was a tremendous racket right over the top of the bunker. It was a Korean P-51 attacking a hill directly in front of our hill. The Korean P-51 was one of four making passes directly over us and dropping some large bombs into the hill. It seemed that they were coming down so low that their propellers would dig up our hill and all of the trenches were full of soldiers watching the planes making their attack. The last plane of the four made a low pass over our hill toward the hill to our front and did not pull out. It made a tremendous fiery explosion and dug quite a crater, which I photographed. It looked as if the airplane never made any attempt to pull out even though his engine was whining very loudly. The U.S. Air Force sent an officer to question us if the plane had received any ground fire or if we knew why it did not pull out but I do not think anybody heard any kind of AA or knew why the plane just bored into the mountain. I remember one time I was in my tent sound asleep one night when I was awakened and told that the Captain wanted to see me. I got up and quickly dressed and went to the CP where the Captain told me that we had lost contact with our Forward Observer on the hill and to get my party together immediately and find him. I found my Sergeant and he contacted the other two men and with some rations, bug-out bag, two radios, telephone, and two spools of wire we were off. I looked at my watch as we cleared the battery area and it was exactly 15 minutes since I had first left the Captain. We went to the hill and it was fairly quite at that time and when I got to the bunker I found the Lieutenant apparently sound asleep with a telephone at his head and his enlisted men gone. I shook the Lieutenant and said, 'John if I were a Chink, you would be dead now.' He threw the cover back exposing his .45 and said, 'You're lucky you don't have slant eyes.' It turned out that his telephone lines had been cut, probably by a mortar, and his radio's were both dead and his enlisted men were out trying to find the break. We had a C rations can of beans and a cup of coffee and I gave him one of my radios and we left. We got back to the battery just in time to have breakfast. The next day I was rotated back to the hill.

Shortly after that, I had been on the hill at the OP for about five days with the weather miserably wet and cold. Both of my wool uniforms were soaked and quite muddy and a British Lieutenant offered to loan me a British uniform. I appreciated that very much because I was really quite miserable and clothes just do not dry out when the humidity is around 100% in a bunker. The British have their rank and identification sewn on their uniforms, so I just pinned my bar and crossed cannon on the collar along with the British identification. I think there is an unwritten rule some place that says that Artillery Captains, Majors, and Lt. Colonels are to never visit an OP Anyway, I never heard of one of them going that far forward. But low and behold, our Battalion Commander picked just that time to visit our OP I was on the other corner of the hill when the Corporal ran up and said the Colonel was there and wanted to see me. I ran down the trench line to the OP and reported to the Colonel and quite frankly I never gave any thought to the fact that I was wearing a British uniform. For a moment he looked at me and then started chewing on me in good OCS fashion for being out of uniform and almost making me think I was a traitor. You would have thought I was wearing a Chinese communist uniform instead of a British uniform. I told him about my uniforms being wet and he told me to change into one immediately. I ran into the bunker and picked the wettest and muddiest uniform and put it on rather quickly then reported back to him. I think he then understood why I was wearing the British uniform but he was not going to back down. We went over the firing information and I described the target area. I described things on the Chinese side that I did not even know, but it seemed to impress the Colonel. After reviewing my *Interdiction Schedule* for the next night he seemed quite satisfied and left. I sure wish some mortars had come in while he was there to give the old boy a show, but the Chinese would not cooperate. After the Colonel left I changed to the warm and dry British uniform.

On January 29th, 1953 the British 1st Commonwealth Division was rotated out of the line till the 8th of April and the American 2nd Infantry Division was rotated in. Artillery wise, things were rather mixed up. The 2nd Division Artillery was in support of the 1st Capital ROK Division troops, so the British left their artillery in support of the 2nd Division. Since the British Artillery needs British observers to direct their artillery, their Forward Observers stayed with the 2nd Division on the line. We continued to maintain and man our own OP's for our own artillery. It was nice to be with some Americans for a while on the hill. An American will tell you clearly what they want. A British soldier quite properly will use words such as, 'It would be nice if you would place a few rounds in a certain area' Or, 'Do you think you might rock them a bit?' or words to that effect. An American would say,

'Get some fire on that damned target.' The 2nd Division almost doubled the listening posts out at night and had patrols going out virtually every night. The British never asked me for my plans on interdiction fire for the night, but the Americans always wanted to review and study it in detail and invariably they wanted much more fire. It seemed that the British artillery seldom fired unless there was a flap going on or unless they had a defined target. The American artillery will fire at anything and everything day and night. The interdiction fire at night was planned fire on enemy trails, trench lines, bunkers, roads, or any place we just thought some Chinks might be. The British officers many times expressed the thought that we were wasting much ammunition, and they were right. But, I am sure a lot of it was not wasted also. Invariably, if the American Infantry wanted a target hit they came to me instead of the British for two reasons. First, I did not procrastinate or question the value of the target, but just fired on it. Secondly, they loved the heavy 100-pound rounds we fired instead of the much smaller British 25-pound rounds. One thing we really liked about being with the 2nd Division was the hot meals. They brought at least two hot meals up to the line virtually every day. We cut back considerably on our C rations, but not on our peanut butter and jelly. Also, we were able to get water from the American outfit we were with on the hill.

During my last tour on the hill we received considerable incoming of both 76.2mm artillery and 82mm mortar from the Chinese. We spent all our time trying to locate the firing locations and the Signal Corps got into the act also. A photographer showed up on the hill and said he wanted to take some pictures. I thought that was nice and was ready to pose but he had different ideas. He set up a camera directly on top of our OP and waited around till dark. After dark he would open the shutter for a time exposure and close the shutter within ten to twenty minutes. Any gun flashes were clearly shown on the developed film the next day as white spots and we did locate some 76.2mm guns firing this way. Mortars, our chief worry, would not show up because they were fired from more concealed locations. Many of the pictures showed a rather large quantity of flashes, which were due to our artillery shells exploding in the Chinese hills. It was quite apparent that the tempo of the enemy firing was increasing and some times we were receiving incoming rounds constantly. Near the end of my last tour the enemy was firing almost constantly. One day I was calling fire on every checkpoint in my sector but could not see to do any adjusting. The Assistant S-3 called me and said that he noticed that I was firing checkpoints only and was not doing any adjusting fire. I told him that I had been back and forth to both sides of the hill and all I could see was smoke and dust and I couldn't make any adjustments. Occasionally when the Chinks stopped firing I could pick out some additional positions where they might be and did some adjusting but they soon started firing again making observation very difficult. I had one and one-half tours with the 2nd Division. On the second tour I received a call from the Captain telling me that he had received a call from I Corps and they wanted me there within two days. Nobody told him that it was just to go to the Artillery School and I suppose he thought I either had political influence or possibly an important assignment. Anyway, I very reluctantly left the battery the next day. On March 3rd, the Chinese attacked the hill I had left and there was some bloody fighting for several days. The 2nd Division was relieved on April 8th and the 1st British Commonwealth Division came back on the line.

I arrived back at C Battery, 936th Field Artillery Battalion, on June 10th after attendance at the Artillery School. PFC Eisenberg's Jeep trailer was loaded with my rolled up mattress that I had acquired from another officer at IX Corps that was rotating back to the States. It was a nice thick mattress and really very comfortable, especially with the foam rubber pillow that I had acquired. The Battery Commander welcomed me and then, spying my Jeep trailer full of mattress, he said, 'We don't live here the same as the people do at Corps. I'll give you one hour to get all your belongings down to one air mattress, duffel bag, and a fuse box.' Then he added, 'Get your Forward Observer party ready because you go on the hill at 0700 tomorrow morning.' He pointed to a small tent and said that was home. I gave my wonderful mattress to PFC Eisenberg but kept my foam rubber pillow. Otherwise, I was in pretty good shape. My Forward Observer party consisted of Sergeant Jackson, a Corporal and PFC and I discussed everything with Sergeant Jackson so as to be ready for the hill in the morning. I was much better prepared and sure of myself this time. The next morning we went to the hill, which was Little Gibraltar. It was next to the First Capital ROK Division, known as 1st Capital ROK Division. This time, going up the hill I did not fall on my face and did not make an ass out of myself. Sergeant Jackson had been on the hill only once before and it was the first time for the Corporal and PFC, so I felt like the 'old hand.' The Lieutenant I replaced was glad to get off the hill for he had been there for almost two weeks running and was getting pretty tired of it. Further, he was due to be rotated back to the U.S.

The 1st British Commonwealth Division was back on the hill but this time we were with the Canadians. Their officers were all right but some of the men were pretty rough. Many of them had joined the Army to stay out of jail and in talking with some of the lieutenants there was some question whether they should be immediately sent to jail and their own officers usually carried a cocked pistol at night. We stayed pretty much to ourselves like we did with the British. The Canadians did not put out very many patrols and only about two listening posts and even some of these were not every night. I did feel some concern especially since the Battle of the Hook had just ended in that area and the Chinese were expected to attack at almost any time. We quickly settled into a routine with morning meetings and trying to locate mortars and enemy artillery. The first week was rather uneventful except for a sniper that kept taking pot shots at us. He could not hit anything but it was a little disconcerting to step out of the bunker and hear a bullet plink close by. We knew about where the sniper was but not precisely and working with the Canadians we watched very intently with binoculars, offering the sniper targets to shoot at and finally we located a very small hole in the opposite hill that he was firing out of. This was a Chinese hill on our left front side named 'John' that was about 400 yards away. This hill was a problem because the Chinese could see behind our hill pretty well from this location. The Chinese had tunneled through the hill and had made only a very small opening almost obscured by a bush. The British brought up a Centurion tank with its high velocity 75mm gun and we strung a telephone line to the tank so as to tell them when to fire. The tank bore sighted directly on the tiny hole and we put our 20-power scope watching for any sign of anybody being there. It was very monotonous watching one single spot and after a couple of hours I gave the job to Sergeant Jackson. He had been on the scope only about fifteen minutes when he saw a flash of light and called the tank to fire. The shell went almost directly into the hole and exploded behind the sniper, blowing him out onto the side of the hill where he laid until dark. We had no further problem from snipers.

We had been a little short of ammunition for a few days and had not been able to fire on everything. Actually, the battery had plenty of ammunition but I presume the Corps might have been below their full compliment of ammunition until another ship came in. Finally, the word came down to start firing for we had plenty of ammunition. I started firing on just about every place I thought the Chinese might be. After about two hours of fire missions a British Captain came to the bunker and said; 'I say old chap, what's the target out there?' I told him what I was firing at and he said, 'Oh, that's not much of a target. You're only going to antagonize the bloody bastards and they'll drop some more mortars on us and get somebody hurt. Just save your ammunition till we really need it.' Ok, I quit for awhile. Soon the Colonel called and I explained what the British commander of the hill said and he told me that I take orders from him and not the British, 'Get to firing!' So, I started firing again, and again the British Captain came back. I told him what my orders were and he left. A short time later Sergeant Jackson came into the bunker and told me that the British had put up a big antenna right on top of our bunker. I went out and looked at it and it was about like a tall flagpole that was sure to attract some attention from the Chinese. I looked up the Captain that I had talked to and told him that we were about to have an international incident and lets talk about this. His points were good that he did not want to attract a lot of enemy fire just because we had artillery ammunition and he understood my dilemma. We finally came to an agreement that I would continue to fire but would not fire within 500 yards from a line we agreed to on a map. This would place the fire out of his immediate sector but would still allow all the interdiction fire we wanted to shoot at night and during the day on the reverse side of the Chinese hills. He had nothing to say about firing into the Capital ROK sector or other British or Marine sectors that could be seen from my bunker. He was only concerned about firing in his immediate area. So, firing continued and especially at night and the flag pole antenna came down. I call that international negotiation.

The negotiations were finally going well at Panmunjom where the peace talks were in progress. These talks had been going on since about June of 1951 but it looked like they were finally going to be finished and a cease-fire would take place. About three days before the cease-fire took place I spotted six enemy soldiers very far to our left and clear over in the Marine sector near a river. The river had a crook that made it easy to spot their location on the map and I called immediate fire on them. After three adjustments I asked for fire for effect and got them. Since we all knew the cease-fire was imminent I suppose I should not have fired on them but by this time it really didn't bother me the least bit. I knew they would have fired on me if they had had a chance and they were still dropping mortars on our hill every day so as far as we were concerned the war was still on. On the afternoon of July 26th we received word that the armistice would go into effect at 2200 on July 27th. We were also instructed to do no more firing unless the Chinese made an attack. I received a call from the Battery Commander to leave the OP at 1000 on July 28th and report back to the Battery and we were easily ready to leave at 1000.

A peculiar incident happened during the last day of July 27th. My crew and I were in the bunker talking and not even bothering to do any observing and we heard a small arm firing. Assuming that it did not concern us we paid no attention but soon a Canadian sergeant asked for me to come with him for the Brigadier wanted to speak to me. I did not know a Brigadier would even be on the hill but since it was the last day I suppose he probably thought it was a good time to be there. The Brigadier told me that one of my men was out in front of the MLR down at the base of our hill firing his carbine. I told him that it wasn't my men but he said it was an American and for me to go get him. I looked over the edge of the hill and sure enough there was a man in American clothing firing a carbine toward the Chinese line. He was too far away to hear me yelling and I told the Brigadier that we needed to shoot near him and attract his attention then motion for him to come up. There was no way I wanted to go out front of our hill in broad daylight and make a good target for the Chinese mortars. But, the Brigadier told me to get down there and get him before the Chinese were provoked into firing a lot of mortars. I went down the hill after him and when I was about twenty feet from him I jumped into a hole and hollered for him to come to me. I kept down in the hole and he walked up to the edge and stood there. I said, 'Do you know where the hell you are?' He said something and I said, 'Why are you here in the first place?' I think I used a bit of profanity in expressing my thoughts. He said he wanted to fire his carbine and thought it was a good place. He had come through a valley between the hills and had not come over the top of the hill. I told him that for some reason the Chinese had not dropped any mortars on us but they probably will and for him to run to the top of the hill.

The man started up to the top of the hill with me behind him while my ears were well conditioned for the sound of a mortar coming in. About half way up he was going entirely too slow and I passed him and made it up to the top a few minutes before he got there. I don't think he was as inspired as I was. Just the day before the Chinese would have blown us completely away. I took his name, rank, serial number, and unit number. He was in the Air Force with a ground controller unit and had no idea that he was in front of the MLR. I dismissed the man and reported to the Brigadier and told him that I would make a formal report about the incident. The Brigadier was not a happy man.

I was on the hill the day the armistice was signed. It was a very quite day. The Chinks tried to shoot leaflet shells at us, but the leaflets drifted back to their side every time. Finally they just gave up or ran out of shells one. The ROK's fired practically all day long. About 8pm they opened up with everything they had, rifles, pistols, mortars, machine guns, artillery, and I imagine sling shots! I watched the tracers from a .50-caliber machine gun firing a steady stream of fire for several minutes. They absolutely had to burn the barrel out of that gun. They fired continuously until about 9:45 and then it began to slacken up. By 10 o'clock they had stopped. Everything stopped at almost exactly 2200 and neither the British nor the Marines had fired a single round. At 10pm the silence was the most eerie I had ever heard. For days there had been a continual crump of artillery and mortar up and down the line, but then there wasn't a sound. I was standing on top of the bunker and a thick fog was rolling in, blanketing out the entire line. Where at ten minutes till 10 o'clock you could see very plainly, by 10 o'clock you couldn't see a single landmark. It was as if God were blotting out the whole battle line. At 10 o'clock the Chinese started shooting flares into the air. The red, yellow, green and blue colors, diffused in the fog, lighted the whole line. They were so thick that a Canadian remarked to me 'that every Chinese must have been issued a flare pistol.' There was almost a complete blanket of them covering the Chinese lines in front of the British Commonwealth up to the border between the British and the ROK's. The flares were thick up to the border but from the border with the ROK's there were none. Not a single flare. Obviously the terrific pounding the ROK's had given them just before the cease fire that night had had some effect, or else the Chinks were afraid to fire a flare pistol. The flares kept up for about 15 minutes. All the time, there were shouts going up from both sides, but they were all individual shouts and none in unison. I stayed up till midnight, but didn't hear another sound after 11 o'clock. One of the men woke me up at first light on the 28th and told me to look at the hill John. John is the hill directly to our left and rear. There are four of them - Matthew, Mark, Luke and John. John is about 400 yards from the OP and is really nothing but a mound of dirt 150 meters tall. All, and I mean every bit of the vegetation, is completely gone, shot off. The day after the armistice you could have sworn that nobody could be within a mile of the hill and definitely not on the hill. I myself fired several rounds into it when one time the Chinks started to build a bunker on it. The next morning at first light we heard Christmas music being played by the Chinese and looking across the way we saw they had banners out on their hill and there must have been 200 soldiers out there waving and hollering. They were waving, playing Silent Night, Jingle Bells and several Chinese pieces on a public address system. We were moved off the hill by 10 o'clock in the morning of the 28th. I took some pictures of the Chinks with their banners, flags, and signs. At approximately 1000 we were loaded in the Jeep and pulling away from the hill for the last time. I felt that it was an historic occasion for me for how many people have the opportunity to be on the front lines when a war is over."

**2nd Lt Willard Holman**
**75th Field Artillery Battalion 1952-53**

"I was drafted in October 1950 after graduating from Cornell University in June 1950. I graduated from Artillery OCS at Ft. Sill, Oklahoma in May 1952. After three months of troop duty at Camp Rucker, Alabama, I was ordered to Korea, Far East Command. My unit assignment was IX Corps, 75th Field Artillery Battalion, a battalion of 155mm howitzers. We were in a position around Kumhwa at the time, in the central front, where I served from December 1952 until October 1953. When I arrived at the 75th, all new officers were required to be Forward Observers for three months. During this time there were constant probes by both sides, and the major portion of my FO duty was with the 9th ROK Infantry Division. Later in my tour, the 75th was also attached to the 2nd, 3rd, and 45th Infantry Divisions. The 75th was known as the 'Fightin' Six Bits'. We had two Ops, OP1 and OP2, both of which were in the Kumhwa area. The major terrains that I adjusted fire missions on were primarily Papa San, which was Hill 1062, Snipers Ridge, Jane Russell, Triangle Hill and the Boomerang. The enemy we faced at this time was Chinese.

After enduring the first incoming rounds that proved someone was trying to kill me, my most vivid memory as an FO was being cold and dirty, a miserable feeling. I adjusted and observed many fire missions including the 75th 155s, plus on many occasions 8" howitzers and 4.2 mortars. As to a specific fire mission, because there were so many, the most vivid that comes to mind is when the Marine Corsairs would attack the position that I would mark with white phosphorus rounds. In reality my experience as an FO was easy compared to my duty at the firing battery, Baker battery. Some time in the spring of '53, a decision was made to use 155s to fire destruction missions against cave entrances and trench lines. The 155mm is not as accurate as an 8" howitzer, however, there was only one 8" near Kumhwa. I volunteered for this duty and for two months I was on the MLR commanding two howitzers. In addition to the fire missions from battalion FDC, the majority of the fire missions were computed at this forward position FDC. It was dangerous, and we survived plenty of counter battery fire. Also, anyone entering the position during day light was under direct enemy observation. Needless to say, I was not bothered by senior officers wanting to visit the forward position. The gun crews were rotated on a weekly basis and my impression was they preferred being away from the firing battery even with the increased risk. As the result of this experience of commanding a 'mini' firing battery, I later was appointed executive officer of Able Battery for the remainder of my time in Korea. The last few days prior to the cease fire, I recall we fired constantly day and night. Then at 10pm on July 27th, it was quiet, what an eerie and welcomed experience."

# Chapter Six

## *1953 – On the OP*

The turn of the New Year brought about the fourth year of battle for the U.S. and the UN. What is commonly referred to as the 'hill battles' era, which had started roughly midway through the prior year, continued and became the norm for the rest of the war. After the White Horse action in October 1952, which was one of the single most large scale attacks by the CCF in the entire war, small actions and limited objectives became the enemy's means of gaining ground to use as bargaining chips at the truce talks taking place in Pan-mum-Jon. Bunkers and positions were set, with the notion of movement to different locations at a minimum. Overhead cover for many of the Corps 155mm units, which started in late 1952, was completed. Combat actions, being light throughout the winter due to the extreme cold, began to pick up again in January 1953. By March of that year, the total output of U.S. rounds tripled, making the monthly firing rate some of the highest for the war. As 1953 moved on, and the truce talks became more and more closer to a completion, artillery Forward Observers played a crucial roll in keeping the CCF at bay. Even up to the last weeks of the war, including the last major action undertaken by the CCF of the war, the Battle of the Kumsong Salient, FOs were firing mission after mission supporting the infantry, and to ensure the MLR held steady. The FO of July 1953 also witnessed one of the most unusual events in modern warfare, the July 27th Cease Fire, when death and destruction reigned one minute, and the next there was an eerie quiet that spread across the Main Line of Resistance...

**Sergeant Clyde Fruth**
**90th Field Artillery Battalion 1953**

"I joined the Illinois National Guard soon after the Korean War started. There was a rumor that we would be activated and several of us wanted to go in together. The rumor was correct and we did get activated. After fifteen days leave in the fall of 1952, I was shipped out of Seattle Washington. I was assigned to Able Battery, 90th Field Artillery Battalion, 25th Infantry Division. We fired the 155mm howitzer, and by the time I got to the 90th, we were mostly in the Kumhwa Valley. I arrived in Korea in December 1952 and departed August or September 1953. I spent time after basic training in radio school as well as artillery training as a radio/telephone operator and a Forward Observer. Within 24 hours after arrival in my unit, I was up at the OP calling in fire missions. All my action was from the OP position starting with the Kumhwa Valley area which was a part of the Iron Triangle. From there we moved to the Chorwon Valley Area. We manned several OP bunkers in these areas. Later we moved father west to the bolder complex of Vegas, Reno, Berlin, and East Berlin area. This is where some of the bloodiest battles late in the war were fought. This entire area was part of the famous Iron Triangle. The Forward Observers were a magnet for enemy artillery and motors. Thus, there was a lot of 'hit the dirt' practice. I was usually too busy with that and fire missions to be scared. That came later when I spent two days back in our battery and would get the shakes. A lot of time was spent looking for artillery that was firing at us. It's a matter of get them before they get us. You didn't have time for your mind to wander. You were just too busy. Of course we supported the 14th, 27th, and 35th regiments of the 25th Division, but there were others like the Turks, what fighters! And also Marines, and some ROK units. The infantrymen were always glad to see us. They knew we were going to take some of the pressure off them. We did support some ROK infantry however I don't remember which ones. When I first entered the Kumhwa Valley area, I think that area was mostly held mainly by North Koreans. However the balance of my time there it was the CCF. They all looked the same when I was calling in a fire mission.

I don't recall names of OP's except for 'Lobster' OP #2 which was named after our own 90th Field Artillery Battalion. I guess this was the only V.I.P. OP I was ever in. Once there were nine generals from the Army, Air Force and Marines there, plus the officers from the Navy! The view from this OP was tremendous. Our battery usually manned only one OP at a time unless we took three guns forward at which time the FO's operated in the open, no bunkers. I can still visualize the view looking north from most OP's. From March '53 thru July 27th of '53, the hot spot was the Iron Triangle. From my bunker it was like viewing your neighbor through your picture window. We generally had three members of our FO party, a 2nd Lieutenant and two enlisted men. Most of the time there would be only one or two on duty in the OP bunker at a time. The third would be sleeping or eating etc. unless things were getting hot. At which time we were all busy. One on phone/radio, one on BC Scope and the third with binoculars, or all three with their faces in the dirt ducking incoming. We always had one person at least looking for targets. I had a phone line to a tank on the backside of the hill and when I would find a moving target that required immediate attention, I would call the tank commander. They would pull upon the hill and would be providing fire power within minutes after I gave him the location. A fire mission with artillery would have let the target escape, it would have taken too long. One fire mission I recall was when I observed the enemy in the process of setting up a 76mm. They had just pulled it out of a cave or tunnel and were getting ready to pound somebody and I called in a fire mission. The first round was over by a couple hundred yards. I was very familiar with the area, but knew I didn't have a lot of time or they'd pull back into the cave. Without time to do much thinking, I guessed 'drop 300 yards'. Bingo! Direct hit on the 76mm and about eight or nine enemy all KIA's. They had only gotten off two or three rounds before we got them. When we were under major attack, all units of artillery, motors, rocket launchers, etc., were assigned specific areas to fire on. Thus, there were only special targets that we were calling fire missions on. This was at night. During the daylight hours we were working primarily on our own, searching for targets if there were none presenting themselves.

Once while there was a semi-lull in the activity I sighted twenty-some enemy bringing up supplies to their front line troops. They would go down behind the hill and return in ten to fifteen minutes. There was one place where the trench they used was very shallow and they would become visible only to our area. After seeing this same supply chain twice, I had confidence they would continue the supply route. I picked up the phone to a Marine tank a hundred yards to my right and gave him the information, coordinates, and what to look for. I could see them return, coming over the hill a few seconds before the tank commander, due to our line of vision. I gave him notice so he could be ready and when he saw the first five enemy, he cut loose with the 90mm and the .50's. He was right on target with the very first high explosive. They continued to fire with the 50's and he threw two more 90mm rounds in on them. Then some of the ammo they were bringing up exploded. I don't believe there were any survivors. With only weeks to go before the cease fire we got overrun. Thanks to infantry reinforcements we were saved from becoming POW's. This was at an OP with the Berlin complex to our right and the Nevada cities ahead and to our left, the west portion of the Iron Triangle."

**1st Lt Eugene Tinory**
**92nd Armored Field Artillery Battalion 1952-54**

"When I completed my Boston College ROTC course, basic training, and Artillery course at Fort Sill Oklahoma, I was sent directly to Japan for pre-combat training and then to Korea. When I arrived I was assigned to the 92nd Armored Field Artillery Battalion, IX Corps, 8th Army in Korea, and was there for eighteen months. The 92nd fired the 105mm howitzer and then the 155mm self-propelled howitzer. Our location was between Kumhwa and Chorwon Valleys, above the 38th parallel in North Korea. I was assigned as a Forward Observer while a member of Headquarters Battery, and participated in all of the battles occurring between 1952 and 1954 in the area of Kumhwa and Chorwon. I fought both the Chinese and North Koreans. The Chinese troops were used as if they were expendable and sent against us in swarms. They used bugles as a psychological warfare device. The most intense was the battle of the Kumsong Salient. I participated as Ammunition Train Commander delivering 155mm howitzer rounds to our forward artillery batteries, and also as a Forward Observer. Being a Forward Observer was lonely, scary and stressful. We realized that we could be overrun and fired at any moment and that the enemy had us in its target sites as much as we had them in our sites. My enlisted men were my main support and much credit is given to them for their support, knowledge courage and ability. I was never a 'moving' FO, like those that were with the infantry units in direct support, and so have no experience in 'the trenches' but rather I was always in a bunker on a stationery hill bunker location. I remember our unit manning one OP, but don't have the exact names for the hills. I participated in numerous actions from the hill, namely the location and destruction of enemy moving and still targets. The life of a FO was similar to the life of any combat participant except that you felt that you were constantly in the sights of enemy weapons and a prime target since we were the eyes of the artillery. We conducted fie missions which were significant in holding the line and the destruction of enemy ordinance and personnel. The illumination of the front lines was a most impressive at night when night turned into day at intervals during massive firing.

Some things stand out in my mind, the visit of Marilyn Monroe was memorable as were the visits by other USO entertainers. It was my delight to entertain the troops on our portable organ, powered by foot-especially at Christmas time and other holidays. Other positions I held in Korea were Mess Officer, Troop Information and Education Officer, and Club officer. When a senior officer suggested one Christmas that I gather up all of the eggs in the mess hall for the purpose of making eggnog for the officers, I refused, considering this most inappropriate. The loss of one of our men who drowned during one of our swimming breaks in a local river was traumatic and a terrible waste of a young American. Our R&R break to Japan was most memorable."

**2nd Lt Ronald Freedman**
**48th Field Artillery Battalion 1953**

"I enlisted on 23 May 1951 as my final year in college was approaching the end, and I had the opportunity to become a 'Contract OCS Candidate'. I went to Korea assigned to the 398th AAA Battalion, and we embarked on the N.S.T.S. Liberty ship, the General Mark. L. Hersey, in mid November 1952 at Staten Island N.Y. We stopped at Fort Buchanan, Puerto Rico and picked up approximately 900 enlisted members as replacements for the 65th Infantry Regiment, and two Medical Service officers. We then stopped at Cartagena, Colombia, and boarded a full battalion of Columbian enlisted and officers who were to relieve the Colombian Battalion in Korea at that time. We stopped in Colon, Panama for refueling and then went on to Hawaii. Then to Yokahama, and picked up replacement GI's for Korea. We arrived in Korea at Inchon early in January 1953, and entrained for

K-55 at Osan. The 398th was a semi-mobile AAA unit consisting of quad 50's and 40mm cannons. I was with the 398th until late April of '53, when I requested a transfer to a light field artillery unit as an FO. I was transferred to the 48th Field Artillery Battalion, I Corps, and we fired 105mm howitzers in close support, usually for the 17th Infantry Regiment of the 7th Division. Our Battalion Commander was Col. Joseph S. Kimmitt, who was an outstanding leader. By the time I arrived in Korea, we were fighting mainly the Chinese, who I think were part of the CCF 23rd Army. There didn't seem to be any North Korean units in the fighting around our area.

When I first arrived at the 48th and went up 'on the hill' I was assigned to OP '29' on Hill 329, which was known as the 'Generals OP'. This had a commanding view of T-Bone, Yoke, Arsenal, Erie and Alligator Jaws. All of these hills mentioned were in the west central area of the Korean front. I also served on OP '38' on 'Bob and Hope' Hill, which was at the very easternmost OP in the I Corp sector until I was reassigned to OP '13' on Hill 347. I picked OP 13 as it had the best view of Porkchop, but I'll never pick 13 ever again! The 7th Infantry Division had I believe approximately 38 OPs across it's front. The 32nd Regiment had from OP 29 to 38. I was attached to 'George' Company of the 32nd although I had very little contact with them. Besides the hill names already mentioned I recall 'Ice Cream Cone' and Outpost 'Yoke', which was manned by the Ethiopian Kagnew Battalion. They had their own FO's as they were the only unit in all of Korea to speak in their native tongue, or 'clear voice' as it was called.

In the Generals OP (OP 29) life was a little different than the others only in that we had a woven rug on the dirt floor, jeep windshields in the event of bad weather, a very large overall space, and we had a blanket curtain across the rear of the OP where we could light candles and write letters etc. The action on this hill at times could be heavy as it supported the T-Bone complex, and the EEFK's, Ethiopian Expeditionary Forces in Korea, in OP 38, it became a little hairy as the OP was at the end of the trench line, and was all by it's lonesome. I could hear the chinks calling us at night. 'George Company 32nd Infantry, Eetowah!' which was Korean for 'come here'. There were two hills across the valley from me that I used to fire H&I missions at. They were known as Upper and Lower Horseshoe, and were a favorite place for our patrols. We rarely had any thing to shoot at during the day, and sometimes we fired missions at boulders or some type of object to keep ourselves busy. Mostly every thing happened at night from about 2200 to 0200. The Chinks could be discerned by their blue-green tracers, and the GI's by the red-orange colored ones we used. Often when the enemy attacked they would send up flares. Usually a green flare signified an upcoming infantry deployment, and red meant for the artillery to start. However, I saw lilac, and orange, and other colors and had no idea what they meant as usually nothing happened after that.

When our planes flew supporting flare dropping missions there was a noise like 'boing' as the parachute opened. One night I could see hundreds of parachutes lying all over the valley below. By sunrise they were all gone. I had a crew of three enlisted men, a sergeant, a corporal, and a private. We had our own jeep and trailer, but that was kept back at Battery because we were in a very static position, but it used to come to the bottom of the hill for us so that we could be taken to a showerhead unit where we would get all new underwear, socks, and fatigues after we showered. The old uniforms were given to the ROKS we were told. After I was wounded the sergeant at the clothing counter wouldn't give me new fatigues as the medics had torn mine all the way down in the left leg and arm. A lieutenant straightened it out for me. Chow was served at the bottom of the hill and in the open. Everything was powdered usually like potatoes, eggs, milk, and the water to mix them with had a terrible taste. Yoo-Hoo became a favorite very quickly. When I ate with the Ethiopians they had one bottle of Hot Sauce for two men every other day. It killed me to eat anything, as I couldn't get it down. I eventually stayed in the OP and had someone bring me mail, Tootsie rolls, and the compressed cocoa bars from the C rations. Our latrines were ammo boxes on the rear slope of the hill. During late June the monsoons hit, and I remember the rear wall next to my cot collapsing from all the rain. Sandbags filled with the local clay started to compress, and everyone was ordered to sleep outside. I stayed in the OP and slept in my clothes and raincoat every night. I had my carbine with two 30 round banana clips taped together, and a round in the chamber with the safety off on my window ledge every night. I also had a .45 with a round in the chamber but the safety on. My crew slept in their own hootchie about 75 yards away. I was alone from midnight until dawn every night. They worked the dawn to midnight shift, but if there was a flap on they all came running down to the OP. Their hootchie had 4x4's as supports inside, and the strung commo wire to make up their bed springs. I had two telephones, an A and a B line and my radio, which hardly worked due to all the interference from the Chinks and the terrain problems. In the static part of the war we were never in the trenches except under dire conditions.

I remember starting a number of secondary fires one night when I was shooting at the Horseshoes. And I recall using my friend Bud Gaynors' quad 50's, he was with the 15th AAA Battalion when we were shooting at some Chink First Aid men. They arrived on the scene at Arrowhead with a stretcher, but threw it down and started to fire their AK 47's at some target. I called Bud, who was an old basic and OCS buddy, and gave him the coordinates. It only took a few minutes and soon the four of them were on the ground. They stayed there all afternoon, but next morning they were gone. I also fired 4.5 mortars at three guys with towels around their necks one day. They were coming down the slope of the Lower Horseshoe. As an FO with Charlie Battery of the 48th I was watching the June and early July attack on Arrowhead from my OP '38' on 'Bob and Hope' Hill. Arrowhead and White Horse were not in my sector, but I fired missions anyway at targets of opportunity.

On 10 July 1953 I was reassigned to the 32nd Regimental Combat Team, which I don't believe ever materialized, as the Regimental Forward Observer along with 1st Lt. Raymond E. Barry, who was CO of Baker Battery of the 48th, and was assigned as Regimental Artillery Liaison Officer. It was here on 11 July 1953 that we were both WIA, Barry receiving very serious neck and facial wounds, and I only was hit by shrapnel in the knee and arm. We were told early on the 11th that a full-blown counter-attack was to take place, and from our view atop Hill 347 we would have grandstand seats from which to do our job. Instead we spent the day keeping the enemy busy, and covering for our infantry as they left the hill for the Chinks. There was no hill left by the end of the day. On Porkchop on 11 July I fired missions all day. We knew that the Chinks had a gathering point somewhere out of our vision behind Porkchop and in front of a large northwest southeast running ridge called Hassakol. That place had no coordinates that I knew of but I was told to keep up the fire in the 'rats nest'. I had arrived there on Porkchop that morning with the call sign of 'Quinine Oboe Uncle 595', and that was a mouthful to get out during a tight moment. We were required to use only correct radio terms. Around 1400 'Quinine Oboe Uncle' wasn't answering me but whenever I used that name someone would say 'Gallivant Charlie 555 do you read me?' No one had told me there was a change in our Signal Operating Instructions and I was to become 'Gallivant Charlie'. I caught on quickly as to who I was, but it was a terrible time to change names and numbers. Ray and I kept up firing until 1600 when our bunker was destroyed, and Ray and I were hit. He was severely wounded as he partially covered me as our OP was destroyed. Ray was eventually sent home and spent a year recuperating in Houston. I was slightly wounded, but had to stay in the battery area until 23 July when I was called upon to accompany King Company of the 32nd, led by a Lt. Armour, on a dislodgement of the enemy at Outposts Dale and Westview. Fortunately, we had to return our ammo as the enemy pulled off the hill, and I went back to the Battery until the end on 27 July 1953. Lt Ray Barry and I both received Silver Stars for the Pork Chop action, his in late August 1953, and mine just recently on 11 Nov 2000. Mine was delayed for 47 years until I found that Barry was alive."

**Sergeant John Oakley**
**980th Field Artillery Battalion 1953**

"I was drafted. After training, I was on a troop ship departing out of Seattle bound for Korea on January 1st, 1953, it took about 16 days. When I arrived I was assigned to the 40th Infantry Division, 980th Field Artillery Battalion, Baker Battery, we fired 105mm howitzers. I served in Korea from January till May 1953. When I got to Baker Battery, the captain said he needed an FO so I was drafted into the job. I went up on the hill in places like big Papasan, the Punch Bowl twice, and Luke's Castle. While serving as a Forward Observer, we were on look out two hours off and four hours on, twenty-four hours a day seven days a week. We usually supported the 223rd and 224th Regiments of the 40th Division, I also remember supporting a ROK unit on Luke's Castle but can't remember which unit. During my time in Korea, I think we only fought the Chinese, no North Koreans. Life in the trenches was a blur of being constantly by phone lines day and night, fire missions and getting shot at. Some of the more memorable fire missions I shot were against troop movements at night, and when we would spot artillery in the open. Calling a mission, we kept it short and sweet, 'Fox Obie George. Coordinates such and such, V.T. fuse, in effect. Will adjust.' It was all a mind boggling experience, sometimes fun and sometimes hell."

**Corporal Donald Olson**
**213th Field Artillery Battalion 1953**

"I got there, Korea, sometime in January 1953, and was assigned to the 213th Field Artillery Battalion, which was a 155mm unit when I got there, and later on they converted to the 240mm howitzer. As we were sitting around at the 213th waiting for our assignments, somehow the topic of maps and compass reading came about, and I had been in the Boy Scouts, and my high school science teacher was a bombardier on B-29's, so he taught us map reading and compass work, and somehow the next day I got elected to go with Corporal Jack Randall and 2nd Lt. Nathaniel Eek up to the Forward Observer post. From there on that's where I spent my time, any time the battery sent men up there. It was usually Corporal Randall and I and one of the lieutenants. A couple times I we got split up, and we'd get put on different OP's. We got shell fire usually every time we were up there, maybe not like the infantry sometimes, because of less activity in our sector at that time, like at Kumhwa. At White Horse, there we got more artillery fire in, usually every day we'd get some in, sometimes more sometimes less, sometimes there won't be any. You always had to have someone in the bunker, or stuff would disappear out of there, sometimes you'd see a ROK soldier stick his head in there, and he'd think no one was in there, and he'd come in and check and see if there was anyone in there, and if there wasn't, why, a lot of your equipment would disappear all of a sudden! So you kinda had to watch both sides there sometimes! When it got muddy or rainy, the trucks couldn't make it up the hill, then you had to walk down and carry supplies up, and that would be quite a hike, because it was steep hills. When we would get shelled sometimes, and I had my camera, and I'd try and take pictures, but it wasn't a very good place to take pictures, cause you'd have to hold your camera above the hole and guess just about what time a shell was going to hit, and I know one time I jumped in a hole and that was on White Horse, incoming rounds were coming in, and this hole was filled with water, it was only deep enough for me to crouch, so here I was crouching down in that cold water. That was bad, that was cold! I was wet up to my armpits, and was pretty stiff by the time I got back to the bunker. But still, you sat there until, usually it was about four or five rounds at a time, one right after another, but then sometimes it would be only two, or then just one. I guess they were just trying to keep us on our toes.

You'd call in that you were going to fire a fire mission, what the target was, whether it was an artillery tunnel or a bunker or whatever, and that had to be approved. Then you called in your coordinates first, then your azimuth, your compass reading, then you called in your elevation. Of course you got this off the map, but then when you also locked in on a position with the B.C. scope, you could read what the azimuth and elevation was. Usually the elevation was down, unless we were firing on top of Papa-san Hill and the elevation was high, cause the hill was so high, it looked right down our throat. And then you would give the comment 'will adjust', then if you got a round in there, say the round landed to the right, you would tell them where the round landed, and you would say something like 'fifty yards right' and then they would know if the round landed to the right of you from your perspective, but from where the guns were fired, they weren't all lined up straight in a row, so they would be sitting back a ways and had a different angle to the target, and you would be looking down at the target from another angle, and you would be giving a different direction, it would be 'over and to the right' from where the guns were firing. So, they would adjust fire that way, but usually you wouldn't have to do any adjusting with the 240mm, because you would give the right coordinates and azimuth, and the target was hit usually with the first round! Sometimes it would take three or four rounds to zero in with a 155mm howitzer, and I think the main reason for that was the movement of the gun every time you fired, because that just sat on the front pad between the two wheels, and when you fired it would jump up and come back down. We had logs dug into the ground too, where the trails were, and those things would vibrate, and one side of the gun might move ahead slightly from the other side. When you looked through the panoramic scope at the aiming lights, that would change your deflection off a couple of degrees, and of course, a couple of degrees back there could mean, if they were firing two or three miles, quite a spread then. Sometimes when you fired a mission, all your rounds would go all around the target, the first three or four, and then you'd get a strike. The 105's did the same thing, taking more rounds to zero in on a target. Every morning you'd have to fire at a base point to make sure you had zeroed in one gun.

On the 240's, each gun was zeroed in individually, but you didn't do it every day, because you'd knock your base point out, there'd be nothing left of it because it was such an explosion. Usually, if you didn't hit your target on the first round you'd get it on the second because the 240mm howitzer was so accurate. They shot such high angle, there was quite a bit of difference between when they would notify you 'on the way' which meant that they had fired until you watched the round land, why it seemed it took three times as long with the 240 for that round to land than with the 155's. With the 155's they would say 'on the way' and then sometimes they would follow that with 'contact' when the rounds were supposed to hit, because they had it timed. If you took your eyes away from the B.C. scope just for a second, you know, maybe just to rub your eyes, or blink, you'd miss where the rounds would hit. Of course you'd see the dust and dirt, but you wouldn't see exactly where the rounds hit because it would take quite a while for the dust and dirt to settle. I know the infantry guys didn't like it when we fired the heavy stuff too close to their lines because they heard the impact more so than we did depending where they were. It was quite a noise. Usually the officer in charge ran the fire missions, and sometimes we did depending on circumstances, they wanted to give us experience in case something happened to them, we could take over. They wouldn't let us fire on Mortar Ridge with the 240's, they said it was too close to the MLR, and I remember two reasons, first they didn't want to expend these 240mm rounds on personnel, they were supposed to be for bunkers, artillery positions, ammo dumps, supply dumps, stuff like that, and then secondly was that they didn't want to waste ammo on enemy personnel that close to the lines, they wanted the 240s to be for the bunkers, and let the other artillery pound these smaller positions. How far ahead of the lines Mortar Ridge was, I'm not sure, but I know we could have dropped in one 240mm round on 'delay' and there would have been no hundred and fifty coming out of that ridge, I know that! They would have been buried down there and they never would have got them dug out, because there wasn't much rock, there was mostly dirt and sand, at least that's the way it looked from our position. We would have been able to cave in everything they got on there. The 240s could go down, they had the penetrating ability of on the average thirty-two feet. At the time I was a PFC, and you don't ask too many questions, and if you do ask, you don't get many answers from higher ups!

The last day of the war, everyone was using up all their ammo. It was just pure, that's all you could hear, was the continual roar of our artillery. It started in the afternoon, I think guys were figuring out to get rid of their odd lot ammo powder and 'projos' and they were gonna use them up, because they knew they were gonna have to move back, and the more they could fire, pick out targets, fire on that, they wouldn't have to move all that stuff. About nine thirty, quarter to ten, it started slacking off, I'd say about quarter to ten, or maybe ten of ten, everything stopped. There were a few rounds back and forth even after ten o'clock, but I think guys were trying to get the last round in, or fire off some more ammo. You'd fire one, and pretty soon the Chinese would fire one. It was, that intermediate stuff went on, probably a half an hour or so afterwards, as I recall. And then the next morning, everyone started coming out of the trenches on the front lines, standing up looking at one another. I remember binoculars were pretty scarce, because everyone wanted binoculars to look at their enemy. The Chinese, they came out in some form of light, real light colored, quilted uniforms. They came out of that one hill, Mortar Ridge, it must have been a hundred, hundred and fifty that came out of there. They must have been down deep, you'd think a small ridge, a small hill like that, they would never put that many men on there, so they must have been really in there. They just kept pouring out of there, and you wondered where they stayed, so they must have been really deep. The morning following the cease fire, that was quite a deal to see all them Chinese come out of those tunnels and the tops of these hills, and then we had to start giving personnel counts, on how many where on each hill or ridge, and I suppose they were doing the same things. I was doing a little sipping there with some booze we had hidden, and about that time, I was looking through the binoculars, and Lt. Hank Sobieski was on the B.C. scope, and we were comparing numbers afterwards. I was sipping out of my canteen cup, and Jack Randall said 'you can't sip at that and look through the binoculars at the same time', so I gave him the binoculars and I just kept sipping! At that moment, that was more important than the binoculars! I remember a bunch of officers from headquarters coming up that day, and I think they must have smelled some spirits on our breath, and they weren't too pleased about that! After we rotated off the hill, Jack and I never went back up there again. I was down in the battery for a few days afterward, maybe a week, and then I got transferred to the switchboard bunker, and I took over as the senior switchboard operator."

**2nd Lt Robert Lusk**
**38th Field Artillery Battalion 1953**

"I was called to active duty in the fall of 1951 from the Officer Reserve Corps. While in college, I elected to take ROTC for reasons of both patriotism and $2700 per month during my third and fourth year of ROTC, and received a reserve commission as a Second Lieutenant in Field

Artillery. After attending the Officer Basic Field Artillery Course and serving as a cadre officer and instructor in the Field Artillery Replacement Training Center at Fort Sill, Oklahoma for a year I was ordered to FECOM in the fall of 1952. I reported at Camp Stoneman, California for transportation to FECOM in early January 1953. Most of those reporting at that time were sent by ship but I was told when I checked in that I would be sent by air because qualified Artillery Forward Observers in Korea were in short supply. The plane I was transported in had mostly FO's and surgeons as passengers. Not very comforting! When I arrived at Camp Drake, Japan I was sent almost immediately by train to Sasebo to take the Pusan ferry to Korea. In Pusan they put us on a train north to Yong Dong Po. The train burned soft coal and the cars had only open windows. The train went as fast as it could. It was a freezing cold ride with coal dust and cinders blowing into the cars. We were aware railroad security and guerrillas were a very real problem, and we actually passed a still smoldering train on its side where a trestle on the southbound rails appeared to have been blown up. At Yong Dong Po there were 2 ¼ ton trucks waiting which took us to Second Infantry Division Rear late at night. The next day I was assigned. Several rides later through DIVARTY and the 38th Headquarters I arrived at the firing battery positions of Battery 'B' about dusk. I met the Battery Commander who told me I would be an FO but would be kept in the battery position area a couple days for acclimation and to do some artillery position survey work. I would be available for perimeter defense at night

The 38th Field Artillery fired 105mm howitzers. It was a light artillery battalion usually with a direct support mission. It was usually, but not always, assigned as the direct support field artillery battalion for the 38th Infantry Regiment of the 2nd Infantry Division. Direct Support means, among other things, that the 38th was responsible for sending artillery FOs to every infantry company of the 38th Infantry Regiment committed to combat. Battery 'B' sent FOs to companies of the 2nd Battalion of the 38th Infantry, and in my case I was normally assigned with Fox Company of the 2nd Battalion. From early 1953 until late June the infantry of the Second Infantry Division was either in the Commonwealth Division area with Commonwealth artillery direct support, in reserve or involved in the prisoners of war problems. I'm not too sure what the assigned mission was for the infantry during this period or if it was in reserve for the 8th Army or a particular Corps. I am aware that the 2nd Infantry Division field artillery battalions were not in reserve and were always committed to some sort of support missions in combat. When I first arrived at Battery 'B' we were participating in firing to support defensive positions including 'flash fires' and patrol activity of the ROK Division and at times firing 'flash fire' concentrations for the U.S. 7th Infantry Division on Pork Chop Hill. This continued until late April 1953.

When I joined the 38th Field Artillery we were in support of the 1st ROK Division in the I Corps area. Later we were in support of the 2nd ROK Division on White Horse in IX Corps area. Then we were in support of the U. S. 3rd Infantry Division in the IX Corps area. The missions were direct support or reinforcing support. At one point I remember being told we were a 'flap' battalion. IX Corps would send us where additional fire support was needed most urgently. What all of this meant to me personally was that I served as an FO with a number of different infantry companies of different infantry regiments and divisions. Since FOs were usually in short supply, the ROK and US companies I served with were glad to have an FO even if he was not from their own organic artillery. I remember one incident, which I was later teased about, that happened in one of the sudden changes in the battalion's support mission. I was the FO with a ROK company on the MLR in the Whitehorse area. One night the battalion moved after dark without any warning to the committed FOs. The battalion's fire support was needed in the U.S. 3rd Division area because Outpost Harry was being attacked. The next morning I took my FO team back from a position on Whitehorse to the old battery position to find out what to do and where the battalion had gone. The Battery First Sergeant was still there to meet some new replacements due in that morning. He told me where to go to rejoin the battery. Before going I decided to get showers for my men and me in a makeshift shower stall the battery had rigged out of a stack of old ammo boxes surrounded by sand bags with two fifty-five gallon drums of water on top heated by emergence heaters normally used in mess halls. The problem was that the makeshift shower stall was within line of sight of Chinese held hills. It had not drawn Chinese artillery fire that day until it was my turn to take a quick shower with a couple of the new replacements sharing the stall at the same time. We were all three nude and soaped up when the Chinese chose to shell us. The first round was at least fifty yards away. The two replacements were obviously frightened. I was too but I wanted to calm them so I remained calm and said something to the effect that the Chinese couldn't hit the broadside of a barn. I said we should get the soap off and then run for a nearby bunker. About that time the next Chinese round hit right outside the shower stall. The explosion knocked the stall partially down with us in it. A flying board from an ammo box hit me in the back knocking me down and caused the water drum to spill its remaining water down on us. The three of us got up off the ground and ran fast to the bunker nude. Of course those in the battery area observed us. When the Chinese ceased firing I retrieved my clothes and left for the trip to the new battery positions with only a bruised back and a humorous story. I did have another shower episode a week or so later though. I had a member of my FO team who had volunteered to come to Korea from a disciplinary barracks in the states. He was a good soldier in combat. He could splice and lay new wire in combat situations faster than anyone else I ever had. He was always courageous under fire and always executed orders immediately. His known weaknesses were drinking, chasing women. gambling and fighting. I made the mistake of letting him go to a shower point accompanied only by another FO team member. He took off to find "a woman" according to the other team member when that team member returned. A day later he was back courtesy of the MPs. They caught him drunk in a Korean village the same evening he ran but kept him until he sobered up. I obtained another volunteer to replace him.

I expected and was told that every young field artillery lieutenant served as an FO when first assigned to the 38th Field Artillery Battalion. I do not know when I first heard this but it was no surprise when I arrived at the 38th Field Artillery HQ and Battalion Fire Direction Center, the S-3, Major Blatt, briefed me about the battalion and what he expected from me, and he told me what I should expect from him. I remember Major Blatt said when I called in a fire mission to FDC it would be fired without any questions being asked. He said the 38th Field Artillery Battalion had great pride in firing missions fast and accurate. He said he would initially rely upon my judgment that each fire mission I called in should be fired. He said he might question my judgment afterwards and raise hell if he disagreed but he would not delay the fire mission. The full responsibility was mine as it was for every other FO from the battalion until he had some reason to question the individual FO 'judgment' based upon that FO's performance. He also told me not to worry about any rationing of rounds. He would worry about that. If I believed the specific fire mission was essential I should fire the mission. He told me I was responsible for my team being trained and be able to move, shoot and communicate in a prompt, accurate and professional manner. I should know my terrain so well I should be able to call for all anti personnel fire missions to be fire for effect on the initial rounds. He said most fire missions would be fired using high explosive HE shells and proximity VT fuses. He said the norm was to use six pieces in the initial rounds, and explained to me what the battalion called 'flash' fire missions. A 'Flash Mission' was a call by the FO for final defensive protective fires by all artillery available at maximum rates of fire. When I left him I had great respect for him and confidence that I would be well supported. I felt a great responsibility to perform to the very best of my ability. My Battery

Commander did keep me at the battery position for a couple days. This was important to me. I learned a lot about the battery and battalion procedures in addition to getting a little bit acquainted. The short stay increased my confidence in my abilities to call for fire missions, plan defensive fires for all crew served weapons, plan and organize perimeter defenses, help plan patrols, use my individual weapon, utilize a number of individual combat skills and teach others many of these skills. I learned that all enlisted members of Forward Observer teams from Battery 'B' were volunteers for the assignment. Men volunteered for FO teams because they earned one more point per month toward rotation back to the states. New FOs and new enlisted volunteers were put with experienced team members. This meant I had an experienced team to break me in. After that I was responsible for quickly training new volunteers as they arrived. It was not hard to do because all were highly motivated and realized their lives depended upon it. I also had to give up trained team members for new FOs. Under this excellent system the majority of every FO team was usually veteran.

A few mornings after I joined my battery I was sent to relieve the senior Forward Observer of the battery on a 1st ROK Division company size outpost, Outpost Queen. We were furnishing direct support to a regiment of the 1st ROK Division. Needless to say, I went with some unspoken anxiety. I remember the day vividly. I was driven to near a Main Line of Resistance infantry position. A ROK infantryman guided me to Outpost Queen. We both had flat board back packs. I carried my weapon, a case of C rations and a few hems of personal gear. The ROK carried a five-gallon can of water. We had to go down a steep hill, cross a little valley and climb a steep hill to the company positions on the top. Outpost Queen was very close to Chinese occupied positions. So close that we were within easy range of light mortars which fired at us off and on every day. The entire approach route of about one mile was under Chinese observation but they did not fire at us. I knew enough to keep about 50 yards behind the ROK. When we got there I was puffing. The veteran FO was ready to leave as soon as I arrived but I asked him to brief me on the terrain before he left. He did so but made it short. He took me through a tunnel to a forward slope hole for observation. I stood up to look out more thoroughly. He hit me hard with his shoulder and dragged me down. He said something like 'You son of a bitch, you are going to be alive when I leave here. Take my advice. Learn to duck. Don't show yourself here needlessly. They will fire at us when they see us here. For the first two or three days rely upon your team to break you in. If you last three days you will probably know how to do your job.' It was good advice. While I was on Outpost Queen I directed artillery fires on Chinese bunkers, Chinese infantry and Chinese mortar positions. I was involved in obtaining and reporting on air support by Marine Corsair fighter-bombers using both napalm and machine gun suppression on Chinese positions close to me on Outpost Queen.

We had daily incoming Chinese artillery, mortar and sniper fire. There was no all out attempt by the Chinese to take Outpost Queen while I was there, thank heavens, but I heard they did take Outpost Queen later when our unit was in another sector. When serving with a ROK infantry company there was a great incentive to communicate all involved even though we spoke different languages. I remember that when they wanted to call the FO they would yell 'Yapo.' I believe 'puk yak po' meant machine gun. Funny about what words took priority isn't it. There were some stories about how the ROKs would try to steal from other units. Well, when you are with a ROK unit doing what was important to save the lives of all concerned the situation was vastly different. On one occasion one of my men could not find a razor he had. I told the ROK Company Commander about the missing razor. In a short time an obviously beaten up ROK soldier returned the razor to me with a bigger ROK right behind him in a threatening posture. On an outpost as remote as Queen we did not want to make any more trips in the open for supplies than we had to. We had been told it was not safe to eat the ROKs chow. However, after awhile eating only cold C rations gets tiring. ROK offers to trade some of their food for some of our C rations led me to accept the offer for our team at least part of the time. There were no ill effects but Korean food is really different to say the least. We were not always quite sure what we were eating. I remember well the very chewy and smelly octopus. It was sort of like chewing smelly pieces of small garden hose. No complaints, mind you. Several of the ROKs wanted to socialize with my team. One ROK sergeant I remember wanted to have us join him in singing from a small hymnal he had. He also got across that his home was in North Korea and he was a Christian. One morning he came to me with two gifts. One was the ear of a Chinese soldier he had killed in a hand-to-hand fight while the sergeant was on patrol the night before. The other was the burp gun of the Chinese soldier. I tried out the burp gun immediately on the back slope of Outpost Queen. Unfortunately for me the chamber was still filled with the former owners blood. I spattered the blood all over myself while firing it. I thanked the proud sergeant and gave both to members of my team. When I was replaced on Outpost Queen I was assigned to the firing battery doing various jobs knowing it was only temporary before going back on the bill. While in the firing battery I learned how 'flash fires' were handled there. Every man worked hard to keep the howitzers firing as rapidly as possible continuously. Every man, including the battery commander, took turns at the exhausting ammo preparation and cannoneers jobs. When relieved at one job you did something else. All of the trucks were being used to haul in more ammunition. The battery was a virtual beehive of frantic activity. This type of firing was difficult but contributed to unit cohesiveness and pride, and I always thought it is also part of the reason the U. S. fired more artillery rounds in Korea than in World War II.

When we left the 1st ROK Division in late April we moved to the IX Corps area. The first battery position area there was partially behind a small hill on the front slope of a somewhat higher ridge bordering the Chorwon valley. Basically it was on the south edge of the Chorwon valley. Most of us considered it to be an undesirable position but assigned to us because other batteries, including a battery of 240mm howitzers, had the nearby positions behind the ridge. The Battery Commander did get a commitment to have engineers immediately help dig in our howitzers. The engineers had tanks with dozer blades, heavy timbers and lots of sand bags. Three of the six howitzer positions were within line of sight of Chinese positions. The dozers quickly dug out six circular gun positions about three feet below the ground surface. The rear two thirds of each dug in gun position was covered with a carport like structure of 12x12 timbers covered with dirt and sandbags on the sides and top. I was charged with planning a perimeter defense for the battery immediately. It was the most vulnerable position we were ever in while I was with the battery. The top of the small hill in front of part of the battery was too far away to be quickly occupied by men from howitzer positions. If we did send some of the limited battery members to occupy it there would be difficulty in coordinating the very thin perimeter defense because of the distance. However, if occupied by the enemy it would make the Battery position untenable even at night. I decided to dig foxholes for a few men on the right front and left front of the battery positions. Both avenues were open and easily approached from the Chorwon flats by deep patrols or by a breakthrough. We would send our two bazookas to the right front because of the road there. Two howitzers on each side would be assigned direct fire zones as part of the perimeter defense of the battery positions. The section chiefs prepared range cards and were responsible for having a few rounds prepared in advance for possible use in short order. Because of the limited manpower available we planned to use the perimeter defenders sort of like a maneuver element sent where most needed. We could not effectively defend all around from this position.

I did not stay in the new battery position more than a couple days before I was sent to FO with a 2nd ROK company on a slope of Whitehorse. It was a relatively quiet front there at the time. The only fire missions I remember were occasional attempts to knock out bunkers. From there, I went to the new battery position behind the 3rd Infantry Division. We dug foxholes in the rice paddy area of the battery and spent the night. We were sent to FO with a company of the 7th U.S. Infantry Regiment the next day. They were located in the 'boomerang' area below the high imposing Hill 1062 called 'Papasan' held by the Chinese. We drove down a valley directly toward 'Papasan' then turned to the left behind the low hill mass at the foot of Papasan to get behind our new infantry company's positions. The valley was a mortar and artillery alley for the Chinese. They shot at us as we drove as fast as we could down the road in the valley in the broad daylight. There was one very close round. When we stopped behind the low hill mass of the boomerang we found a big piece of shrapnel in our spare tire behind the back seat of the jeep but not one of the four of us was even scratched. I was there only a few days, and there were no major attacks during this time. I remember that Papasan was so big and imposing it was not hard to pick out distant points on it as well as close up points. The Chinese moved around quite a bit on the more distant higher reaches even in the daytime. We could see groups of them a frequently every day. We often shot at them but the daytime shooting results were usually poor because they would move out of sight so quickly. I had many questions from men of the *r'* Infantry Regiment about whether or not I was pan of a relief of the 7th by a regiment of the 2nd Infantry Division. I kept telling them that my battalion was reinforcing their own artillery and had nothing to do with relief as far as I knew. I was their short time FO because their direct support field artillery battalion was short of FOs. Moving around so much, going to so many infantry companies made it possible for me to keep learning more good techniques in planning final defensive fires. I started volunteering more and more to help the infantry integrate all their crew served weapons with all the other artillery, mortar, tank, quad fifty AA weapons, etc. which might be available. An example of this was the use of quad fifties in indirect fire on avenues of approach. I liked using the quad fifties at night for interdiction missions as well. The quad fifties had a psychological warfare side to them in that there were a lot of tracer rounds. The Chinese hated them. I was told the Chinese referred to them as 'raining death.'

From the 7th I moved two or three regiments west to the western end of the U.S. 3rd Division's MLR. I believe the U.S. infantry company I went to was the 15th Infantry Regiment but it could have been the 5th Regimental Combat Team. I was there only a couple of days. These days were quiet as to patrol activity. There was a considerable amount of incoming artillery and mortar rounds. The positions were in the Chorwon flats to the left of and not far from Outpost Tom. There were foxholes and trenches but all had water in them. It required frequent bailing and digging to prevent them from caving in entirely. It meant we lived in the water and mud. Our feet, clothing and all of our equipment were wet most of the time. My next move was to go with 'F' Company of the 15th Infantry Regiment. It was on the MLR to the right rear of Outpost Harry. From this ridge I could see Outpost Harry to my left front. I had excellent observation of the approaches to Outpost Harry from the Chinese held hills on its east flank. There was a narrow draw between 'F' Company and the company on its left directly behind Outpost Harry. The problem was that the Chinese attacks on Outpost Harry were at night when observation was limited for directing artillery fire. Efforts to provide illumination included not only artillery illumination rounds and air dropped illumination rounds but also the use of searchlights directed at low clouds to diffuse the light from the searchlights. I arrived there several days after the major Chinese attacks on Outpost Harry. There was nightly action but it was patrol activity by both sides. After a couple days I was ordered to leave this company. I was to find Fox Company of the 23rd U.S. Infantry Regiment, 2nd U.S. Infantry Division, to become its FO. It was to relieve the

Infantry Regiment on the left flank of the 3rd Infantry Division. The 23rd was the first regiment of the 2nd Infantry Division to go on line. I was surprised to be the FO for Fox Company of the 23rd because the 38th Field Artillery usually furnished the direct support for the 38th Infantry Regiment when the 2nd Division was committed. The 37th Field Artillery Battalion usually was in direct support of the 23rd. When I arrived at Fox Company of the 23rd it was planning to go on line the next night. There was already an FO team from the 37th Field Artillery there. It had arrived hours earlier. The company commander had just learned the 38th would be furnishing direct support, so the FO team from the 37th left. I learned the reason the 38th Field Artillery was to support the 23rd rather than the 37th was that our battalion was already in the area and knew the terrain better. This was the only company commander I had difficulty working with. He had recently volunteered for a second consecutive tour in Korea to get the company command and a promotion. He was overconfident in his own ability and pretty full of himself in my opinion. When I learned the positions we were going to occupy I told him I had been there. I volunteered to help integrate the planning of defensive fires of infantry crew served weapons with mortars and artillery. He didn't exactly refuse the offered help but he put me down like what could an artilleryman know about good fire planning for infantry crew served weapons. Not a good way to start for either of us.

When with 'F' Company of the 23rd Infantry Regiment, I was again in the Chorwon flats on the left flank of Outpost Tom. It was difficult to get hot food to the company in the flats once each day because of exposure to direct observation and fire by the Chinese. Therefore, each night a tracked armored personnel carrier would come through the area with cans of hot food. Timing would be different each night and speed in unloading the cans along the line sometimes resulted in the daily hot meal lacking in completeness. We might be short meat or vegetables or something else in our particular part of the company position. But it was great to get a hot meal every day. This company was on the extreme left flank of the regiment. The weather was damp and the water table was near the surface of the ground. This meant our trenches were like drainage ditches or muddy bathtubs. I inherited a small low bunker from the previous unit. It was constantly fill of water up to about 18 inches below the ground level. We would bail it out frequently with our helmets but the bottom line was that we were wet all of the time and lived in the muddy water. That is where I first got the fungus infection in my ears. Since my little bunker was the most prominent position in the company area, we often experienced direct fire from the Chinese. One afternoon during one of these episodes, the company commander called me from his position and ordered me to provide him with a 'shell rep.' Shell Reports are in a specified format. In examining a shell hole you can often retrieve the fuse of the round. You are then enabled to take a rough azimuth reading back toward the weapon from which it was fired. I told him I would take a shell rep but that I was trying to triangulate on the direct fire weapon of about 75 or 76mm in caliber. Triangulation is working with another observer in a different location to get the angles from each observation point to the direct fire weapon as it fired. By knowing the coordinates of each observer the location of the direct fire weapon could be plotted where the angles crossed. Very accurate fire could then be brought on the direct fire weapon. In the flats this method was quite useful because of the difficulty in estimating distance accurately. The other observer was having trouble seeing the flash of the direct fire weapon so some time was passing. ***A*** few minutes later the company commander called me back wanting to know where his shell report was. He was quite angry and accused me of being afraid to go out or have one of my men go out while being fired upon. I had to explain about the triangulation as soon as he stopped raving. I told him I would still get him his shell rep but that I would proceed with the triangulation attempt first.

The other FO never did get an angle reading for me so I just used my own direction with a distance estimate to fire on the enemy weapon. It was silenced but I never was sure whether I got it or they just chose to move it somewhere else. I then got the shell rep complete with a fuse I dug out with an entrenching tool. I reported the incident to the artillery liaison officer at the infantry battalion operations center so that he would know in case the infantry company commander complained about me to the infantry battalion commander. The liaison officer was upset about the attitude of the company commander and later spoke to the infantry battalion commander who did not back up his ambitious company commander. Needless to say, my relationship with this company commander was cool at best but I sensed that my men and the infantry platoon in the vicinity of my bunker thought the company commander got what he had coming to him. Fortunately for me I did not have to hang around many more days. The 38th Infantry Regiment was going on line to replace a regiment from the 3rd Infantry Division. An FO team from the 37th replaced us with Fox Company of the 23rd and we went to Fox Company of the 38th Infantry Regiment. We were in the same position as I had been with on the right rear flank of Outpost Harry. Once again this made it easier for me as I already knew the terrain and knew most of the defensive fire plans needed. I just had to work the new people into the plan and make the adjustments needed or desired by our home infantry company. The most serious problem was that the new company commander was the opposite of the last company commander with the 23rd. This new company commander was a very nice person but lacking in confidence. He had difficulty making prompt decisions. Those around small unit leaders quickly sense confusion, incompetence or lack of confidence or dedication. One night the company had a patrol out. The patrol leader and I had gone over his planned route and planned several concentration points for artillery support if the patrol got in trouble. We agreed upon code words for each of the concentrations. The patrol leader was to radio me code words for any of the preplanned concentrations he wanted artillery fire on or adjustment from. I had asked FDC to be prepared to fire the concentrations immediately. FDC had settings ready to transmit to the artillery pieces. The patrol left after dark. The company commander and the company First Sergeant were with me in my small bunker on the forward slope of the hill. Even though it was dark, I could vaguely see some of the terrain in the valley the patrol was planning to cross. This terrain was on the right flank approaches to Outpost Harry.

All of a sudden a firefight began in that valley. I could dimly see almost exactly where it was. It was at one of the points the patrol leader thought there could be an ambush. A concentration had been planned for this very situation. It immediately became chaotic but there was no radio message. I immediately called in a fire mission anyway but ended the transmission with something like, 'At My Command, Fire for Effect' so that the howitzers would be ready. With the telephone line still open I then asked the company commander for permission to fire even without the radio message, but he seemed confused. The First Sergeant quickly said 'Shoot if you can Lieutenant'. I then simply said 'Fire' into the phone and the immediate reply from FDC was 'On the Way'. Because of the detailed preplanning with the patrol leader and FDC I was able to have six rounds of accurate fire for effect on the way in less than one minute from the opening of the firefight. The patrol got back. I believe it lost only one man. It easily could have been more. The patrol leader said he was able to disengage and withdraw when the artillery rounds began arriving in front of them. In the chaos of the firefight they just didn't try to use their radio. The company commander later denied his confusion but his panic had cost him true control of his company. The First Sergeant, the patrol leader, who was a platoon leader and I had a tight bond thereafter. Tragically, this platoon leader was killed on the night before the ceasefire. He was killed while running or walking up a trench away from my position and about ten yards from me. He had brought me a canteen cup of coffee and we had been visiting in my small bunker about cars and home. I remember well one thing he told me. He had said that we were good friends then but after going home I probably couldn't take him into my parent's home. He was a black ROTC graduate from the University of Michigan. I denied this to him but neither of us was certain we believed this. I certainly understood where he was coming from. Remember this was just after integration in the army and before the big civil rights movements.

I was an FO with different companies of the $1^{st}$ and $2^{nd}$ ROK Divisions, companies of the $7^{th}$ and $15^{th}$ U.S. Infantry Regiments, and companies of the $23^{rd}$ and $38^{th}$ Infantry Regiments, $2^{nd}$ Infantry Division. The reaction was uniformly positive. The explanation is simple. By performing your job well you helped keeping them alive as well as yourself my experience was that combat is a strong motivator to do your job to the very best of your ability. When new enlisted men joined my team they were highly motivated to learn all they could about doing their jobs and those of the entire team well. I always maintained we each had to be prepared to do every job. All of our lives could depend upon it. They wanted to learn all they could to accomplish this as rapidly as they could. It was not unusual for them to sit and practice wire splicing for speed, correct radio operating procedures, picking our terrain features and translating those into fire mission commands without any prompting. In fact, I expected it of them. I encouraged questions and I asked questions. This practice and my team's routine practice of offering to assist the infantry in all matters relating to planning the best use of crew served weapons in integrated defensive fires had the effect of in infantrymen seeking my team out with questions and for advice. Confidence is contagious and word gets around quickly too. I was pleased that 81mm mortar men and 4.2 mortar men from infantry battalion and regimental levels would closely coordinate with us when they had confidence in us. There was a set sequence in calling a Fire Mission. The whole procedure was referred to on occasion as 'A system designed by geniuses for execution by idiots'. Every person on the FO team and every member of every Fire Direction Center knew the sequence of a fire mission by heart. You had to be able to do this automatically in the worst chaos imaginable. Chaos is when the most important fire missions seemed to be needed, and the need for accurate and prompt fire of sufficient volume was essential to staying alive and holding positions. The artillery's mission is to be able to move, shoot and communicate. Two of these are invoked in the Fire Mission. My battalion's pride in being fast and accurate with the delivery of fire was about the most important thing in our lives.

In my combat unit experience in Korea most of the Observation Posts were usually on high hills to the rear of the Outposts and MLR. It is possible an Observation Post could be on the MLR but I did not see any such situation. Observation Posts were usually manned by Artillery Forward Observers from artillery units with general support or reinforcing missions. These were normally the medium artillery battalions, 155mm howitzers, organic to the infantry division or artillery units of various calibers directly assigned to a Corps or to $8^{th}$ Army. I was with a light 105mm towed artillery battalion. Our normal mission was direct support, direct support reinforcing or reinforcing. Most of the artillery Forward Observers from light battalions such as the $38^{th}$ were assigned to accompany individual infantry companies in combat. We would seek out positions in the company area from which we could best furnish fire support. We would, however, often call our positions Observation Posts and these might occasionally be referred to as 'OP Able' etc. using the letter designation of the infantry company. If the infantry company went into reserve the artillery Forward Observer would usually be reassigned to another infantry company on the MLR or an infantry company on an Outpost. The $38^{th}$ Field Artillery could be called upon for 16 FO teams to be with supported companies of infantry. Battery 'A' furnished the FOs for the $1^{st}$ Battalion of the $38^{th}$ Infantry Regiment, Battery 'B' furnished FOs for the $2^{nd}$ Battalion and Battery 'C' for the $3^{rd}$ Battalion. Since the Dutch Infantry Battalion was attached to the $38^{th}$ Infantry Regiment each of the $38^{th}$ Field Artillery Batteries furnished four

FO teams, one for each of the infantry companies of the supported battalion and one for a Dutch infantry company. Most of the FO teams from my battalion were on Outpost Queen, Whitehorse Mountain, Outposts Tom, Dick and Harry, the Boomerang and other hill masses in the areas occupied by the infantry units we were supporting during the time I was in combat in Korea. I was personally on Outpost Queen, Whitehorse Mountain, the Boomerang and a few other no-name hills. Life as a Forward Observer was full of changes. I was never bored but quite tired most of the time. There was never enough sleep. One infantry company commander said that any officer in combat was not doing his job if he got more than four hours of sleep in a twenty-four hour period. Life was full of danger, full of decisions, full of moves, full of challenges. Trenches are miserable places to live, or rather exist. Add to this that most of the fighting was at night because of the accuracy, volume and nature of artillery fire in the daytime. We used 'VT' or variable time fuses most of the time. This meant our rounds were exploding about twenty feet above the ground to get maximum antipersonnel effect by the shrapnel. The Chinese reciprocated with accurate artillery fire. Trenches, foxholes and bunkers were essential at the MLR and in the battery positions. After while you become accustomed to it. I do not mean you lost your fear, but you realized you had to do your job even with it. The GIs would say you had to know when to duck and when not to duck. You simply could not hide yourself or stay down too much. Water in the trenches, foxholes and bunkers added to the discomfort and dangers. For example, I got a low-grade fungus infection in my ears. Water and freezing also added to the potential for bunkers and tunnels to collapse on men. In summation, trench warfare was miserable.

We were in this position when the ceasefire occurred. We had been hearing rumors that the Chinese were building up for a big attack in our sector so we were suspicious that the Chinese might not observe it or get the word immediately. It was late evening when the ceasefire occurred, but we thought things might start up again. We knew we were to withdraw from the now demilitarized zone, and were dubious about withdrawing from our positions within 48 or 72 hours because of our increased vulnerability while withdrawing and immediately thereafter. We stayed on alert most of the night. It was eerily quiet at first and then we could barely hear voices shouting or singing. It was the Chinese. The next morning I saw more Chinese than I had ever imagined in front of us and on the right flank of Outpost Harry. They easily outnumbered us by multiples. The Chinese waved to us. We knew we could not take everything with us in the limited time we had and we did not want to leave valuable defensive and offensive assets behind. The plan was to take out all we could, destroy the rest and destroy our fortifications. The infantry did not have sufficient mobility to take out all that needed to be taken out. Since most of the artillery was already behind or could move behind the demilitarized withdrawal lines more easily, most artillery FO teams stayed with their infantry to assist them in withdrawing. I had one jeep and trailer at my disposal for such use around the clock and we were able to get some of the artillery prime movers and ammo trucks to assist also. We could not get vehicles up the steep mountain to where our positions were so everything had to be carried down hill about one quarter of a mile to the highest point we could drive. During the last day of the withdrawal I saw and heard a large explosion in the positions to our left. For almost fifty years I thought it was in the French positions. At the time I heard that a number were killed but the cause was a mystery to me for almost fifty years, until I finally found out it was a Chinese POW that had thrown a hand grenade into a pile of munitions.

When the withdrawal was over and we were in our infantry company's Dew area I laid down on the ground next to the Company headquarters area in exhaustion and slept quite a few hours. When I finally woke up, infantrymen were moving about all around me. My team was also just starting to get up. We were closely bonded with the infantry company. I called my battery on an infantry line and was told to return to the unit. Before leaving I visited with the company commander. He said they were taking up defensive positions but wanted to make us honorary members of their company and award us their skull and spear unofficial battalion insignia. My team and I were very pleased. Field Artillery FO teams at that time were envious of the infantrymen receiving their coveted Combat Infantryman Badges while field artillerymen had no comparable badge. It was stressful being an FO but there was also a sense of pride of personal and unit competence. My thoughts were pretty focused on doing my job well. I believed my team and the units we were with depended upon me knowing what I was doing and that I would do it well. At times you depend upon inner strengths.

I was in Korea from early 1953 until late November 1953 when I went back to the United States by ship on the Christmas rotation quota. I could have gone shortly after the cease-fire by applying to do so but mistakenly decided I would rotate anyway in early September. Unfortunately for me I had become Gunnery Officer, Assistant S-3, for the battalion by that time. Too many experienced officers had applied for early rotation and battalion tests were scheduled for early November. Therefore I was held over for the convenience of the Army until after the battalion tests even though my two years would be up in mid October. The trip home took about three weeks at sea. The ship had about 60% Marines and 40% Army. There were very few Marine and Army officers. As I recall, we were all company grade officers. We were charged with maintaining order, etc. Most of the Marines and Soldiers were to be released from active duty upon return. The attitude was happy and carefree, and gambling and fights were occasional problems. I was assigned as permanent officer of the guard. I had my problems not only with the occasional disorders but also in recruiting Marine and Army members of the guard force to handle the problems. The potential inter service rivalry was of concern to me. I remember how worried I was when we were only about a day or so out of San Francisco harbor and the ship picked up commercial radio. The radio broadcast was put on the ship public address system. Most were interested to hear U. S. commercial radio for the first time in since leaving for Korea. The very first commercial news broadcast included a sentence near the end of the news that 'The USS General Pope is due to dock tomorrow at Fort Mason with 3300 battle weary Marines.' There was no mention of the Army troops. I thought there would be big fights but there was some kidding and an incident or two but nothing of any great importance, I was relieved. I guess everyone was so happy to be arriving they did not want to risk court martial charges on their last days of military service."

**2nd Lt John Fisher**
**10th Field Artillery Battalion 1953**

"I was drafted in November 1950 and went thru 8 weeks of infantry basic training and from there to Aberdeen Proving Grounds where I became an instructor in the anti-aircraft gun control repair area. I applied for OCS, went to leadership school, and then entered OCS at Fort Sill in December 1951. I graduated in June 1952 and was shipped to Korea in December. When I arrived on January 6th 1953, I was assigned to the 10th Field Artillery Battalion, and went up to the line at their reserve position on the same or next day. In April '53 was assigned to Air Observation section. The 10th Field Artillery was a 105mm unit, however with a large enough target you could obtain division artillery. The 10th Field position was an area where no major battles were fought in 1953, except for the Chinese assault on the ROK division on our right flank which gave way. This affected us and the air section was moved to the rear. Some of the 3rd Division artillery was overrun, I believe one unit was the 555th, but the only action was patrols and probes by the Chinese, but some outposts were really hit hard and overrun for a time. The area we were located was a quite area on the line, and in the air section I felt it was doubtful they could hit us. On line and in the air, we just looked for targets of opportunity to keep us busy. I usually was with company 'H' 7th Infantry Regiment, and we were not in the trenches with the infantry, the FO had a private bunker-observation post, but the infantry also had bunkers. We were stationed on OP 'Sugar' in 3rd Division area, which was between Kumhwa and Chorwon over looking the Chorwon Valley looking north. From what I remember each battery had one Forward Observer team directing fire. We fought the Chinese, I had no particular thoughts concerning them, they were just an enemy and for an FO, a target. I think back on it, and I realize how lucky I was that there was not more activity in my area. In my area it could have been considered dull, but I was one of the very, very lucky ones. To fire a fire mission, we all used the same routine, one gun to locate the target and the battery adjusted when the target was fixed. I do remember one mission in which we were shooting a direct fire tank mission. There was an observation hole or more likely a ventilation hole for a Chinese troop bunker or cave, and they stayed out of sight in the daytime. We used to shoot at this hole all the time, but no direct hits. One day we failed to see the tank round explode, however about a minute later a big puff or cloud of dust came pouring out of the hole. They must have had a surprised look on their faces when that one went off!"

**2nd Lt Richard Jaffe**
**57th Field Artillery Battalion 1953**

"Upon graduation from Class 19 of Field Artillery Officer Candidate School at Fort Sill, Oklahoma, on 15 July 1952, I was commissioned a Second Lieutenant and ordered to duty with the XVIII Airborne Corps at Fort Bragg, Norm Carolina. By February 1953, as a 24-year-old 'shave tail', I had reported to the 7th Infantry Division, just south of the 38th parallel in Korea. I was assigned to the 57th Field Artillery Battalion, a 105mm howitzer outfit, then in support of the 31st Infantry Regiment. The war at that point had become a politico-military stalemate, not unlike the trench warfare of 1917 France, but with mountains. I got my first taste of combat on 25 March 1953 when I was detailed to an infantry company that was in a blocking position in a valley a few thousand meters behind the main line of resistance. My briefing for this assignment had been minimal and boiled down to 'stick with the company commander'. Unfortunately, The Chinese picked that night to attack and take Old Baldy from us. The next 24 hours became a mélange of scrambling up and down mountains with the infantry and ducking incoming artillery and mortar fire until the situation stabilized. My only function during this whole time was to call in sortie smoke rounds to mask our company's movement through a valley and then, later, to lift some of our own HE fire that was dropping too close to us. Early in April 1953 I was assigned as a Forward Observer atop hill 200 in a position designated 'OP 15' about300 meters east of Pork Chop Hill. Shortly after occupying this position, I got a call from the Fire Support Coordination Center of a 155mm howitzer battalion from another division that was moving in to provide additional artillery support to us. They asked if I would conduct a registration for them. Of course I agreed and asked them to give me a 'splash' five seconds before impact. About ten minutes later, simultaneously with their 'splash' warning, the initial round passed so low over my bunker, I thought it was coming in the back door and going out the front. I do not exaggerate when I say I could have lit a match on the side of that round as it screamed overhead! Despite my having been taught at the Field Artillery School that the FSCC was responsible for clearing the friendly mask, I immediately asked the FSCC to give 'Angle T' which was the angle formed by the intersection of the Gun-Target and the Observer-Target lines. The response was 'Wudda ya want that for?'. 'Just give it to me or I'm not continuing with this registration' I said. About ten minutes later, they called me back and told me what I already knew, the Angle T was zero! I told them to mark that last round as just barely clearing the mask and in less-than-polite terms told them how close they had come to destroying my OP and its occupants. I have often reflected how fortunate it was that I was awake and alert when that class was taught back at Fort Sill.

The Chinese conquest of Old Baldy had placed the American outpost on Pork Chop Hill in great peril as the Chinese Communist Force now was looking right down their throats. At 2100 on 16 April, EE-8 field telephones began ringing in command posts all along the 7th Division front. The battalion S-2 relayed an intelligence summary warning of an expected broad-based attack in our sector starting at 2300. The information had been gathered from reliable agent sources and had been the basis for increased readiness for the past week. The anticipated assault was just two hours away but such warning calls had become almost routine. 300 meters west of me in 'OP 16', which shared a bunker with the 'Easy' Company CP on Pork Chop, 2nd Lt Harvey D. Anderson received the same message. So, too, did 2nd Lt Herbert W. Linn on 'OP 14', which was located on a higher hill some 400 meters southeast of Anderson. The three of us were assigned to Battery 'B' of the 57th, and although we were inexperienced, our close friendship enabled us to work well together to get the job done. At precisely 2300 hours, I stood at the north opening of OP 15 staring intently at the invisible Chinese positions 1000 meters away. Suddenly the entire northern horizon erupted in a series of rippling flashes that illuminated the intervening mountains against the pulsating light. With the veteran assurance born of three weeks' experience on the line, I turned to my recoil sergeant and said 'Looks like those B-29s are giving them hell with radar bombing tonight!' My sergeant, with the superior knowledge that seven months on the MLR had given him quickly, corrected me. 'No, Sir! Those flashes are from enemy artillery firing at us!'

Seconds later, one of the most intensive artillery bombardments in the history of modern warfare began as a preface to the Chinese infantry's assault on Pork Chop Hill. As the 122mm Soviet-made shells began screaming in, I dropped to my knees below the lip of the aperture and grabbed the field telephone, yelling 'The shit has hit the fan! Give me some flares over Pork Chop!' In the next second, the roaring crescendo of exploding shells was punctuated by the blinding flash of direct hit on our OP. The explosion blew off part of our overhead cover and caved in the rest in a jumble of broken timbers and slashed sandbags. This result bore mute testimony to the superiority of the Chinese method of tunneling into the forward and reverse slopes of hillsides, as opposed to our building positions up from the crest. I lay on my back, dazed but still clutching the telephone handset and buried up to my neck in debris. As I recovered my senses, I instinctively drew the telephone to my ear, pressed the butterfly switch and gasped 'Give me Flash Pork Chop!' This was the signal to initiate a preplanned, variable-time fused artillery concentration designed to decimate assaulting enemy infantry in the open by exploding 20 meters overhead. Unfortunately, the severed wires dangled uselessly from the EE-8 handset, and I realized I had a communications problem. I took a quick inventory of my body and appendages and was surprised and elated to find everything intact and in working order. Grinning with the realization that I had survived the blast without a scratch, I dug myself out of the rubble and helped my recon sergeant dig himself free. He did not seem to he hit either, but complained that he was not able to see. The flash from the exploding shell had singed his eyelashes and eyebrows. He had been temporarily blinded. Fortunately, he recovered his vision the following day. Luckily, we both had been spared by a defective shell resulting in a low-order burst with minimal fragmentation. My first priority was to restore communications with both OP 16 on Pork Chop and the FSCC. After leading my blinded sergeant to a safer location in the other leg of our partly demolished L-shaped bunker, I crawled back to the corner of the 'L' and turned on our 610 FM radio. I made contact with Anderson on Pork Chop and asked him if I could be of any help. By this time, the remnants of a Chinese assault company were storming the crest of Pork Chop, tossing hand grenades and spraying AK-47 fire into the Easy Company OP bunker. Anderson was wounded, as were most of the other occupants of the CP. When I called him on the radio and asked him if I could help, the first thing that popped into his head, and has remained burned into my memory ever since, was, "Sure thing, Dick, you can come over here and take my place!' Anderson's radio antenna had been blown away in the initial barrage, drastically limiting his transmitting range. However, since we were less than a quarter-mile apart, we could communicate clearly. His initial request was for the continuation of 'Flash Pork Chop' as the best defense against the marauding Chinese infantry overrunning his position. For the rest of that endless first night of what went down in history as 'The Battle of Pork Chop Hill', I provided Andy's link to the FSCC, relaying his requests for fires, reinforcements, supplies and medical assistance.

From his superior vantage point on a higher hill between and behind the other two positions, he was able to observe the area throughout the action. In spite of the constant hail of artillery and mortar fire Lt. Linn continued to adjust illuminating flares and the 'friendly' VT fire over Pork Chop. The Chinese suffered severe casualties from the firestorm and shell fragments and were unable to consolidate their initial advantage by taking and holding Pork Chop. 'Easy' Company of the 31st was relieved the next morning by the remnants of 'King' and 'Love' Companies. The fight raged on for another day and a half, with 'Easy,' 'Fox' and 'Able' Companies of the 17th Infantry Regiment fed into the rotating meat grinder that Pork Chop had become. The artillery of both sides pounded away with lethal efficiency. Pork Chop was essentially a massive artillery dual with the recurrent infantry efforts unchanged by both sides repeatedly disrupted by the deadly storm of exploding artillery shells. By the second day, the supporting Amen-call fires had consumed a total of 77,349 rounds. Anderson was evacuated safely to Japan, where he recovered from his wounds while lc3nxitig to relax in positions other than sitting. For his cool performance under fire on Pork Chop, in addition to the Purple Heart, Andy received the Silver Star. In an ironic footnote to history, three months after the great battle for the bloody hill ended, our forces abandoned Pork Chop as part of the general line-straightening that followed the end of hostilities."

**1st Lt Henry Kreutzer**
**3rd Battalion, 11th Marine Regiment 1953-54**

"I joined the Marine Corps PLC program during my freshman year in college. I was going to New York University at the time and a Marine Corp Major talked to the Physical Education majors about joining. I remember two of us signed up and we were supposed to get to go to two summers, six weeks each summer, of training. The year was 1949. I later transferred to SUNY Cortland, graduated in June 1952 and went on active duty with the USMC in July 1952. After five months of Marine Corp basic school I was assigned to the Naval Gunfire School and then as a replacement to Korea. I left for Korea March 1953 from Camp Pendleton, by way of the CBR school in Eta Jema Japan. When I arrived in Korea, I was assigned to 'H' Battery, 3rd Battalion, 11th Marine Regiment, we fired 105mm howitzer. We supported the 1st Marine Division, part of I Corps, and we were just east of Panmunjom and about thirty-five miles north of Seoul. I was with the 11th Regiment from early April 1953 until about March 12th, 1954. As a battery officer, I was assigned by our battery commander and attached to an infantry company as a Forward Observer, whenever the infantry company was on the MLR or in a blocking position. Part of the time the 1st Marine Division was in reserve. During that time the Forward Observers stayed with the battery and did Fire Direction Center duty.

During my time, most of the battles were outpost battles. They included the Vegas and Berlin outposts. We fired mostly continuous patterns of fire to designated areas. For me, I was mostly concerned with localizing machine gun fire and pin pointing mortar muzzle blasts, so we could return fire. There was an urgency because we felt we had to get them before they got us. We did. Our fire was very accurate. We were confident we could put rounds on target with our first mission, since guns were checked in everyday in late afternoon before the action began. Action was mostly at night. I was surprised that the Chinese fired at us at night with a machine gun, since the muzzle blasts and tracers made it easy for us to accurately return fire. We supported the 5th Marine Infantry Regiment fighting the Chinese. We worked well with the infantry. We had a well built bunker and their mortar spotters came up to use it. They felt good about our ability to give them artillery support. We didn't support any ROK units, but we did have Korean Marines on a different sector of the front, but they had their own artillery battalion. My OP was 'Five B' or 'Five Baker'. They were given a number and letter because we also had a 'Five Alpha'. We regularly manned three OPs, which covered three infantry companies, and in our case about five thousand yards of front line. From near the truce zone at Panmunjom, our western most OP was near their and I was on the eastern most which was near Bunker Hill and the Chinese Outpost 'Yoke'. I was located opposite of outpost Yoke and near Bunker Hill. Also 'Todak-san' was in our view which was a commanding mountain held by the Chinese. I have forgotten the name of our outpost, but I think is was 'Aggie' or 'Esther'? The hill my OP was on was another 'no name' hill in Korea.

It was hot in July of 1953 as we spent the whole month on the hill. Rats were a problem. They would sometimes walk in front of our bunker aperture at night as we were monitoring patrols. Our observation bunker was on top of the hill. It had 12x12 lumber and about five layers of sandbags on top. An overhang came out about two feet in the front and the aperture was an opening about eight inches high and four feet long. Screening wire was placed over the aperture to protect against grenades. A trench line in the back of our OP led to our living bunker which was on the reverse slope, about ten yards back. Everyday from about 1pm to 4pm we received incoming rounds from the Chinese, which were a mix of mortars or 76mm artillery. At 3pm everyday I would go to the company CP bunker, which was about forty yards away, and we would have a briefing of the patrols going out that night. Our company would send a patrol out every night. I would monitor on the phone line the patrol until they came back to our lines because they would string wire. By 1am or 2am my sergeant would take over the watch, with one other and I would go to sleep. We had an old, beat up radio but we listened to music from armed forces radio from Tokyo. Most of the evenings were quiet, except once in a while a patrol would be hit. Sometimes we would report readings on an air strike or a rocket attack by our unit. In the trenches we ate a good deal of peanut butter and jelly on biscuits. We had big cans of jelly and peanut butter. Sometimes we would heat a can of rations and on some occasion go down the reverse slope for about a half mile to a mess hall for a hot meal and a hot shower and clean uniform. The showers were open, since the summer was hot. It was a relief. We had an old canister stuck in the side of a trench for a relief tube and an outhouse that was just a seat only on the reverse slope for anybody's use. This could get precarious when the incoming rounds came in. It was a difficult climb up the hill, so if you went back down for a hot meal and therefore it was not done too often. Marines reverted to canned rations and heated them with a little gasoline burner, but the water did not taste good because it had to be purified.

The fire mission I recalled the most was when a machine gun opened up on our position and started strafing the whole company. Because the burst came from an easily pinpointed position, I was able to call a mission and have six rounds of 105mm on target within a few minutes and that was the end of that firing. The platoon was much relieved at the turn of events. Calling a Fire Mission, it went something like this 'This is OP Five Baker. Fire Mission. Machine-gun firing. Coordinates so-and-so, one battery. Fire for effect', and the response after six rounds have hit target was 'On target. Possible two KIA. End of Mission.' The cease fire was signed on July 27th 1953 while I was in OP Five Bravo. We then had three days to take our bunkers down and bring our equipment back three miles from the front. We had to dismantle the bunkers and carry all the lumber to a trench about one hundred yards away. Those 12x12's were heavy! That whole area is now the DMZ. At 10pm on July 27th the ceasefire went into effect and we went to sleep the next morning. The Chinese were all over their hills covering over their trench lines. During the war, you hardly could find the Chinese during the day!"

**Sergeant Antonio Montalvo-Nozario**
**999th Armored Field Artillery Battalion 1953-54**

"I first got into the military by the Puerto Rican National Guard, then after that I volunteered as regular Army. I volunteered to go to Korea and was assigned to the 999th Armored Field Artillery Battalion. The 999th was a 155mm self propelled unit, and then I was further assigned to the 32nd Infantry Regiment of the 7th Infantry Division as part of a Forward Observer team. We adjusted fire for not only the 155mm, but also 81mm and 4.2 inch heavy mortars. I was in Korea from January 1953 to April 1954. I believe I was originally assigned as an FO by a simple verbal order of one of the battalion officers. We participated in the winter 1952-1953 campaign and the spring and summer campaign of 1953. My only thoughts during this whole time centered on getting back to Puerto Rico safely. By this time in the war, we were fighting mostly the Chinese on our sector of the front. The 999th usually manned two or three OPs at any given time, I served on all of them, they were in front of the Alligator Hill, the 'Ice Cream Cone', and Pork Chop Hill. Life as a Forward Observer was just like that of an infantryman, cold and tired. The most significant time for me was during the battle of Pork Chop Hill. I remember before the battle it was a continuous fire mission day and night for many days. To call in a fire mission, we had three telephone lines or could make radio calls. I was wounded while at the 999th AFA and did not receive my Purple Heart because I was told all records accidentally destroyed in a fire at the St Louis Army Archives."

**2nd Lt. Henry J. Sobieski**
**213th Field Artillery Battalion 1953**
*Lt. Sobieski is the author's father*

"I enlisted in August 1948. At first I wanted to join the Air Force, but when I talked to the recruiter he said 'We met our quota, we're filled up', so I decided to try the Army. They wrote me up, put me on a bus to the Sckullkill Arsenal in Philadelphia, where I took my physical and entrance exam, and I was sworn in that same day! After basic, I got orders to Germany and was assigned to the 709th MP Battalion, Company 'A', in Frankfurt Germany. By 1950, the Korean War had started. My enlistment was up in August of 1951 and I didn't think I would go there, but President Truman issued and Executive Order extending the enlistment of all those who were getting out for one year. I applied for OCS, was accepted, and sent to Fort Dix in August 1951 for the Leadership School. After graduating I became a drill instructor at the Leadership School, where I also taught physical training and use of the bayonet. By January of 1952, we were told that the quota for MP OCS was two per month for Ft Dix, so I decided to change my service career from Military Police to Anti-Aircraft Artillery OCS at Ft Bliss, Texas. However, they were no longer accepting candidates and we were transferred en masse to the Artillery OCS at Ft Sill. After graduating from OCS in July 1952, I was assigned to the 369th Field Artillery Battalion at Ft Sill. The 369th was using 105mm howitzers, but in December 1952, I got orders to go to Korea, but first was to report for special training in the 240mm howitzer before going. I learned that the 240 was not in operation in Korea but we were going to put it there. Our class size consisted of two majors and six 2nd and 1st Lts that were to be the nexus for two firing batteries. The majors were to become battalion executive officers and the Lts to become battery executive officers, two battalions and six firing batteries. After specialized training we got orders to go and got priority Military Aircraft Command transport to Japan. The flights were on DC-4 aircraft, about twelve hours each flight from San Francisco, to Hawaii, to Wake Island, to Tokyo Japan where we were sent to Camp Drake. From Camp Drake we boarded a train to Yokahama and there we boarded a ship.

We sailed from Japan on up to the Yellow Sea, and we docked at Inchon. That took about five days. I was issued my combat harness, carbine, and other things, and in the middle of the night, we were ordered to debark from a one man ladder on the side of the ship into a waiting LCI. All this was done in the dark, no lights. In the distance, I could see flashes of light and thunder, and I knew this was the sound of artillery, what sounded like exploding rounds, not outgoing. After getting on a train that took us to Yong-dong-po, we finally were dropped off and I spent the night in a Quonset hut. It was winter, and there was no heat, blankets, anything. It was cold! We were there a couple of days and then I got my assignment to the 213th. A deuce and a half came by from the Battalion, and I got in and off we went. I reported in to Lt Col. Charles Jorgensen, the Battalion Commander, in the HQ bunker that was built on the side of a hill. He assigned me to Baker Battery, and on my way there, I could hear our battery pieces firing in the distance. We pulled up to a bunker and the jeep driver said 'That's the officer's bunker, you're to report in there'. I went into this bunker, and low and behold, it was filled with other officers, and they were having a party in celebration of my arrival! What I didn't know at the time was that to fool me, they had all changed ranks, and there was this older officer with 2nd Lt. bars on, and I thought 'Where'd they get this guy from?' Turns out he was the battery commander of Charlie Battery, Captain Buris C. Dale, and we later became good friends. I couldn't figure out what was going on, here I am in a combat area, and there's artillery pieces going off, and here's all these officers having a good time!

All of us new officers were sent up to OP 'Love' on White Horse Mountain to get acclimated with the front when we would be assigned as a Forward Observer, and a battery officer took us up. When we got there, the ROKs were sending out a reinforced platoon, and we were able to observe some of the action. I was in the trenches right next to a .30 caliber air cooled machine-gun section that was firing at a North Korean position in front of us. I stuck my head over the trench and watched the ROKs go from one enemy bunker to another, clearing them out, with mortar rounds bursting around them, and as I looked at the ridgeline in front of me, I could see the flashes from the enemy guns. Those ROKs did a good job. A couple of days later, I went up to OP 'Item' on Hill 278, and was shown all the key reference points, and Dagmar Hill was pointed out to me, to the left and in front of our position. In March, right before the Chinese overran Old Baldy, I was with the forward platoon for the first time. We were right behind a South Korean 105 outfit, and this position was right with the infantry, and we were firing all the time. Whenever we got counter-battery fire, I was instructed, if I could, to call it into HQ, 'Notice Baker' with the code word 'Spark plug'. One time I was laying on the ground, and we were getting counter-battery fire, and I had the EE8 phone in my hand, and I called up Battalion HQ, and the officer who answered was, I think, drunk, and I was yelling 'Spark plug! Spark plug! Notice Baker Spark plug!' and he said, 'What's Spark plug?' and after a few minutes, I couldn't get him to understand, so I hung up, right in the middle of this counter-battery fire.

I remember the first time I was assigned to OP duty, my team was assigned to OP Item. This OP was located to the left of White Horse, with Dagmar Hill to the left of the OP and Porkchop to the far left and Old Baldy slightly in front of it. The 213th supported the 2nd ROK Division, with the U.S. 7th Division manning Porkchop and a Columbian unit on Old Baldy. The rotation policy was for each FO team to be on the OP from Sunday to Sunday, at which time they were relieved by another FO team. Our teams consisted of a lieutenant and two enlisted men. It was customary to line up the battery and ask for two volunteers by stepping two paces forward. I was fortunate to have two men who had been on the hill before step forward one of which was Sergeant Bruce Graham. We took with us one fifth of liquor, Canadian Club, a case of beer, brand unknown, a couple of cases of 'C' rations, and as much charcoal as we could handle. Charcoal does not give off smoke, although I'm sure they, the Chinese, had us well zeroed in. We loaded our supplies including weapons onto a ¾ ton truck and started out. The men were armed with Garand rifles, and I had a carbine with three thirty-round clips taped together. Grenades, flak jackets, and multi ammunition were already at the bunker on the hill. The ¾ ton truck could only take us so far, and the road seemed to almost go straight up. We reached a kind of 'parking lot' where the other FO team on the hill had parked their truck, and we got out and started to carry our gear the rest of the way. The climbing of the Korean hills was brutal, but soon we arrived at the OP. We relieved the other team, and they were glad to go. The lieutenant I was relieving pointed out the key reference points from which to direct artillery fire, and they left.

That night, Sunday, was exciting. It was cold, and the only light in the bunker was a candle or a gas Coleman lantern. A firefight broke out in our sector and the bullets were flying and the artillery was exploding. It was dark and I could only see the flashes of exploding shells and artillery muzzle blasts, ours and the Chinese. What fascinated me the most were the tracer bullets. Depending on how a bullet strikes the earth, stone or target, it either penetrates or bounces. The streaking tracers from both sides would go flatly for a few seconds and then, depending on what it hit, ricocheting every which way. The noise of all of this was deafening. Near midnight, a Korean officer and several of his men entered our bunker. Since we supported the 2nd ROK Division, we were in their trenches and there were no restrictions on access to each other. Since none of us could speak each other's language, we began by sign language. I gathered he was a company commander, a captain perhaps. He pulled out a map and indicated to me that the enemy was in the sector he was pointing to and that he wanted artillery fire to drive them out. I called the Fire Direction Center on our EE8 wire system, and gave them the co-ordinates. After a few minutes they called back and refused to fire the co-ordinates. They said the Chinese had penetrated the 'No Fire Line', and didn't want to fire on friendly troops. I tried to convey this to the ROK officer, but he became furious. He angrily let us know that he opposed the decision. He was waving his arms and yelling and using a crude form of sign language to let us know that. Finally, I ordered them out of our bunker. They either didn't know what I meant, or refused my direction, so I pulled out my .45 sidearm from my holster and began to wave it at them, the ceiling and the entrance to the bunker. At last they realized I wanted them to go, and they silently filed out. So what if they took casualties from friendly fire. They had suffered so much anyway. After this exasperating experience, I looked down and noticed that one of them took my Army winter issue gloves, the ones that were two-piece, black leather with wool inserts. I realized that my hands would be very cold for the balance of my stay on the OP. The firefight settled down into almost nothing in the early hours of the morning, and we couldn't help but think it was diversionary.

The next morning, all hell broke loose. The three of us were very tense. Radio reports plus rumor from the American units in the sector reached us that the Chinese were launching a full scale attack on Old Baldy and Pork Chop. It was reported that the Columbian unit on Old Baldy had 'bugged out', ran away and left their casualties and equipment to the Chinese. Things were glum. I think each one of us thought about what we would do if we had a direct attack on our position. It was drummed into me from the moment I arrived in Korea that the Korean soldier would most likely 'bug out' than fight. After Old Baldy was taken, the Chinese continued their assault on the U.S. 7th Infantry Division on Pork Chop Hill. During the day, while it was relatively quiet in our sector, I stood in the trenches and focused my field glasses on Pork Chop. It was too far away to see the trench fighting, but I could follow the sound and sight of exploding artillery, and the movement of the fire line. This was especially evident at night. During the night we used many illuminating shells to see where the enemy was. But what is not widely known is that also at night, we would fly an L-19 observation plane along the length of Pork Chop and the rest of the front, to drop illuminating flares over the battlefield. I would watch as enemy tracers would reach up to the sky to shoot it down, but to no avail. I could hear the airplane engine and as it approached Pork Chop, the pilot would cut its engine and silently glide over and drop its illuminating flares, then after passing, turn its engine on, turn around, cut its engine and repeat the process. On Thursday, I believe, the radio reported bad news. One of our L-19's was shot down. No parachutes. Another spotter plane reported that the Chinese were taking away one of the crew as a POW and presumed the other was dead. A decision was made to bring artillery fire onto the plane and the Chinese around it, which we did.

While on the OP, we were shelled regularly, we took a lot of incoming rounds. I remember some of the shellings very clearly, sometimes because of the devastating feeling that the rounds could come through the observation slit and get me. The fire would come in and cease just as unexpectedly. One time, I was in the 2nd ROK Division trenches, when a U.S. Sherman tank pulled up to the trench line not more than fifty yards from me. I watched with fascination and a little amusement as to what they were going to do. The hatch opened, the tank commander climbed out and leaned on the back of the turret, and with field glasses began to direct tank fire on positions in front of us. This must have riled the Chinese, because they responded. I heard the unmistakable whistle of incoming artillery and ducked in the trench, but not before seeing the first round of 'willie peter' explode about seventy-five feet in front of his tank. I watched him scramble back into his tank, pull the hatch shut, and back off the hill in a hurry. He got out of there fast! After the shelling stopped, I pulled myself off the bottom of the trench and scrambled back to the bunker. I hollered if anyone saw any muzzle flashes of the enemy guns, but it happened too quick. By Wednesday, three days after relieving the other FO team, I still had not gone to the bathroom yet, i.e. defecated. I finally felt the urge, and fearing of being caught outside during an artillery barrage, this happened to an officer I knew at a later date, so I used the tunnel from our bunker to the OP. The tunnel was about four feet high and about forty feet long, so I dug a hole about halfway and went. Also, by the third day, our provisions were gone. In three and a half days, the three of us drank the 5th of Canadian Club and the case of beer, and had used up all of our supplies. I sent the private on our team back to the ¾ ton truck to go to the battery and bring up what he could. A couple of hours later, he called on the radio and said he would be late because the battery had undergone heavy shelling. No casualties, but the #6 gun got shrapnel in the tube which damaged the lands and grooves. While he was gone, Sergeant Graham and I got caught in an artillery barrage while we were in the 2nd ROK Division trenches, and I thought it was the end. But as suddenly as it started, the barrage stopped.

From Friday till Sunday, we received sporadic artillery fire, all the time small patrols were going out causing firefights, but nothing major was happening. On Sunday morning our team was expected to be relieved. I anxiously awaited the arrival of the new FO team. But, the most disheartening news came. We weren't going to be relieved. The fighting around Pork Chop required mop-up operations, things had to be in order, so we were to stay on the hill for another week. Our second week wasn't as eventful as the first as the U.S. 7th re-established itself on Pork Chop. We continued to take artillery and small arms fire, and the usual firefights broke out from patrol action. Finally, the second Sunday came. The men asked if they could fire their Garands at the enemy lines to celebrate. I was in the bunker and said 'go ahead'. I was getting my gear ready to leave and I could hear the cracking of their rifle fire. Suddenly, without warning, the enemy hit us with artillery fire. I could hear them scrambling off the top, into the trench, and into our bunker. In hindsight, I shouldn't have let them do it, but we all laughed. Late Sunday morning, the replacement FO team arrived and relieved us. We arrived at Baker Battery in time for lunch. I had not bathed or shaved in two weeks. I stunk. Captain Helm ordered us to a 7th Division shower point. Most of those there were in the fighting around Pork Chop. There was no laughing or kidding around, like in basic or OCS. The mood was somber, quiet. After showering, I received a new set of underwear and uniform, and we returned to the battery area and were given a days' rest. I found life as an FO was a combination of being lonely and worrisome at times, but the sights were fantastic. The days were long and companionship was scarce, serving with the ROKs most of the time. The food was rations only, usually eaten right from the can, and almost always cold. Candle light at night was supplemented usually by the gas Coleman lantern. We were fighting the Chinese, and I can remember thinking 'what happened to the North Koreans?'

By June of 1953, I was an executive officer of Baker Battery, and 1st Lt. 'Dutch' Rehm was CO, and the 240mm howitzer was fully operational and shooting fire missions almost day and night. We had been moved from Chorwon to Kumhwa, the far right of the base of the 'Iron Triangle'. It was called the 'Iron Triangle' because of the railroad line shaped in the form of a triangle that connected Chorwon and Kumhwa at the base and in our lines with Pyongyang in their lines. We were supporting elements of the U.S. 3rd Division. Our Observation Post was called 'Blaster' and the enemy held Papasan Hill and Mortar Ridge. Both were almost directly in front of the OP, and to the far left was Outpost Harry. We fired many missions during the siege of Outpost Harry, and during the Kumsong Salient battle, we watched as lines of South Korean troops were heading south, and the U.S. 3rd Infantry Division was rushed back to stem the tide. I remember during sunset one day, several of their trucks loaded with infantry came into our battery area. The men were silent and glum. When it got dark, they moved out. All the while, we were firing, firing like hell, and this went on for several days. During the daytime, I remember that our Air Force jets were dive-bombing some positions in front of us, and I would see tracers reaching up into the sky after them. We continued to execute many fire missions and nearly exhausted what was available to us from the nearest ammunition supply point, finally after several days the situation became stable, and we recovered what we lost initially. Immediately after the Kumsong Salient Battle, I was ordered to man OP Blaster. Rumors had it that the war would end soon but everyone was still shooting. A couple of days before the truce, F-84 fighter-bombers were hitting positions in front of us on Mortar Ridge, that was a show! That week, I remember one particular fire mission, when I suspected enemy movement to the left of Papasan and called for artillery fire. It was at one of the reference points, and I had a suspicion that something was right behind the hill that the reference point was at. There was some sort of activity going on back there, and there were no spotter planes flying that day, and figured that I would drop a few rounds behind there and see what happens. So I fired on it, and after zeroing in and firing for effect we got a secondary explosion going almost straight up in the air. I radioed battalion to cease fire, end of mission, secondary explosion. Baker Battery did very well with a 240 fire mission. If we started from scratch, it took about eight or nine rounds to completely destroy a target. Some cases, it was only three or four rounds, but it wasn't always that easy.

Calling a fire mission, we would call the FDC and say something like 'This is OP Blaster, have fire mission for you, suspected enemy position. Coordinates are such and such, will adjust'.

Also, sometimes we assisted other battalions, I can recall registering a 155mm 'Long Tom' unit onto a hill right next to Outpost Harry. We also used reference points, and while I was on OP Blaster, I think one of them was a Chinese bunker, an observation post, and every day, a couple times a day, I would swing my BC scope to each one of the reference points to be prepared in case there was an attack from any one of those areas. You could call a fire mission by saying 'Fire Mission reference point such and such, two hundred yards right, drop four hundred', A day or two right before the armistice, I was traversing my scope, and I went to this one Chinese bunker, and I said 'Where the hell did that one go?' During the night, they closed it up and moved it! One day it was there, and the next it was gone! My CO called the OP early in the day on the 27th to tell us that the war would end on that evening, July 27th. All firing was to cease by 10pm on July 27th. During that last day, there was sporadic fire, but after sunset and darkness began to set in, all hell broke loose. Tracers were flying and bouncing all over and the unmistakable blasts of artillery and tank fire were there. It was like the fireworks on the 4th of July. It seemed to me that it lasted for hours. I gathered we were using up our ammunition so that we would not have to cart it back, and so were they. It was a magnificent spectacle. As the cease-fire time approached, things began to slow down, and at 10pm it stopped but not completely. There were no more explosions, but an occasional rifle or pistol round went off until one or two in the morning. With that, the OP Blaster team stood down. In the early morning it was strangely quiet. We looked through our bunker slit and could see many Chinese standing on the ridgeline in front of us. We got out and stood too. So did the 3rd U.S. Infantry. Many more Chinese and U.S. soldiers came out of their holes, and we all stood there looking at each other. They in their off-white quilted uniforms and us in our combat fatigues. Just looking and staring at each other. Occasionally someone on their side and someone on our side would go back into a bunker. I was amazed how many of them were there. Hundreds. And Mortar Ridge, which we plastered. They even came out of there. Their tunnel system must have been deep, intricate and protective. The first couple of days, we did nothing except look at each other. Then, orders came from battalion to report a count on how many we saw. A live body count. And so every hour on the hour, we called in our count, until we were relieved a week later in August. I don't know how long this practice continued, but I understand other follow on teams had to do it. With my relief, the war ended for me."

***Name withheld***
**1st Field Artillery Observation Battalion 1952-53**

"I volunteered. I was serving as a Flash Ranger in the 449th Field Artillery Observation Battalion at Ft. Bragg, NC, when there was a critical need for my MOS in Korea. As a Flash Ranger, we served as 'spotters' and directed fire onto enemy artillery and mortar locations. We use BC Scopes, the M-1 Aiming Circle and other calibrated devices from fixed locations to pin point targets and call fire missions. I was sent to Korea and assigned to the 1st Field Artillery Observation Battalion, Baker Battery, in December 1952. Our battalion call sign was 'Nathan Hale'. We were considered a front line support unit, part of X Corps. Able and Charlie Batteries were assigned to IX and I Corps, respectively. My unit was along the 38th Parallel about fourteen miles in from the Sea of Japan, and I was there from December 19th 1952 until November 2nd 1953. We were in support of several U.S. National Guard units from the 40th and the 45th Infantry Divisions. We also supported several ROK divisions during the time before the war ended in July. As for who we were fighting, the information that we had was that for the most part it was the North Koreans who were in front of us, but there were times when the Chinese relieved them. Operating as an FO, sometimes we were directly involved in close skirmishes. I was a wreck the first few times I was in direct contact with enemy small arms fire. The first few times that I had to return fire, it was without looking directly at a target. I just raised my carbine over the edge of the trench and fired. Some later engagements were a bit different. I think it was April 16th 1953 that we were hit by what looked like a major force of Chinese troops. I got in a few well aimed shots and was able to see the result.

Baker Battery was responsible for four OP's. I served on all of them, but spent most of my time on OP#2, which was located on Hill 812. Life as an FO was lousy most of the time. We ate C Rations most of the time, and were permitted to get off of the hill about every two or three weeks for showers at the shower stations, and get some clean clothes and some 'B' Rations. About once a month, we had a medic come up to check us over for lice and spray for the mice that could cause Hemorrhagic Fever. We slept on the 'Hot Rack' system. Four guys on the hill, but only three bunks and they were made from tree branches and commo wire. We used inflatable mattresses and army blankets, and had the Coleman Stove for heat and often warmed our C Rations on it too. We only moved into the trenches when a fire fight broke out and thank God, that was not too often. One mission I remember well was when I had noticed a supply movement of oxen and Shetland ponies being shepherded by enemy troops but by the time 'Fire Mission' was called and the unit was ready to fire, the 'train' had gotten past my zone of responsibility. An officer in an 8-inch battalion asked if I wanted to fire the mission and establish a 'Concentration Number'. I said I would. Using a single 8-inch round, I got the desired placement and the other three howitzers fired and landed all of the rounds in a nice tight pattern. The mission was marked 'Concentration 570 How'. It was several days, perhaps even a week before the oxen and the ponies showed up again. I grabbed my EE-8 telephone, gave it a crank and spoke with someone in my FDC. I asked for 'Concentration 570 How' and then waited. In about one minute the area was blown to bits. There appeared to have been two or more secondary explosions. The next day, the OP had a visit from a Lt. Colonel who looked through our BC Scope at the area, shook my hand and told me I would be promoted to PFC! We were a unit that used the 'Triangulation' system to locate our targets. Our FDC would decide which OP was in the best location to complete what any two or three OPs had started.

At some point near the end of the war, our OP was fired upon from long range by a 76mm weapon. I was just coming up from meeting the jeep from battalion HQ. I had the mail, some fresh water on my 'choggie board' and was carrying my carbine. I sensed the incoming round and jumped to my left and fell about twenty feet down hill. I don't think I hurt anything, but for a week, I did not leave the bunker. I was there when the war ended on the 27th of July. We were told at about 10am that all firing would end at 10pm. Around 6pm, there was firing coming from just about everywhere. Small arms, artillery, everything. And then, at exactly 10pm. it all came to an end. The lack of noise was disturbing. The next day, North Korean troops were in our trenches begging for C Rations. The hugged us when we gladly gave away the Ham and Lima Beans."

**Sergeant William Thomas**
**38th Field Artillery Battalion 1953**

"I was married before I got drafted. I got married in September and went into the service November. I took training in Fort Bliss, TX outside of El Paso. When I got to Korea and the 38th Field Artillery Battalion, there were several of us 'new' rookies that came in early spring. We were there several days when we were called to the CP and were told about the FO's and that it was a volunteer group. We then went to chow and were told to think about it. At 2:00 pm we reported back to the CP to be told we had volunteered, and I was put with Lt. Bob Lusk, and some went with Lt. Allison. The first OP I was on was White Horse Mountain with the ROK Division. We then went to the Chorwon Valley with the 23rd Infantry Regiment, 2nd Infantry Division to relieve the 3rd Division. That's where our bunker was in the rice paddies and got about six inches to a foot of water in it every time it rained and the North Koreans could see us every time we came out of the bunker. I was glad when we went to the Kumhwa sector. We were up in the hills there, but our bunker was out in front of the MLR. I was up staying at the bunker they had for all of the enlisted men. Our bunker got hit with a round up in the right corner. We all hit the floor. LeRoy Daulb was in the top bunk in his sleeping bag. Well when he hit the floor, he got turned over in it and he was screaming that they got him and he was blind. We got him turned over the right way and he wasn't hurt. We never let him forget it. It was around this time they hit our outhouse. It was a ten-seater. They probably thought it was some command center with everybody going in and out of there! The guys in the OP bunker at the time were Mitchell, York, Noel, EJ Banad, Daulb, Wade, Carter, Tyler, myself and DeMuseo. Some of these guys were ready to rotate home. It was right about that time they sent some of us back to where the observer planes were and had us trained as air spotters. It was kind of fun going up in the planes, we flew up over where our OP was. We went up once a day for about two weeks. When we came back to the battery we were put in charge of our OP's. There was me, and three others with me. I was in charge as I was a sergeant, and from then after I was at the OP till I rotated home. After getting home, I had six months to serve here in the states at Fort Meade, Maryland."

**1st Lt Al De La Garza**
**57th Field Artillery Battalion 1953**

"During the battle for 'Old Baldy' in March 1953, after we had been under mortar and artillery barrage for 23 hours straight, I got orders to take my radio and move out, by myself, to West View and set up an OP there for the night. They said for me to leave my crew behind so they could brief the new FO with Charlie Company and his crew who were coming onto the hill. So I put my radio on a back pack and got it up on my back. If you remember those 610 radios, they weighed about 60 pounds or so, and they were worthless. Left over WWII junk. One little bump and the crystals were out of alignment and the radio was useless. Anyhow that's all we had, right? So I took off for West View. Half-way there, at the base of Baldy, the barrage suddenly let up and within ten minutes the Chinks were in our trenches. I ducked into a Listening Post manned by two Colombians and a machine gun. In order to get into the LP bunker I had to take the radio off my back and leave it at the entrance of the bunker, remember that whip antenna, it was about six feet long? My thoughts were to pull the radio off my back and call in 'Flash Baldy', which I had fired a few days earlier in another attack. But just as I pulled the radio off my back, the Colombians challenged me. By the time I convinced them who I was, maybe thirty seconds or so, and I turned around, my worthless radio was gone! So, based on what good fortune Lt Felger had when he called in his 'Flash' fire, one can only wonder if something similar might have happened to me had I gotten a chance to call in Flash Baldy. Somebody called it in a while later because there were dead Chinks three deep all over the top of that hill, I saw them! Oh well, I came home safe and sound, and maybe my little ole Bronze Star ain't too bad after all."

**1st Lt Crosby Lawlor**
**424th Field Artillery Battalion 1953**

"I was called to active duty on 4 Sept 1950. After OCS I was assigned in March 1953 to the 424th Field Artillery Battalion, we were an 8-inch howitzer battalion assigned to IX Corps. I was the battalion Recon Officer, and one of my duties on occasion was to be a Forward Observer. We usually manned two OP's during this time, and it was, at times, boring, exciting, confining, uncomfortable, dangerous, and I wish I were home. Being an FO on a hill with the Capital ROK, the enemy knew where you were so you'd better keep your head down. It was quite an experience. To fire a mission, it was routine, call for the mission and fire about 4 rounds. We always had incoming too. I remember being bracketed one time, and by July of '53 we were shelled all the time we were there. Mostly when I served as an FO, I was on a hill serving with the Capital ROK Division and the 3rd Infantry Division. I didn't know and didn't care who I was fighting against, but I suppose it was the Chinese with incoming rockets that were Chinese or Russian made. We had two OP's OP 'Right' and 'Left', which were both located in the Kumhwa Valley. I think I spent at most 3 or 4 weeks not consecutive, on the OP's. In July of '53 I was on OP 'Right' and Lt. Frank Wilkinson was on OP 'Left'. At this time we were constantly being shelled. A day or so after, I was relieved, and Frank was overrun and killed, he left a wife and a daughter.

Being the Recon Officer, I had many duties. Of course survey, we did targets, OP's and new positions. We had to key data on hang fire positions in case we had to move. That occasion came in July of '53 to move 'A' Battery to a new position. It was all surveyed with coordinates and all. We also manned the OP's, usually two members of the survey section went to the OP with an officer either from HQ staff or with me. I was all over our sector to all the batteries for one reason or another. I even remember the 213th Field Artillery 240mm howitzers were down the road from us. They were the big ones that used two tractors to get into place. Moving about I could be doing anything, from bringing USO entertainment, delivering liquor rations, or delivering ammunition. I also pulled duty nearly every night in the Fire Direction Center controlling fire missions and harassing and interdiction requests. The FDC crew was amazing and very competent. As to my survey crew, they were the best and taught me my job. I am still amazed at the talent, skills, and resiliency of those young men who were so capable. Only a short time before they were laborers from all walks of life, farmers, clerks, mechanics, students, salesmen. But they were able to lean new things quickly and well. To see the FDC and survey crew work you would think they were at it much longer than they were. Also the wire and radio crew were real craftsmen. I remember being without wire and low on power for the radio when a line crew came to us on the OP, stringing wire in the midst of heavy shelling. Also the radio crew during the Chinese offensive in July set up a radio relay station to keep 'A' Battery in control with HQ. The communication officer was a former radio and TV specialist and did an incredible job with his men."

**2nd Lt (George) Sam Buck**
**39th Field Artillery Battalion 1953**

"I enlisted just before I was drafted, and I was sent to Camp Stoneman, California in February 1953, and shipped out on Orient Airlines to Camp Drake, Japan. I spent approximately one week there, sent to CBR Warfare School in Eta Jima, Japan for two weeks and then to Sasabo, Japan for an overnight cruise to Pusan, Korea where we were met by an Army band playing 'If I knew you were coming I'd bake a cake'. Not funny at the time. We were moved from the harbor by open 4X6 trucks thru the streets of Pusan with crowds lining the streets, some were giving us 'the finger'. I spent a few days at the Repo Depot in a quonset hut, and we were given a day or two to roam the area. We visited, of all things, a United Nations Cemetery near by. Then we boarded 'The Pusan Express', a narrow gauge passenger train with many windows shot out. I was the Car Commander of my car. Each time we stopped, I had to issue a clip with 5 rounds of ammo to four guards and post them on each corner of our car, then before we moved, I had to get the guards back on board and collect the ammo from them. We left Pusan in the afternoon and rode all night arriving at Seoul the following morning. The cars were very primitive with wooden seats and a hole in the floor for a latrine. Our door between the cars fell off, making a regular wind tunnel and we almost froze during the night. At Seoul, we were loaded on open trucks and taken to the 3rd Division rear for a few days of briefings and then back on the trucks for a night journey, driving blackout, to the 39th Field Artillery Battalion headquarters. I was assigned to C Battery, a 105 Howitzer unit somewhere 4 to 6 miles behind the MLR. We were in direct support of the 15th Regiment, 3rd Infantry Division. I was usually assigned as an FO by my Battery Commander, Capt Bray. The other FO's for the battery were 2nd Lt Russ Wagner and 2nd Lt John Gallaspy.

As an FO, I was treated just like a company officer and had the full support of the Company Commander when I would spot dereliction of duties or infractions of anyone on the Out Post. I would spend my days in the Observation Post as it was equipped with a 50X BC Scope and I also would use the apertures of the machine gun and fighting bunkers to locate targets of opportunities. The nights I spent with the Commander and XO as they were in telephone contact with the Listening Posts and Patrols who were out in front of our forward trenches. I was able to call fire missions that I had bench marked as well as shoot some flares if an area needed illuminating for them to see what was in front of them. I think the infantrymen felt like I was one of them and I took all of my orders from the Company Commander as he was responsible for the defense of the Out Post and not my Battery Commander.

I joined King Company, 15th Infantry Regiment, 3rd Infantry Division in April 1953 on Outpost Dick as their Forward Observer. The Company Commander was 1st Lt Martin Markley. My first day on line was a Sunday, my 23rd birthday. A Chinese division was located to our front harassed us with artillery, mortar and sniper fire day and night, and we returned the same hospitality. Our patrols, consisting of eight or nine GI's plus several listening posts, would go out just after dark and would return before daybreak. This static position was located just to the right of Chorwon Valley. My first day on OP Dick, the FO whom I was replacing and the XO were showing me around the OP when an enemy round came in they both hit the ground and there I stood, not realizing it was incoming, I was cautioned to hit the ground when we were getting shelled. I explained that I thought it was out going. They said, 'You don't know the difference between incoming and out going?' They weren't sure that I was going to last very long up there if I was that dumb. I'd had many hours on the Firing Range at Fort Sill adjusting fire and the shells going over our heads. After that embarrassment, we went a little further and I heard a shell and I hit the ground hard only to look up and see those two standing there laughing at me. They said, 'You don't know the difference do you?' I never made that mistake again! On OP Dick we had a much more relaxed time. We had considerable sniper fire and a lot of mortar and direct fire especially during daylight hours. I was constantly looking for targets of opportunity, however, we had orders not to call fire missions unless we saw at least 10 of the enemy. Occasionally, when calling a fire mission, we would get a message that we had expended our quota of ammo for the day. On OP Harry, we were harassed day and night by machine gun, direct fire weapons and mortars. We got very little sleep but did have adequate drinking water and C rations. Capt Markley did what he could to try to get some warm food up to us when he could. We were constantly moving from the CP to the OP day and night, rain or shine.

Around the middle of May 1953, a company of Greek Hellenic Forces replaced King Company on OP Dick. We didn't want the Chinese to know what was going on, as a company just new to the Outpost would be very vulnerable to an attack within the first night or two. We exchanged positions five men at a time, taking close to a week to get our company off and the Greeks in position. Lt Markley and myself were the last to leave as the new company commander had to be sure he understood how the Outpost was laid out and to be familiar with the Chinese defenses. The same with the Greek Forward Observer taking my place, as he had to learn the sector we were defending and every artillery and mortar positions. There was only one interpreter for this operation so there were lots of charades going on, in desperation locating an interpreter. We had a humorous experience after going to these lengths to keep our transfer a secret. The last night before Lt. Markley and I left the Outpost, a speaker out in the valley said 'Sayonara King Company, we will get along better with the Greeks than we did with you'!

King Company then went in reserve for some needed rest and training to keep them sharp. I went back to my battery and being a new 2nd Lieutenant, I was assigned Safety Officer during the nights. That job entailed using a gunner's quadrant on the breach of a 105 Howitzer to be sure the elevation and site was set correctly to avoid firing on friendly forces. One night around the 1st of June, as I was watching a rare movie, a runner from our Battalion gave me a message to rendezvous with K Company, 15th Infantry at these coordinates. I then located my Recon Sergeant, a ROK by the name of Sgt Kim, who spoke very good English and was a real asset to our team, my radio operator and my driver. We had to be very careful, as the edges of the road had not been completely cleared of mines so we had to take it slow and easy. Our jeep and trailer was always on the ready and we left about 9:30 at night, driving black-out to a little schoolhouse at a cross roads some two or three miles behind the front lines. King Company's trucks were all parked around the school and the men were lounging around in the dark. The company officers were inside the small building with blackout curtains covering the doors and windows. By candlelight, they were going over a map and getting ready to move out to take responsibility for defending a critical combat outpost located forward of the main line of resistance (MLR). The US 8th Army had designated this defensive position 'Outpost Harry'. Lt Markley was in the lead jeep and my jeep and trailer was second. The rest of the company was mounted in trucks and we drove blackout up to just behind the MLR, also known as the front lines. There, we parked the vehicles and moved out in column formation across the front on foot and headed North without making any noise. A few times we would come to a fork in the trail and Markley would post Lt Richards, the Company Executive Officer, or me there to direct the men to the correct trail.

Searchlights located behind the MLR shined their powerful lights over us into the eyes of the Chinese soldiers located in positions north of Outpost Harry to prevent the enemy from seeing us. We finally reached an orchard at the base of Outpost Harry without being discovered. We could almost smell the Chinese, they seemed that close. It is important to realize that King Company was now 1,000 yards in front of the MLR, beyond the effective range of the automatic weapons belonging to the friendly units located there. From now on, King Company could only rely on its own organic weapons and supporting artillery and mortar fires for its defense. We scattered out under the shattered trees waiting for daybreak before we made our move up the hill. Finally, Markley gave the order to move in-groups of five so as not to attract too much attention. I was the second man behind the ever-present Markley who led the first group up the hill. Considerable incoming artillery and mortar fire began to impact on the hill. We had hardly any protection and at places the hill was almost straight up. I was loaded down with my M-1 carbine, flak-jacket, steel helmet, six grenades strapped to me, an EE 8 telephone, a roll of commo wire and a PRC radio on my back. I never thought I would make it to the summit, but there was no place to stop to catch your breath. After we reached the positions on top, we found Outpost Harry to be well fortified with trenches and bunkers arranged so that each bunker could keep the enemy off the roof of another. My observation post was on the forward slope and equipped with a BC scope. There was just enough room to sleep two. The command post was located just on the rear side of the front trench. It was protected by about six feet of overhead made out of railroad ties and sandbags. I usually spent the nights with Markley and Richards.

About the second day on the Outpost, orders came through promoting Markley to Captain. Richards and I took two of his silver bars and made a Captain's insignia to celebrate Markley's promotion. For some reason, he didn't want to use my gold 2nd Lieutenant bars. Our intelligence informed us that the Chinese were building up behind two hills directly in front of Harry called 'Star Mass' and 'Camels Bank'. Star Mass was connected to OP Harry by a saddle. It was considerably higher than OP Harry, and the Chinese had excellent observation on our position. Intelligence estimated the build up to consist of three divisions of Chinese, and Outpost Harry was the closest 8th Army outpost to this buildup and our resources consisted of a company plus heavy weapons or approximately150 men. We knew for several days that we were going to get hit and our orders were to 'Hold At All Costs'. The Chinese wanted this vital piece of real estate as it looked straight down on our main line of resistance and then they would have a clear shot at capturing Seoul just before the armistice. If that had happened, the line dividing North and South Korea would have been south of the 38th parallel instead of where it ended.

One of my first jobs on the Outpost was to register defensive fire around the three sides, one gun at a time, so that we would have a wall of steel protecting OP Harry. After I had all the guns registered, Captain Markley asked me to show him where I had placed the fire. As I was showing him, he spotted this rather deep gully right out in front. When he said that he wanted a round placed in the bottom of this gully, I explained that I had one on the far bank and 105's have a dispersion bracket of 50 yards so some of the rounds would land where he wanted. He informed me that he wanted to see a round in the bottom of the gully, as it offered the Chinese cover on the natural approach we knew the Chinese would take to attack the outpost. I asked the Captain to get our company buttoned up and I would see what I could do, but I was afraid I might put one in our trench. He took off to make sure everyone was inside their bunker and I called fire direction center a very unorthodox fire command 'a RCH (red cunt hair) left and repeat range'. I soon received a 'splash' from FDC informing me the round was on its way. The next thing I heard was the blast of the shell to my left rear. I ran back to the impact area, afraid of what I was going to see. Would you believe the Captain forgot about three engineers digging in a bunker in the area? The round landed on the edge of their hole, blowing dirt all over them, they were both scared and mad, and after I found they weren't hurt, I got out of their sight as quick as I could without telling them that I was the FO!

We knew several days before, that we were going to get hit but didn't know when. Intelligence requested that I indicate on my map where the smoke shells were landing as that was the way the Chinese were marking their approaches to OP Harry plus they were using red, blue and green smoke shells that must have meant something to them. It appeared most were landing on both sides, indicating the Chinese would mount a pincher attack. I called the coordinates of every shell I saw throughout the day of 9 June 1953. At about 2100 hours the following day, 10 June, all hell broke loose with the Chinese firing their artillery and mortars. They fired a 'Time on Target' and then continued to pound our hill. It was a tremendous barrage. One thing the Chinese were not hesitant to do that night was to attack through their own artillery fire, thinking we would be in our bunkers and they would be on top of us before we could defend ourselves. They lost many of their soldiers to their own artillery fire, and to ours, but they succeeded in reaching the outpost and commenced their assault. We had planned to fight the enemy outside our bunkers under a covered position erected in the trench, but incoming artillery fire blew up our position and pinned us inside the bunker.

Anthony J. Sobieski

I was in the command post with Captain Markley and Lt. Richards. We started hearing the bugles, whistles and burp guns all around us. Richards shouted that the enemy was in the trenches. As Markley and Richards were firing over my head to keep the Chinese out of our bunker, I was on my radio to the Fire Direction Center requesting to have our artillery fire on ourselves to clean out the enemy out of the trenches. We knew that the Chinese were in the open, while our men were inside bunkers, so we felt this was the best way to hurt the enemy before the Chinese overran the hill. The next thing I heard was that unmistakable sizzle of an armed grenade behind me. Before I could complete radio transmission, it went off and Markley and Richards were hit by shrapnel and fell unconscious. American artillery opened fire on top of our position anyway, once FO's on the MLR realized we were being overrun. I ran to the door where I had left my carbine, grabbed it, and shot a Chinese soldier coming through the door. Another grenade was thrown in. I hovered in the corner of our bunker and put my head down against the blast, then I stepped back in the door and shot down another Chinese soldier trying to run in. This went on at least three or four more times before my hand, arm and leg went numb from the exploding grenades.

I switched hands and laid the barrel of my carbine on the edge of the doorway. I let the Chinese soldier almost run into me before I fired. The next grenade that was thrown in exploded and knocked me off my feet. I fell partially on the Captain. I tried to work a bullet into the chamber of my carbine and prepared to fire again. I heard some conversation outside the door and then I saw a Chinese with a flashlight creeping in. My carbine was lying across my lap but when I pulled the trigger, nothing happened. The Chinese soldier started to search the other side of the dark bunker, looking at Richards. I wiped my bloody hand on my face to play dead. He then checked out and searched the Captain. He took the Captain's carbine. When he searched me, he took my .38-caliber automatic handgun and my carbine, and then he left the bunker. Almost immediately, two Chinese came in carrying one of their wounded and the next thing I felt was one of their guards squatting near my feet at the edge of the doorway. Several more of their wounded were brought in and laid on the floor near Richards, Markley and myself. Each time someone came through the door, the guard would slide his rifle butt up my leg that was cut up from shrapnel. I knew if I moved he would kill me.

A little later, Lt. Richards started to come to and was moving and groaning. After some conversation with their wounded, the guard got up and shot him. A short time later, Captain Markley started to cough up something and the guard shot him, but I could tell Markley was still alive as I could feel him moving. Due to the darkness, the Chinese couldn't see him very well. A while later, a shell landed outside the door of our bunker filling it with fire and shrapnel. I could feel the guard lurch and fall over. I think he was the only one hit. That left Captain Markley and I alone with four or five wounded Chinese lying inside. Just after daybreak the next morning, I heard GI voices. I could tell there was still hand-to-hand fighting in the trenches. A GI came busting through the door, seeing the Chinese on the floor, and started firing. He probably thought they were going to try to kill him, but I knew they were wounded and shouted 'Cease fire - GI!' He stopped and said, 'Ok Doc' and took off. At that tine, one of the wounded Chinese rose up to a sitting position and was looking for something to kill me with. I started looking too and all I could find was a flashlight. When I shined the light directly into his eyes, he froze. Finally a GI came in and saw what I was trying to do and the wounded Chinese soldier lay down not moving. Then we looked at Captain Markley. His head was split open from one ear to the other and bleeding quite profusely. His eyeball was lying on his cheek. I'll never know why, but I cleaned the blood and dirt out of the socket with my fingers and put the eyeball back in place. What is hard to believe is that he still has that eye going on 50 years later and has a little vision in it.

My replacement Forward Observer found me but he had lost his radio operator to a direct hit and he was hit badly in both feet. He tried to get me on his shoulder but neither of us had the strength to get out. I kept telling him to leave me and get out himself, if he could, as it didn't appear we both were going to make it in the shape we were in. He told me he wasn't going to leave me and we were going to make it. Then I saw two medics had Captain Markley on a litter. It was very hard going, as the trenches were full of bodies both Chinese and American, as well as commo wire and all kinds of debris. All I could do was pull myself with my left arm and try to kick with my left leg, as my right side was useless. On the way down the hill, we were in the way of the replacements trying to drive the Chinese out of the trenches. After we arrived at the foot of Outpost Harry, we spotted an aide station a short distance away with a big Red Cross on it. Did it ever look good! Before we could get to it, the Chinese opened fire on it so we gave up trying to get there. The other FO spotted a US tank and took off his T-shirt and got the tanker's attention. They came over and helped my partner down the turret. I was hurt too badly to get inside the tank and one of the tankers asked if I could hang on to one of the steps on the rear. I told him I could and away we went toward the main line. The machine gunner on the turret was spraying anything and every place that could hide a Chinese. We got away from the fighting and the crew spotted a jeep with two litters sticking out. We were loaded on it and taken to the Regimental Aide Station just behind the front lines.

At the Aide Station, they bandaged our wounds and were told our next of kin would be notified. We were transported by ambulance to a MASH unit that night. I was left on my old dirty and bloody stretcher when they carried me into the operating room. I remember looking up and seeing a star shining through a tear in the top of the tent. After the shrapnel was removed, we were not sutured until we got to Japan, needless to say, there was a lot of swelling and we were still loosing blood. We were then put on a hospital train and taken to a building that appeared to be a school. Rows and rows of wounded GI's on stretchers lay there, sitting on saw horses in this large auditorium. Finally, we were put on a plane for Yokohama, Japan where I spent 30 days in traction and then on a plane to the Army Navy Hospital in Hot Springs, Arkansas. I find it hard to believe that I survived the worst nightmare of my life. I wouldn't have if it had not been for men like Captain Markley, Lt. Richards, who never made it home, and the FO whose name I never got who wouldn't let me quit until we got off that damn hill."

**2nd Lt. Gaylund Adams**
**213th Field Artillery Battalion 1953**

"I got to the 213th Field Artillery Battalion and was assigned to the HQ Battery in January of '53. I moved over to Baker Battery in the spring, when the OP was in front of Papa-san Mountain. The 213th had just gotten the 240mm howitzers, and we had started to use them. When I went in originally, I was assigned as the Motor Officer of HQ Battery, and I got it up and running pretty good, but all that time I was doing Forward Observer work out of the HQ. We had two observation points on the front lines, OP 'Love' and OP 'Item'. From where they were, we could see Porkchop Hill over to our left there. This is where I did my stint as an FO while I was in HQ Battery. For a twenty-two year old kid, it was kind of tough, when you're young you're not afraid of much because you didn't know any better. It was interesting, we would sit up there in that bunker, and anything we would see move, if we got it authorized, we'd fire into it. The two OP's were built differently. OP Love was self-contained, everything was all in one bunker, the sleeping stuff and everything. Over on 'Item', when you came out of the observation bunker, you were exposed to the enemy, they could see us move back into our bunker where we slept. An interesting thing was that the toilet was just a box with a hole in it, but it was right in sight of the enemy observation post. It seemed like every time somebody would go out there, they'd start to adjust mortar fire on us! I remember running back into the bunker a few times just as I was finishing things up! We were in support of the ROK Army, and I got the impression that they really weren't dedicated to what they were doing, and they would run at the drop of a hat, it seemed like. Of course, their officers would threaten them, they would shoot into the ground at their feet, it looked like an old western movie. Just crazy. Their officers would threaten them if they didn't come out of their bunkers and fight that they would shoot them. When the spring thaw started, you could tell when the ground started to thaw out, because body parts would start to straighten out, sticking out of the ground in places, it wasn't too great a place to eat a meal, a hundred feet from all that. Of course, all we ever had up there was 'C' Rations to eat, and you could get into the bunker and close the door and get rid of the smell pretty good. After a while everything they would send up there started to taste the same, whether it was corn beef hash or hamburger paddies and stuff.

When we moved over into the Chorwon sector, we didn't even have our OP bunker built yet, and I remember laying there at night with no protection, and there would be our outgoing rounds right over us, not necessarily just our 240's, but also there was a 105mm battery sitting right on the road beside us, and we were as close to the front as they were. It wasn't that far back from the OP They had these older Koreans from the local towns lug these twelve by twelve timbers up the mountain, a bunch of them, and it took a long time to build that bunker. If you were looking north, Papasan was just to the east of us. The Air Force would come in there with napalm a lot, the Chinese were really dug in on that mountain. Those 240's really would really tare things up, I remember one fire mission, it was in the evening, and I observed this bunker across from us, with smoke coming up out of it, maybe they were cooking or something was on fire, well, I kept adjusting fire till we hit that thing, just dead on, I could see it in the BC Scope, it blew logs and sandbags and everything straight up in the air, and I knew we got a direct hit on it. The fire mission I remember most was the one when the Chinese were coming up the mountain at us, they were trying to take our hill that night, and we already had intelligence that they were coming. I was trying to adjust our 240mm fire, and a rocket battery was behind us, back a ways behind a hill, and as soon as they fired the Chinese could see where the fire came from, so that battery would fire and do a quick 'March Order' and take off like mad, and I was adjusting fire for our outfit, the rockets, and then there was an Air Force plane dropping flares for us, and that got kind of hairy for a young lieutenant trying to see. I rotated home in September 1953, and took the USS Nelson M. Walker transport ship home. I think it was kind of a rotator. I sat in Seoul for a week or so, because there were so many people asking for an early out. It certainly was a great day when I got on that ship, I remember going out on the LST, and we got on the ship, and we had a great meal that first night, white tablecloths and napkins and silverware, it wasn't the old canteen and mess kit. It sort of brought me back to reality a little bit, that things weren't so bad after all. It was a big difference from sitting in the snow up on the OP trying to eat, and when I would sit my cup of coffee down in that metal cup that went with the canteen, by the time I would get around to drinking it, it would have a little bit of ice on top of it."

## 1st Lt Harvey Anderson
## 57th Field Artillery Battalion 1953

*Author's note: Lt Anderson passed away after our initial contact, and I regrettably was unable to interview him for this book. However, listed below is a newspaper account from the Army Times dated June 17, 1953, recounting some of his actions in Korea. This type of article was a regular occurrence in either the Army Times or the Stars & Stripes, telling the story of the Forward Observer and artillery in Korea.*

3 Artillery FO's Show What Teamwork is Like

WITH THE INF. DIV., KOREA—Three Forward Observers from Btry. B. 57th FA Bn., recently gave a good demonstration of the teamwork it takes to win a battle. The trio, 2d Lts. Harvey D. Anderson, Richard E Jaffe and Herbert W. Linn, were manning adjacent observation posts with the same infantry battalion when the Chinese launched an assault on Pork Chop Hill. The attack was prefaced by an intense artillery and mortar barrage which knocked out all wire communication. Within a very few minutes the three PO's had restored communication with their radios. The Chinese came up the hill at a dead run—through their own slackening barrage—and, in the vicious hand-to-hand fighting which followed, swarmed through the trenches and over the bunkers. Anderson, in observation post atop Pork Chop, remained at his radio, giving tense, textbook-like accounts of the situation. Time after tie the enemy hurled grenades through the door and apertures. Though wounded by fragments, he stayed at his post, finally calling friendly artillery fire in on his own position. Linn, from a vantage point on a hill to the rear of the other two positions, maintained observation of the area throughout the action. Although his bunker came under a withering, hail of artillery and mortar fire, he continued to adjust illuminating flares and friendly artillery fire on Pork Chop. Anderson's transmissions, though weak, were picked up by Jaffe in an observation post east of Pork Chop. Jaffe then relayed his buddy's reports and requests for fire and reinforcement. At one point during the action Jaffe asked, "Is there anything else I can do for you Andy?" "Sure!" replied Anderson. "You can come over here and take my place." The trio kept it's vigil throughout the night, and the vital communication enabled friendly infantry to coordinate their reinforcing elements. The counterattack cleaned out the remaining enemy on the hill and information gleaned from a Chinese prisoner testified to the efficiency of the teamwork. The prisoner, who was one of the subsequent assault waves, reported that his group ran into one of the worst artillery barrages he'd ever seen and that only one or two men from his company survived it. Anderson was awarded the Silver Star Medal for his valorous performance during the action.

**Sergeant Michael Schack**
**37th Field Artillery Battalion 1953**

"Upon graduation from high school in June of 1952 I worked as a laborer for a brick mason. In October he left for Florida to spend the winter and left me out of work. There weren't a lot of folks around for draft table guys so a friend and I enlisted into the army. I went to Fort Riley Kansas and had eight weeks of infantry basic and eight weeks of Field Wireman School. After completing my training I received orders for FECOM or Far East Command. When we reached Korea, I landed in the 'repo' depot of the 2nd Infantry Division, eventually being assigned to 'A' Battery of the 37th Field Artillery Battalion, 23rd Infantry Regiment. It was in May sometime towards the end of the month. We spent a couple of extra days at the repo depot doing a lot of bayonet training, as they said we needed it. I think we took it a little more seriously than we did in basic. The 2nd Division was part of the IX Corps and the 37th Field Artillery was in direct support of the 23rd Regiment, which was in reserve at the time. In Korea artillery units were temporarily assigned to ROK units when the Infantry went into reserve, and we were supporting the 2nd ROK Division on the left hand portion of the Chorwon Valley. I was on guard duty one day in the battery perimeter when I was relieved and told to report to the commo section bunker. When I arrived they were getting ready to draw cards to see who was going to the 'hill' as a wireman or as FO crew. Being naïve, I volunteered to be the one. I think when

I heard the 'Are you sure?' I knew it may have been a mistake. The next thing I knew I was with the driver over in supply getting a 'flak jacket' and we headed off to Arrowhead Ridge.

It was a long, steep, and arduous walk in the trenches up to the OP. I was introduced to the FO, a Lt. Hausnick and the recon sergeant, Sgt Short. The driver was a guy from my own state, Bob Lindeman who lives about seventy miles from me. Our driver came up daily with mail, ammo, 'C' rations, and anything else we could get. We were the only GI's on the hill, except for two guys from a sound and flash crew who were also with the 23rd. Their bunker was close to ours. They had speakers that would pick up the sounds of the incoming and would get back-azimuths to the guns. Our bunkers were in two parts. The OP was where the aperture, B.C. scope and maps were and adjacent were our living quarters. Our bunks were engineer stakes with wire, and the bunker itself was made of timber, sandbags and rock, including chicken wire out in front of the aperture to catch any grenades. The ROKs occupied the trenches and maintained two outposts directly in front. They had the CP dug down to the center of the hill damn near. I didn't have any artillery training at the time so it was 'OJT'. When I pulled duty in the OP I was fortunate in that Sgt. Short had balls like bushel baskets and was on his second tour over there. The lieutenant usually stayed in the OP most of the day and Short and I split the nights. Of curse if anything happened everyone was awake. I remember on one of my first nights, two patrols got in a firefight. I thought it was WWII and woke everyone up needlessly. We used empty hand grenades, pipe cleaners, and gas for candles. Occasionally when we made one, we'd throw the fuse over on the sound and flash crews' bunker, then we'd get on the sound power and ask them if they could pick up anything. We ate C rations from WWII and had a one burner stove to heat them on. There was a pill we could light and it would heat them too. Sometimes our driver would bring up dried chicken soup and it was a real treat. We spent our days sand bagging the crapper we shared with the sound and flash guys. One of them wouldn't leave the bunker and he used his helmet and through it out. We also added burst plates to our bunker and occasionally screwed off down by the river, which ran behind the hill. The ROK soldiers were friendly and some of them would salute us out of fear or ignorance. Occasionally I'd return their salute. Few of them spoke English, but we managed to communicate. We even ate some of their Kim Chi once.

The war was fairly stable in May and June, but we always received incoming mortars fire, and patrols would get into firefights sometimes. We could observe 'Pork Chop' to our left at night and would report to S2 about flares, etc. The 7th Division finally gave the hill up as it wasn't worth the lives I guess. We started to receive some heavy artillery sometime in June. The Chinese were registering on our hill for a couple of days. We went out and took some shell reps, and they were Chinese Corp artillery pieces 122 guns I think. One of the rotating band pieces they said was from some naval gun they must have chogeyed up the hill. S2 told us that there was a buildup and we had our driver spend some nights at the bottom of the hill across the river. We were finally attacked one night which was preceded by an intense artillery, and mortar fire. The Chinese overran the outposts but were driven out by the ROKs and our artillery. We fired just about every 'X Ray' on the map. These were locations we had pre-registered on. FDC had them too, so they knew the elevation and deflection and coordinates. It scared the hell out of me the incoming was about one a second for a while. Our phone lines were both out so we had to use the radio. When the Chinese withdrew our officer got on the radio and said 'We had several direct hits on the bunker, the bunker is still standing and all men are OK.' He didn't encode the message and was relieved to the Division rear, I'm not sure that was the reason, but he left shortly after. The next morning I went out and restored our telephone lines at the rear CP at the bottom of the hill, the ROKs had several bodies lying in rice bags to be hauled away. Several more were going in and out of the aid station that had been wounded. Seeing the bodies kind of unnerved me. I stuck to the trenches a lot more. The Chinese had left a wounded soldier out in front of us. The ROKs sent two guys after him and after a brief encounter when he threw a potato masher type of grenade they subdued him. We watched them through field glasses and the B.C. scope. We later learned he was with a Chinese engineer battalion that were there to destroy bunkers. They had supposedly only recently arrived in Korea. He seemed quite defiant when he saw us. I'm sure the ROKs gave him an attitude adjustment. We had our driver bring us V.O. or Seagrams that we bought from the supply sergeant. We paid $10.00 per bottle for stuff he paid $1.75 for in the rear. We weren't supposed to have any alcohol on line, but who was to know since we were the only GI's there! We drank it warm and straight.

When we were in the OP we spent most of our time looking at the Chinese targets, especially after we took some incoming mortar fire. We could only get a fire mission if we had at least ten CCF in the open, or an enemy active mortar, unless we were being attacked. Needless to say any puff of smoke, dust, flash, or movement became an enemy active mortar. After the mission was over they always asked for surveillance. If the mortar fire stopped, we give them an 'Enemy active mortar destroyed and two CCF killed'. We weren't always sure but eighteen rounds of V.T. should have killed something. It felt good when we were pretty sure. According to the 2nd Division history book for this time frame they fired eighty-six thousand rounds of artillery 105 and 155, and one million rounds of .50 calibers into enemy troops mostly in front of Arrowhead and White House. When calling a fire mission, in most of our cases the FDC knew our coordinates so we would call 'Fire Mission' then we would give the coordinates or an X-Ray number. We would give them the shell then the fuse, which was usually V.T., and then we gave them the target. Once the info got to the guns they would give us an 'On the way'. We would answer with an 'On the way wait'. Then you just waited and watched the rounds land in the target area. It is a good feeling to know that they're landing on someone else, but the Chinese seldom exposed themselves in the daylight. We would test our radio frequency each day and sometimes the gooks would get on our frequency and make so much noise we couldn't transmit. Short would get on the radio and use every profane word he could think of, I doubt they understood him, but in the end we would need to change frequencies. The ROKs had an officer that would come into its OP daily and map out their patrols so we didn't fire on them. The Chinese also played oriental music over loud speakers at night. It sounded like a one string band and some really high-pitched singing. It must have had some psychological effect on the ROKs though, as we could sometimes hear them cursing.

If we had a target where we hadn't pre-registered the guns on an 'X-Ray' number, we would need to fire a mission by using coordinates, or azimuth if FDC didn't know our position, and we would adjust one gun until we were on target, fifty yards. We also gave the type of shell and fuse. Once we were on the target, we would usually get a 'battalion one round'. They would give us an 'On the way' and we would say On the way wait'. Sometimes we could hear the rounds going over us. V.T. would detonate when it was within twenty yards of the ground. Once in a while they would detonate before it reached the target, but not too often. A GPS would have been great in those days. We had a lot of X-Rays on the map and added new ones regularly. They were mostly areas that the Chinese were likely to use in an attack and defiladed areas out of reach of small arms fire. We moved over to White Horse Mountain, a hill to our east on the other side of 'Sausage'. Another crew moved into our bunker on Arrowhead. Only a day or so later the Chinese attacked Arrowhead again. This time in broad daylight, which was unusual. We watched some of it through a 20-power scope. They overran the outposts again. We heard that a member of the FO crew was killed, but I never verified it. We moved again from White Horse to a hill called '369' because of the elevation. It was by outposts

'Tom Dick and Harry'. We sewed on 3rd Division patches as a cover, because the 2nd was relieving the 3rd in the sector. They had suffered mammoth attacks on Harry prior to our arrival. We were attached to Baker Company and relieved a company on Outpost Harry. If I remember right, it was about eight hundred yards in front of the MLR. The Chinese were so close, I had to disconnect the ringers on my field phones. There was just one company of infantry in a perimeter of defense on Harry. Everyone had automatic weapons except for an M1 with a rifle grenade flare, to signal 'Flash Harry' if all of our communications were gone. That would bring our fire on our gun positions if we were overrun. Only the company commander could order it. Harry was a scary place and we rotated one week on and one week off with Able Company. That FO crew had a wireman by the name of Red Harrelson, but I don't remember the recon sergeant's name. I don't remember any of the teams being wounded. Someone was firing counter mortar fire I remember, and we were taking hits on the OP I think our FO got it lifted. I remember about the second night on Harry, the Chinese loud speakers came on and they said 'Welcome 2nd Division. So nice to see you again. Soon you will be taking a glorious journey home.' I don't think our patches fooled anyone. They also played some Kay Star or Joni Jones stuff.

We got along with the infantry guys just fine as I recall. On one occasion my phone line went out right after dark. I had to go to the checkpoint which was outside of the perimeter. I went to the rear CP to find out about any flares or bouncing betties, etc. The officer sent a BAR man with me when he found out I was alone. I assure you I liked the infantry just fine at that point. There were reports of a Chinese patrol, but the only problem I had was remembering the password to get back inside the perimeter. The OP was subject to sniper fire and the trenches needed a lot of repair, as did the bunkers. Aerial photos of the Chinese positions 'Star Mass' I believe showed all kinds of caves dug into the hill. A rumor was circulating that they would give a Silver Star to any officer and radio-telephone guy who would sneak behind the Chinese and adjust fire from there. They supposedly had an officer and were going to pick a radio-telephone operator. I didn't volunteer this time. The Chinese made a large attack on the Capitol ROK Division on our right flank at the end of July. They overran the ROKs and elements of the 555th Artillery. In fact they were reported to be about five miles behind us. Units of the 2nd Recon and some 3rd Division units were put back on line and closed the break. Finally we got the word that a cease-fire had been reached, and the firing was to stop at 10 pm on Monday the 27th. Both sides fired everything they could that evening. It sounded like all hell broke loose. The gun batteries even took some incoming. Then it got eerily quiet. It was strange not to hear the quad fifties especially.

After the ceasefire we went up on Harry to clean up and get ready to pull back. Sometime in the morning there was a terrific explosion back by the MLR. We thought the damn war started again. When we got back there, we found out an ammo dump in a personnel carrier had exploded killing five or six men from 'B' and 'C' Companies. It was a real tragedy, to make it through the firing only to be killed in an accident. I have a picture of the 'after', but there's not much to see."

### Sergeant Roy Portelli
### 461st Infantry Battalion Heavy Mortars 1953-54

"I was drafted in November 1952 and was sent to Korea by boat in May of '53 from Ft. Lewis, Washington. I was then assigned to the 461st Infantry Battalion Heavy Mortars. We were a 4.2 inch mortar unit that was attached, I believe, to I and sometimes X Corps around Kumhwa and Chorwon. I served with the 461st in Korea from May 1953 to May 1954. As a Forward Observer, we alternated between FO duties and the Fire Direction Center. The largest action that I participated in was the Pukon River action of June 14th through the 16th. Being an FO caused you to run the gamut of feelings, frightened, observant, anxious, and fascinated. I believe we supported the ROK 5th and 8th Divisions at different times, and fought mostly the Chinese. We usually had one OP called 'Native OP', and we moved about on six different hills. Many days and nights it was monotony, just harassment fire, one round every hour or so. If we saw the CCF in groups of two to four, it not enough to fire a round. By 1953 the front was stalemated, we FO's lived in reinforced bunkers dug by preceding ROK troops. For days we observed the enemy, doing nothing other than awaiting the jeep that would bring the hot chow. On June 14th of 1953 at the Pukon River two divisions attacked the 5th ROK Division. We began to fire on the troops but they broke through so we abandoned the OP's. As I went through the company the men had wrapped burlap bags around the tubes and poured water from helmets to keep the tubes cool since they were just putting in the shells without measuring the charges. When it got too close with the shells going only two hundred yards on max charge, they folded up the guns and we all took off. Calling a fire mission, we would call FDC and explain what we had, giving distance and azimuth. The CO would approve it or not. If firing started we would spot impact of the rounds and call for adjustments. When we had gotten fairly on target we informed the CO and he would order one platoon, two, or the company to fire full affect. After June 15th the 461st had lost thirty of its' thirty-six guns, and one hundred and ten of it's one hundred and sixty vehicles. In order to get rearmed, the 8th Army sent us replacement weapons for the 4.2-inch mortars, which were equivalent to 107mm. These were 155mm mortars, yes 155mm, and we tested them. They were fired with a lanyard and max range was two thousand yards, which we deemed unacceptable. The colonel ordered 4.2 inch replacements, which we finally got."

**Captain Stuart W. Reid**
**213th Field Artillery Battalion 1952-53**

"The battlefield area depends entirely upon the prospective of an observer. The ground Forward Observer is limited in range, based on where he is and how far he is to the target to adjust fire. The Aerial Observer can see for miles in all directions, we used to fly at 8-10,000 feet on a regular basis. On a clear day we could see the Yalu River. The only limitations we had were the range of the various weapons that we fired. Lt. Paul Braner, another Aerial Observer with the 213th, and I called in the first 240mm round fired in the Korean War. It was at a target called 'The Donut'. The first round was on target and hit right in the center! That was on May Day, May 1st, 1953, but it seems like yesterday. I'll bet it woke up the neighborhood! We took a lot of pride in flying the dawn patrol. Normally, we would be over the front lines well before daylight and used to adjust fire on enemy artillery fires and convoys. During my time with the 213th, I flew two hundred and fifteen missions of two to three hours each and was awarded seven Air Medals. And for the record, we were shot at every day on every mission."

**2nd Lt Samuel Cantwell**
**300th Armored Field Artillery Battalion 1953**

"I volunteered to go to Korea for two reasons. First, my father was one of the first 300 aviators in WWI, and second, having missed out on WWII I felt since it was the only war for which I might be eligible, I concluded it was then or never. I was a Forward Observer for the 300th Armored Field Artillery Battalion, Battery 'A'. we fired the 105mm self-propelled howitzer, and were part of the 5th Army Armored Artillery Group of 70 guns including 105's, 155's, and 8 inch howitzers. I was there from June through July 1953, where we were in support of the 6th ROK Division. There were 18 guns in this Wyoming National Guard Unit and over 70 guns ranging from 105mm to the eight inch, all self-propelled, a cannoneers' dream! After about two days orientation, I was sent up to my first of two observation posts where I spent three weeks. We were general support of the 6th ROK in the Kumsong region a bit north of the 38th parallel. It was generally desultory action, mostly light infantry patrols and continuous exchange of mortar rounds.

Upon my return to base, I was taking my first and last shower, when a sergeant pulled me out to say I was to saddle up immediately and get back that evening to another OP, which was about 10 miles east of my earlier position. Just before I struggled up the hill again, I helped myself to two quart bottles of Asbehi beer complete with the rice straw covers. A whole carload of the stuff had been 'liberated' by some enterprising GI's. My time at the base artillery battalion was about three days before I was sent up to the first of two OP's. Up I went with a wireman and beer. I passed Lt. Ed Atenasio. He was reported to have taken a direct hit and I was to be his relief. I knew Ed from OCS at Ft. Sill. Thankfully, he seemed OK, with only a minor hand injury. No time for BS, so on we went. I parked my two treasures in a dent along the trench leading to the bunker, but I never got a chance to have a sip!

The bunker had been in place since the US Civil War, I think. It was a stone cave about four feet around and three feet high with an 'L' shaped entrance sand bagged on both sides. There were two observation ports about four inches high and eight inches wide commanding a great view of a very large valley below and about twenty feet ahead of the 6th ROK infantry. To my left and a bit south was Capitol Hill, I think, and also not too far from Pork Chop Hill. I was guessing based on the position of the last OP I had, now occupied by Lt. Ed Baldwin. I no sooner got my radio in place when I got my first and only telephone message 'We are expecting an attack tonight'. Not the most welcome news, but that's what I went through all that training for. Sure enough, a red tracer right, green center, and white left, and away they came. No bugles, not so much as a 'by your leave', just straight on. It was 1900hrs, 13 July 1953. Given that the bunkers had been in place forever, the first thing that happened, they registered their guns on our position. Being carved out of rock helped a lot. I, of course, called for VT, which is murder for troops in the open but no problem for us.

About 2300hrs, the 300th ran out of VT. I then asked for and got WP and by 2400hrs got the word via radio 'sorry, we are out of that stuff too'. They then asked, 'What now?' Easy problem, that, considering the circumstances. About that time, Ed Baldwin, who unaccountably couldn't reach the 300th, I was relaying his missions, told me via radio 'All is quiet here, I'm going to bed'. I was too busy to argue, but on reflection, I could hardly believe it. I did have a weak connection with what I assumed was a ROK officer via the trench behind us. He whispered that the Chinese were on top of my bunker 20 feet away. We continued to get hit by our own shells, at my request until about 0200hrs when I was told I had to change location. Now I wasn't about to tour the area, so nothing for it but to burn the maps, shoot up the radio, and wait, and I did a lot of waiting for John Wayne and the cavalry to come riding up. About noon on the 14th a burp gun opened up on the sandbagged entrance to our bunker. Nothing further happened, so we just waited some more. My concern was what to do with a handful of hand grenades. I concluded that was too depressing and I'd wait until later to worry about that. During the night a lone ROK soldier had come in out of the rain and when a second blast of rifle fire worked on those bags again, I asked our guest if knew the word for surrender. He did and we walked out into a drizzling rain, hands up. There then was an interesting ceremony. The language barrier meant we acted on hand and arm signals. They took off our helmets, we silently shook hands with each, and gave us each a cigarette! I later learned that it was the same with others as well. I wasn't thinking about insignia, so didn't think to try to remove my brass bar. The result was I got the rapt attention of three out of five guards for what became a group of about 15 POWs, all but two of us

GIs. When we came out of the OP, I had to step over the body of a Black American soldier. He lay in a trench behind our OP looking as though he simply went to sleep. A small patch of brain tissue was the only indication of a wound. That has returned to haunt me many times."

**Sergeant (Arthur) Max Sarazin**
**1st Signal Battalion, 1st Marine Division ANGLICO 1953**

"I joined the Marines right out of high school and was assigned to 1st ANGLICO at Camp Catlin in Hawaii in March 1952. I went to Camp Pendleton, California on maneuvers and then back to Camp Catlin with orders from Colonel Lewis B. 'Chesty' Puller's outfit. Lots of rubber boat drills, landings from LCVP's and an LCM, and firing howitzers and naval gunfire at Makua Valley and Kahoolawe in Hawaii, then finally an amphibious assault on the Island of Maui. We flew to Korea in April 1953 and went by 6x6 from Kim-po Airfield to Inchon where an LST took us to meet an LCM which landed us on Sok-to. I was with 1st ANGLICO, USMC, First Air & Naval Gunfire Liaison Company at Sok-to, Korea. We had a couple 90mm guns and plenty of sea power including the Battleship USS New Jersey, a couple LSMR's, US Destroyers, a Dutch and a New Zealand Frigate the HMS Kanarie which we could direct fire from. Also nearby was a Carrier for air support. There were plenty of gun caves protecting their shores as constant targets, plus we caught plenty of troops in the open as well as activity in the villages. Our 90mm guns were very accurate, but didn't provide the devastation of naval gunfire.

We held the Islands of Sok-to and Ch'o-do on the west coast of North Korea outside of Pyongyang and I was on Sok-to. The rest of my outfit was in Wonson Harbor. ANGLICO called in Naval Gunfire for the Inchon invasion, and Air Support to fight their way out of the Chosin Reservoir. I arrived for the Spring Offensive, and final fighting in the assault before the Truce. Being in ANGLICO there was a feeling of power and doing my job as a US Marine. We supported the Korean Marines, known as the KMC's. Our trenches and bunkers were at the top of hills for visibility, and the infantry trenches were lower where they wouldn't be so obvious. The KMC units also supplied infantry support for us, and while I was there I think we fought mostly North Koreans. Our OP's didn't have names, we just went up to the 'OP'. We went down to the CP every third day for a warm meal and to clean up. It was a long steep walk but there was a shortcut, a small path thru a minefield which we were forbidden to take. One night I 'lost' the path and was on my hands and knees feeling my way along. I was sure I was going to have a date with 'Bouncing Betty'! That was my last trip thru a marked minefield. We had two OP's that were regularly manned. One each on Sok-to and Ch'o-do at the entrance to the harbor and river into Pyongyang, and at least three more in Wonson Harbor. Our presence on the enemy's side of the MLR was always a thorn in North Korea's side. Being an FO, there was a feeling of accomplishment of a job well done. Many hours spent watching the enemy and looking for targets. There was lots of rain in April of '53, and the trenches and bunker got flooded till we dug deeper towards downhill. Nothing was dry, and we lived like rats.

I remember a particular fire mission that I called, it was like chasing the enemy around with a 90mm till they ducked into a grove where I figured I wiped them out. Today I realize they probably had tunnel entrances in there and most of them probably survived, though. One time a round from an enemy gun cave landed about 300 yards off the stern of a New Zealand Frigate. By the time I raised them with my AN/GRC-9 radio a second round landed a hundred yards off their bow. They were bracketed, and they weren't even aware of this until I brought it to their attention! They escaped at full speed with black smoke pouring from their funnel. Another time a North Korean work party came out of their gun cave with pick and shovels to repair damage. I called rounds in and worked my way up to the opening to get into the cave before they could close the steel doors. I was using the Dutch Frigate which had a German howitzer in the turret and was very accurate. Finally I thought I lost a round with my last final adjustment, when all of a sudden smoke came pouring out of the cave. The round had gone right in! Then I immediately called in a Fire for Effect. Calling a Fire mission was always an adrenalin rush. We alerted the gun crew with the words 'Fire Mission' followed by azimuth, coordinates, target description, close or deep support, which by this means 50 yards or less is close support in the Marines, number of guns we wanted, type of ammo, type of fuse and the words 'Will Adjust'. We had 72 hours to get below the 38th parallel, trying to get out of North Korea when the Truce was signed. The US Navy couldn't get us and finally a filthy South Korean LST picked us up and took us to Paengyang-do where a Greek C-47 flew us back to Munsan-ni."

**Sergeant Joseph Delfino**
**980th Field Artillery Battalion 1953**

"I was drafted and was sent to Korea during the fighting and was an FO for the artillery with the 40th Infantry Division. I was assigned to the 980th Field Artillery Battalion, Baker Battery, we were a 105mm howitzer unit in direct support. We were located in the Punchbowl in Kumhwa Valley, near Heartbreak Ridge, Bloody Ridge, Luke's Castle and Sandbag Castle sector from April 1953 to September 1953. I was a communication chief, MOS 1542, but during the fighting, we all had to pull FO duty. I was usually assigned by the battery commander, and the work was, in a word, dangerous. We fought against the Chinese and the North Koreans, and we had one OP for each battery I believe. Our OP call sign was 'Glacier Baker'. We usually were next to other FOs from the infantry, and our main job was to support the U.S. and ROK infantry on the line."

**2nd Lt James Moroney**
**39th Field Artillery Battalion 1953**

"I was a 1952 ROTC graduate of Boston College and was ordered onto active duty at Ft. Sill on July 19th, 1952. I was stationed at Ft. Polk, Louisiana when my orders came through, directing me to report to Ft. Dix N.J. for shipment to Japan. I sailed out of New York to Puerto Rico, then through the Panama Canal to Hawaii and then to Tokyo. The whole trip took thirty days. I had more sea duty than some sailors I know! After about three weeks of waiting and schooling, I went by a small ship to Pusan, then a train North to Seoul and by truck to the 3rd Infantry Division, where I was assigned to the 39th Field Artillery Battalion. My MOS was 1189, FO, and that is what I did. We were a track drawn 105mm, but the guns were so entrenched that it would have been a job to tow them. Baker Battery had many Koreans on the guns. Known as Katusas, they were integrated into each section and did a good job. I got there in late April of 1953 and was evacuated as a battle casualty on or about June 11th of the same year.

In May and June of 1953 the war had slowed down to a crawl. We all knew that peace talks were going on but no one dared hope that things would end. Even the higher levels were trying to keep things quiet, so no large battles were waged. However, we sent small patrols out every night from the Main Line of Resistance and the Chinese were doing the same thing. At times, these patrols would bump into each other and to the men involved that was a battle. As an artillery Forward Observer, I supported two units of the 3rd Infantry Division from my OP on the MLR. One was an infantry company whose designation I forget, the other was a tank company. I also joined Baker Company of the 15th Infantry Regiment of the 3rd division on Outpost Tom where we had nightly probing attacks by the Chinese. These experiences were interesting and exciting but not real battles.

Being an FO on the hill, it was like nothing I had been trained for or even heard about. Let me explain what I mean. My first Observation Post was in a rice paddy. The water had long since drained away but the position was low and I could see very little from the observation ports. We had to fix that. The bunker flooded out in a rain storm. We had to fix that. We were the left most company on the left of the whole 3rd Division. There was only an empty space between our left flank and the next division, a Korean outfit whose bunkers I could barely see. When asked about who or what was defending that space, the infantry CO said not to worry about that as the whole gap was covered by mines which had been positioned by other divisions in days of yore. When liaison with the Koreans to our left was mentioned, it was dismissed as not to worry. We had no land line link with them, no radio contact and no one on either end who could translate Korean or English. This very green, very junior, very inexperienced 2nd Lt went back to his wet, no-see post and made sure that the prearranged defensive artillery concentrations were current and known to the 39th Battalion Fire Direction Center. I never had to use them but it was a comfort to know that they were there and ready to go. Being with the tanks, which of course were dug into the MLR trench as armored pillboxes, was an active time since the Chinese seemed to fear them and shelled us a lot. One night the tankers built a large bunker to be used as a latrine and just for fun put an old bed spring on top of it in an upright position. The Chinese seemed to think that it was some sort of new Radar and blew the whole thing back to dust. No one was hurt so we thought that it was quite a joke. We already were just a little crazy.

My first job with the infantry was rather quiet. The company commander liked his mostly peaceful sector and did nothing aggressive to irritate the enemy. He told me to be cool, that his people would know if we were being attacked long before I would and that he would tell me if we needed defensive fires. It was an arrangement that worked. If we were poked by the Chinese, I would be told to drop a few discouraging concentrations and soon the Chinese would go away. It was not glorious combat but the enemy never got through so, I guess we were doing our job. Then, one night the situation changed when a company of tanks rattled and groaned its way into the infantry position. The tankers liked to work with us since we could get permission for them to fire their tank cannons. We did this a lot. The tankers would whoop and holler and we even hit a few targets, mostly caves. When I was on Outpost Tom, the infantry CO, Captain Tart of Baker Company, 15th Infantry Regiment, knew what artillery fire could do and told me to be easy to find on the hill and to stick close to him. I did this on 'Tom' and later on 'Harry' until they carried me off the hill as a battle casualty on June 11th or 12th 1953. We always were up against the Chinese. I thought that they were brave soldiers who were not afraid to die. I did my best to accommodate this rather puzzling predilection. The few prisoners I saw seemed poorly equipped, with flimsy shoes and thin uniforms. However their brass belt buckles were always shined, their weapons were clean and functional. However, they all seemed to be sick with some kind of cold, runny noses or a cough. I did not hate them. They were soldiers doing a dirty job, as was I.

Baker Battery 39th had three Forward Observation teams. I know that we manned a post on the MLR to the left of OP Tom. We also manned 'Tom' and I was attached to Baker Company of the 15th when we went onto 'Harry'. The 15th Infantry seemed a little light because I think that the heavy weapons were left on the MLR. Our main reason for being there was to act as an in your face force, to dare the Chinese to attack. They did just that about every night with small probing patrols. All of these actions took place in the dark, so there were no Fort Sill style fire missions of targets that you could see. I called in mostly concentrations and rarely adjusted fires. It may seem crazy but that's the way it was. I adjusted flare drops from Air Force planes, smoke concentrations to cover a daylight evacuation of wounded from Tom and a Time on Target to rattle a Chinese patrol in addition to some fire missions during night time attacks on Harry. I had all the professional equipment that I needed, a 20 power scope, commo radios and EE8s, an emergency switch-board device which were little plastic plugs which glowed if you had a call, you could attach to each other for a variety of stations, compasses, and a Battery Commander's scope. We had plenty of tools. We also had plenty of food since the battery would send us things like whole eggs and canned bacon, onions, and coffee in addition to the c-rations. We also could eat with the infantry at their daily 2:00am hot meal. This was while I was on the MLR. It was tougher on Outpost Tom where we only had the c-rations. The whole time I was in combat, my mess equipment was a spoon and a can opener. I had a canteen but no cup and drank from a tin can. It was basic but effective. I was healthy, strong and adjusted to the life. My little team washed and shaved almost every day. There was a creek to the rear of our OP, the one in the former rice paddy, where we could sponge down if it was quiet. We all had our duty to fight, to win, to stay alive. I have never regretted my actions in combat, just wished that I could have done more.

On the MLR life was like a World War I movie. Our positions were deep and things were mostly quiet, a few hectic nights some shelling, a little patrol work. On Tom with Capt Tart things were more active. We slept during the day and were up all night every night. We did not patrol from Tom but the Chinese hit us about every night. The listening post would hear movement, Tart would call the people back to the hill, then we would pop a few flares. There they were, outlined in the dark. The infantry would start up their small arms fire. I would call in a few of my favorite old concentrations. Then the Chinese would drop mortar rounds on us and pull back. After that, quiet and strained listening, hoping that they would not come back. In the morning, the infantry first sergeant and I would go through the attack area to collect enemy hand grenades which we would toss out from our northern slope, just for fun. One morning, with our jacket pockets stuffed with Chinese grenades, we heard 'pop-fizz', the tell tale sound of an activated grenade fuse. What to do? We both knew that we were about to be blown apart due to our own stupidity and could only hope that the end would be quick. Then whoosh a flare shot into the air. We had set off one of our own trip flares. We looked at each other's pale fear drained face and laughed. We were both more than a little crazy combat soldiers. We did not go grenade hunting for a few days after that.

Harry was another story completely. The march up was a horror parade, dead dismembered bodies, mostly Chinese but some Americans were piled high on either side of the trench and some times in it. The slope seemed to be straight up and Tart kept on saying 'keep going Moroney, keep going'. Only death himself could have stopped me, I was young and a soldier. On top of Harry, Tart began to sort things out, positioned his men and released me to the Artillery OP. Once there we established commo with the Mortar OP people and our Battalion Fire Direction Center. Then crump, crump, crump, incoming artillery right on my bunker and the whole hill started to jump. I could see exactly nothing since the bunker was caving in on me and my radio man and we were about to be buried. We worked our way out on our bellies. The main radio was gone, no phones and only a hand radio which soon exploded at my feet. I was doing no good where I was, so back to the Company CP and Capt Tart for orders. The CP was also being pounded but holding together for once. The only radio working was set on some strange frequency. I was talking to Americans trying to put some fire on 'Star Mass' but they would not believe who I was. We tried every thing to identify ourselves, Tart even said to tell them that he recently 'got his tracks', made Captain, but no go. Then over the air came the voice of a classmate from Ft. Sill, John Gallaspy of Louisiana who said that he knew me and if they did not honor my calls for fire he would call them in himself. That did the trick and we got blind, no adjustment fires all around the hill. Good but not good enough because now there were Chinks on the hill who had run right through their own artillery and mortar fires. We now started a discussion in the CP on the advisability of on position fires. I said 'yes' others counseled 'no' because perhaps all of our troops were not under cover. Tart had been in touch with the platoons and said 'Do it', and I did. 'Fox Oboe Baker, Fire Mission, Chinks in the open on Harry, coordinates of Harry, request HE with variable time fuse, request all available artillery, spread fire over the hill, will adjust'.

With that a grenade landed at my feet. Now I was at the bunker door, ready to adjust fires if needed, doing a little shooting at the Chinese running past and I thought, 'damn, another hand grenade incident' and was trying to push it outside with the butt of my carbine when boom! then nothing. I regained consciousness to find the carbine blown apart, a broken leg and a gentleman of Chinese persuasion coming through the door. When I went into the Army, my father gave me a German P38 from WWII. He said I might need it in a tight spot and this was the spot. I pulled it out and shot my enemy with every round the pistol had, then passed out. It was still dark when I next came around. The shelling had let up a little, both theirs and ours, and I saw no more figures running past the door but I could not move my body from the hips down and the dirt was starting to bury me. Subsequent rounds only added to my plight. Being buried alive in a bunker doorway in Korea did not appeal to me. 'Do something Jimmy, don't let the bastards grind you down' I thought to myself. Then I noticed that at least part of my problem was the dead Chinese soldier on top of me. My upper body had been protected by my flack jacket so I used my hands to dig my self partially out and to push the Chinese off. That was better, at least I had some feeling in both legs, it was mostly pain but I could tell that while the left leg was broken, I could push a little with the right one. I gradually worked my way deeper into the bunker and again passed out. My next memory is of the sun light coming through the doorway and seeing American figures going past. We were being reinforced or perhaps relieved. Tart was out with them telling them the situation and ducking incoming mortar rounds. After a while, a 2nd Lt came in looking for him. We talked briefly and he asked if he could help me. My only thought was that if he ran across a Medic he could send him in. He said 'Well, I guess I had better be going', stepped out side and was immediately blown up by a mortar round that detonated on his helmet. There was nothing left at all. He seemed a good sort but was gone in an instant. By this time I was unconcerned in my own existence, things seemed to be running on automatic. I had been seriously wounded but had not lost a lot of blood, still had my wits and was one tough Boston Irishman who was very hard to kill. Besides, we were being reinforced, maybe even relieved. We were all set. Then a soldier came in wearing a gold leaf and I knew that if a field grade was on the hill we were really in deep trouble. He asked what my problem was and I pointed out my broken left leg which was now at an odd angle to the rest of me, various slashes, holes, gaps and wounds to head and body. I guess that convinced him and he got a medic in to treat me.

The Medic gave me some morphine, got a stretcher and some bearers but could not load me on it in the bunker. I would have to get out of the bunker myself, which I did, after saying a little pray out loud in Latin and elbow crawled, dragging myself behind. On the way down the trench line I met and talked with Frank Codd, a fellow FO from the 39th. Frank was KIA later that very day. We were under constant if light mortar fire while this evacuation of wounded was in progress. Even when we were at the base of the hill, waiting for transport to the battalion aid station we were under fire and the troops, with a typical American attitude, were yelling, 'Hey, tell those bastards that it's not fair to shoot at the wounded'. When the incoming got too close, a black medic threw himself on top of as many men as he could to protect them with his own body. At a break in the shelling, he lit a cigarette and hesitated before giving it to me. 'Will you take this, Lt?' he said. I said I certainly would and that if we did not hang together we would all hang separately. That ended my experiences on Harry but I do want to say that at the MASH unit I found out I had two broken legs, multiple wounds on both legs, on one arm and my head and a kidney puncture. As I'm writing this, I am touching a piece of Korea imbedded about one finger width away from my right eye. I spent six months in various Army hospitals and was then returned to duty in the US. Told you I was hard to kill! While in the Tokyo Army Hospital, Capt Tart came in to see me. He himself had received three wounds on Harry and as he said 'I had to be ordered of the hill three times'. He also was in the Tokyo Hospital but since we were in different areas, he did not even know that I was there also until he was about to leave."

**1st Lt Joseph Brummell**
**625th Field Artillery Battalion 1953**

"Concerning the last day of the war, July 27th, there were three events on this momentous day I have never related until this time for fear of telling 'war stories'. Thinking back after 50 years I can remember July 27th, 1953 like it was yesterday. I do not wish to imply any acts of heroism or valor on my part, because none existed. I was, however, aware of two firm convictions, number one, there were no atheists in the trenches or bunkers, and number two, that after a few months I was developing an ever widening 'yellow' stripe down my spine. These three events of the 27th are humorous today, even though I could see absolutely no humor at the time. After two years of bickering, the boys at Panmunjon had decided they were tired of this police action as we were.

July 27th, 1953 arrived warm and bright. There was a great hope that at 2200 hours this day, all the shooting would stop. I was a Forward Observer, artillery, manning a battalion OP on Bloody Ridge. We were in support of the 223rd Infantry Regiment, 40th Infantry Division. This OP was located a few hundred yards west of Col. Conklin's Heartbreak Ridge. This OP had a complete view of Mundung Ni Valley that ran due north from the two ridges. In the valley were eight or ten Sherman tanks that had bought the farm in an earlier engagement. Rumors had it that they were from either the 24th or 25th Infantry Divisions. We had been told that the shooting would stop at 2200 hours. We were cautioned to stay in our bunkers and not to take any unnecessary risks. We were told to get rid of a lot of our munitions, in other words to have a mother of all turkey shoots, so we wouldn't have to carry them to the rear. There seemed to be an air of relief with everyone. I could hardly wait to board a luxurious troop ship for a long trip back to Wyoming to see my wife, and for the first time my young son who was seven months old at the time.

Things seemed fairly peaceful until about 0900 hours. It seems the Chinese had received similar orders, get rid of excess munitions. We were being bombarded by 60 and 81mm mortars of U.S. manufacture, but they definitely were incoming. I began to feel that the ancient war gods and the entire Chinese Army were teaming up in a personal vendetta against me and my OP. I was sure that it was meant that I was to atone for all my pasts sins. Looking around I saw that everyone else was being clobbered. About mid-morning I spotted two mortar squads on the forward slope of a hill we called 'Joe Stalin's Nose'. Everyone knows that mortars are never located on a forward slope. The Chinese had a reputation of being excellent mortar men. They were proving it today. I called for a fire mission and it so happens they were located on one of our pre-plotted concentrations. I reported enemy mortars and requested not only my coordinates but also my sobriety. 'Mortars are never located on forward slopes' I thought, this was true but Chinese mortar men had never read the Fort Benning manual on mortar placements. 'Fire For Effect' brought two of the six VT rounds on top of the crews, beautiful air bursts, and the mortars had appeared to be dispatched. This was an unusual fire mission because our smoothbore 105's might land anywhere including Outer Mongolia. At about 1230 hours, against my better judgment, I decided to make my way back to the mess area, for a can of warm C rations and to compare stories with other FO's and the platoon leaders. On the way back to the OP I was forced to stop and visit a friendly 'two holer', a bathroom. This facility was built with sandbags and had a screen door that faced south giving a scenic view of the valley to the friendly south. While enjoying the brief respite, I could hear shell fragments 'thunk-thunk' against the sandbag walls. While enjoying the scenery, I thought humorously how the War Department telegram would read, 'Dear Mrs. Brummell, The War Department regrets to inform you that your husband, Lt. Brummell, died on July 27, 1953, while in defense of his country and the battalion latrine'. Still chuckling about the telegram, I cautiously made my way down the trench to my OP. My wire-corporal, Jolin LaTrace, originally LaTracioni I think, from Brooklyn, met me and said, 'Lt, you aren't going to believe this, but our sleeping bunker is gone, and our driver PFC Gibbs has cracked up'. The top of the sleeping bunker had a hole five feet in diameter. Whatever it was that hit it, penetrated at least four feet of rocks, logs and sandbags. We had rumors that the Russians had given the Chinese some giant mortars, around 240mm I think, called 'Bunker Busters', and this 'Buster' had landed dead center with a fuse delay. A quick view of the interior confirmed that such a weapon had hit our bunker. No injuries, thank God, no one was inside at the time, but normally five of us used the bunker. I made my way to the OP, which was about fifteen feet away. Everyone was naturally shook-up to say the least. Poor Gibbs was cowering in a corner babbling verses from the Bible. He understandably had answered an involuntary call from mother nature, and was indeed hysterical. He survived and was a good soldier.

The afternoon passed rapidly with great expenditure of resources by both sides. As reported by Col. Conklin, it all stopped at 2200 hours. Out came the Chinese loudspeakers playing Glenn Miller and Dorsey along with their usual propaganda. Welcome music compared the Armed Forces Networks that only played Hank Snow and Ray Acuff! As 2200 hours came with a great sigh of relief, and out came a welcome quart of I.W. Harper 100 proof-bonded. Memories of those months on the peninsula come back vividly. To recall a few, the rattling beer cans on our concertina, the reminder of ever present trip flares and unmarked mine fields, the 'Turkey Shoots', the searchlights in the rear with quad 50 half tracks nearby, the Chinese loudspeakers at night, the five day R&R in Kyoto, Hank Snow's 'We're Moving On' or Roy Acuff's 'Wabash Cannonball'. 'China Night over Arirong' played by Army Radio Network, the loved and much respected Katusas attached to us, but the most vivid and respected memory is the lonely Infantry rifleman manning the rifle positions through the long dark night. They were the unsung heroes that helped me survive these months. I will be eternally thankful to them."

### Sergeant Walter Powell
### 143rd Field Artillery Battalion 1953-54

"I enlisted in January 1953, and was being held at Fort Dix, NJ to attend OCS and instructing in heavy weapons training. After two months of this I volunteered for Korea. It took them three hours to cut my orders. I arrived in Inchon on the day of the cease fire, July 27th 1953, and was assigned to 'B' Battery, 143rd Field Artillery Battalion, supporting the 40th Infantry Division. We had 105mm howitzers. After being in the Battery for one month I was so bored I volunteered for the hill. I did not take part in any hostile action having gotten there after the cease fire, and after the 27th all the OP's were put under control of S2. It was a great learning experience and we constantly practiced calling in fire missions. We were there to keep track of the enemy. When we spotted what would be a target we would call in a sighting to S2 and a practice fire mission to the battery. This taught us how to pin point things on the map and how to select the proper shells. While there we were in direct support of the 160th Infantry Regiment, but we actually supported any units that we could direct fire for. Although we were in a cease-fire we kept track of the units opposite us, they were always CCF. When I first went up on the hill we were in Kumhwa. We moved to Chorwon in October 1953, and we stayed there until the Division was sent home in April of 1954.

The battalion manned nine different OP's, and I served on a number of them, but the most the most significant was OP 245 in the Chorwon Valley. This was designated the main surveillance OP in the area, and we had sand tables set up that showed the CCF units opposite us and their suspected strength. Big Brass, Congressmen and Newspaper Reporters were constantly visiting us. We had a set spiel we would go though and then answer any questions that we could. Being the ranking man on the hill it was my job to do the talking. After the division went home I was assigned to the 7th Infantry Division, and when they learned of our OP experience, we were all promoted one grade and sent back up the Hill. We served with all the foreign units attached to the 7th, with all the OP's overlooking the infamous Old Baldy on which the CCF had an OP. We got friendly with the men that manned it, from a great distance of course, and would wave and signal them and they would respond in same. Also we over looked Pork Chop, White Horse, and T-Bone.

Being an FO was both exciting and boring. You are on the front lines realizing that anything started you'd be in the thick of it and the likely target for enemy mortars and at the same time, the day to day routine of looking across the DMZ , and seeing the same thing day after day was quite boring. The only break from this was the occasional going to the rear and having a service shoot, i.e., practicing your FO skills with live fire at an artillery range. After the cease fire we lived in fortified bunkers which were heated but dank, while the infantry lived in tents to the rear of the line. After the cease fire the OP was a target of enemy infiltrators on intelligence gathering information. On one occasion, I left the bunker to use the piss tube, I observed one of these infiltrators on top of the bunker looking down and recording our conversations and taking pictures through the vent pipe which was directly over our map table. As I was unarmed at that time, I went back into the bunker, retrieved my carbine, and alerted other members of what was happening. At this point we all went outside armed to the teeth. The infiltrator heard us coming and fled down the hill. Nine of us opened fire and to the best of my knowledge nobody hit him. He ran into a mine field and was killed. The next day we were overrun by MP's and intelligence trying to determine if he had been alone and what information might have been lost. On another occasion, we were continually buzzed by two Chinese MIG fighters. We reported this to Battalion and within ten minutes two British jets appeared and chased the MIG's north. We could hear firing but could not see the planes. Shortly after this the British fighters returned doing a wing-wag as they passed over our bunker. Later on the CCF started using the DMZ as artillery range. They would walk the shells across the DMZ in a straight line towards our bunker. We assumed this was to let us know they knew exactly where we were and could take us out at any time. This continued for a week. S2 used this episode to establish listening posts with high-tech equipment to pinpoint the exact location of each firing weapon."

**Sergeant Coy Mason**
**49th Field Artillery Battalion 1954-56**

"I was married and had one child when I was drafted, which made it very hard for me. After training I sailed out of Seattle, WA on the Marine Phoenix in October 1954. Upon getting to Korea, I was assigned to 'A' Battery, 49th Field Artillery Battalion, 7th Infantry Division. The 49th was a 105mm howitzer unit and I served with them from November 3rd 1954 to February 15th 1956. I became assigned as a Forward Observer by transferring from the firing battery to the FO group in the Motor pool. Being an FO during the early part of the armistice, I remember it being very lonely, cold, home sick, bad chow, afraid of land mines, skirmishes, terrible weather, little sleep, and thoughts of 'why am I here?'. The 49th supported the 34th Infantry Regiment, and had no problems, we pulled guard duty together on the DMZ beyond Freedom Bridge. I recall skirmishes involving North Korean soldiers being a normal occurrence at the time. This was in the Chorwon Valley area. We had to stay in red alert just about all times, ready to move into action any minute. Being on the hill, it always seemed to be cold, wet, with plenty of anxiety, there were men who froze to death, and also a lot of frozen feet. As the driver for our FO team, I drove a jeep with a trailer with all our supplies, food, ammo, carbines, camouflage, etc. I remember one time we actually had to shoot a live fire mission, and the FO officer called down the mission and dropped the shells too short. We all hit the dirt in a large hole, almost killed by friendly fire. Another time, it was about 0200 hours and we were sleeping under shelter. I was half awake and I heard a noise. We all got our carbines and had a shoot out, we captured one infiltrator with no casualties."

# Glossary

## Common terms used in the artillery

As with any book, to be able to understand what you are reading is always helpful! In that spirit, the following are a list of abbreviations and definitions to help readers better understand the language of an artilleryman.

**Adjusting Fire** - Forward Observer gives corrections of add, drop, left or right to correct fire on a target.

**Aiming Circle** - An optical device with angular scales graduated in mills and used in laying a battery. This device can also be used in surveying.

**Aiming stakes** - Two poles set at a designated distance and angle to the howitzer and used by the gunners to sight on.

**Azimuth** - An angle from true or magnetic north.

**BC Scope** – Battery Commander's Scope – This was one of the most important pieces of equipment that a Forward Observer used. This special type of binoculars assisted the FO to calculate co-ordinates and call fire missions. They had a twin lens viewing scope of usually ten power with reticule for adjusting fire, and were designed so the head of the observer can be several inches below the viewing lens.

**BOQ** - Bachelor Officers Quarters.

**Check point** - A known location within a target area that has been identified, usually with a number, by the fire direction center for future use.

**CSMO** – Close Station Marching Order – This was when all of the batteries of the battalion moved as a unit to a new location to set up new tactical positions.

**Circular Azimuth Overlay** - An opaque circular paper material graduated in mills on its outer circular edge and with vertical and horizontal graduations in yards on the interior of the circle. Used in conjunction with a firing chart to graphically correct for the angle of the observer line of sight to the gun firing line.

**Converge Sheef** – When a battery fires all rounds that converge on the same point.

**Contour lines** - Lines drawn on a map that denote altitudes.

**Coordinates** - A numbered location as determined from the grid lines of a map.

**CP** - Command Post – There was a battalion CP and each battery had a CP. These were where the Battalion and Battery commanders directed their respective units.

**Cut charges** - Powder for many artillery shells comes in multiple bags tied together. This term refers to removing unnecessary bags of powder from the charge before firing.

**Cutting fuses** - An old term still used for setting the proper bursting time on mechanical or powder train fuses.

**Deflection** - The angular measurement from a known and established direction.

**DMZ** – De-Militarized Zone – This is the area that is considered 'no-man's land' the boarder between North and South Korea, agreed upon by both sides at the truce talks.

**Fan** - A plastic device that is oriental fan shape and graduated on one side in yards and the other side in meters. The top wide end is graduated in mills and the narrow bottom end fits in a pin used on a firing chart indicating the gun location. Provides a visible reading of both range and deflection.

**Fire for effect** - Term applies to firing multiple guns on a target after the exact location is known to maximize effect.

**Firing chart** - A large sheet of heavy paper usually with grid lines and used to determine ranges and deflections to targets, located and used in Fire Direction Centers.

**Firing map** - A map used in a fire direction center for reference and to determine locations and elevations of a target.

**Flash reducer** - An extra chemical in a bag included with the regular firing charge to cause the powder to burn more rapidly thereby reducing the flash from the gun. In Korea some 155-mm gun units occasionally fired flash reducer with the regular charge in order to increase range.

**Firing tables** - A book of tables that show a corresponding range that a given charge and elevation will provide.

**FO** - Forward Observer – Usually an officer and two enlisted men comprised an FO team, or sometimes referred to as an OP Team. The officer was the leader, one enlisted man was a radio operator, and the other enlisted man was the recon sergeant.

**Fuse delay** - A fuse of a shell that will detonate after a delay period from impact.

**Fuse quick** - The fuse of a shell that will cause an instantaneous detonation of the shell on impact.

**Gun in battery** - When a gun has been fired the tube will recoil backward and will be returned to its starting position by the recoil mechanism. This term is applicable when the tube is in its normal at rest position.

**HE shell** - High Explosive shell. The HE shell is the most common type of artillery shell.

**H&I** – Harassing and Interdiction – This term is used when pre-selected targets are fired on at pre-set times of the day. Both sides did this. Many times the OP teams were subjected to this, and many times in reports there appears the statement 'Received a number of H&I rounds daily'.

**ILLUM** – Illuminating, or 'star' shells, used for nighttime operations.

**Lands and grooves** - Tubes have spiraling ridges to engage the rotating band on an artillery shell to provide a gyroscopic stabilizing spin. The raised part of the ridge is called "land" and the lower part of the groove is called "groove".

**Laying the Battery** - A method in which the aiming circle is used to get all guns in a battery pointed in exactly the same direction initially upon occupying a position.

**Metro Report** - Information provided, usually by an observation battalion that includes information as to humidity, temperature, wind direction, and pressure of the atmosphere. Used in applying corrections for firing.

**Mills** - An angular measurement in which one mill subtends an arc of one unit in 1000 units.

**MLR** – Main Line of Resistance – This was literally the front lines, what divided the two sides.

**OP** - Observation Post – For the infantry, OP sometimes stood for 'Out Post', which were manned positions out in front of the MLR, to detect and give early warning of enemy attacks and movements. The artillery OP or Observation Post, was usually on the MLR and preformed the same basic function, in addition providing artillery support for friendly infantry attacks in that respective sector.

**On the way** - Information transmitted from fire direction to the FO to tell him that the requested artillery rounds have been fired.

**Powder Train** – The number of powder increments it takes to propel a projectile forward.

**Precision fire** - Firing one round at a time to hit a specific small target. Sometimes corrections are calculated by averaging overs, shorts, lefts or rights.

**Prime mover** - A vehicle used to tow artillery pieces. This was a 2-½ ton truck for 105-mm howitzers and the 13-ton M-5 tractor for the 155-mm and larger guns.

**Rotating band** - A brass band on the lower end of an artillery shell that engages the lands and grooves of the tube to cause the shell to be stabilized in flight due to gyroscopic rotation.

**Ramrod** - A long pole with a flared end used to ram projectiles to seat them in the lands and grooves prior to firing.

**Range** - The distance from one point to another. The term can be used to identify the distance from an observer to a target; distance an artillery piece can fire, or distance from one target to another. The term is also used to define an area used for artillery target practice.

**Recoil** - The movement of a tube backward due to the momentum generated in firing the shell.

**Registration** - A method of firing successive rounds on a known location to obtain corrective data for future firing.

**Reticule** - A graduated scale viewed through an optical device that enables the viewer to make estimates of lateral distance.

**ROK** – Republic of Korea – Usually used in reference to Korean Army units for identification purposes, such as '52nd ROK Artillery Battalion' or '31st ROK Infantry Regiment'.

**RSOP** - Reconnaissance, Selection and Occupation of Position – This was usually done by the one of the Battery Executive Officers and sometimes the Battery Commander. This was an important job because when an order was given to move into an area, consideration had to be given on bringing the maximum firepower of the Battery on the enemy.

**Self contained ammo** - Shells similar to bullets, which include a brass shell with powder, primer, and projectile.

**Separate charge** - Unlike a bullet, the powder is handled separate from the projectile. Also called separate loading.

**Set back** - The inertial effect of rapid acceleration as when a shell is fired. This effect is used to arm some fuses in flight.

**Shell casing** - The brass portion of self contained ammunition that contains the powder and primer. Supports the projectile during loading.

**Shift trails** - To fire into a sector the gun can not traverse to, the trails must be shifted manually on towed guns.

**Shoot** – When a battery has been issued a fire mission, they are involved in a 'shoot'.

**Slip stick** - A slide rule type device containing information of range and corresponding elevation. Used in fire direction.

**Smoke shell** - A shell that produces a large amount of smoke without explosive force.

**Splash** - A term used to tell the FO when his rounds are landing on the target. This information is transmitted five seconds before impact.

**Spread sheaf** - Normally all rounds land in a relatively small concentrated area. If the target is wide, this command is used to order the guns to spread out their impact area.

**Star shell** - A shell that has a magnesium burning material which is set to ignite high in the air and is suspended by a parachute. This type of shell is capable of lighting a considerable area at night.

**Trails** - Long boxed or pipe extensions to howitzers and guns used to both tow and to help anchor the weapon to the ground to absorb recoil.

**Timed fuse** - A fuse with powder train or clock mechanism that will cause the shell to detonate after a predetermined time.

**ToT** - Time on Target - Calculations are provided by fire direction so that all rounds burst on the target at a pre-determined time. This was used when many artillery pieces were fired at a specific target at the same time, with devastating effect.

**Tube** - The barrel of an artillery piece.

**VT Fuse** - 'Victor Tare' – Variable Timed fuses to arm artillery shells so they burst in the air above enemy troops. This was accomplished by a radio signal that emanates from the tip of the projectile (in the detonating charge), and when the shell, after arming in flight, was within a certain distance from the ground, would detonate. The radius of the explosion spread out in a half conical shaped pattern until hitting the earth. VT rounds were usually fired in a ripple pattern so as not to have the shells set each other off in flight.

**Will adjust -** A term used by Forward Observers to inform the fire direction center that the FO will make adjustments of range and deflection after observing the impact of the rounds being fired on the particular fire mission.

**WP Shell –** An artillery shell that contains white phosphorus that produces choking white smoke and can severely burn personnel. Commonly referred to as 'Willy Peter', white phosphorus artillery shells were also used for 'marking' a target or area for further shelling.

# Epilogue

*"Picture yourself as an artillery Forward Observer at a well-prepared defensive position overlooking a large plain dotted by hills, low ridges and a narrow meandering stream. Beyond the plain, about two miles distant, lay a series of higher ridges occupied by the enemy. Intelligence has learned that a huge Chicom force forming behind the far ridge line for several days has moved closer. Because a large-scale attack by this force appears imminent, every unit in your division has been placed on 100 percent alert. All along your division sector other mutually supporting strong points are similarly defended. All weapons are loaded and ready to fire. What seems an unlimited store of ammunition is available within easy reach. Deadly mortars and artillery pieces by the hundreds have been zeroed in, meaning, routes of approach and point targets within assigned zones of fire have been pre-fired. Range, azimuth, and time of flight from the guns to each target have been recorded and given a concentration number, simplifying the FO's job. Anytime he needs to fire on any of the several separate targets, he needs only to state the concentration number and the number of rounds he wants fired. Since gun settings are known, rounds can be fired quickly and accurately. High explosive, or H.E., mortar and artillery rounds are stacked, waiting to be loaded and fired by alert, well-trained crewmen. It's just before dawn and the weather is favorable. All is in readiness for the expected enemy. With a volley of firecrackers, whistles and blaring, off-key sound of bugles the Chinese begin their attack. Seen through spotting scopes and binoculars, we observe the many small figures swarming over the distant hills coming in our direction. They are out of range of our riflemen, who wait. The machine gunners also wait. The artillery FO's calmly call in pre-planned fire commands and concentration numbers to the FDC, which in turn passes the information to the gunners at the batteries. Hundreds of our guns fire, almost as one, reload, and fire again. And again.*

*Within seconds the swishing of the initial rounds sizzle and 'whoosh' overhead as they speed unseen toward their designated targets. Some of the rounds hit the ground and explode, others armed with the V.T. Variable Time fuse explode 40 to 50 feet in the air. You are barely aware of the expletives of awe and amazement from guys within hearing range. You watch as all the expected routes of approach used by those wide columns of two-legged figures disappear in huge flashes of flame, black smoke and clouds of dust of different colors. White hot shell fragments hit the ground and amongst the waves of humanity running toward you. With all those numbers attacking and the volume of our fire, you know some of those bodies have to be pulverized, literally disappear from sight. There are scores of direct hits. You've seen artillery fire many times, but this is different for the targets are swarms of people. A thought flashes. You wonder how many enemy troops that first splash of cascading fire and metal eliminated. The thought passes quickly, forgotten. The men at the FDC need to know what you've just seen so you speak in your phone, 'Target! Repeat Concentration Number Alpha Zero One, Fire for Effect.' You keep firing that particular concentration repeatedly. There's a tremendous amount of smoke, dust, flashes of exploding rounds, and thousands of shell fragments ripping through the target area. There is a slight hope our devastating firepower will stop them and turn them back. But no! Incredibly, you see them bursting through the fire and smoke as though untouched! You call in the next series of concentration numbers, 100 yards close, this time, maintaining fire on the initial targets as well. Your palms are sweating and your ears hurt from the noise of the guns. There is no letup in our artillery fire, but by now the explosions are joined by our mortars, the big 4.2-inch and the 81mm. The smaller 60mm mortar crews wait to fire because the range is still too far. The heavy machine guns open up firing into the air at an angle to take advantage of their maximum range at a near 45-degree elevation. Thousands of machine gun bullets 'plunge' into the masses of attacking humanity, causing additional death.*

*Occasionally smoke and dust lift just enough to see what appear to be 'things' lying on the ground. Some are motionless, others crawling, and still others appearing to be kneeling. You know they are dead or wounded, the latter probably crying out in pain, or for help, but you don't hear their cries because your ears are numb with battlefield sounds of guns firing and explosions. You're concerned about nothing except stopping that flow of specs coming toward you. With each air burst, additional littering of bodies occur but no one notices the attackers are fewer, you know this has to be, but they continue to come, too numerous to count. A sergeant in the Forward Observer party looks through his field glasses and says, 'Jeez, some of 'em don't' even have rifles!' Another says 'Yeah I see 'em but it looks like they're carrying grenades.' It's little comfort to know they are still too far away to throw those grenades at you, but they need to be dealt with before they get within throwing range. Suddenly there is a heavy flash of an exploding round and the group of men we had just seen disappear in black smoke and you think, 'Atta boy, artillery!' maybe it was a mortar round that got them. Doesn't matter, they're gone. There is no feeling of pity, it's them or us. You know the remaining hordes will kill us if they can get close enough to over-run our position. Incredibly, some of the early leaders continue coming, well out front, alone, and still running fast, not aware they will soon be in the gun-sighs of our riflemen. A little farther back are others in clumps of three, five or more. Hundreds of followers replace those who had been in front; lead for a while, killed and replaced by other hundreds who follow. You wonder what kind of people these are, running without seeming to fear into certain death! Have their leaders inspired them? Are they drugged? They stagger, fall, and get closer. The question arises, 'Should we fall back?' We decide not to. It's better to stay where we are.*

*Speaking calmly into the field telephone you ask the FDC to 'Repeat Fire for Effect' over and over on target areas previously fired upon. It doesn't matter which direction we shoot, like liberated ants, they're all over the place. Riflemen fire clip after clip of ammunition, aiming their rifles at maximum range in the general direction of the attackers. The crack of rifle fire blend into the noisy scene so well, all you see is smoke from the muzzles. You can hear the rattle of machine guns, louder than before. Machine gun barrels bend as they become almost red hot forcing the gunners to pause briefly to allow cooling before the weapon jams. A few pour water from their canteens on their weapon to cool the barrel. We start getting mortar fire in on our position. They enemy must have its mortars behind several of those hills just beyond the river. I hate that stuff. You can hear an incoming mortar round, unlike artillery that vies you a chance to duck, except you rarely hear the one's that come right at you. They've got an Observer, too, the way they're walking the rounds in. Wonder where he is? Cr-rackk! A rifle bullet hit somewhere close. It had to have come right into the bunker! Sniper maybe, or was it a random shot? See if you can spot a white puff of smoke just before the next 'crack' sound. That's likely where the guy is shooting from, if it's a sniper. Nothing. Must be just random shots, but they can kill just as well.*

*Through your binoculars you sweep the area for new targets. Get ready to request a separate fire mission in case you see any. Using the mil scales etched in the lens, you calculate yards and distance to add to a request for fire. It is not necessary to rehearse the commands because you have been an FO so long the procedure is automatic. It's comforting to know that they, in the FDC, know you, that you are not a stranger, or worse, an inexperienced guy, 'first time up on the hill'. It's a pell-mell rush now for the enemy to get to where we are, to envelop and smother us with sheer weight of manpower. It appears their horrendous losses are of no concern to their leaders, manpower reserves are committed to continue the onslaught over bodies of their own dead. We wonder, 'Is that their whole army?' How can they keep coming like that, with such butchery among their ranks? Is it discipline? Or fear that they'll be shot by their leaders? On they come. We feel their hysteria, to kill us, take our weapons and the ground we hold. We are barely aware of the wetness of perspiration on our hands. We wipe our hands on our clothes, probably the first real tinge of fear. Well, it'll be harder for them because we are on higher ground. Before they get to us, they have to get through our barbed wire. A slight consolation. We comment aloud, although not to anyone in particular, 'Didja see that?' when we see some of the Chinese who were carrying a rifle fall, their bodies jerking as they do. Other unarmed soldiers following close behind pick up rifles from their fallen comrades and continue running toward us. This happens over and over again. Now and then one of them fires his weapon in our direction without aiming. Others carry rifles like a club, the muzzle pointed to the rear! You begin to wonder when all this butchery is going to stop. Will our ammo hold out? With a start you realize your body is sweating even though your face is dry, and so is your throat. You think of the word adrenaline. Yeah, that must be it. The Chinese keep coming, but is there a slowing of that rush? Certain signs indicate it is. Some attackers have stopped, some are squatting, some are down on one knee, but others keep running in a crouch toward you. By this time, close by infantrymen with their M1 rifles with accurate long-range fire are able to hit many of them. Earlier they had fired in the general direction of the attackers. Because of the Chinese, many of them became casualties from non-aimed bullets.*

*Suddenly the artillery fire lifted, which is understood when the sound of the jet engines roar in on the scene, at the same time we see the planes fly over really low. That made us jump! The 50-caliber machine guns on the planes add a staccato 'brrrrt' sound. Hundreds of small puffs of dirt whip in and around the Chinese masses, obliterating sight of their charge, slowing their pace, but not their movement. Tanks of napalm, bomb-shaped but thinner than a conventional bomb, flip from the planes end over end. When the tanks hit the ground there is a puff of a red-orange fireball. The ball speeds along an erratic path along the ground engulfing the remaining jellied gasoline that quickly spewed from the tank and spread through the ranks of the onrushing Chinese, setting many of them on fire, dropping them like flies in a cloud of insecticide. Heavy black smoke follows the path of fire. If they survive the fire, they cannot breathe because the oxygen is sucked out of the area by the fireball. Others still alive must be screaming with the pain of burning flesh, but of course we can't hear it. Or care. Two other planes follow, drop their deadly cargo and are gone almost as quickly as they appeared. The leading waves of humanity are closer, but the ranks are thinner. They stop and die as they reach the final protective line and get tangled in our barbed wire. A yell, then cheers as our own troops realize the enemy has turned and is retreating back over the hills and ridges from where it had started. Someone asks, 'Did you hear a bugle?' I didn't. If one did sound, maybe that was the signal to stop and pull back. A few final rounds explode after them, out of sight, but undoubtedly causing additional casualties. Our side had fired thousands of rounds of assorted ammunition. It had been like a wall of steel and fire. The ground out front releases wisps of smoke, but the scene is quiet. How long had the attack lasted? No one knows. Everyone is tired, a little shaky. Although we try to sound calm, the sound of our own voices seems to have a higher pitch. Perhaps because our throats are dry. We are elated that it's over, at least for the present. Another attack has been beaten off, another killing phase over.*

*Our infantry commanders ignore normal procedure outlined in tactical manuals, when the enemy runs, counter attack! No, not this time. We don't want real estate. Our mission was, and will continue to be, to kill as many of the enemy as we can by luring them in. If they don't come back, then we go look for them. The worst thing now is to do nothing, so we begin immediately to prepare for the next attack. We dig in deeper, check our weapons, and take inventory of our ammunition stores. Medics scour the bunkers and foxholes for wounded. There are always a few that have to be evacuated to the rear evacuation hospitals or MASH that aren't far behind the firing batteries. We are extremely fortunate this time, there are none KIA. But will we be so fortunate next time? It was a good thing we had the time to prepare our position with dug-in bunkers and zero-in our weapons. It could have been a disaster. How many enemy had there been, 10,000? 20,000? I remembered the largest crowds I had ever seen when I was a kid watching the 4th of July fireworks. I think someone estimated the count as ten thousand on the hill side at Brady Park in the Sault. But that had been in one relatively small area. These guys had been spread all over the landscape, out front, and like onrushing water in a river bed, circled the natural obstructions of higher hills and clumps of trees that were in their path."*

***1st Lt Howard Maki, 37th Field Artillery Battalion 1951-52***

Acknowledgements

There are so many people to thank regarding this book I am not sure where to start! To all the men who answered my original postings for information in the American Legion, VFW, and Korean War Veteran Association magazines, my humble thanks and gratitude for giving your time and memories to me, and for your patience while getting this work published, thank you. To the family members of these veterans, for your care and support of these men through the course of time since Korea, thank you. To Hal and Ted Barker, whose website The Korean War Project, yet again has been an invaluable resource for information and contacts with Forward Observers and all artillerymen of Korea, thank you for the work that you do to keep that website up and running. To Colonel Jack Callaway (Ret), 1st Lt Joseph Reynolds (Ret), and Major Michael Glisson (USANG) for providing wonderful reference, knowledge, and support, thank you. To Miss Hannah Danielle Deal for your typing and transcription efforts, thank you. To Major General Robert H. Scales (Ret), words cannot express the gratitude I have for you taking the time out of your busy schedule to help a fledgling writer with his work, thank you. To my Mom, you are my soul, I love you. To my Dad, what can I say? You don't like to be called a hero, but that's what you are, you are my hero. Last but not at all least, my wife Annie and my son John, I love you, you are my life. Thank you for your support and patience with me.

**About Major General Robert H. Scales, Jr. U.S.A. (Ret)**

Dr. Robert Scales is currently President of Colgen, Inc, a consulting firm specializing in issues relating to landpower, wargaming and strategic leadership. Prior to joining the private sector Dr. Scales served over thirty years in the Army, retiring as a Major General. He commanded two units in Vietnam, winning the Silver Star for action during the battles around Dong Ap Bia (Hamburger Hill) during the summer of 1969. Subsequently, he served in command and staff positions in the United States, Germany, and Korea and ended his military career as Commandant of the United States Army War College. He is the author of two books on military history: *Certain Victory*, the official account of the Army in the Gulf War and *Firepower in Limited War*, a history of the evolution of firepower doctrine since the end of the Korean War. Dr. Scales has also written two books on the theory of warfare: *Future Warfare*, a strategic anthology on America's wars to come and *Yellow Smoke: the Future of Land Warfare for America's Military*. Dr. Scales latest work, *The Iraq War: a Military History*, written with Williamson Murray has set the standard for all future works on the conflict, and has received very favorable reviews by the New York Times. Dr. Scales is the senior military analyst for The Fox News Network, The BBC, and National Public Radio. He is a graduate of West Point and earned his PhD in history from Duke University.

Cover photograph credit: 240mm Fire Mission on Hill 1062, Papa-san Mountain, taken by Sergeant Jerry Sax, 213th Field Artillery Battalion, 1953

# About the Author

Tony Sobieski wears a number of 'hats' working for the U. S. Air Force. As a civilian he is the Information Security Manager for McGuire Air Force Base in New Jersey, and as a reservist he is a Senior Master Sergeant assigned to the HQ Air Force Security Forces at the Pentagon where he serves as the Assistant for Nuclear Security and Integrated Base Defense Policy. Tony also is still actively involved as a U.S. Air Force Phoenix Raven, force protection and anti-terrorism specialists who protect U.S. aircrew and aircraft around the world. After the success of his first book *FIRE MISSION!* concerning the history of his Father's unit in Korea, Tony has become an avid and recognized Korean War artillery historian. Tony's love and respect for his Dad, a Korean War Veteran, and others like him, is the continuing motivation for his interest in the 'Forgotten War'. Combining his military background and using a unique 'matter of fact' interviewing style are becoming Tony's trademark, enabling him to shed light on how American artillerymen lived and died in the wasteland known as Korea. This is his second book.

Printed in the United States
34027LVS00005B/153

9 781420 838367